THE INSIGHT GUIDES SERIES RECEIVED SPECIAL AWARDS FOR EXCELLENCE FROM THE PACIFIC AREA TRAVEL ASSOCIATION.

NEPAL
Sixth Edition (Reprint)
© 1987/88 by APA PUBLICATIONS (HK) LTD.
Published by APA Publications (HK) Ltd.
Printed by APA Press Pte. Ltd.
Colour Separation in Singapore by Colourscan Pte. Ltd.

APA PRODUCTIONS
Publisher: Hans Johannes Hoefer
General Manager: Henry Lee
Marketing Director: Aileen Lau
Editorial Director: Geoffrey Eu
Editorial Manager: Vivien Kim
Editorial Consultants: Adam Liptak (North America)
Brian Bell (Europe)
Heinz Vestner (German Editions)

Project Editors
Helen Abbott, Diana Ackland, Mohamed Amin, Ravindralal Anthonis, Roy Bailet, Louisa Cambell, Jon Carroll, Hillary Cunningham, John Eames, Janie Freeburg, Bikram Grewal, Virginia Hopkins, Samuel Israel, Jay Itzkowitz, Phil Jarratt, Tracy Johnson, Ben Kalb, Wilhelm Klein, Saul Lockhart, Sylvia Mayuga, Gordon MaLauchlan, Kal Müller, Eric Oey, Daniel P. Reid, Kim Robinson, Ronn Ronck, Robert Seidenberg, Rolf Steinberg, Sriyani Tidball, Lisa Van Gruisen, Merin Wexler.

Contributing Writers
A.D. Aird, Ruth Armstrong, T. Terence Barrow, F. Lisa Beebe, Bruce Berger, Dor Bahadur Bista, Clinton V. Black, Star Black, Frena Bloomfield, John Borthwick, Roger Boschman, Tom Brosnahan, Jerry Carroll, Tom Chaffin, Nedra Chung, Tom Cole, Orman Day, Kunda Dixit, Richard Erdoes, Guillermo Garcia-Oropeza, Ted Giannoulas, Barbara Gloudon, Harka Gurung, Sharifah Hamzah, Willard A. Hanna, Elizabeth Hawley, Sir Edmund Hillary, Tony Hillerman, Jerry Hopkins, Peter Hutton, Neil Jameson, Michael King, Michele Kort, Thomas Lucey, Leonard Lueras, Michael E. Macmillan, Derek Maitland, Buddy Mays, Craig McGregor, Reinhold Messner, Julie Michaels, M. R. Priya Rangsit, Al Read, Elizabeth V. Reyes, Victor Stafford Reid, Harry Rolnick, E.R. Sarachchandra, Uli Schmetzer, Ilsa Sharp, Norman Sibley, Peter Spiro, Harold Stephens, Keith Stevens, Michael Stone, Desmond Tate, Colin Taylor, Deanna L. Thompson, Randy Udall, James Wade, Mallika Wanigasundara, William Warren, Cynthia Wee, Tony Wheeler, Linda White, H. Taft Wireback, Alfred A. Yuson, Paul Zach.

Contributing Photographers
Carole Allen, Ping Amarand, Tony Arruza, Marcello Bertinetti, Alberto Cassio, Pat Canova, Alain Compost, Ray Cranbourne, Alain Evrard, Ricardo Ferro, Lee Foster, Manfred Gottschalk, Werner Hahn, Dallas and John Heaton, Brent Hesselyn, Hans Hoefer, Luca Invernizzi, Ingo Jezierski, Wilhelm Klein, Dennis Lane, Max Lawrence, Lyle Lawson, Philip Little, Guy Marche, Antonio Martinelli, David Messent, Ben Nakayama, Vautier de Nanxe, Kal Müller, Günter Pfannmuller, Van Philips, Ronni Pinsler, Fitz Prenzel, G.P. Reichelt, Dan Rocovits, David Ryan, Frank Salmoiraghi, Thomas Schollhammer, Blair Seitz, David Stahl, Bill Wassman, Rendo Yap, Hisham Youssef.

Distributors
Australia and New Zealand: Prentice Hall of Australia, 7 Grosvenor Place, Brookvale, NSW 2100, Australia. **Benelux:** Uitgeverij Cambium, Naarderstraat 11, 1251 Aw Laren, The Netherlands. **Caribbean:** Kingston Publishers, 1-A Norwood Avenue, Kingston 5, Jamaica. **Central and South America; Mexico and Portugal:** Cedibra Editora Brasileira Ltda, Rua Leonidia, 2-Rio de Janeiro, Brazil. **Denmark:** Copenhagen Book Centre Aps, Roskildeveji 338, DK-2630 Tastrup, Denmark. **Europe (others):** European Book Service, Flevolaan 36-38, P. O. Box 124, 1380 AC Weesp, Holland. **Hawaii:** Pacific Trade Group Inc., P. O. Box 1227, Kailua, Oahu, Hawaii 96734, U.S.A. **Hong Kong:** Far East Media Ltd., Vita Tower, 7th Floor, Block B, 29 Wong Chuk Hang Road, Hong Kong. **India and Nepal:** India Book Distributors, 107/108 Arcadia Building, 195 Narima Point, Bombay-400-021, India. **Indonesia:** Java Books, Box 55 J.K.C.P, Jakarta, Indonesia.

Israel: Steimatzky Ltd., P.O. Box 628, Tel Aviv 61006, Israel (Israel title only). **Italy:** Zanfi Editori SRL. Via Ganaceto 121, 41100 Modena, Italy. **Japan:** Charles E.Tuttle Co. Inc., 2-6 Suido 1-Chome, Bunkyo-ku, Tokyo 112, Japan. **Kenya:** Camerapix Publishers International Ltd., P. O. Box 45048, Nairobi, Kenya. **Korea:** Kyobo Book Centre Co., Ltd., P.O. Box Kwang Hwa Moon 1 658, Seoul, Korea. **Philippines:** National Book Store, 701 Rizal Avenue, Manila, Philippines. **Singapore:** MPH Distributors (S) Pte. Ltd., 601 Sims Drive #03-21 Pan-I Warehouse and Office Complex, S'pore 1438, Singapore. **Spain:** Altair, Balmes 69, 08007-Barcelona, Spain. **Sri Lanka:** Lake House Bookshop, 100, Sir Chittampalama, Gardines Mawatna, Colombo 2, Sri Lanka. **Switzerland:** M.P.A. Agencies-Import SA, CH. du Croset 9, CH-1024 Ecublens, Switzerland. **Taiwan:** Caves Books Ltd., 103 Chungshan N.Road, Sec. 2, Taipei, Taiwan, Republic of China. **Thailand:** Far East Publications Ltd., 117/3 Soi Samahan, Sukhumvit 4 (South Nana), Bangkok, Thailand. **United Kingdom and Ireland:** Harrap Ltd., 19-23 Ludgate Hill, London EC4M 7PD, England, United Kingdom. **Mainland United States and Canada:** Graphic Arts Center Publishing, 3019 N.W. Yeon, P.O. Box 10306, Portland OR 97210, U.S.A. (The Pacific Northwest title only); Prentice Hall Press, Gulf & Western Building, One Gulf & Western Plaza, New York, NY 10023, U.S.A. (all other titles).

French editions: Editions Gallimard, 5 rue Sébastien-Bottin, F-75007 Paris, France. **German editions:** Nelles Verlag GmbH, Schleissheimer Str. 371b, 8000 Munich 45, West Germany. **Italian editions:** Zanfi Editori SLR, Via Ganaceto 121 41100 Modena, Italy. **Portuguese and Spanish editions:** Cedibra Editora Brasileira Ltda, Rua Leonidia, 2-Rio de Janerio, Brazil.

Special Sales
Special sales, for promotion purposes within the international travel industry and for educational purposes, are also available. The advertising representatives listed below also handle special sales. Alternatively, interested parties can contact Apa Productions, P.O. Box 219, Orchard Point Post Office, Singapore 9123.

Advertising Representatives
Advertising carried in Insight Guides gives readers direct access to quality merchandise and travel-related services. These advertisments are inserted in the Guide in Brief section of each book. Advertisers are requested to contact their nearest representatives, listed below.

Australia and New Zealand: International Media Representative Pty. Ltd., 3rd Floor, 39 East Esplanade Manly, NSW 2095, Australia. Tel: (02) 9773377; Tlx: IMR AA 74473.
Bali: Mata Graphic Design, Batujimbar, Sanur, Bali, Indonesia. Tel: (0361) 8073. (for Bali only)
Hawaii: HawaiianLMedia Sales; 1750 Kalakaua Ave., Suite 3-243, Honolulu Hawaii 96826, U.S.A. Tel: (808) 9464483.
Hong Kong: C Cheney & Associates, 17th Floor, D'Aguilar Place, 1-30 D' Aguilar Street, Central, Hong Kong. Tel: 5-213671; Tlx: 63079 CCAL HX.
India and Nepal, Pakistan and Bangladesh: Universal Media, CHA 2/718, 719 Kantipath, Lazimpat, Kathmandu-2, Nepal. Tel: 412911/414502; Tlx: 2229 KAJI NP ATTN MEDIA.
Indonesia (excluding Bali): Media Investment Services, Setiabudi Bldg. 2, 4th Floor, Suite 407, Jl. Hr. Rasuna Said, Kuningan, Jakarta Selatan 12920, Indonesia. Tel: 5782723/5782752; Tlx: 62418 MEDIANETIA.
Malaysia: MPH Media Services, Lot 2 Jalan 241, Section 51A, Petaling Jaya, Selangor, West Malaysia. Tel: (03) 7746166; Tlx: MA 37402 JCM.
Philippines: Torres Media Sales Inc., 21 Warbler St., Greenmeadows I, Murphy, Quezon City, Metro Manila, Philippines. Tel: 722-02-43; Tlx: 23312 RHP PH.
Thailand: Cheney, Tan & Van Outrive, 17th Floor Rajapark Bldg., 163 Asoke Rd., Bangkok 10110, Thailand. Tel: 2583244/2583259; Tlx: 20666 RAJAPAK TH.
Singapore: MPH Magazines (s) Pte. Ltd., 601 Sims Dr. #03-21, Pan-1 Warehouse & Office Complex, Singapore 1438. Tel: 7471088; Tlx: RS 35853 MPHMAG; Fax: 7440620.
Sri Lanka: Foremost Productions Ltd., Grant House, 101 Galle House, Colombo 4, Sri Lanka. Tel: (1) 584854/580971-3; Tlx: 21545 KENECK CE.

APA PHOTO AGENCY PTE. LTD.
The Apa Photo Agency is S.E. Asia's leading stock photo archive, representing the work of professional photographers from all over the world. More than 150,000 original color transparencies are available for advertising, editorial and educational uses. We are also linked with Tony Stone Worldwide, one of Europe's leading stock agencies, and their associate offices around the world:
Singapore: Apa Photo Agency Pte. Ltd., P.O. Box 219, Orchard Point Post Office, Singapore 9123, Singapore. **London:** Tony Stone Worldwide, 28 Finchley Rd., St. John's Wood, London NW8 6ES, England. **North America & Canada:** Masterfile Inc., 415 Yonge St., Suite 200, Toronto M5B 2E7, Canada. **Paris:** Fotogram-Stone Agence Photographique, 45 rue de Richelieu, 75001 Paris, France. **Barcelona:** Fototeca Torre Dels Pardais, 7 Barcelona 08026, Spain. **Johannesburg:** Color Library (Pty.) Ltd., P.O. Box 1659, Johannesburg, South Africa 2000. **Sydney:** The Photographic Library of Australia Pty. Ltd., 7 Ridge Street, North Sydney, New South Wales 2050, Australia. **Tokyo:** Orion Press, 55-1 Kanda Jimbocho, Chiyoda-ku, Tokyo 101, Japan.

nepal

Directed and Designed by Hans Johannes Hoefer
Produced by Lisa Van Gruisen
Edited by John Gottberg Anderson

APA PUBLICATIONS

Welcome to Apa Productions' *Nepal*. The *Insight Guide* you have in your hands is the culmination of years of effort by dozens of men and women who love the mountainous land as their own.

Lisa Van Gruisen, a director of Tiger Tops Mountain Travel International in Kathmandu, heads a distinguished team which includes the great mountaineers Sir Edmund Hillary and Reinhold Messner. Nepali writers include Harka Gurung, Kunda Dixit, Dor Bahadur

Hoefer

Van Gruisen

Anderson

Andreae

Bista and Biswa Nath Upreti. Desmond Doig, Kathmandu's most noted expatriate writer, joined with Elizabeth Hawley, Al Read and John Sanday in producing much of the text.

Photographs were taken by Hans Johannes Hoefer, Bill Wassman and Walter Andreae, with additional shots by John Cleare, Kalyan Singh, Max Lawrence and Jan Whiting. Free-lance editor John Gottberg Anderson pulled the final strings together in Kathmandu and at company headquarters in Singapore.

In the possession of these team members as they worked to compile *Nepal* was a first manuscript, painstakingly drawn together in the late 1970s by writer Marcel Barang and editorial consultant Carl Pruscha.

In fact, this book was essentially conceived 15 years ago, when Hoefer paused in the cultural melting pot of the Kathmandu Valley during overland wanderings. Shortly thereafter, he established Apa Productions in Singapore, and the string of culturally oriented guidebooks acclaimed by some as "the best series in the world" began emerging under his creative direction.

In 1973, Hoefer flew from Bangkok, where he was photographing *Thailand*, to Kathmandu, where he met with Pruscha, an Austrian professor specializing in the peoples and places of the Valley.

Pruscha's classic two-volume study of Valley landmarks, *Kathmandu Valley The Preservation of Physical Environment and Cultural Heritage*, was in the preparation stage, then for publication by His Majesty's Government of Nepal in collaboration with the United Nations and UNESCO.

Pruscha agreed to author a guidebook with the assistance of an editorial collaborator.

Hoefer introduced him to Marcel Barang, a French correspondent to various European newspapers and a translator of several early Apa titles from his base in Bangkok.

Meanwhile, Andreae entered the picture. A Hawaii-based financier-photographer whose input launched the highly successful *Insight Guide: Hawaii*, he offered backing to *Nepal* as well.

After numerous false starts, the project finally got underway in 1978. Pruscha and Barang were joined by Andreae, and together this threesome

Wassman

traveled throughout the Kathmandu Valley and the Kali Gandaki River basin of west central Nepal. Pruscha acted as cultural consultant, Barang taped notes for the entire journey and later turned them into prose, and Andreae photographed the

Barang & Pruscha

proceedings. The material they compiled in their dash through the spiritual wonderland of Nepal laid a strong foundation for this volume.

There followed a period of revision and consolidation. To develop the book's introductory and feature sections and to add new material on travel destinations, Hoefer turned to his long-

Sanday

time friend Van Gruisen in Kathmandu. She assigned the text necessary to fill the book's gaps, saw the articles through to completion, then assisted Hoefer and Anderson in the final editing and production phase in Kathmandu and Singapore.

All three of the principals involved in the production of this book long ago adopted nomadic lifestyles. Hoefer, for example, supported his education in printing, book production, design and photography at Krefeld — where he studied under the stern disciplines of the Bauhaus tradition — by traveling between his native Germany and the Middle East every summer, trading German cars for Persian and Turkish carpets. Then he made the overland jaunt to Nepal and Bali, and the rest is Apa history.

Anderson, a native of America's Pacific Northwest, was infected with the travel bug shortly after his graduation from the Uni-

Doig

versity of Oregon in 1971. Between lengthy stints as a newspaper reporter in Honolulu and an editor in Seattle, he traveled for several years in the Pacific, Asia and Europe, living and working at a grassroots level as he wrote about world cultures. Anderson's expertise was solicited after completion of the prestigious Gannett Fellowship program in Asian studies at the University of Hawaii. His first major project was editing *Insight Guide: Burma*, and he interrupted a period of residence in Colombo where he was producing *Sri Lanka*, to serve as *Nepal* editor.

Hillary

Messner

Hawley

Read

Gurung

Bista

Dixit

Lissanevitch

Van Gruisen left her home in Northumberland, England, at the age of 17 to study art history in Paris. Since then, she has worked in Ireland conserving Georgian architecture and coordinating a book on Irish painting; in New York as an art dealer; in London with *Connoisseur* magazine; and in Iran and Turkey researching a film on Marco Polo. In 1972, during Southeast Asian wanderings, she encountered and admired Hoefer's work in Bali.

The following year, she ventured into Nepal for two weeks of trekking — and she is still there. Her art preservation focus has transferred itself to concern for Nepal's cultural heritage and the conservation of the land's rich wildlife and natural environment.

About the same time this project was taking firm shape, a New York-based photographer named Bill Wassman encountered Hoefer and showed him a portfolio of Nepal photography he had recently assembled. Hoefer, overwhelmed by the stunning depth and beauty of Wassman's work, showcased it in many of this book's double-truck and full-page spreads. Wassman is a graduate of Indiana University in comparative literature and anthropology, and has traveled extensively throughout Europe, North Africa and Asia since the early 1960s. He worked as a full-time assistant to famed photographers Eric Meola and Pete Turner in 1973 and 1974. Today, he has several book projects "at various stages of completion."

Desmond Doig, widely recognized as Kathmandu's top expatriate writer and artist, became Van Gruisen's main aide in Kathmandu. He assembled this book's sections on history, arts, festivals, Sherpas, yetis and hippies. He also contributed his knowledge to revisions of other parts of the book, and helped piece together various introductory sections.

Doig came to the Indian Subcontinent in the Second World War, when he served with the Fifth Royal Gurkhas. He has lived in India and Nepal ever since — writing for *The Statesman*, India's premier daily, as well as for such internationally known magazines as *Life*, *Time* and *National Geographic*. He also founded India's leading youth magazine, *J.S.*

Doig has authored five books, the best

(continued on page 338)

13

TABLE OF CONTENTS

Cover
    — by Walter Andreae and
Max Lawrence

Cartography
    — by Gunter Nelles

THE ABODE OF THE GODS

Nestled in the cradle of the highest mountains on earth, it is not surprising that Nepal has come to be known as the kingdom where deities mingle with mortals.

Here are the Himalaya, the "Abode of the Gods." Here, too, is Mount Everest, the world's greatest peak, known as Sagarmatha ("The Brow of the Oceans") by Nepalese. Sherpa artists picture the peak as the god Chomolungma riding a snow lion through clouds of many hues.

Ancient sages sought the highest climes for meditative seclusion, amongst gods who bestowed love or sudden anger on a worshipful people. Here are Gauri Shankar, home of Shiva and his consort, Parvati; Ganesh Himal, named for the elephant-headed god, Ganesh; and Annapurna, the goddess of plenty. The devotion of ages past remains among Nepalis today: whether Hindu, Buddhist or animist, the people of Nepal live close to their gods.

Truth, no less colorful than fiction, has made Nepal one of the world's most incredible countries, a geographical wonder, an ethnological conundrum.

A Land of Diversity

No one taking a daytime flight into Nepal can fail to marvel at the land below. There are the flat, checkered plains of the lowland Terai, the Siwalik (Churia) Hills swathed in hardwood jungles, the ochre-red farmlands of the Inner Terai, the plunging flanks of the Mahabharat range, the deep gorges of turbulent Himalayan rivers, and layer upon layer of foothills blued by distance. Beyond, the Himalaya soar to unbelievable heights along the northern horizon.

This is the home of 15 million Nepalis. These people, their languages and their customs, are as diverse as the terrain. From mountain to mountain, valley to valley, plateau to plain, ethnic groups vary as much as the climate.

Squeezed between the vastness of China to the north and India to the south, east and west, Nepal is the world's most precipitous staircase to the frozen heights of "the Roof of the World." Within a single day, one can fly closely past Everest and its neighboring summits, pause in the emerald valley of Kathmandu, then descend to the plains and ride elephants through tropical jungle and view wild tigers.

Nepal is the world's only Hindu kingdom. King Prithvi Narayan Shah of tiny Gorkha, who unified a country of feuding states and principalities in the late 18th Century, described his kingdom as "a root between two stones." The Gurkha king may not have appreciated the full truth of his words. He knew from his expansionist forays the almost unending size of his gigantic neighbors, China and India; but it takes a study of today's maps to realize the precarious position of Nepal, a rectangle 800 kilometers (497 miles) long and from 90 to 220 kilometers (56 to 137 miles) wide, bent to follow the curve of the central Himalaya, a country the size of Austria and Switzerland combined. Such a land, precariously strategic and beset by the disadvantage of being landlocked, is truly a slender root between two vast boulders, not stones. This fact is cause for as many political headaches among his descendants as it was for King Prithvi Narayan Shah himself.

But for the narrow strip of Terai plain along its southern boundary, and temperate valleys spread across its middle, the country is entirely mountainous. Indeed, many of its high passes along the northern border with Chinese Tibet are perpetually frozen. Yet this is the barrier through which armies, waves of settlers and traders have made their way over the centuries.

Nepalese Geography

This stupendous mountain pedestal causes more than a quarter of Nepal's land area to be over 3,000 meters (9,843 feet) in altitude. It also includes eight peaks higher than 8,000 meters (26,247 feet): Everest, Kanchenjunga, Lhotse, Makalu, Cho Oyu, Dhaulagiri, Manaslu and Annapurna. Mountain relief is asymmetrical, with rock strata inclined to the north, leaving steep south faces. Deep river gorges incise across the range to fall rapidly to the lower valleys. The steep slopes prevent the formation of large glaciers; a snowline varying between 5,000 and 6,000 meters (16,400 to 19,700 feet) also limits glaciation.

Below the Himalaya, running in a similar

A royal elephant carries the King and Queen during 1975 coronation ceremonies.

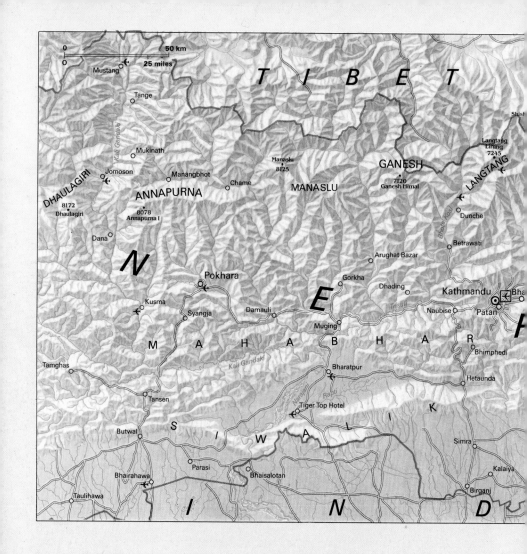

NEPAL AT A GLANCE

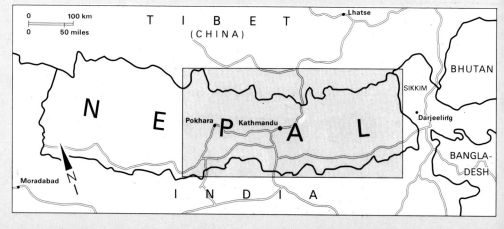

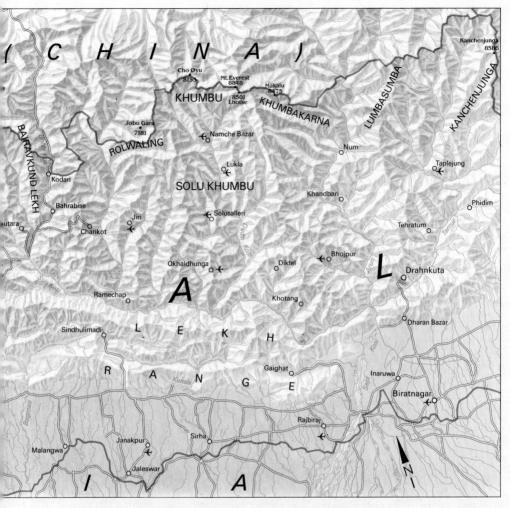

Area: 145,391 square kilometers (56,139 square miles).

Terrain: Heavily mountainous. 14% of the land is cultivated, 13% is pasture, 32% is forested.

Population: About 17 million (42 percent under the age 15).

Government: Monarchy headed by His Majesty King Birendra Bir Bikram Shah Dev. The Right Honourable Marich Man Singh Shrestha is Prime Minister.

Capital: Kathmandu (population 300,000; metropolitan area population 800,000).

Peoples: Tribal groups include Gurung, Limbu, Magar, Newar, Rai, Sherpa, Tamang and Tharu, with diverse smaller groups. Major caste groups are the Brahmins and Chhetris. Large numbers of Indians and some Tibetans make their home in Nepal.

Languages: Nepali 58% (official language), Newari 3% (mainly in Kathmandu), Indian languages 20% (mainly in Terai), dozen or so languages and many dialects.

Religion: Officially 90% Hindu, 8% Buddhist, 2% Islamic. However, Hinduism and Buddhism overlap a great deal.

Highest point: Mount Everest, also known as Sagarmatha (8,848 meters or 29,028 feet, highest point on earth).

Currency: Nepalese rupee (about Rs. 22 equal US$1.00).

west-northwest to east-southeast direction, are two parallel ranges. Ninety kilometers (56 miles) south of the great range, the Mahabharat Lekh rises to elevations between 1,500 and 2,700 meters (4,900 and 8,900 feet). Broad tropical valleys are encased in the range's complicated folds, but only three narrow river gorges slice through it.

Immediately south are the Siwalik Hills which rise abruptly from the Terai plain to heights of 750 to 1,500 meters (2,450 to 4,900 feet). The dry, immature soils support only a sparse population.

In the northwest of the country a fourth, trans-Himalayan range defines the boundary between Nepal and Tibet. Peaks of 6,000 to 7,000 meters (19,700 to 23,000 feet) lie about 35 kilometers (22 miles) north of the main Himalaya; their relief is less rugged, with wind-eroded landforms predominant.

Each of these mountain ranges is separated from the next by lowlands or valley systems. On the south is the Terai extension of India's vast Ganges plain. Twenty-five to 40 kilometers (15 to 25 miles) broad within the Nepalese border, the Terai's gentle topography is in sharp contrast to the rugged relief of the rest of the country.

At a slightly higher elevation, but with similar vegetation, lie the *dun* or Inner Terai valleys between the Siwalik Hills and the Mahabharat Lekh. Until recently, this region was an impenetrable, malaria-infested jungle; today, with much of its indigenous wildlife endangered, it has become Nepal's most populous region. Almost all of the modern industry is in the Terai and Inner Terai, and the flat lands are ideal for growing rice and other grains.

Summers are hot in the Terai and the *dun*, with temperatures often exceeding 38°C (100°F). Winters are considerably cooler, with temperatures down to 10°C (50°F). Rainfall comes primarily in the June-to-September monsoon season, heaviest in the east. The strong, straight *sal* tree, compared by some to the mahogany for its durability, and the *kapok,* or silk cotton tree, are frequently seen in Terai forests.

Between the Mahabharat Lekh and the main Himalaya lies a broad complex of hills and valleys. This *pahar* zone has been heavily eroded by rivers and streams. Here is the traditional heartland of the Nepalese people, and here is located the Kathmandu Valley.

Nepal's capital is a city of about 300,000, at once medieval and modern. Despite its 1,331-meter (4,368-foot) elevation and the snowy summits looming at its northern horizon, Kathmandu has a mild climate. Summer maximums are about 30°C (86°F) and mean winter temperatures about 10°C (50°F). Winters are sometimes frosty, but are dry and snowless, while summer monsoons bring substantial rain. The moderate climate permits three harvests a year and small plantings in between. Oaks and alders are oft-seen trees, and rhododendron and jacaranda are beautiful when in bloom. Visitors often are surprised to learn that Kathmandu's latitude — about 27°40' North — is the same as that of Florida and Kuwait, and slightly south of New Delhi.

Beyond Kathmandu, high in the mountains, thunderstorms are frequent and winter frosts limit agriculture. Nevertheless, potatoes are grown to 4,000 meters (13,100 feet), and barley even higher. The mountain population finds sanctuary in isolated valleys, where juniper and birch share the terrain with sub-alpine grasses.

There is a distinctly alpine climate in the highlands above 4,000 meters. Summers are short, winters severe and dry, with high snowfall, low temperatures and strong winds. In western Nepal and north of the Himalaya, there are elevated *bhot* valleys reminiscent of Tibet, with broad, open profiles and arid climate — particularly where the Himalayan rainshadow blocks out the monsoon rains.

People of the Valley

It is much more pleasant in Kathmandu. The Valley is a veritable crucible in which, over the centuries, many races, religions, languages and customs have been molded into a handsome, artistic people. Kathmandu's Newars are a striking example of the ethnic evolution of Nepal.

Most chronicles mention an original Valley people and an original mountain people. But no one knows where they came from. Over thousands of years, migrants from north, south, east and west settled in what is now Nepal.

Opposite, the eyes of Swayambhunath; overleaf, map of the Kingdom of Nepal.

Saints, like the immortal Guru Padma Sambhara, walked the length of the Himalaya to Tibet from distant Swat in today's northernmost Pakistan. The guru spread the teachings of Tantric Buddhism as he journeyed, an example of how one man, let alone a migrating people, could influence the lands he visited. Another was the *sadhu* Ne Muni, who may have given his name to Nepal.

It was not uncommon for warring Himalayan kingdoms or principalities to invite an Indian or Tibetan prince to lead them in battle and accept a vacant throne. Such foreign royalty, with its inevitable entourage of soldiers and retainers, remained to settle and intermarry, leaving its own peculiar mark on the population of its adopted land.

Tibetan influence is seen in the story of the beautiful Buddhist goddess Tara. In historical reality a Nepalese princess of the 7th Century who married into Tibet and took as her dowry the Buddhist religion, "Green Tara" has long since been deified. It is romantically believed that the powerful King Tsrong-tsong Gompo invaded Nepal to woo and wed this legendary beauty. More likely, he took her as part of the tribute he extracted from a subject people.

The King's far-reaching conquests left a residue of Tibetans all over the northern region. These include the Tamangs, a gentle artistic people whose name suggests they were once Tibetan cavalry or the grooms of Tibetan invaders. Sherpas migrated from the far north-

eastern Tibetan province of Kham. The people of Mustang are unadulterated Tibetans.

Meanwhile, people of Tibeto-Burmese stock and Indo-Aryan languages spread throughout the hills, valleys and plateaus of central Nepal. The south was overrun by a bewildering variety of Indian peoples.

A review of Himalayan history uncovers even more confusing facts. There are distant connections with Alexander the Great's Greeks, whose invasion of India left a legacy in the western mountains. People of Polynesian blood may have visited the far eastern Naga Hills. Neither of these groups may have reached Nepal — but then again, they might have.

Legends, more forthright than history, traditionally told the Nepalese people all they needed to know about their origins, attributing unknown beginnings to great heroes or gods. But in the sudden explosion of modern education, legends don't carry the same meaning they once did.

In the last two centuries, a measure of popular mobility — brought about by population pressure and, more recently, by political unification and development of communications, — has started to alter age-old patterns. Still, the sense of belonging to one nation may not have spread to all the diverse peoples of this land. To this day, it is not uncommon to have hill people refer to Kathmandu as "Nepal" — even though they all recognize King Birendra Bir Bikram Shah Dev with great reverence and affection.

No fewer than 36 languages and dialects are spoken in Nepal. Similar diversity is observed in rites and religions, with wide variations between one ethnic group and its immediate neighbor. The prevailing pattern is of Hinduism in the south and Buddhism in the north; but animist rites and shamanistic practices, known as jhankrism, have survived in a highly integrated form. Both major religions coexist in most of the country. It is only in the heart of the land, in the Kathmandu Valley, that they merge, so that Hindu and Buddhist share the same festivals and the same places of worship. This unique blend of religions has created a homogeneous and sophisticated culture and civilization.

But if Kathmandu has long been considered to be Nepal, Nepal is not only Kathmandu. Think of the capital as a marvel of a microcosm, a flawless emerald in a filigree setting.

The colorfully clad Royal Cavalry, left; and right, crossed *khukris* atop a ceremonial mace precede a parading Nepalese soldier.

A HISTORY BATHED IN LEGEND

In the distant dawn of unrecorded time, so legend tells us, the Valley of Kathmandu was a turquoise lake. Upon this lake rested a wondrous lotus flower, from which emanated a blue light of awesome magnificence. This was a manifestation of Swayambhu or Adhi-Buddha, the primordial Buddha. So beautiful was the lake, so sacred the flame, that the devout came from many lands to live in caves along its shore, to worship and meditate.

From a mountain retreat in China came the patriarch Manjushri. Wishing to worship the flame more closely, he sliced the restraining Valley wall with his flaming sword of wisdom, draining the water and allowing the lotus to settle to the Valley floor. There Manjushri built a shrine that was to grow into the great stupa of Swayambhunath. He also founded a city of perishable wood and clay called Manjupatan, reaching from Swayambhunath to Pashupatinath, and bestowed upon one of his followers the kingship of the Valley.

Another version of this legend has the Hindu deity Krishna hurling a thunderbolt at the Valley wall to release the waters of the lake. Flaming sword or thunderbolt, there is to this day a gorge at Chobar as narrow as a blade. Below it, enshrined in a temple, is a stone shaped vaguely like Ganesh, the elephant-headed god; some believe it is Krishna's thunderbolt.

Both legends are as acceptable to modern science as legends can be. Geologists have confirmed that the Kathmandu Valley was indeed under water at one time.

Krishna is said to have peopled the Valley with Gopalas, or cowherds, who built a city and established the legendary Gopal dynasty. The Gopalas were later absorbed by the Ahirs, one of several successive waves of Tibeto-Burman migrants. These people probably came from today's north Bengal, after sweeping across the hills and valleys of northeast India from Burma and beyond. Or perhaps they descended in plundering waves from Tibet, Mongolia and China.

The Kirati Culture

The coming of the Kiratis in about the 8th or 7th Century B.C. is nearer recorded history. These apparently fierce tribal people may have been the Kiriaths of Old Testament Babylon.

They invaded from the east, established a kingdom in the Valley of Kathmandu, and left a legacy of outstanding kings in the rich fabric of early Nepal.

Yalambar was the first and best remembered Kirati king. Legend credits him with meeting Indra, the lord of heaven, who strayed into the Valley in human guise. He had the dubious honor of being slain in the epic battle of the *Mahabharata*, in which gods and mortals fought alongside each other.

There were 28 Kirati kings. In the reign of

the seventh, Gautama Buddha and his beloved disciple Ananda are believed to have visited the Valley. There are stories of how the Buddha dwelt awhile in Patan, where he elevated the blacksmith caste to goldsmiths and bestowed upon them the name of his own clan, Sakya.

By then, the Kiratis had developed their culture to a point where the 4th Century B.C. chronicler Kautilya describes them as exporting 20 different grades of woolen blankets, carpets, treated skins and hides. They were

Preceding pages, Swayambhunath penetrates the morning clouds. Left and above, the patriarch Manjushri depicted on a *thangka* and in bronze.

largely sheep breeders and shifting cultivators; irrigation was unknown to them.

Two centuries later, the great Indian emperor Ashoka, who embraced Buddhism and set to converting everyone in his huge empire to the new religion, visited Lumbini — the Buddha's birthplace — and raised an engraved column. He is said to have also visited the Kathmandu Valley, where he erected stupas at the four cardinal points of Patan, and may have enlarged upon the stupas of Swayambhunath and Bodhnath. His daughter, Charumati, married a local prince, Devapala. They founded the cities of Chabahil and Deopatan close by the holy shrines of Pashupatinath and Bodhnath. A stupa and monastery in modern Chabahil are said to date back to Charumati.

When the Kirati dynasty came to an end, so did its crafts and architecture. But though the Kirati people vanished from the Valley, they

Manadeva II rode to battle, his mother either accompanied him or sent a close confidant.

In 602, the first Thakuri dynasty began with the ascent of Amsuvarman. He inherited the throne upon the death of his father-in-law, the Licchavi king Vasudeva. Amsuvarman himself was not a Licchavi. He may have been a Gupta from northern India. His palace in Deopatan, not far from Pashupatinath, was so fabulous it has passed into legend.

Amsuvarman married his sister to an Indian prince and his daughter Bhrikuti, perhaps as a token of vassalage, to Tibet's powerful King Tsrong-tsong Gompo. Bhrikuti is believed to have taken as part of her dowry the begging bowl of the Buddha and other artifacts of Buddhism. She is a legendary figure, considered an incarnation of the Green Tara of Tibetan Buddhism, subject of countless *thangkas* and images. Tsrong-tsong Gompo's second wife, a Chinese princess, became known as the White

remained in the mountainous east, where they are considered to be the forebears of the Rai and Limbu people.

The Licchavis and Thakuris

The last Kirati ruler of the Kathmandu Valley, Gastee, succumbed to a Licchavi invasion from India in about 300 A.D. The Licchavis were probably Rajputs from today's Bihar and Uttar Pradesh. They brought with them the first golden age of Nepalese arts, and introduced the division of society through the Hindu caste structure.

The Licchavis gave Nepal its first great historical figure, Manadeva I, in the 5th Century. An inscription in stone at Changu Narayan, dated 467 A.D., confirms him to be a king of considerable talents, responsible for conquests in the east and west. While Licchavi sculptors created masterpieces in stone, King Manadeva's politicians and widespread armies consolidated the kingdom.

His successor, Manadeva II, had a tremendous mother fixation which is known through royal inscriptions: Mom's virtues were extolled almost more than those of her son. When

Tara. She took with her to Tibet an image of the Buddha and her unshakable faith. Together, the princesses converted the king and Tibet.

Chinese travelers who visited Nepal after Amsuvarman's reign were awed by his legacy. The palace, said Yuan Chwang, was seven stories tall and ornamented with gems and pearls. Golden fountains shaped like dragons gushed clear water. The king sat upon a lion throne, wearing golden earrings, jade, pearls, crystal, coral and amber. Officials and courtiers sat on the ground to the king's right and left, and hundreds of armed soldiers kept guard.

The people of the Valley, wrote this Chinese pilgrim, bathed several times a day. They wore a single garment, and pierced and enlarged their earlobes as a form of beauty. They loved theatrical performances and the music of trumpet and drum. Traders exchanged copper coins with a portrait on one side and the figure

A portion of an ancient Licchavi inscription at Changu Narayan, above; and an image of the fabled Green Tara of Swayambhunath, right.

of a horse on the other. There were copper utensils, houses of carved and painted wood, and "sculpture to make one marvel."

The 'Dark Ages'

There were two more Thakuri dynasties after the one founded by Amsuvarman. The Thakuris of Nuwakot, a settlement to the northwest, imposed their might in 1043, and a second Rajput dynasty assumed command of the Kathmandu Valley in 1082. Despite turmoil and strife in the Valley and the thrust of more than one foreign invasion, trade and commerce flourished and settlements grew all along the trade routes. The capital was forever expanding, and numerous monuments to the glory of various gods were erected.

Two kings of this long, rather obscure period, generally known as Nepal's "Dark Ages," deserve to be remembered. Gunakamadeva, a 10th Century ruler, is generally credited with founding Kantipur, today's Kathmandu (although some scholars place Kantipur's origin in the 12th Century).

This king is also said to have inaugurated the three great festivals of Indrajatra, Krishnajayanti and the Machhendranath Jatra. Legend says a god came to the Valley in disguise to watch one of these festivals. He was recognized by powerful Tantrics who bound him with a spell until he promised them a boon: a celestial tree. From this tree's wood was constructed a large building, known as the Kasthamandap or "House of Wood." It gave

its name to Gunakamadeva's new city.

In 1200, King Ari-deva assumed the title of Malla and in so doing founded a new, highly accomplished dynasty. It is said the king was wrestling when told of the birth of his son. Immediately he bestowed the title "Malla," meaning "wrestler," upon the infant. Nearer the truth, perhaps, is that intermarriage, court intrigue and power struggles swept the Mallas to the throne.

The Early Mallas

The early Malla period is often thought of as a stable age of peace and plenty, when art flourished and traders brought riches and recognition to the Kathmandu Valley. But hardly had the Malla rule begun when a terrible earthquake struck the Valley cities and killed thousands of people. Then foreign invaders from the northwest plundered the weakened Valley, setting fire to village and town. Patan was laid waste in 1311.

The most important figure of ensuing years was the Raja Harisimha or Hari Singh. He came to the Valley between 1325 and 1330 from Tirhut, a kingdom in the foothills south of Kathmandu. Some believe he was a conqueror who vanquished the cities of Bhaktapur and Patan and ascended the throne of Kathmandu, bringing with him South Indian retainers known as Nayars — from whom the Newars may have got their name. Others maintain he came as a refugee, expelled from his kingdom by the Muslim invader Ghiyas-ud-din-Tuglaq, to live in Bhaktapur but not to rule there.

Whichever version is correct, King Hari Singh made a lasting and valuable contribution to Nepal's religion. He brought with him the royal goddess Taleju Bhawani, and this South Indian deity remains to this day the royal goddess of Nepal.

The early Malla monarchs held absolute power by divine right: they were considered to be incarnations of Vishnu, as are the present Shah rulers. Although the Mallas were Hindu Shaivites following strict Brahmin rituals, they were tolerant of Buddhism, which was widespread at the court and among the people — especially in its Tantric form, the cult of Vajrayana.

A feudal administrative structure was imposed, dominated by an aristocratic elite whose powers at times overshadowed those of the sovereign. Below them, Brahmans and Chhetris

A carving of Vishnu Vikrantha dating to Licchavi times, found at Changu Narayan; and right, the medieval-looking Kasthamandap, monopolized all offices of profit around the palace. Next on the social ladder were the traders or farmers, divided into 64 strictly enforced occupational castes.

Patterns of Settlement

To protect themselves from invaders and bandits, and to preserve the limited arable land, villagers clustered together in compact settlements on upland terraces and along the main trade routes. Houses were built of brick and tile and streets were paved with bricks. In some cases, protective walls were erected around the villages. The caste system ensured a tightly knit social fabric and easy domination by the rulers.

It was during this early period that hill peo-

the sword. "The whole of Nepal was ravaged by fire," said a chronicler of the times.

The passing of the Muslim storm from India — short-lived in the Kathmandu Valley — had swept away most of the Brahmin empire. Waves of refugees from northern India forced their way into the mountains of Nepal. Here they established small Rajput fiefdoms and kingdoms, 46 in all, ruled by Hindu princes or chieftains who had fled the Muslim invaders. It was from one of these, the mountain-perched kingdom of Gorkha, that the present Shah dynasty emerged four centuries later.

Rise and Fall of a Dynasty

By this time, the Valley not only had been divided among the three principal cities; it had

ple from the west began to settle on mountain slopes surrounding the Valley. Unlike the lower hill dwellers, they lived in scattered hamlets of thatched mud houses, clearing the forests and building terraces on which they grew maize and millet.

An era of progress was followed by a period of great instability that split the Valley, pitting king against king, royal princes against parents, and feudal lords and aristocratic families against their monarchs. Into this confusion swept the conquering Muslim hordes of Shams-ud din Ilyas of Bengal. These armies destroyed temples and religious foundations, desecrated images, shattered Pashupatinath, and greatly damaged the stupa of Swayambhunath. People and their priests were put to

been fragmented so that feudal lords controlled new fiefdoms about the Valley. Rivalry between the three cities grew so severe that walls were erected. The cities were built in concentric patterns around the kings' palaces, with the higher castes in the immediate vicinity of their rulers and the lower castes on the periphery. Each city developed independently in keen competition with its neighbors. The rulers led lives of amazing affluence, luxury and indolence.

Then in 1372, King Jayasthiti Malla took Patan and established the third Malla dynasty. Ten years later, he moved his capital to Bhaktapur. A new and durable age began. Civil strife was quelled and the Valley unified. The caste system was reinforced, recognizing both the social differentiation and the occupations of the people.

Though storms continued to sweep the Malla scene, by the 15th Century a wonderful age of art and culture had blossomed. Newari was introduced as the court language and everywhere, in all three cities and many of the small towns, a renaissance flourished. Most of the great buildings, the fine woodcarving and powerful sculpture one sees today, belong to this period. A prime patron was King Yaksha Malla (1428-1482), who also expanded his territory as far as the Ganges River in the south, the border of Tibet in the north, the Kali Gandaki in the west, and Sikkim in the east.

Upon his death, the kingdom was divided between his three sons and his daughter. The ensuing small kingdoms, though related, were

for textiles, demand for which was growing. All exchanges were done in Nepalese currency.

The Birth of 'Modern' Nepal

But the political rivalries among the divided kingdoms led to the Mallas' demise. In western Nepal, the Gorkha kingdom was subjugating minor principalities and growing in strength. Finally, King Prithvi Narayan Shah summoned his forces to invade the Kathmandu Valley.

How alluring the lush Valley and the rich cities must have appeared to the mountain king. Little wonder he was obsessed with the conquest of the Valley. In 1768, after 10 years of preparation, siege and attack, Kathmandu fell to Gorkha on the day of the festival of Indra and the Virgin Goddess. The Malla age

soon warring among themselves. Conflict continued for almost 200 years.

A good deal of the land available for cultivation in the Valley had been cleared by this time, and irrigation had become sophisticated. In the 17th Century, maize and other cash crops like chilies, sugar cane, ginger and turmeric were introduced, which greatly enhanced trade. The Valley was not only providing passage for goods between its northern and southern neighbors; it was also producing goods for export: unrefined sugar and mustard-seed oil for China and Tibet, metal ware and religious instruments for India and Tibet. Cottage industries had developed with the introduction of sugar and mustard-oil presses, as well as the use of spinning wheels and looms

was at an end.

Prithvi Narayan Shah was the ninth king of the Shah dynasty of tiny Gorkha, about halfway between Kathmandu and Pokhara. His ancestors were believed to have been Rajput princes originally from Udaipur (Rajasthan). Fleeing the persecutions of Muslim invaders, they had first settled in the Kali Gandaki river basin, and conquered Lamjung and Gorkha in the mid-16th Century.

The new Shah rulers, transferring their seat of power to Kathmandu after its conquest,

A 1793 view of the Kathmandu Valley, above; and a 1975 depiction of Gorkha King Prithvi Narayan Shah surveying the Valley prior to his conquest.

undertook to expand and consolidate their territory. But in 1790, their troops met Chinese resistance while marching to Tibet, then a vassal of China.

In the clashes that followed, the Gorkha rulers sought the help of the British East India Company, whose traders and troops were then busy instituting British rule in India. A British envoy arrived in Kathmandu in 1792. He was too late: 70,000 Chinese troops had invaded Nepal, and the Tibetan war ended in defeat for the Gorkhas. The Nepalese signed a treaty pledging them to desist from attacks on Tibet, and agreed to send a tribute every five years to the Chinese emperor in Peking. This practice was discontinued only in 1912.

The British emissary, Col. William Kirkpatrick, was not the first white foreigner

to have entered the Valley. In the 1730s, the Malla kings had allowed the establishment of an Italian mission of Capuchins. But the padres were expelled by Prithvi Narayan Shah, who charged that foreign priests supported their religion first with trade and later with guns.

A 'Treaty of Friendship'

At the turn of the 19th Century, Nepal signed a commercial treaty with the British. But England was becoming increasingly concerned with Nepal's territorial expansion: by 1810, the kingdom extended from Kashmir to Sikkim and was double its present size. Frontier disputes with the British in the Terai led to a full-scale war of almost two years.

The 1816 "Treaty of Friendship" that ended it was most unfavorable for Nepal. The Gorkhas' expansionist ambitions were checked in all directions. The eastern and western borders were fixed in their present locations; Sikkim became a British protectorate; most of the rich Terai was taken away from Nepal; and a British resident was established in Kathmandu. The Nepalese were so resentful of his presence that he was settled on land they considered lethally malarious and infested by spirits. In fact, the resident found it to be a very healthy location.

The treaty also provided equal opportunities for Nepali and Indian traders to establish commercial enterprises in each other's countries, paving the way for the expansion of Indian business interests in the kingdom. Nepalese trade with Tibet was not immediately affected, but Kathmandu's monopoly was taken away when Britain opened a new trade route to Tibet at the beginning of the 20th Century. This 1816 treaty was abrogated only in 1923.

After the so-called "honorable defeat" of 1816, the Nepalese rulers, distrustful of all foreigners, closed their borders, not to be reopened until 1951. The British resident and his successors were the only aliens within Nepal's frontiers for well over a century. The Nepalese retained full control of the country, with emphasis on military preparation, and kept "a standing army of brave soldiers always ready for war or plunder," according to one British account. Between 1819 and 1837, the strength of the Nepalese army jumped from 12,000 to 19,000 men, with twice as many men in reserve.

There was one more aftermath of the 1816 conflict. The gallantry of the Gorkha soldiers had so impressed the British that they inducted them into the British India army. Since that time — through two world wars and dozens of lesser conflicts, including the 1982 Falklands crisis — the Gurkhas have earned fame as outstanding soldiers for the British and Indians. (See the feature article on Gurkhas.)

The Fashionable Ranas

In 1846, after a period of bloody palace intrigues, a young, shrewd and opportunistic Kathmandu army general named Jung Bahadur Rana had himself designated prime minister and later "Maharajah," with powers superior to those of the nominal sovereign. He made the office hereditary, establishing a line of succession that would pass first to his brothers, then to their sons, and in so doing inaugurated the century-long Rana oligarchy.

Political enemies were assassinated or persecuted, and the power structure was reorganized to the sole benefit of Jung Bahadur Rana himself, his immediate circle of relatives and friends, and his successors. The Shah kings were kept under strict vigil in their own palace and were no longer permitted to exercise authority.

As soon as he had firmly established his rule, Jung Bahadur Rana took the highly unorthodox step of traveling — at a leisurely pace and in full royal regalia — to England and France in 1850. Upon his return, no doubt duly impressed by what he had seen, he launched an architectural vogue of neo-classical palaces. Moreover, he proved his progressive inclinations by abolishing the practices of *suttee*, immolation of widows on their husbands' funeral pyres, and restricting the application of capital punishment. Ladies of the court were forced into crinolines and bustles, amazingly contrived from saris of added length, and wore ringlets, kiss curls and heavy makeup. Men wore fanciful European attire and uniforms.

A later prime minister abolished slavery and reformed the forced labor system introduced by the first Shah rulers, easing the lot of agricultural workers. Another prime minister built a school, a college and a dispensary in Kathmandu. Yet another started a newspaper, and one dared to emancipate women by starting a college for them. All these institutions remain today.

In spite of these advances, the most valid criticism that can be leveled against the wealthy Ranas is that during their 104-year reign, they simply did not do enough for the country. If Kathmandu, the seat of their excesses, could feel neglected, it can be imagined how deprived people were in the rest of the country. The huge palaces the Ranas built, the grandiose but spurious lives they lived, contrasted sharply with the austere houses of Kathmandu, the mud huts of village Nepal, and the lifestyle of the common man.

Agricultural methods improved little during the Rana period. Irrigation, in fact, receded in later years. Land was unequally distributed to Rana friends and relatives. In fact, although the king retained rights of property to all land, his holdings were allocated to feudal military overlords acting as local representatives of the central government.

Major changes began taking place during the years following World War Two:

•The union of India, freed of British rule in

1948, swallowed 500 autonomous principalities and a few kingdoms. India considered its northern border to be defined by the Himalaya Mountains.

•China's revolutionary labors resulted in its independence in 1949. A year later, the new People's Republic of China annexed Tibet. Thousands of Tibetan refugees fled to Nepal; some settled in the Kathmandu Valley, while others remained in the Buddhist border areas of the north.

•Within the kingdom, tensions were growing. A "liberal" Rana prime minister proposed a new constitution offering a measure of people's participation through an administrative system known as *panchayat*. Democratic in character, this would have involved a council of village elders, or *panchas*, solving problems

locally, with leaders elected to a national *panchayat*. But this reformist was soon replaced by a hard-liner who saw the solution in increased isolation and authoritarianism, a concept not shared by people fired by the ideal of freedom.

With the support of the Indian Congress Party, opponents of the Rana rule — including some prominent Ranas — joined the Nepali Congress Party under the leadership of B.P. Koirala. The rightful sovereign of Nepal, King Tribhuvan, still powerless in his palace, was heralded as the embodiment of the democratic aspirations of his people.

In November 1950, the king, on the pretense of taking his family on a shooting picnic, escaped to the Indian embassy in Kathmandu, and from there fled to India. In Delhi, he was

Preceding pages, Rana princesses, circa 1910; left, Jung Bahadur Rana with his three wives; above, Chandra Shamsher Jung Bahadur Rana.

welcomed by Nehru as Nepal's reigning monarch. In King Tribhuvan's absence, the Ranas chose his four-year-old grandson, Prince Gyanendra — who had been left behind by the royal hunting party to allay suspicion — to replace him. The child was proclaimed and crowned.

At this point, Koirala and his backers stepped in, with India's blessings if not her weapons, and called for the overthrow of the Rana tyrants. The "freedom fighters" liberated most of the Nepalese Terai, set up a provisional government in Birganj, and engaged Rana troops in battle. But the action was not decisive, and eventually India presided over a compromise agreement between the rival parties.

years after the King's 1955 death that his son, King Mahendra, finally promulgated a constitution that provided for a parliamentary system of government.

The first general election in Nepal's history was held over several weeks in February and March 1959. It was widely assumed that none of Nepal's many fledgling political parties would gain a clear majority, and that King Mahendra would thus be able to manipulate the political scene as actively as in previous years. But the Nepali Congress Party, whose members described themselves as social democrats, surprisingly won a substantial majority of seats in the new parliament.

Koirala, the party head, was a charismatic figure with a large personal following — and strong convictions about how the government

On February 18, 1951, King Tribhuvan returned from his self-imposed exile with garlands of flowers around his neck, and began a new rule with a cabinet that was half Rana aristocrats, half Congress Party commoners. A few months later, the Rana prime minister was forced to step down. He went to live in India, thus ending more than a century of extravagant, despotic rule by the Ranas.

Upheaval and Panchayat

King Tribhuvan opened Nepal's doors to the world, establishing diplomatic relations with many lands. But his 1951 promise to establish a truly democratic government did not achieve immediate fruition. In fact, it wasn't until four

should be run. As prime minister, his views frequently clashed with those of King Mahendra. The Shah ruler did not want himself relegated to a ceremonial role. So at noon on December 15, 1960, he took actions to assure that would not occur.

Declaring that politicians had led the nation to the brink of chaos, and that foreign political concepts did not suit his Himalayan kingdom, King Mahendra suddenly sent army officers to arrest the cabinet. He followed this action with

A royal hunt in south Nepal, above; and right, a rare photo showing (at far right) Rana Prime Minister Juddha Shumsher Jung Bahadur Rana (1932-1945) with King Tribhuvan. Third from right is Crown Prince Mahendra (King from 1955 to 1972).

the announcement that he himself had taken over direct rule. Political parties and their activities were banned, parliament was dismissed, and a 21-month experiment with democracy came to an abrupt end.

Two years later, King Mahendra announced a new national constitution establishing a system of indirect government. Local five-man *panchayats* chose representatives to district *panchayats*, which in turn sent delegates to a national *panchayat*, a legislative body with few real powers. The prime minister and his cabinet were chosen by and were responsible to the King. Political parties remained outlawed, and freedoms of speech, press and assembly were greatly curtailed.

King Mahendra died in January 1972 and

Violence broke out in Kathmandu on April 23, for the first time in living memory.

The following morning, King Birendra told his people on Radio Nepal that a nationwide referendum would be held to determine whether the citizens of Nepal wished to continue the existing system of government, under which party politics were forbidden, or to replace it with a multi-party system.

The King's announcement immediately brought peace to the troubled land. It was followed by a royal proclamation granting considerable freedom of expression and assembly. At the same time, former Prime Minister Koirala, who had been either jailed or in self-exile since 1960, was allowed to go free and campaign for restoration of party politics.

was succeeded by his son, the youthful King Birendra. The new king affirmed his belief that a political system truly suitable to Nepalese conditions had been well established. His government, he said, would turn its efforts towards improving the standard of living of his people, who were becoming increasingly aware of their poverty and lack of progress on an international scale.

By the spring of 1979, popular discontent with insensitive and corrupt officials, arbitrary tax assessors, steeply rising prices, and inadequate supplies of such basic necessities as rice and drinking water, reached a climax. The frustration erupted in public demonstrations which spread throughout the kingdom.

Koirala lost the May 1980 referendum to a vote of 55 percent in favor of the existing system. But by then, the King had declared that whichever side won the plebiscite, the national legislature would be directly chosen by the electorate. The prime minister would in turn be elected by that legislature, and his cabinet would be responsible to it. The national constitution was amended by the King to put these changes into effect, and a year later, in May 1981, the first general elections were held under the partyless system.

The King, however, reserved the right to name one-fifth of the members of the legislature. He retained ultimate authority, and Nepal continues as a strong monarchy in which the King really rules his people directly.

NEPAL TODAY

Century after century, Nepalis have carved a precarious living from the steep slopes of the Himalaya and its foothills.

Generation after generation has farmed the terraced fields that wrinkle the hillsides of a country where only 10 percent of the land is arable.

But if the past has been threatening, the future overwhelms the Nepalis with Himalayan odds.

Population is increasing at a rate of 2.6 percent per year, and land productivity has fallen. Massive deforestation has caused landslides, and the whole mountain ecology has been thrown off balance. There seems to be little hope for the poor Nepali farmer clinging to the thin skin of topsoil on which his life depends.

Land Reforms

In the last three decades, various governments have tried to tackle the problem in different ways. In 1955, in an attempt to give the lower classes greater opportunity, the system of *zamindari* (absentee landlords) was abolished and a comprehensive land-reform plan was announced. The plan didn't become effective until 1964, when a ceiling on land ownership was established (allowing farmers up to 17 hectares in the Terai, 4.11 in the hills and 2.67 in the Kathmandu Valley).

Prior to these reforms, 450 families owned all the farmland in the kingdom. The tiller, surviving on the edge of poverty with neither incentive nor capital to improve his lot or his crop, was laden with debts, inherited and contracted. The Land Reforms Program abolished sub-tenancies, fixed rent at 50 percent of produce, and took various measures to liquidate peasants' debts and secure compulsory savings from the farmers.

After seven years, however, not even half of this target had been met. The reform had actually institutionalized inequalities between landowners and tillers. Redistribution did take place, but landowners used convenient loopholes to beat regulations by transferring property deeds to family members. Money lenders still supply 79 percent of farmers' credit, despite the recent activity of several development banks.

Preceding pages, American diplomats pose with the court of Mohan Shamsher Jung Bahadur Rana about 1950. Left, His Majesty King Tribhuvan.

In July 1976, after the failure of the land reforms had been tacitly accepted, the government gave the go-ahead to organize embryo cooperatives, known as *sajha*, under the aegis of local village leaders. These have been slow in finding a solution to problems.

Success Stories

There are bright spots in Nepal's development struggle. About 3,000 kilometers (1,864 miles) of viable motor roads have been built, and 40 airstrips have been constructed in remote parts of the country otherwise accessible only by weeks of trekking.

Four power stations, generating 80 megawatts of electricity, are in operation, and this is only the tip of an iceberg: Nepal's hydroelectric generation capacity is 83,000 megawatts, probably the highest per capita potential in the world. The most recent addition to the national grid is the Kulekhani Project, which stores monsoon runoff in a valley south of Kathmandu and can generate up to 60 megawatts of peakhour power. Partly because of this project, electricity became available in Kathmandu 24 hours a day in 1982.

The biggest development effort has probably gone into education. Long-time trekkers often comment on the number of village schools that have sprung up in the past 20 years — a trend obvious because new schools often are located on exposed ridges that previously had been ideal camping places. Official figures show the literacy rate nearing 25 percent, or about three million persons; 25 years ago, there were no more than a few thousand students from privileged families.

Food: The Best Medicine

But Nepal is still beset with many problems, chief of which is rural poverty. Hunger, premature death and inadequate housing are rampant. There are only three doctors in Nepal for every 100,000 people, and only one per 100,000 outside of the Kathmandu Valley. One child out of every five dies in the first few weeks of life, and 35 out of 1,000 die between one and four years of age. Contributing to this tragic statistic are malnutrition and poor sanitation. One report says that the only medicine most Nepali children need is a well-balanced diet. This would cure most fatal complications of dysentery and pneumonia.

In the hills and mountains, farmers produce barely enough to feed their families for six or seven months of the year. When the off-season arrives, they must seek temporary employment or migrate to the Terai or India for work.

The Terai has often been called Nepal's grain basket because of the surplus food it produces, but even this surplus has been steadily declining in the face of migration from the hills and from India. Demographic pressure, fragmentation of the land, and falling productivity may soon force the Terai to deal with the same problems currently facing the people of the mountains.

Nine percent of Nepal's population has emigrated to India for permanent work. Nevertheless, population is increasing at an alarming

which are absorbed by India and do not earn hard currency.

Maintaining the Peace

Sandwiched between two colossal neighbors, Nepal is constantly trying to keep both India and China happy. King Birendra's proposal to turn Nepal into an internationally recognized "Zone of Peace" has been endorsed by 80 countries, including China. India has rejected the proposal, emphasizing the "kinship of countries on this side of the Himalaya."

Nepal, however, is not confined to the southern slopes of the Himalaya. Its territory stretches over the mountains into the trans-Himalayan region, and Nepalis insist they are as much a part of Central Asia as the South Asian subcontinent.

rate. Despite a family planning program financed mainly with foreign aid, there are 270,000 extra mouths to feed in Nepal every year. The annual rate of population increase in the mountains is 1.8 percent, the hills 2.6 percent, and the Terai a whopping 4.2 percent. Some pockets of the Terai even show 6 percent annual growth. If present trends continue, the Terai population will double in less than 10 years, with disastrous results. Although grain production is increasing in volume, the population is climbing even faster.

Few if any of Nepal's mineral resources can be exploited industrially. Industry is confined mainly to the Terai belt, with a few factories and workshops in the Kathmandu Valley. Jute represents 90 percent of all exports, most of

China has taken an active part in the development of this Himalayan kingdom, mobilizing tens of thousands of Nepali workers to build and maintain important segments of all-weather roads. Strategic considerations have prompted India and various other foreign powers to offer additional aid; as a result, parts of Nepal never before accessible have been linked by roads.

Nepal's geographical juxtaposition between India and China may be its best guarantee of survival as a Himalayan buffer state. Neither of the two powers would tolerate political

Singha Durbar was built in 1911 as the home of the ruling Rana prime ministers. Today it houses various government offices.

encroachment by the other in Nepal, but the Indian subcontinent has always been politically volatile, and Nepal cannot afford to relax its vigilance.

Dependence on India is almost complete. Eighty percent of Nepal's trade is with her southern neighbor. The Indian market also has a mighty hold on the tourism industry, Nepal's biggest foreign exchange earner. Indeed, India is in a position to call the shots in the economic sphere. With no other access to the sea, Nepal must trade with India.

This overriding dependence often disturbs Nepalis, creating uneasy feelings of potential political intervention by India. Certainly, Indian pressure could bring Nepalese industry to a standstill, should a crisis arise. This fear has sometimes led to fierce anti-Indian demonstra-

ning and population control. Direct Soviet aid, once notable, has dwindled to nothing. Through barter deals with India, the U.S.S.R. supplies most of Nepal's crude oil needs.

Nepal's government still relies heavily on foreign aid and expertise in its development programs. By international standards, this aid — while steadily increasing — is still negligible. But aid is a mixed blessing. The heavy reliance on foreign funds is criticized in influential circles by Nepalis who feel a loss of sovereignty. King Birendra himself has stressed the importance of self-reliance. Economic necessity may dictate otherwise, however.

After a tremendous increase in tourism through the 1960s and 1970s, arrivals have leveled off at about 160,000 visitors per year. For the first time since 1955, the total number

tions in Kathmandu and in some towns of the Terai.

Trade relations have been adjusted several times, taking into account transit facilities in Indian ports for goods bound for Nepal. Goodwill and detente now appear to be the order of the day, thanks in part to a certain rapprochement between India and China.

Foreign Aid: A Mixed Blessing

If the rivalry between the two "big brothers" has been put to good use by Kathmandu, other foreign powers and international agencies have also contributed to Nepal's development efforts. American and British aid has been especially noteworthy in banking, health services, education, agriculture, family plan-

of visitors actually declined in 1981. Tourism, despite the growth in trekking, remains confined largely to the Kathmandu Valley.

Fortunately, so do the after-effects and cultural fallout. The fragile, somewhat artificial wealth carried by tourism has brought an overdose of westernization to Kathmandu's traditionally conservative social structure. The society has become generally service-oriented. Antique thefts and hard-drug usage, while hardly rampant, are a fact of life. And the almighty rupee has found a niche in the pantheon of gods.

King Birendra in ceremonial dress graces the 100 rupee note. With the rapid increase in tourism, money has an increased importance in society.

AN ETHNIC MOSAIC

Mutual tolerance and peaceful co-existence have been the basis of social harmony and cultural synthesis since the dawn of our country's history.
— *His Majesty King Birendra, May 17, 1982.*

Nepal is a veritable mosaic of dozens of ethnic groups with their own unique languages, cultures and religions. But it nevertheless has a tradition of harmony rather than conflict. Society here has always been accommodating to new ideas, new values, new peoples from afar.

In this land of ethnic elements as diverse as its landscape, the principles of integration and synthesis were accepted from ancient times. The earliest distinguishable races of Nepal were an intermixture of Khas and Kiratis with other immigrant groups. Today, a striking example of this amalgam of north and south, of Tibeto-Burman and Indo-Aryan stocks, are the Newars of the Kathmandu Valley. (See the chapter on "Daily Life" for a discussion of these people).

Watch the faces of the Nepali people passing you at any busy intersection in Kathmandu, and you will soon discover what a fascinating melting pot of Himalayan cultures the city is. But if you wander from the Valley to Nepal's outlying regions, you will find many isolated pockets of distinct peoples and cultures.

The Tamang 'Horse Traders'

Outside the rim of the Valley, and well beyond it, live the Tamangs. Tamang means "horse trader" in the Tibetan language, but no one knows whether they ever traded in horses. Today, they are mostly small farmers; some work as porters and craftsmen, especially in wicker work and carpentry. Their elaborate two-story stone-and-wood houses are clustered along cobbled streets.

Tamangs are often seen in the streets of Kathmandu carrying large *doko* (baskets) by headstraps. The men and boys are dressed in loincloths and long, usually black tunics; in winter, they wear short-sleeved sheep-wool jackets, frequently with a *khukri* knife thrust in the waist band. Women wear short saris of homemade cotton, and blouses adorned with a few ornaments.

Preceding pages, a face on the streets of Kathmandu; left, a Tamang woman adorned with traditional jewelry and embroidered jacket.

Tamangs are Lama Buddhists, as are most upper Himalayan peoples. They have *gompas* (monasteries) in every sizeable village. The gods, religious paintings and texts, festivals and ritual ceremonies are all of Tibetan style. Some northern peoples follow the Bonpo religion, generally considered the pre-Buddhist religion of Tibet; but both religions have priests and deities, and variations in the rites appear to be minimal. Whereas a Buddhist walks to the left of a shrine and spins his prayer wheel clockwise, a Bonpo believer walks to the right and spins his prayer wheel counterclockwise.

Like most of Nepal's peoples, the Tamangs retain *jhankris* (shamans) in addition to their *lamas* (priests). These *jhankris* conduct religious ceremonies for communal and individual well-being: their ritual procedures involve trance and possession to drive away spirits for the sick or dying, to recover lost souls, and to perform various seasonal agricultural rites, such as making sacrifices to ensure good crops. Not surprisingly, many of these shamanic rites are quite similar to those once found among the peoples of Mongolia and Siberia.

Polygamy is not uncommon in the hills, even though the government has restricted it and family economics are a limiting factor. There is an ambivalent attitude regarding sexual activities, with money as a soothing influence. If a Tamang man abducts the wife of another, for example, the new husband compensates the ex-spouse with payment of about Rs. 1,000. Adultery is punishable by lower fines.

Life on the World's Edge

The high Himalayan settlements of Tibetan-speaking peoples perch precariously on mountain ledges and fragile slopes. Life here is a very delicate balance of hard work and social frivolity, tempered by a culture deeply founded in ancient religious tradition.

The best known of the high-mountain peoples are the Sherpas, inhabiting central and eastern regions of Nepal. Although the name "Sherpa" has become synonymous with "mountain guide," it is only those in the Everest region who have achieved relative prosperity through mountaineering and trekking.

The southern limits of these Himalayan regions — places like Phaplu, Junbesi, Tarkeghyang, Sermathang, Marpha and Jomosom — are sometimes thought of as attractive, even

romantic, examples of high-altitude settlements. Indeed, many are. But the extreme north and other communities on higher slopes are not very comfortable or prosperous. These border settlements are few and far between; interaction with the inhabitants of other villages requires long journeys. Villagers therefore develop a lifestyle of constant mobility for their economic, social and cultural activities.

Among the inhabitants of these hardy climes are the 6,000 to 7,000 people of Mustang. They live in oasis villages on a reddish-brown rock desert, fighting a constant bitter wind to farm grains and potatoes in sheltered plots.

Long-distance trade is an integral part of socio-cultural interaction, not just an economic behavior. When, during the 1960s, the barter trade between the border people of Nepal and Tibet was reduced to a trickle, many thought the Chinese authorities in Tibet had intentionally stopped the trade. In fact, trade was not discouraged — but social interaction was. And with a ban on long-term credit arrangements, as well as on *chhang* drinking, dancing, singing and sometimes intermarriage, trade was no longer attractive to the mountain peoples.

The hard grind of daily life in the high Himalayas is interrupted by seasons of feasts and festivals, marked by drinking, dancing and general merry-making. Most festivals are of a religious nature and center around the temples and monasteries, with rites conducted by *lamas*. These festivals are spread out through the full-moon days of May, June, July, August and November in different sections of the Himalayas. They include the Dumje and Mani Rimdu rites of the Sherpas of Solu-Khumbu; the Yartung festival of Muktinath; and the Dyokyabsi fest of Mustang.

The Clever Thakalis

Among the most interesting northern peoples of Nepal are the Thakalis. Residing in the upper Kali Gandaki river region, astride a seam of cultures, languages, ethnic groups, climatic conditions and historic traditions that are worlds apart from one another, Thakali society has necessarily been open but alert and vigilant. Over several centuries, the Thakalis have successfully integrated Lamaism and Hinduism into their own colorful faith, and have mastered the arts of trade and commerce to emerge as perhaps the most successful entrepreneurs in Nepal. Their careers began with the salt trade between Tibet and India, but to-

day they have spread into all spheres of contemporary life — including construction, politics, business, academia, arts and literature.

The secret of this expansion is the *dighur* system. A group of friends or relatives pool a given amount of money, sometimes thousands of rupees each, and give the whole sum every year to one among them. The recipient uses the loan as he sees fit; whether he loses or gains money is his own affair, and his only obligation is to feed the *dighur*. When everyone in the pool has taken a turn, the *dighur* is automatically dissolved. An interesting self-financing device based on mutual trust, the system does away with interest rates and presupposes stability of currency.

A good example of Thakali behavioral patterns can be seen in the village of Marpha. A

casual glance at this community shows a strong sense of organization, discipline, cleanliness, and far-sighted vision. Marpha is picturesquely wedged between steep sandstone cliffs on one side and a small ledge of cultivated fields overlooking the Kali Gandaki on the other. Along cobbled alleyways, whitewashed mud houses with flat roofs surround a succession of courtyards where livestock feed on fragrant juniper boughs, which the people also use to make tea. There is running water and a drainage system, an exceptional phenomenon in Nepal.

Most Thakalis are small farmers, growing barley and some potatoes. Savings are often invested in herds of yaks grazing the upper pastures of the valley. These long-haired Asi-

Tibetan-speaking inhabitants of the Muktinath Valley, left; and right, study of a young Thakali merchant.

atic oxen are good providers: the females, *naks*, give milk; their cheese is sold as well as used for home consumption. The beasts' rough wool and hides are used in clothing, tents and pack saddles.

People of the Middle Hills

The various peoples living in the temperate zone of Nepal's middle hills are sometimes erroneously referred to *en masse* as Gurkhas. The British and Indian armies have famed Gurkha regiments, named after the soldiers from the former Kingdom of Gorkha. But there is no single ethnic group today called Gurkha. By tradition, most Gurkha soldiers come from the Gurung, Magar, Rai, Limbu, Yakha and Sunuwar ethnic groups.

Magars are quite predominant numerically. They have earned a reputation for martial qualities both within and outside of Nepal, though they are basically self-sufficient hill peasants. They grow rice, maize, millet, wheat and potatoes, depending upon the suitability of the terrain they occupy. Spread out all over western and central Nepal, from the high Himalayan valleys to the plains of the Terai, the Magars — a Tibeto-Burman race — have adopted whatever language, culture, religion, style of dress, and even architectural style is dictated by their area of settlement.

The Gurungs are similar in many respects to the Magars, but generally live higher and further east, along the Kali Gandaki watershed. Farmers and herders they cultivate maize,

millet, mustard seeds and potatoes. Cattle are kept and buffaloes provide meat, but sheep are of paramount importance. Families own perhaps a dozen sheep each, grouped in village flocks of 200 to 300. Four or five shepherds — accompanied by fierce mastiffs — take them to the upper pastures from April to September, when shearing is done. The flocks return to the village in October for the feast of the Dasain festival; then they head south for the winter, sometimes as far as the inner Terai hills. Wool is soaked and washed, but used undyed when woven in traditional patterns by Gurung women.

Rai, Limbu, Yakha and Sunuwar people of the eastern hills, like Magars and Gurungs, favor military service to all other professions, perhaps because soldiers return home with added prestige and income. But the majority of them stay home and practice the subsistence-level agriculture of the middle hills. While subtle differences exist among them, their lifestyles are similar. They are nominally Hindu, although some have adopted Buddhism in a unique melange typical of Nepalese religion.

Brahmans and Chhetris

The ubiquitous Brahmans and Chhetris, along with the occupational castes of Nepal, have also traditionally played an important role in Nepalese society. Originally from west Nepal, the majority have a preference for the temperate middle hills, although they have dispersed in all parts of the Terai.

Orthodox Hindus, they believe in a hierarchical caste structure. "Caste," a word originally brought to Nepal and the Indian subcontinent by the Portuguese, is easily misunderstood by outsiders. In fact, it is not as exotic as usually portrayed. Most societies in the world have hierarchical systems based both on birth and pedigree as well as wealth and position, groups with whom they prefer to socialize and intermarry, and groups whom they consider different. Hinduism merely institutionalizes it.

In Nepal, the Hindu caste system socially and ritually defines all people by the group into which they have been born. It is elaborated into a number of rules for eating, marrying, working and touching. But as strong and persuasive as this system is, Nepal has been unique in the Hindu world for the degree to which economic, political and romantic deviations from the caste norms are accepted and incorporated into society.

A jovial woman from the Mugu Valley smiles at a visitor, left; and a colorful Rai maiden takes a break in her working day, right.

Brahmans and Chhetris are, like their neighboring ethnic groups, predominantly subsistence farmers. However, the literary and priestly tradition of the Brahmans has facilitated their taking important roles in modern Nepalese government, education and business. Similarly, most of the ruling families, including the famous Ranas, have been drawn from the Chhetri caste. Together, the Brahmans and Chhetris have provided the *lingua franca*, Nepali, and the main cultural and legal framework for Nepal's national identity.

Peoples of the Terai

The Terai Hindus — especially the high-caste people — are more orthodox and conservative than the hill people, and are somewhat

throughout most of the western Terai. Rajbansi, Satar, Dhimal and Bodo people live mainly in the far eastern districts of Jhapa and Morang. Moslems are found mostly along the central and western sections of the Terai.

The Tharus are probably among the most ancient people inhabiting the Terai. Still numbering about half a million, they live in scattered villages. Their spacious houses with latticework walls are decorated with animal and fish designs. In most areas, their agriculture is stationary but primitive; however, in the Deobhuri valley of western Nepal, Tharus run an elaborate and well-maintained traditional irrigation system. They breed a few sheep and goats, hunt with bows, and fish with jute nets.

The bejeweled Tharu women, noted for

inhibited by their rigid values and attitudes. Although the caste system has lost its legal support, the higher castes still control almost all the region's wealth and carry considerable political clout. Movement back and forth across the India-Nepal border is basically unrestricted, especially for marriages and socio-economic relations, thus cementing caste ties.

Villages are clusters of 30 to 100 or more dwellings, most of them with bamboo walls plastered with cow dung and mud, and topped by thatched or tile roofs. Concrete walls and flat cement roofs are signs of wealth.

Non-caste ethnic groups, such as the Tharu, Danuwar, Majhi and Darai, live mainly along the northern strip of the eastern Terai and

their austere mien, usually marry early. Their lovers must often work for their parents-in-law, sometimes for two or three years, before they "earn" the right to marry. Age defines authority in the family; the old man is the overlord and the mother or elder sister rules over the female side of the household.

Living as they do in the realm of tigers, crocodiles and scorpions, Tharus venerate animistic spirits as well as some Hindu deities. A village god is worshipped by each community at a small raised shrine.

A shy Brahman bride gazes through her wedding veil, above; and right, a hardy Chhetri woman wears a traditional cotton outfit and bead jewelry.

A UNIQUE VISION OF THE DIVINE

Every day before dawn, when sacred cows and stray dogs roam aimlessly in empty streets and when farmers are hurrying to market with their loads of vegetables or chickens, devotees of Nepal's religious cults wake up their gods in sacred temples.

As the misty rays of dawn begin to stream through the doorways, men, women and children set out for Hindu and Buddhist temples, carrying ritual offerings — *puja* — for the multiple gods of their pantheons.

They carry small metal, usually copper, plates piled with grains of rice, red powder and tiny yellow flower petals to scatter on the deities' images. Afterward, they mix the offerings with clay, and apply a small amount of the mixture to their own foreheads, between the eyes: this is *tika*, a symbol of the presence of the divine.

Puja such as this is made at any and all times in Nepal, for any occasion or celebration. It is a cornerstone of Nepali religion, inherited from the most ancient of ancestors. Offerings renew communion with the deities most important to each individual's particular problem, caste or inclination.

Some of the devout have a special sequence of offerings, carefully arranged in a partitioned copper tray; they go from god to god for the best part of the morning. Others arrive with a couple of cups of yoghurt or *ghee*, and perhaps a few coins for the priests. Still other people may stay near their homes, contenting their deities by throwing rice, powder and petals on a particular rock or tree.

Ritual sacrifice is Nepali religion's other "cornerstone." Whether for a wedding or initiation rite, a seasonal festival for a deity, or a blessing for the construction of a house, sacrifices are carried out with utter simplicity or with utmost pomp and ceremony, from the Himalayas to the Terai.

The sacrifice of a chicken, goat or buffalo, always a male animal, is not only a way of slaying a beast in the presence of the divine. It also gives an "unfortunate brother" a release from his imprisonment as an animal, and the opportunity for rebirth as a man.

At the time of Nepal's biggest feast, the Dasain festival of early autumn, some 10,000 animals, mainly goats, are sacrificed in the

Preceding pages, a priest sits at Budhanilkantha. Left, sacrifice of a goat near Sankhu's Bajra Jogini; right, a Hindu devotee applies *tika*.

space of a few days. More commonly, there are biweekly sacrifices of chickens and goats at the Dakshinkali Temple — to the fascination of tourists crowding outside the sacrificial pits. In other lesser known temples and courtyards, such sacrifices are a normal Friday and Saturday occurrence.

In Nepal, obedience to the gods' laws and placation through ritual are a part of every person's daily routine. Each individual partakes in the divine in his personal way. For the common folk, this often involves a matter-of-fact repetition of gestures. But it is part of an all-

pervading perception of religiosity, enhanced by a strong sense of human dignity.

Religious Mainstreams

The two main spiritual currents underlying the religious practices of Nepal are Hinduism and Buddhism. It is often hard to distinguish the two, especially since they are interwoven with the exotica of Tantrism on a background of animistic cults retained from the distant past. The result is a proliferation of cults, deities and celebrations in variations unknown elsewhere on earth.

With such diverse beliefs, religious tolerance is of the essence. In fact, proselytism is forbidden by law — with a lengthy jail term awaiting offending parties, converter and convert.

The bulk of Kathmandu's Newars can be called Buddhist, in the sense that their family priests are Tantric Buddhist priests rather than Hindu brahmins. Such classification, however, has never prevented a villager from worshipping Tantric Hindu gods who are the village's patron deities. By becoming a follower of the Buddha, one does not cease to be a Hindu. Buddhists, in fact, regard the Hindu trinity of Brahma, Shiva and Vishnu as *avatars* of the Primordial Buddha, and give the triad important places in the Buddhist cosmogony. Hindus likewise regard the Gautama Buddha as an incarnation of Vishnu. It has been said that, if one asks a Newar whether he is Hindu or Buddhist, the answer will be, "Yes." The question is meaningless, implying an exclusive choice which is foreign to the religious experi-

ence of Nepal's people.

The political leaders of the Kathmandu Valley have always been Hindus, but most of them have consistently and equally supported development of their peoples' other faiths.

The 7th Century King Narendradev, for instance, received Chinese Buddhist travelers with utmost respect, and took them to visit all the Buddhist temples and monasteries in his realm. Chinese journals describe the king as a devout Buddhist who wore an emblem of the Buddha on his belt. But inscriptions left behind from Narendradev's reign insist that he regarded Shiva as his principal god.

Beginning with the time of King Jayasthiti Malla in the 14th Century, growing pressure was put on Nepal's population to conform to

the social structure of Hindu society. Even the Malla family deity, the goddess Taleju, was an import from south India. This trend was strengthened when the present Shah dynasty acceded to the throne over 200 years ago, adopting as its patron deity a deified Shaivite yogi, Gorakhnath.

The Rana prime ministers increased the caste differences in their century of power, enhancing the wealth and power of the ruling class. At the same time, innovation in religious arts was discouraged, with material wealth shifting to earthly "lords." Architects turned to building palaces rather than temples, and little was left for beautification of the religious heritage. The current government, however, realizes the importance of religion and promotes this cultural legacy.

The Hindu Heritage

Nepal's religions actually had their origins with the first Aryan invaders, who settled in the north of India about 1700 B.C. They recorded the *Vedas*, a collection of over 1,000 hymns defining a polytheistic religion. Out of this grew the caste-conscious Brahminism, linking all men to the god-creator Brahma. The brahmins, or priest class, were said to have come from Brahma's mouth; the Chhetris, or warrior caste, from his arms; the Vaisyas, artisans and traders, from his thighs; and the Sudras, or serfs, from his feet. This same general caste classification persists today.

As Brahminism evolved into modern Hinduism, people of the subcontinent began to feel increasingly that existence and reality were subjects too vast to be encompassed within a single set of beliefs. The Hindu religion of today, therefore, comprises many different metaphysical systems and viewpoints, some of them mutually contradictory. The individual opts for whichever belief or practice suits him and his particular inclinations the best.

Hinduism has no formal creed, no universal governing organization. Brahmin priests serve as spiritual advisers to upper-caste families, but the only real authority is the ancient Vedic texts. Most important is that the individual comply with his family and social group.

Different sects have developed a particular affinity with one or another deity — especially with Brahma "the creator," Vishnu "the preserver" and Shiva "the destroyer."

Most Nepali Hindus regard Brahma's role as

Popular image of the terrifying Seto Bhairav, left; and a priest at Bisket ceremonies during the Nepalese New Year, right.

being essentially completed. Having created the world, he can now sit back astride his swan and keep out of everyday affairs. Both Vishnu and Shiva are very important in Nepal, however.

Vishnu, whose duty it is to assure the preservation of life and of the world, is traditionally considered to have visited earth as 10 different *avatars*, or incarnations. Nepalese art pictures him as a fish, a tortoise, a boar, a lion, a dwarf, and as various men — among them Narayan, the embodiment of universal love and knowledge; Rama, a prince; Krishna, a cowherd and charioteer; and Gautama Buddha, who corrupted the demons. The King of Nepal also is regarded as an *avatar* of Vishnu.

The stories of Rama and Krishna are parti-

habharata epic, particularly in that portion known as the *Bhagavad-Gita*. In this important story, Krishna appears as a charioteer for the warrior Arjuna, who meets an opposing army manned by his friends and relatives. Arjuna is reluctant to strike until convinced by Krishna that he must be true to his own role in life; he goes on to battle and exterminates the opposition.

Nepalis love the many tales of Krishna's pranks and antics as a cowherd. It is said he once appeared to the *gopis,* the cowherd girls, in as many embodiments as there were women, and made love to each of them in the way she liked best.

But for all the devotion paid to Vishnu and his *avatars*, it is Shiva who gets the most attention in Nepal. Those who worship Shiva do so

cularly important to Hindus. Rama is the hero of the *Ramayana*, perhaps Asia's greatest epic tale. The ideal man, Rama is brave, noble and virtuous. His beautiful wife Sita (whose legendary home of Janakhpur in the eastern Terai is a site of pilgrimage for Hindus) is the perfect wife, loyal and devoted. On a forest foray, Sita is captured by the demon Rawana, who carries her off to his lair on the isle of Lanka. Rama enlists the help of the monkey people and their general, Hanuman, as well as the mythical eagle, Garuda. Together, they rescue Sita and slay Rawana. Sita proves her purity after the abduction by entering a fire and emerging unscathed. In Nepal, Hanuman and Garuda — Vishnu's mount — are revered.

Krishna is the central figure in the *Ma-*

not out of love of destruction, but because man must respect the fact that all things eventually will come to an end, and from that end will come a new beginning.

Like Vishnu, Shiva takes different forms. He is Pashupati, who guides all species in their development and serves benevolently as the tutelary god of Nepal. He is Mahadev, lord of knowledge and procreation, symbolized by the *lingum*. And he is the terrifying Tantric Bhairav, depicted with huge teeth and a necklace of skulls, intent on destroying everything he sees — including ignorance.

One of Shiva's sons, by his consort Parvati (also known as Annapurna, goddess of abundance), is the elephant-headed god Ganesh. It is said he was born as a normal child, but had his head accidentally severed, and the elephant's head was grafted onto his neck. It is Ganesh's responsibility to decide between success and failure, to remove obstacles or create them as necessary.

The idea of "new beginnings," made manifest in the doctrine of reincarnation, is what keeps the Hindu caste system strong. Hindus believe they must accept and act according to their station in life, no matter what it may be. Their birthright is a reward or punishment for actions — karma — accrued in a previous life. Their behavior in this life will help determine their next one.

Teachings of the Buddha

Brahminism was the dominant faith in India

at the time of the emergence of Buddhism in the 6th Century B.C.

The religion's founder, a Sakya prince named Siddhartha Gautama, was born about 543 B.C. (the actual date is disputed) near present-day Lumbini in Nepal's western Terai. Raised in the lap of luxury in a royal palace, sheltered from any knowledge of the suffering outside its walls, he was married and fathered a child.

At the age of 29, he convinced his charioteer to take him outside the palace grounds. There, the sight of an old man, a crippled man and a corpse — and his charioteer's acknowledgment that "it happens to us all" — persuaded him to abandon his family and his lavish lifestyle for that of a wandering ascetic.

For more than five years, Gautama roamed from place to place, nearly dying of self-deprivation as he sought a solution to the suffering he saw. He finally abandoned his asceticism, and while meditating under a pipal tree near Benares, India, oblivious to all distractions and temptations, he became enlightened. One must follow the Middle Way, he declared, rejecting extremes of pleasure and pain.

Now known as the Buddha, the "Enlightened One," Gautama preached a doctrine based on the "Four Noble Truths" and the "Eightfold Path." We suffer, he said, because of our attachment to people and things in a world where nothing is permanent. We can rid ourselves of desire, and do away with suffering, by living our lives with attention to right views, right intent, right speech, right conduct, right livelihood, right effort, right mindfulness and right meditation.

The "self," said the Buddha, is nothing but an illusion trapped in the endless cycle of samsara, or rebirth, and created by karma, the chain of cause and effect. By following the Buddhist doctrine, the Dharma, he said, one can put an end to the effects of karma, thereby escaping samsara and achieving nirvana, which is essentially extinction of "self."

Gautama preached his doctrine for 45 years after his enlightenment, finally dying at the age of 80 and transcending to nirvana. Nepalis claim he may have visited the Kathmandu Valley with his disciple, Ananda, during his ministry.

In the centuries following the Buddha's life, many doctrinal disputes arose, leading to various schisms in the philosophy. Most important was the break between the Theravada or Hinayana school, which adhered more closely to the original teachings and today predominates in Southeast Asia and Sri Lanka, and the Mahayana school, which spread north and east from India.

It was Mahayana Buddhism which took hold in Nepal. One of the central beliefs of all Mahayanists is that one can achieve nirvana by following the example of bodhisattvas, or "Buddhas-to-be." These enlightened beings have, in the course of many lifetimes, acquired the knowledge and virtues necessary to attain nirvana, but have indefinitely delayed their transcendence in order to help other mortals reach a similar state of perfection.

The Buddhist emperor Ashoka of India's Maurya Dynasty made a pilgrimage to the Buddha's birthplace near Lumbini in the 3rd

Two portraits: one of tne Dalai Lama is paraded around the grounds of Bodhnath, left, while the Most Respected Tarig Tulku poses at right.

Century B.C. He or his missionaries may have introduced some basic teachings while building stupas in the Kathmandu Valley. Nearly 1,000 years later, in the 7th Century A.D. the Tibetan King Tsrong-tsong Gompo invaded the Valley and carried back a Nepalese princess as his wife. Both the Nepalese lady ("Green Tara") and the king's Chinese consort ("White Tara") were Buddhists, and they persuaded him to convert to Buddhism.

Tibetan Buddhism

Since that time, Tibetan Buddhism has exerted a significant influence on Buddhist belief in Nepal. Altered in part by the earliest religion of Tibet, known as Bon, it has taken on a unique form in the world of Buddhism.

pilgrimage among Tibetan people to discover where their leader was reborn immediately following his physical death. The correct child is determined by his recognition of possessions from his previous life.

Tibetans believe there are, at any one time, several hundred more *tulkus,* people identified in similar fashion as reincarnations of other important religious figures. These people generally go on to become leading monks themselves.

There are four chief sects of Tibetan Buddhism, most important of which is the *Gelugpa*, or Yellow Hats. Although himself a Yellow Hat, the Dalai Lama preaches free access to all teachings, including the *Kargyupa* (Red Hats), *Nyingmapa* (Ancients) and *Sagyapa* (People of the Earth). Each of these groups has made important contributions to

The shamanistic Bon faith, elements of which still exist today in Tibet and some remote corners of Nepal, has certain affinities with Buddhism. Bonpos (followers of Bon) claim their religion was carried from the west, possibly Kashmir, by their founder, gShen-rab, who (like the Buddha) endured great hardships and meditated to achieve his spiritual knowledge. In medieval times, interchange between Bon and Buddhism led to a mutual adoption of parts of each other's pantheon under different names.

The leading figure of Tibetan Buddhism — its pope, as it were — is the Dalai Lama. Every Dalai Lama is regarded as the reincarnation of his predecessor. Upon the death of a Dalai Lama, a party of elderly monks goes on a

Tibetan Buddhist doctrine.

Tibetan Buddhism stresses the inter-relatedness of all things. Universal cosmic forces and the energies of the individual human being are one and the same, and through the faithful practice of meditation, one can learn to apply one's knowledge of these energies. This can involve an altered state of consciousness: skilled Tibetan monks are said to be able to levitate, to travel across land at the speed of the wind, and to perform other actions which Westerners tend to relegate to the realms of the occult.

Learning proper meditation, under the

Tantric erotica from the Halchok temple, left; and a sculpture of the god Shiva and his *shakti* Parvati, right.

guidance of a personal teacher, is the first step toward understanding the doctrine of interdependence. The most important tools of meditation are *mantra*, or sacred sound, and *mandala*, or sacred diagram. In *mantra* meditation, chanting of and concentration on certain syllables, such as "*Om mani padme hum*," is believed to intensify the spiritual power of those indoctrinated to the meaning. *Mandala* meditation requires one to visualize certain circular images to assist in orienting the self to the total universe.

Another important aspect of Tibetan Buddhism is the perception of death and dying. Accounts of pre-death and post-death experiences are an integral part of Tibet's religious archives.

Because mental and emotional states are believed to have an effect on afterlife and rebirth, the dying person — accompanied by family, friends and *lamas* — meditates through the period of transition from life to death. This makes it easier for his spirit, or consciousness, to give up its residence in the body.

The Tantric Cults

All of Nepal's religions, whether Hindu, Buddhist or otherwise, are strongly influenced by the practices of Tantrism, a legacy of the Indian subcontinent's medieval culture. While the Moslem conquest, the British *raj* and modern secularism largely eliminated Tantrism elsewhere, it has lived on in Nepal.

Tantra is originally a Sanskrit word, referring to the basic warp of threads in weaving. Literally, Tantrism reiterates the Buddhist philosophy of the interwovenness of all things and actions.

But Tantrism, with roots in the *Vedas* and the *Upanishads,* pre-Buddhist Brahministic verses, is more than that. In its medieval growth, it expanded the realm of Hindu gods, cults and rites, and added a new element to the speculative philosophy and yogic practices of the time. Within Buddhism, it created a major trend called Vajrayana, the "Path of the Thunderbolt," which reached its greatest importance in Nepal.

The *vajra*, known as the *dorje* in Tibetan Buddhism, is a main ritual object for Tantric Buddhist monks. It is a scepter, each end of which has five digits curved in a global shape, said to represent the infinite in three dimensions. It is the symbol of the Absolute, a male instrument, and has as its female counterpart a bell or *ghanta*.

The prolific Tantric gods are represented in numerous human and animal forms, often with multiple arms, legs and heads as symbols of the omnipresence and omnipotence of the divine. Many of these deities have a terrifying appearance, like forbidding Bhairav, bloodthirsty Kali or ambivalent Shiva, who in the Tantric pantheon is both creator and destroyer. Their appearance is said to reflect man's when confronted with unknown forces.

Opposed to contemplative meditation, Tantrism substituted concrete action and direct experience. But it soon degenerated into esoteric practices, often of a sexual nature, purportedly to go beyond one's own limitations to reach perfect divine bliss.

Shaktism is such a cult, praising the *shakti*, the female counterpart of a god. Some ritual Tantric texts proclaim: "Wine, flesh, fish, women and sexual congress: these are the fivefold boons that remove all sin."

At a higher level, Tantrism is an attempt to synthesize spiritualism and materialism. Practitioners seek to expand their mental faculties by mastering the forces of nature and achieving peace of mind. In the sexual act is seen wisdom, tranquility and bliss, along with — of course — the mystery inherent in human union.

The image depicting sexual union is called *yab-yum*, perhaps not entirely unlike the Chinese *yin-yang*, a symbol of oneness in polarity. In several locations in the Kathmandu valley, *yab-yum* and other erotica are carved in wooden relief on the struts of temples. The significance of these artistic expressions depends less on what they show than on who looks at them.

THE VALLEY

Nowhere in the world can one find the same concentration of culture, art and tradition that exist in the Kathmandu Valley. To the majority of Nepalis, the Valley *is* Nepal. This concept, which stems from the land's early human history, was magnified during the cultural heyday of the Mallas when the Valley flourished as a center of art and architecture. Later, the Valley's petty kingdoms were unified by Prithvi Narayan Shah, and the Valley then became the fulcrum of Nepalese power and politics.

Due to its inaccessibility and the fact that it was closed to the outside world until the early 1950s, the Kathmandu Valley still remains a place of mystery. Although Western influence has made its mark on Kathmandu itself, it is easy to walk back into history and become totally immersed in imageries of the medieval period.

Kathmandu is the crossroads for the numerous tribes and ethnic groups, more than 30 in all, inhabiting Nepal's highlands and lowlands. They come to the Valley on pilgrimages, seeking the favor of a special god or perhaps honoring an ancestor. In a way, every visitor to Nepal and the Kathmandu Valley is a pilgrim, whether he has come to gaze upon the fabled Himalaya or to relax in the peaceful, almost biblical environs of the Pashupatinath temple. The essential experience is the same.

Flying into the Valley is another such experience. On a clear day, you can see the crystal-clear snow-clad peaks of the Himalaya from the Annapurna Massif to the Everest range. From the foothills surrounding the Valley, a maze of river courses fan through the flat land. Descending into the basin, you can pick out key landmarks like the hilltop temple of Swayambhunath and the large Bodhnath stupa encircled by dwellings and monasteries. The sharp eye may even spot Changu Narayan, atop a ridge that was once a peninsula in the Valley's primeval lake; or Kirtipur, a fine village perched on a rocky hilltop, an oasis in a sea of agriculture.

You can't miss the main cities of Kathmandu and Patan, once feuding petty kingdoms, now merging into a common urban sprawl. A little further east is the Valley's third major city, Bhaktapur. Within each city is a concentration of temples, outlining the main palaces and Durbar Squares. The large white neo-classical palaces built by the Ranas are easily identifiable.

And then, with a rush, the runway comes toward you. As you skim past a group of Chhetri houses — the straw-roofed brick residences of local farmers — you have arrived in the center of the Kathmandu Valley. Ahead of you is the excitement of a melange of peoples and cultures found nowhere else on earth.

DAILY LIFE

The Valley of Kathmandu is a world in itself. In sharp contrast to the rural hills, where the only two directions are up and down, it is an oasis of flat land where life can move as it may.

Flying into the Valley, the hills suddenly open out. Green terraced hillsides descend stepwise down the Valley's rim to the flatness below. Three-hundred sixty degrees of blue hills encompass this emerald Himalayan gem. Red-tile roofs of tiny doll houses strike a pleasant harmony with the flat expanse of green below an azure sky.

Many thousands of years ago, the only inhabitants of this lush and fertile valley floor were *gopalas,* or cowherds. The Kiratis and the Licchavis, who followed them, left little lasting cultural legacy; but under the Mallas, there was a renaissance. Patronized by the nobility, Newar artisans constructed the temples, *bahals* (monasteries) and *chowks* (courtyards) that constitute the manmade environment of the Valley today.

As time went by, the growing importance of the Valley as a trading post between Tibet and India laid the framework for the emergence of a unique culture. The exceptional fertility of the former lake bed contributed to the dominance of the agricultural population. Even today, Kathmandu's artisans, priests and traders maintain this intimate link to their precious land.

Building Close to the Land

The Valley's Newar settlements reflected this pattern. But there was something about these settlements that was unusual for an agricultural community — their compactness. Located on the spines of ridges, Newar houses clustered around sites of religious significance, expanding on the basis of the joint character of their family structure. Villages expanded laterally along these upland plains, leaving the more fertile low-lying areas for farming. In this way, organic wastes ultimately found their way to the farms, adding valuable nutrients to the soil.

The Gorkha invasion of 1768 brought a concept of nationhood into this ancient and traditional milieu. With the establishment of the capital of a united Nepal in Kathmandu, the tightly knit homogeneity of the Valley was interspersed with new values. The Gurkha settlers had more independent family units which spilled over the traditional urban precincts.

What one sees today in Kathmandu is precisely this mixture: a medieval township that finds itself in the midst of the 20th Century, a blending of the essence of old Kathmandu with the effects of latter-day migration from outside the Valley. A charming air of rural life pervades even the city's commercial center.

The urban framework reveals a genuine sense of aesthetic perfection and a deep understanding of integrated social functions. Space is arranged, combined and organized in-

to a subtle succession of buildings and courtyards, of ornamented facades and sunken fountains, of open spaces peopled with statues, monuments and decked temples.

Each new step opens unexpected vistas and perspectives. As you walk along the maze of narrow streets, you get glimpses of ancient courtyards through a succession of doors opening on dark passages. While statues of gods grin and groan, you pass open shrines, small temples set back from the street, and large pagodas towering over the squares.

Chubby smiling faces appear fleetingly fram-

Images of childhood: noses run as a young Kathmandu girl carries her baby brother, left; in Patan, above, a little boy drags a little toy.

ed in dark rectangles of ornate windows. Painted eyes protect carved doors, as other eyes peer unobserved from behind trellised wood.

Everyone goes about his daily chores, working or playing, perhaps idling in the sun, shifting with its rays, seeking the shadow in times of summer heat and sunshine in the cold months.

The Divine in the Worldly

Lost in a maze of wondrous eye-catching detail, it takes time to realize how well thought-out is this integrated urban universe. It is a chain of neat architectural patterns reproducing the basic rectangular motif of the Newari house, with variations adapted to the configuration of the terrain and the needs of men and gods. In a valley where there are said to be more religious monuments than houses, it is sometimes difficult to tell the difference between the divine and the worldly. In fact, houses can be built only with divine permission, which must come prior to the foundation-laying ceremony and again after the roofing of the house.

Concrete cubes are fast replacing the old mud-brick buildings that are being torn down in the heart of the city. But a great deal of construction following traditional building techniques is still taking place in Kathmandu's suburbs.

Bricks are manufactured near the construction site by a couple of men who dig the mud, mix it with water, stuff it into a simple wooden mold, and leave stacks of these bricks in the sun to dry. Although fire-baked bricks and cement are increasingly being used, they are more expensive, and it is the sun-dried "raw" bricks that mix best with the clay cement. The walls of buildings are made of a double line of gray bricks stuffed with clay. Beams and wood rafters are set in place and covered with planks, then are topped by a layer of mud on which the tiles are fixed. Even though this mud is cooked to prevent tiny seeds from germinating, grass grows in roofs by the time a couple of monsoons have passed.

The Family Unit

Just as the house is the basic architectural unit, so is the extended Newar family the cornerstone of society. The family is both a support and a refuge, the main system of social insurance and security. From early age, the individual learns how to fit within the social nucleus and how to relate to the clan and caste, through respect for relatives and patron deities. Sometimes, joint families include three genera-

tions with 30 or more members. Family life is marked with rites and obligations that the individual does not dream of dodging.

If the family is the basic unit of Newar society, then the *guthi* is on a slightly higher plane and symbolizes a deep aspiration to community living. Often as night falls, you may hear voices and accordion notes pouring from the upper windows of ordinary houses. Inside, there is a *guthi* meeting where relatives and companions get together to have a good time, chatting, sucking at the *hookah* and generally relaxing.

Newars derive substantial advantages from belonging to various *guthi*. These brotherhoods maintain local and communal services, organize feasts, festivals and proces-

sions, arrange burials, maintain family sanctuaries, care for the ailing and elderly, and even assist in the collective preparation of fields.

Guthi are indicative of the social rank and the economic potential of each family. They also offer a channel for going beyond caste barriers. There is even a possibility of buying one's way into a better *guthi*. This institution, present in the Valley from the time of the Mallas, has been both a factor of social integration and a means of perpetuating cultural values and achievements.

Images of growing: classmates in a village school, left; and a makeshift brass-and-drum corps serenading outside a bride's house, right.

Ceremonies of Daily Life

From birth to death, special rites and celebrations mark the important events of one's existence, assuring a symbiosis of body and soul with the divine. This deep relationship between man and god is reaffirmed through daily rites. In some of these, man symbolically becomes the god himself, strengthening his sense of sacredness and self-respect.

The birth of a child is supervised by a community midwife, and is a joyous affair. The midwife assists in the delivery, and after cutting the umbilical cord and shaping the child's head, anoints the newborn with mustard oil. This oil is regarded as therapeutic, and is used for massaging both baby and mother.

The *pasni* (rice-feeding) ceremony is the

child's next important occasion. In the presence of family and priests, the seven-month-old child is dressed in finery and fed rice presented on a coin by all members of the family. He is shown several objects on a tray: a heap of earth, paddy (unhusked rice), bricks, toys, rings, a pen and ink-pot, and a book. It is said his parents can tell the child's future profession from the object he first picks up.

The mother takes her baby everywhere, either on her back or in one of the many folds of the *patuka* around her waist. She takes the child to the fields, where it rides piggy-back while the mother works. But as soon as the baby can walk, the child is left in the custody of an elder brother or sister. The mother con-

tinues to go about her daily chores or prepares to have another baby.

Rites of Initiation

Childhood is a time of fun. Young boys push bicycle tires with sticks for hours on end, running alongside the street traffic. Girls play hopscotch on temple steps, keeping a quiet vigil on nearby toddlers. Kite season brings them all to the rooftops to try to catch the wind, or down to the streets to chase falling kites.

Initiation to adult life comes early for Newar children. All the girls in the family are "married" to the god Narayan before they reach puberty. They take a ritual bath and make a trip to the local Ganesh temple, where they undergo the symbolic rituals of a typical marriage — nails varnished red, vermilion smeared on the central parting of their plaited hair. The human marriage that will take place later, when the girl is in her teens, will be her second. Technically, this means that the girl will never be a widow and will also make divorce a mere formality.

The initiation of boys follows a different pattern. A lad of 13, draped in saffron robes, may clutch an alms bowl and a long curved stick as he makes his way from door to door in his introduction to Buddhist monastic life. If the child is Hindu and belongs to a Brahman or Chhetri family, this is the time of the sacred thread ceremony. He must wear this thread around his shoulders constantly, changing it only on the full-moon day of July/August, when the old thread is tied to the tail of a cow.

The Marriage Celebration

Marriage comes next. Traditionally, the parents make the match; but young Kathmandu urbanites are increasingly making their own free choices.

First, there is an official engagement ceremony, when the boy's parents send gifts of betel to the girl's parents. The girl's parents make a display of feigned reluctance, and the boy's representatives make very literary speeches extolling his virtues. After this hilarious exchange, and acceptance of the young man by the girl's parents, the wedding may proceed as planned.

Dates for weddings are fixed according to astrological calculations. Certain seasons are considered most auspicious, but for marriage at short notice, an astrologer can be paid to "fix" a suitable date. Spring is the most popular time

Images of adulthood: family men share a *hookah* at a *guthi* gathering, left; and two businessmen share an early-morning conversation in Kathmandu.

for marriage, and Kathmandu often resounds with the music of two or three marriage bands making their way simultaneously along the New Road to or from the bride's house.

Weddings are long affairs and stretch on for the better part of a week. In Newar families, the groom sends a *pathi* (almost a gallon) of milk to the girl's mother as a token of compensation for the milk the girl sucked as a child. After dusk, the procession forms. Drummers and musicians make their way to the girl's house with the boy sitting at the back of a decorated chauffeur-driven car. (Before the advent of motor vehicles, he was carried in a palanquin.) The visitors remain for a while at her home, sitting on chairs or in the courtyard

chewing betel, that stimulating mixture of betel leaves, araca nut and white lime so popular in South Asia.

The bride does not show herself yet. She leaves at midnight and spends the night at a friend's house. It is only on the following day that she is received at her future husband's home. She distributes betel to each member of his household, lastly to her groom. Then the betrothed partake of the same food, and the bride bows down at the groom's feet.

The ceremony will last two or three more days, and each night the young woman goes back to her parents' house. On the last evening, after an offering of musk — believed to be an aphrodisiac — the marriage can at last be consummated. The end of the ceremony and the

beginning of life in common is marked by a merry wedding banquet where the couple introduce their friends to each other. It is traditional that the bride should act shy and show herself aggrieved when taking leave of her parents ... though not so upset that tears will ruin her makeup!

Old Age and Death

In a country where death comes early (the average life expectancy is 44 for males and 47 for females), age is respected and celebrated. The old are venerated, and when an aged relative reaches the auspicious age of 77 years, seven months and seven days, there is a reenactment of the *pasni* ceremony that all children go through when they are seven months old.

The old man is hoisted on a brightly decorated palanquin and paraded through the streets of the town. If he has a wife, she follows in a second palanquin and is carried around the village with respectful pomp. The old man wears a symbolic golden earring to commemorate this event, and carries it for the rest of his life.

When death finally comes, the deceased is borne on a bamboo platform to the banks of the river, usually in the pre-dawn hours. Traditionally, the dead must be carried to the cremation *ghats* by their survivors; nowadays, they sometimes make the trip in the back seat of a taxi. Occasionally, musicians precede the funeral procession, playing slow music.

At the riverside *ghats,* sons walk around their parent's corpse three times, carrying the butter lamp that will be placed on the face of the deceased. As the priest sets the pyre ablaze, the dead person's relatives get their heads shaved and ritually purify themselves with a bath in the river. The ashes are then scattered in the river. The priest carries the soul of the dead to the abode of Yama, the god of death, where it will merge with the divine.

Elsewhere in Kathmandu, life goes on. On the streets, in the *bahals,* in the temple squares and on rooftops, Kathmandu endures, caught in transition. It is a transition from the old, to which the town clings with the tight bonds of Newari tradition; and a metamorphosis to the present, a reality that has come with the town's jet-age links to the rest of the world. Riding on this tightrope are Kathmandu's inhabitants, who are born, who live, and who die in the Valley world.

Images of death: an old woman breathes her last at a Bagmati River *ghat*, left; and a ritual cremation, right, helps the soul leave the body.

THE ARTISTIC HERITAGE

The great civilizations of the Kathmandu Valley are justly famous for the masterpieces of art they produced. In architecture, sculpture, painting, metalwork, literature, music and dance, the various groups of people who have made the Valley their home have left a marvelous legacy.

Of the earliest settlements, little remains. There are the two great stupas of Swayambhunath and Bodhnath, whose origins are lost in time. There are the four stupas built at the cardinal points of Patan about the 3rd Century B.C., reputedly by the Indian Emperor Ashoka. The mounds are inviolable; they might contain relics of an unknown art form. Other remnants have vanished completely.

Licchavi Classics

The first golden age of Nepalese classical art, left to us in durable stone sculpture, dates from the Licchavi period of the 4th to 9th centuries A.D. Entirely religious in character and Indian in origin, it proclaims an age of amazing accomplishment — from the colossal image of the reclining Vishnu at Budhanilkantha to hundreds of beautiful small works of classic simplicity scattered about the Valley, all masterpieces of incalculable value.

Stone inscriptions at the ancient temple of Changu Narayan tell of King Manadeva I who — apart from commissioning places of Hindu and Buddhist worship — built a palace many stories high, a wonder of the age. Probably it was made of wood, for it has vanished without a trace.

In fact, no early remnants of wooden artistry have been found, even though wood must have preceded stone as a material for construction, and certainly for carving. The carvings of the 12th and 13th centuries — the earliest known in the Valley — are masterly. These include the struts of the Hanuman Dhoka and the Basantapur Tower in Kathmandu, the Uku Bahal in Patan, and the Indreshwar Mahadev temple at Panauti, all of them almost Licchavi in their elegant simplicity. But by this time, the golden age of classic Licchavi sculpture had come to an end, and an early Malla renaissance in stone, metal and paint, as well as in wood, had begun.

Preceding pages, Vajracharya temple dancing in classical Newar style. Left, an 8th Century Licchavi stone carving of Vishnu at Changu Narayan.

This renaissance was spurred by the genius of the Newar people. Into the Kathmandu Valley crucible had been poured the culture and talent of people from India, Tibet, China, Mongolia, Central Asia and perhaps Burma. Their influences melded into a new, completely indigenous style. Religious symbolism, Hindu and Buddhist, was paramount. It decorated temples, religious courtyards, palaces and the homes of the rich, extolling the virtues of deities and of monarchs who had assumed divinity.

By the time of the Mallas, metal was preferred to stone for image-making, even for large-sized statues like the handsome golden kings of Kathmandu, Patan and Bhaktapur. These include the stately goddesses Ganga and Jamuna in the old royal palace at Patan, and the two exquisite Taras at Swayambhunath. Important temples were crowned with gold, fused by a mercury process. Goldsmiths, silversmiths, and workers in bronze and other baser metals developed their skills to a fine degree.

Other artisans likewise flourished: wood-carvers, ivory carvers, masters of terra-cotta, and brickmakers. Licchavi purity was smothered in amazing outpourings of ornamentation. During the centuries of Malla rule, Newar artisans touched almost every exposed surface of temples and important buildings with the magic of their many-faceted creativity.

Tibetan Influence

In the late 13th Century, a Newar architect and master craftsman named Arniko was invited to Tibet. He took a party of 24 assistants with him to build important stupas and cast historic images. So great was Arniko's fame that he joined the court of the Ming emperor of China as "controller of the imperial manufactures." The multi-tiered pagoda-style roofs so much a trademark of East Asia' owe their origin to this remarkable man. The modern highway from Kathmandu to the Chinese Tibetan border is appropriately named in honor of him.

Other Newari artists were also invited to Tibet, and in time, this new Tibeto-Newari style began influencing the art of Kathmandu. The gem-like Golden Gate of Bhaktapur (1754), renowned as the Kathmandu Valley's outstanding single work of art, owes its brilliance to this intercultural melange. Chinese and Tibetan symbols, like dragons and phoenixes, began appearing among familiar Newari symbols. Traces of Muslim influence can be seen in late Malla architecture, notably in the old royal palaces of Kathmandu and Bhaktapur.

While Bhaktapur produced marvels in wood and continued a virile tradition of stone sculpture, Patan was the city of metal workers. Their excellence is best seen in the 14th Century Kwa Bahal, or Golden Temple. So enchanted were Tibetan visitors to this city of artists, they called it Yerang, "Eternity Itself."

With the passing of the Malla dynasty in the 18th Century, Newari art floundered. It was even suppressed during the 104-year reign of the Rana prime ministers. Since the Shah dynasty regained power in 1951, there has been a revival of the arts. Much of the work done today is merely as a craft for tourist dollars, devoid of vision and grand purpose.

But for a short while in the 1970s, a true renaissance took place. The Valley's craftsmen displayed their latent abilities when UNESCO set about to restore the old royal palace in Kathmandu and the West German government involved itself in the renovation of some important buildings in Bhaktapur. The old arts and crafts, indeed, are still alive. With adequate patronage, they can be very impressive.

Devotion Through Painting

Newari painting had its origin in illuminated religious manuscripts dating from the 11th Century. Done in simple natural colors over crude ink drawings on strips of palm leaf, or on the wooden covers in which manuscripts were bound, these earliest painting are Indian in style and Buddhist in inspiration.

Brahminical manuscripts began to appear in the 15th Century. Strong paper started to replace palm leaves some time later, and by the 19th Century, illuminated manuscripts were on their way out. Visitors must beware of purchasing the many "old" manuscripts peddled on the Valley's streets and in some of its shops today. Almost all of them are fakes.

The Newars employed a miniature form of painting, distantly related to the Indian Pahari school. This style endured through a transition to painted scrolls in the 14th Century, and later to murals. The painting became highly sophisticated. Significant influence came from Tibet, where *thangka* or scroll painting was well established.

Between the 14th and 16th centuries, Newar artists were invited to Tibet to paint scrolls and monastery murals. They left an indelible stylistic imprint on Tibetan art; at the same time, they themselves partook of the exotic styles of China, Kashmir and Central Asia that met and mingled on this high plateau. By the 18th Century, the Tibetan art of *thangka* painting had been introduced to the Kathmandu Valley.

Newari painting, known as *paubha* or *pati*, serves a variety of religious purposes: worship, meditation, glorifying deities, obtaining merit, recording festive events and consecrating temples. The detail of these paintings is so exquisite, the drawing so brilliant, that the Newar artists have left a clear record of the rituals, dress and customs of centuries past.

The best examples of traditional painting, including the long scrolls often used for worship, hang in the museums in Kathmandu and Bhaktapur. Other fine 16th to 18th Century paintings are found in Swayambhunath, in Kirtipur's Bagh Bhairab, and in Panauti's Brahmayani Temple.

Thangkas for Tourists

The *thangkas* displayed in the Valley's shops are largely done for the benefit of tourists; painted by contemporary Newar and Buddhist Tamang artists, their colors are modern, and many are smoked to appear old. One shop in Bhaktapur sells *paubhas* painted in Patan. Otherwise, traditional Newar art is rarely seen. Hopes are that it will endure, because it has a rare charm and a smoldering beauty all its own.

Newar artists belong to a unique caste, the *chitrakar*. They are found most extensively in Bhaktapur, where some belong to a cooperative turning out modern *paubhas* and purely decorative pieces of art. Most of these artists are contracted to decorate temples and private houses with painted motifs for festivals and marriages.

Some of them make and paint brightly colored papier-mâché masks representing popular deities. Once used only for ceremonial purposes, these masks are now made in all sizes for sale to tourists. They are even incorporated in a very recent innovation, string puppets.

Some Tamangs, calling themselves *lamas*, operate small ateliers in Kathmandu, Patan and Bhaktapur. Most of the *thangkas* found in the Valley's shops are turned out here. Many Tamangs paint in their distant villages until they have a sufficient number to sell in the Valley or to export to India.

Genuine Tibetan *lama* artists can often be seen painting at the great stupas of Bodhnath

Bronze temple guardians such as this fierce beast at Patan's Kwa Bahal are found everywhere. Metal workers flourished during the early Malla period.

and Swayambhunath. A dedicated few strive to maintain traditional standards, using muted stone colors and time-honored laws of proportion and subject matter. There is a single Tibetan artist at Bodhnath who turns out applique *thangkas* of unusual beauty.

Outside of the Valley, there are as many styles of art as there are ethnic groups. In the distant Sherpa district of Khumbu, for instance, two brothers paint landscapes in *thangka* style. Elsewhere, brilliant artists may spend a lifetime unknown. One cloth painting, carried to Kathmandu after having been purchased for a single rupee in a hill village, has been adjudged a masterpiece of Nepalese art.

In Kathmandu, the Nepal Association of Fine Arts has a large fellowship of young artists painting in numerous styles and media. The NAFA has a permanent gallery, and holds regular exhibitions of members' work.

Two Nepalese painters who have won recognition at home and abroad are L.S. Bangdel, working in Kathmandu, and Laxman Shrestha, resident in India. Their abstract canvases exude the essence of this country's mountains. In a strange, luminous way, their work can lay claim to the same ancestry as the *thangkas* and murals of traditional Nepal.

The Gilded Word

The written word in Nepal dates at least to Licchavi times. Chronicles of gods and kings, and later of royal achievements, laws, and life at court, were carved in stone in the Pali or Sanskrit languages.

Probably predating these records — no one can know by how many centuries — were the lyric odes passed orally from generation to generation. So rich is this particular art form today among the peoples of Nepal's mountains and valleys, it is easy to believe that troubadours composed and sang of their kings' battles and gods' loves when the Licchavis were carving their masterpieces in stone.

The famous 17th Century King Pratap Malla of Kathmandu let himself be known as the "King of Poets," so presumably poetry flourished in his time. Even today, Nepal's kings and queens like to be known as poets and songwriters. Their creations are frequently recorded or played over Radio Nepal.

Remarkably, it wasn't until the 18th Century that literati began expressing themselves in Newari, the language of the Valley, or

Nepali, the *lingua franca* of the kingdom, introduced by the Gorkha conquerors. Early Nepali literature's brighest star was the 19th Century poet Bhanubhakta, whose name is a household word wherever Nepalis are found. Two poets of almost equal stature are Motiram Bhatta, known for his gentle eroticism, and Leknath Poudyal, a recently deceased 20th Century poet of growing reputation.

The years of political unrest preceding the Rana overthrow in 1951 influenced a number of writers. Because of the threat of oppression, their writing was stilted and heavy with symbolism; besides, in a country where illiteracy was rampant, their words were aimed at a small educated elite. B.P. Koirala, the former prime minister who spent many years in jail or in exile, is the author of many short stories and novels belonging to this period and later. The works of Balkrishna Sama, a poet, dramatist, novelist and artist, also come from this era.

Today, late 20th Century authors tend to indulge in experimental styles and themes, and await the verdict of acceptance. They thrive despite the small audiences they command (mostly outside Nepal) and in spite of the lack of translation and distribution. As Nepalese literacy improves, the fame of some is bound to grow.

Songs of Life

Music is a main artery of Nepal. It is an important, hauntingly beautiful accompaniment to life itself. It follows a man from birth, through courtship and marriage, attends his religious ceremonies and harvests, follows him abroad and welcomes him home again, enriches his vocabulary of love and desire, tells of war and Gurkha heroism, and trails him to his death.

Everyone sings. Married women sing for the long life and well-being of their husbands. Young girls flock to the Teej dance festival and sing to attract worthy partners. During the festival of Tihar, bands of singing children, teenagers and adults "carol" through the streets, entertaining all who care to listen, collecting funds for some cause.

When you are in the city, you will hear music everywhere, from dawn worship to the late-night chanting of hymns. When you walk in the mountains, you will hear the throb of drums and distant echoes of song. So persistent is the Nepalese flute, you might think you are being followed through street, forest and field by Krishna himself.

Professional musicians known as *gainis* were once found everywhere. Whole families traveled together, and one could almost watch

The intricate woodcarvings on Kathmandu's Hanuman Dhoka palace mostly date to the time of the Mallas. This is a typical example.

the repertoire of songs being passed from grandfather to father to son. They sang old legends of gods and larger-than-life mortals, of love and impassioned happenings. To a song dedicated to Krishna and the *gopis,* they might add tongue-in-cheek twists — suggesting a certain tenderness between Queen Victoria and the first Rana prime minister, Jung Bahadur; or telling the story of the first ascent of Everest, with Tenzing pulling Hillary to the summit.

These delightful troubadours traveled from village to village, from festival to festival, accompanying themselves on four-stringed *saringhis* — a type of viola carved from a single piece of wood and played with a small horizontal bow to which tiny bells are sometimes attached. Their traditional function was for information as much as for entertainment. Among the illiterate masses, their religious songs conveyed a more immediate message than the teachings of priests or the carvings on temples and palaces.

Today, they are slowly dying out. Perhaps the young are turning to more lucrative means of living. Or perhaps they are wilting before the invasion of Japanese transistor radios and cassette players.

Religious music is played on a wide variety of instruments, from drums to cymbals, flutes to harmoniums. It is the preserve of the *damais,* whose normal occupation is tailoring. In recent times, these *damais* have grouped themselves into uniformed, cacophonous walking bands. They are *de rigeur* at large weddings, where they play popular Hindi film music, often unrecognizably.

At the great stupa of Bodhnath, another kind of music can be heard. It is echoed in Nepal's far northern monasteries, wherever Buddhist *lamas* sit to pray or observe festivals with sonorous pomp. Huge, collapsible metal horns, smaller trumpets, thigh-bone flutes, cymbals and conches create sacred Tibetan music. Belching, tearing, grunting, wailing shafts of sound are held together by human chanting. There is also a happier Tibetan sound — folk music played on the colorful *damiyen,* a brightly painted ukulele-like instrument which sets feet stomping in rousing dances.

A Multitude of Dance Forms

Folk dances are everywhere in Nepal. They are performed in village clearings, in fields, in cramped houses, in temple courtyards. At festival time, when hill people converge on Kathmandu, there are outbursts of folk dancing throughout the Valley cities. To the sound of simple musical accompaniment — drums and voices, sometimes flutes or small hand cymbals, and the jingle of tiny bells worn around the dancers' ankles — an amazing variety of steps are executed.

Every clan has its own dances. These vary from the innocently naive to the sophisticated, as when women form arabesques with brass platters in each hand, on which are placed lighted candles. In some of the dances, a distinctly Cossack influence is notable: performers squat on their haunches, kicking out their legs as they bob or spin up and down and around, settling on their haunches again without missing a beat.

Classical dancing is the domain of the Valley's Newars. The delicate dance of the *kumari,* which appears to have much in common with Indian Bharatanatyam and Thai dancing, is as fragile as the tinkling wind bells of the Newari homes and temples. The more vigorous dances of Manjushri and Vajra Yogini are an exciting contrast. Seldom seen today, these dances have been encouraged in recent years, and a small revival is now taking place.

More frequently performed are the masked dances of Bhaktapur. These are at once primitive, lordly and aggressive. They tell of ancient battles between the gods and the forces of evil. Seen best by firelight, they are naively magnificent.

These masked dancers are not to be confused with the Nawa Durga dancers. Tantric devotees don masks to walk, swirl and leap through the streets of Bhaktapur, Kirtipur and the village of Thecho. Considered by most to be possessed by the deities they represent, they are worshipped as such.

Centuries ago, a Malla king decreed that the dancers of Thecho must annually dance all the way from their village to his court at Patan, or be fined. Similarly, the masked Bhaktapur dancers appear in Kathmandu once a year at the festival of Indrajatra. Valley residents believe that as long as these sacred dances are performed in the streets, powerful deities will mingle with man, and the Valley will remain in the abode of the gods.

A storyteller draws a crowd to hear his tale during the Budhanilkantha temple festival. The oral tradition is still strong throughout Nepal.

EXPLORING THE VALLEY

There are two ways of discovering the Kathmandu Valley: from the inside out, or from the outside in. We recommend the latter.

The typical visitor arrives by air, heads directly to his Kathmandu city hotel, and explores the Western-influenced urban center from its Durbar Square. He will perhaps make excursions to Patan or Bhaktapur, marvel at the prayer wheels of Swayambhunath or Bodhnath, then depart for his next destination.

But the visitor who really wants to know the Valley, to feel its pulse and get to its spiritual roots, should start his exploration well beyond the city limits. In ages past, when the Valley floor was filled with water, the only settlements were near shrines and pilgrimage sites in the surrounding hills. They remain today, more ancient than Kathmandu itself. When the waters of the Valley lake drained and the rich basin took a form much like it has today, the network of routes connecting these various sites provided the framework around which the new cities grew.

These ancient shrines are the keys to unlocking the mysteries of Kathmandu city itself. And they are not difficult to reach. Because of the Valley's compact size and its relatively flat terrain, one can travel by foot or bicycle — or if somewhat less adventurous, by car — to innumerable shrines and temples, each with a story of its own to tell.

In the following pages, we have presented the Valley's outlying shrines in a systematic fashion, by religious function. Thus the great Buddhist stupas are discussed first; followed by shrines to the important Hindu deities Vishnu, Shiva and Ganesh; then shrines to female deities; and finally nature sites.

With this background thus established, we take you into the cities of man, the metropolises of Kathmandu, Patan and Bhaktapur, and the strings of smaller villages which have radiated in all directions from the cities.

Preceding the descriptions of these destinations is a listing of various walks in the Valley. These excursions serve to tie some of the shrines to the villages and thus to the cities, providing the visitor a broad base of understanding of the Valley residents' lives.

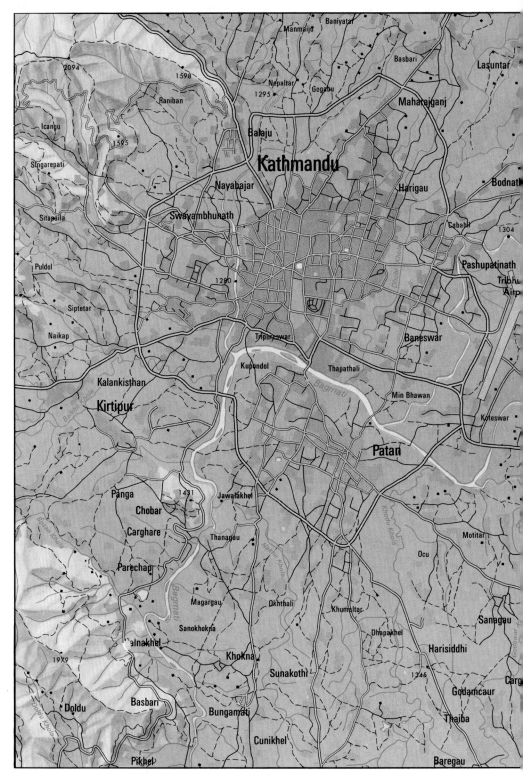

Maßstab 1 : 75 000

109

WALKS AROUND THE VALLEY

There are many very beautiful walks within the Kathmandu Valley that combine cultural experience and natural heritage. For the majority of them, it is necessary to hire a car or taxi to reach the starting and ending points. Most of these walks can be accomplished in a day. On all of them, you will sample the rewards of getting off the beaten track: the serenity of the countryside and the drama of mountain views. Most walks also will take you to sites of great spiritual importance.

1. Nagarkot to Changu Narayan. This is a splendid and varied walk for persons who do not like climbing hills. It can be done comfortably in just over three hours. Begin by driving toward Bhaktapur, and just before reaching that medieval city, taking the left-hand fork to Nagarkot. About halfway to Nagarkot village, the road rises to a saddle; it is here the walk starts. A gentle uphill grade leads through a pine-tree plantation for about 20 minutes; the trail then levels out, following a saddle that juts into the Valley. There are gorgeous views across the Valley to the Himalayas.

The trail passes through several little Chhetri settlements. Soon, the gilded roofs of Changu Narayan appear above the clustered houses of Changu village. As you climb the stone-paved street leading to the temple, note the quantities of stone sculptures littering the roadside. After marveling at the beauties of Changu Narayan temple (see page 122), cross the courtyard and leave through a doorway on the western side.

Ahead, you will see the meandering Manohara River, and just beyond it, the road at Bramhakhel. Aim for a point northwest of Changu Narayan where a collection of small houses and a little tea room encourage you on your descent. On the river plain at the foot of the hill, you might find a makeshift bridge; otherwise, take off your shoes and wade through the soothing waters. Follow a dike through the maze of paddy fields back to the road, where your car should be waiting.

2. Sankhu via Bajra Jogini to Nagarkot. This is a good hard day's walk combining culture with spectacular mountain views. A 12-mile drive past Bodhnath, skirting Gokarna forest on your left, will bring you to the ancient and interesting little town of Sankhu, a post on the old trading route between Kathmandu and Lhasa. Continue in a northeasterly direction until the road finally peters out. This is where the walk starts.

An uphill climb leads to the important temple of Bajra Jogini (see page 136). From here, take the pathway east behind the complex, through a stand of pine trees. The trail wends its way, often rather precariously, down the slope and back to the main trail between Sankhu and Helambu. The paths merge near a cluster of tea houses where you can refresh yourself with a cup of *chiya* (tea).

There is a long climb ahead. Follow the main trail for awhile until you notice a well-worn side trail on the right. This takes you in a southeasterly direction up a rather uninviting steep hill, across a rickety bridge, and through a forest. As you rise out of the Valley onto a grassy saddle, you get your first glimpses of the high snow peaks of the Himalayas. A fairly well-marked trail follows the ridge; in the far distance, you can make out the army encampment at the top of Nagarkot Hill. Soon the track dips and turns to the right, twisting through shrubs as it climbs a smaller ridge branching from Nagarkot. Eventually you reach a large white cheese factory. Many small houses in this area have been converted into lodges, where you can get tea or a well-deserved Star Beer.

If you want to be alone, you can easily find a secluded hilltop from which to watch the sun set over the mountains. This is undoubtedly one of the best panoramic views of the Himalayas. If you wish, having located your car, you can drive higher, above the army checkposts. From here it is possible to see Mount Everest, small and unimpressive though it may appear at the eastern end of the scenic vista which continues all the way to the Annapurnas and Dhaulagiri in the west. The drive back to Kathmandu takes about 45 minutes.

3. Ichangu Narayan to Balaju. Begin by driving to Balaju, where you must acquire tickets to enter the Jamacho Forest Reserve. Then take the Ring Road to the crossroads on the west side of Swayambhunath, and turn onto the dirt road leading west toward the stone quarries. Keep going as far as you can, past the scarred hillside, and take the trail leading toward the little settlement of Ichangu. This is a wide, well-worn trail bustling with activity. You might even witness the sacrifice of a goat at one of the small shrines along the uphill slope. Approximately one hour of walking takes you to the little temple complex of

Ichangu Narayan (see page 125).

Beyond the temple compound, the trail narrows, sometimes becoming indistinct. It twists uphill through terraces of wheat and maize to a grassy saddle adjacent to the enclosure wall of the Nagarjun forest. At a passage through the wall, a military guard will ask to see the entrance ticket you purchased in Bulaju. Then you enter the Jamacho reserve, a forest of beautiful pines which is the home of bears, leopards and a multitude of birds.

Follow the path in a northeasterly direction to the top of Nagarjun Hill, where there is a small white *chaitya* serving as a pilgrimage center during festivals at Balaju. On the hill's eastern slope, about a kilometer apart, are two small hermits' caves containing Buddha images (see page 148). The descent to Balaju is fairly easy, with excellent views across the Valley to the Ganesh Himal range.

4. Budhanilkantha to Kathmandu. This pleasant afternoon's walk through the paddy fields northeast of Kathmandu begins with a visit to the reclining Vishnu of Budhanilkantha (see page 121). From there, head in an easterly direction along the base of a wooded hill, then take a concrete bridge across a small river to a village. Follow the river's west bank to a steep gorge, where water-powered mills grind local corn. Then cross another bridge and climb a grassy slope past a two-tiered temple to the village of Tupek.

The trail skirts the southwestern edge of the village, where intensive rice cultivation takes place. A little further, at the village of Lasuntar, the trail drops down a rather precipitous gorge. At the bottom, a stream will lead you through a maze of paddy to the Dhobi Khola river. Cross the river, climb the hill on the opposite site, and proceed through another village to the Ring Road.

Across the road is the shrine of Dhum Varahi (see page 125), unmistakable in the clutches of an enormous pipal tree, isolated on what has become a school football field. Near here, the track turns into a motorable road which leads to Hadigaon, one of the oldest settlements encompassed in Kathmandu's urban sprawl. It is easy to catch a taxi from here.

5. Gokarneswar to Bodhnath via Kopan. This walk leads through one of the more remote parts of the Valley. Start at the Gokarna Mahadev temple (see page 130). Cross a small bridge below the hamlet of Gokarneswar, turn left (northwest), and follow a well-marked trail up a rather steep grade. Traverse paddy and maize fields and a bamboo grove to a saddle on a ridge marked by a pipal tree. The tea shops here will point you in the direction of Kopan.

Cross the main trail and head downhill to a grassy meadow, enjoying superb views of the northern part of the Valley as you look toward Budhanilkantha. The path follows the edge of a forest plantation, crosses another main trail, then climbs a small hillock on top of which are the monastery and settlement of Kopan. This is a Tibetan refugee center with as many as 120 young novices and a smattering of intense-looking Westerners. The monastery and main temple are worth a visit. You may even be offered some Tibetan butter tea to give you strength for the remainder of your walk.

You can see the great Bodhnath stupa to the southwest of the monastery. Follow the motorable road down the hill and across a small river bed. From here, all trails lead to Bodhnath — provided your bearings are right. The stupa is surrounded by several recently constructed monasteries full of friendly monks (see page 117).

6. Kirtipur to Patan via Chobar. Take a morning taxi or bus to the town of Kirtipur, atop a rocky hill, and spend a few hours wandering around this fascinating Newar settlement. Then head off by foot toward Patan.

The ridge route leads from the southeast corner of Kirtipur past a tumbledown stupa, then climbs slowly to the village of Chobar overlooking the Bagmati River (as well as a large cement factory). There are several important shrines here, including the Adinath Lokeswar (see page 143). Leaving Chobar from its southeast corner, cross the main road and make your way to the Jal Binayak temple complex at the mouth of the famous Chobar Gorge (see page 134). Here you can cross the Bagmati — which drains the Kathmandu Valley — noting the chasm allegedly cut by Manjushri's sword. The suspension bridge here was manufactured in Scotland and erected at the beginning of the 20th Century.

The trail crosses a large grassy slope, a favorite picnic ground for area residents, then climbs a hill to meet the main trail from Bungamati and Khokana. You can follow this motorable track back toward Jawalkhel, on the outskirts of Patan; or cross the road and continue down into the beautiful Naku Khola river valley. A trail leads to southern Patan. If you've had enough walking, you can hail a taxi from the Ring Road.

This is by no means an exhaustive list of Valley walks. Remember that local people walk everywhere. It is easy to break off the usual routes and travel anywhere your fancy may take you.

BUDDHIST SHRINES: THE EYES HAVE IT

Atop a green hillock west of Kathmandu, at the point where the legendary patriarch Manjushri discovered the lotus of the ancient Valley lake, stands the great stupa of **Swayambhunath.**

On all four sides of this ancient structure, looking out in all directions at the Valley below, are painted the eyes of the Buddha. Their gaze is one of compassion, an omnisighted stare from beneath heavy black eyebrows. Between them is a mystic third eye, symbolic of true wisdom. The nose, with the appearance of an incomplete question mark, is the Nepalese number *ek* or "one," a symbol of unity.

There is little doubt that this sacred site was established more than 2,500 years ago. Well before the advent of Buddhism, there must have been a monument here: a projecting stone which later became the central element of the stupa. Emperor Ashoka may have visited in the 2nd Century B.C., and an inscription dated at 460 A.D. says King Manadeva I carried out construction work on the site. By 1234, Swayambhunath was an important center of Buddhist learning, closely linked with Lhasa.

The shrine was destroyed by a Bengal sultan's troops in 1346. But it was rebuilt, and in the mid-17th Century, King Pratap Malla made several renovations. He improved access to Kathmandu with a long approach stairway and a bridge across the Bishnumati River; he also built two new *shikharas* (temples) and added a big *vajra* (symbolic thunderbolt) to the top.

Today, 300 flagstoned steps lead to the terrace on which the stupa is built. Three stone Buddhas, daubed with yellow and red, sit at the bottom. At regular intervals up the steps are pairs of stone animals, the vehicles of the gods. These beasts are harmless; not so the monkeys, who slide down the stairway's metal handrails and pilfer anything visitors fail to protect.

The construction of a stupa adheres to specific rules, and Swayambhunath is a model of its kind. Each segment has a symbolic meaning. Its dazzling white hemispherical mound represents the four elements — earth, fire, air and water. The 13 gilded rings on the spire are the 13 degrees of knowledge, and represent the

SWAYAM-
BHUNATH.
1-stupa
2-gumba
3-Singu Bahil
4-Harati Ajima
5-Shantipur Blɗ
6-Karmaras Gur
7-Pratappur Ter
8-Anantapur Te

The eyes of Swayam-bhunath.

114

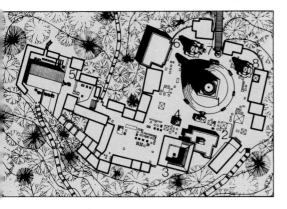

wheels, each turned by the faithful during a clockwise circumambulation. In their actions, Buddhist devotees symbolically turn the wheel of the law, representing the cycle of life and death.

In the *gompa* (monastery) facing the stupa, there is a service every day at 4 p.m. Onlookers are fascinated by the incense, the chanting and the deafening sound of trumpets. At other times, you will often see families exiting the *gompa* after meeting with the *rimpoche*. The father may be wearing a red ribbon around his neck. He takes his shoes off, kneels and prostrates himself several times in front of the main shrine. His wife and daughters, bejeweled and wearing their best saris, imitate him. They dot their foreheads with *tika,* the votive vermilion.

Images of the goddesses Ganga and Jamuna, masterpieces of Newari bronze art, guard the eternal flame in a cage behind the stupa. Here, on behalf of the faithful, a priest makes offerings to the sacred fire, symbol of the first appearance of the Adhi-Buddha.

At festival times, a human sea sweeps around the stupa. There is *puja, tika,* vermilion powder galore, the lighting of hun-

ladder to *nirvana,* which itself is symbolized by the umbrella at the top.

At the four cardinal points, four niches — richly adorned with repousse copper work — shelter the same number of Buddhas. These *dhyani* Buddhas are in four separate postures of meditation. One of these primary niches is abutted by another niche containing a fifth Buddha, facing the stairway. It is flanked by two pairs of benign, sculpted monks. At the sub-cardinal points are images of the Taras.

Around the stupa runs a row of prayer

dreds of small butter lamps, the making of offerings, and picnicking under the many trees. A delightful legend relates how Manjushri had his hair cut at Swayambhunath, each hair subsequently becoming a tree, and the lice becoming monkeys.

On a neighboring hill stands another more subdued stupa, flanked by a *gompa* and a shrine dedicated to Saraswati, the goddess of wisdom and learning. School children bring their pen and ink here to be blessed during Panchami Basant, the festival of knowledge. Monkeys here are particularly mischievous.

At the foot of the hill, the new Tibetan refugee community has spread. More *gompas* are being built in triumphant shades of white, red and black. Lower down, a small community of foreigners attempts to blend itself into the landscape, under the all-seeing gaze of the stupa's eyes.

Bodhnath's Simple Beauty

The other great stupa of the Valley, and indeed, the largest in all of Nepal, is **Bodhnath.** Sitting on flat land as a crown above pastel-painted facades of shops and houses, it is directly opposite Swayambhunath from the orientation of the old Royal Palace.

Bodhnath's great size and its red, white and blue-painted eyes, more remarkable even than Swayambhunath's, give it a striking appearance. The stupa combines planes and surfaces in a manner that can only be called simple, even austere; but it is done with a powerful effect. Built on concentric, gradually ascending, terraces — with the overall pattern of a *mandala* — the monument has a wide flight of steps leading to its base.

Along the stupa's base is a ring of 108 small inset images of the Buddha Amitabha. Surrounding the triple deck of platforms is an almost round brick wall with 147 niches, holding four or five prayer wheels each. Bodhnath's powerful silhouette is not interrupted by other structures; instead, the stupa shape is strongly emphasized by smaller stupas lying to its east, below the main stupa.

Goose Girl's Legacy

Worshipped only by Tibetan Buddhists, this stupa has always been linked to Lhasa. Its origin is a bit obscure. Legend says it was built by a woman named

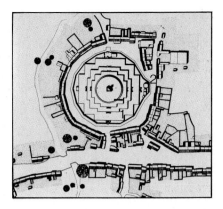

Kangma, born in supernatural circumstances as a swineherd's daughter after being banished from Indra's heaven for stealing flowers. In adult life, widowed with four children, she accumulated a fortune from her labors as a goose girl. She requested the king to give her as much ground as the hide of a buffalo would cover, so that she could build a temple to Buddha Amitabha. The king agreed. Kangma shrewdly cut the hide into thin strips, joined them, and stretched them out to form the square on which the Bodhnath stupa now stands.

A complete township has been built around Bodhnath. New monasteries great and small, chapels, private houses, shops, country liquor bars, lodges and carpet factories are all recent additions to the neighborhood. The small shops around the stupa are an inviting place for visitors to buy a variety of exotic items.

Mantras and Incense

At the start of the Tibetan New Year, normally in February by the Western calendar, people from far and near come to Bodhnath to watch *lamas* perform year-opening rites. Tibetans from the northern regions of Nepal, Buddhists from India and Ladakh, Sikkimese, Bhutanese and others arrive in traditional brown and dark blue dress, heavily decorated with corals and turquoise. Among the human tide, a few men sport Western garb but wave smoking incense sticks in their fists. Professional beggars chant *mantras* and clap their hands. Nearby crouch a few old women whose wrinkled hands mechanically count the beads of their rosaries.

On the stupa, the devout hoist long rows of multicolored prayer flags, blessing them first with juniper incense. They gather to pray in a colorful ceremony under the direction of magenta-robed *lamas* who blow great copper horns. At the climax of prayers, all throw fistfuls of *tsampa* (ground grain) into the air.

At the main entrance to the stupa, a dozen *lamas* position themselves in a double line. Other *lamas* walk majestically between them, holding a large portrait of the Dalai Lama under a canopy. People lunge forward to touch the portrait, tripping over themselves. The *lamas* retire into the monastery, some of them to prepare for hours of masked dances they will perform for spectators in a nearby field.

Other dances are performed in a monastery courtyard by professional troupes from Tibetan centers in India. There is much merriment and drink flows freely. The celebrations go on into the night, long after sunset fires the snow peaks and stars wheel about the soaring gold finial of the great stupa.

The Chaityas of Chabahil

The stupa at **Chabahil,** about 1,500 meters west of Bodhnath, is basically of the same type as its towering neighbor,

but is much smaller and more primitive looking. Its brick, stepped tower is too big for the rather plump, hemispherical mound on its narrow platform, but it is typical of the early stupas built in the Valley.

The village of Chabahil, just across the Dhobi Khola river from Kathmandu, has almost merged with the capital through 20th Century urban sprawl. But during Licchavi times, it was an important rural settlement of its own account, situated at the junction of the Valley's two main roads — the one across the Bagmati River leading to Patan, and the one from the Kasthamandap leading between India and Tibet.

King Ashoka's daughter Charumati, who lived here, is said to have been responsible for the construction of the stupa. She and her husband later retreated to two Buddhist monasteries they also built. One of those monasteries is supposedly the same one located nearby the stupa.

Around the Chabahil stupa are small votive Licchavi *chaityas* (reliquaries) in stone, with many of their small niches

Celebrating Tibetan New Year.

CHABAHIL.
1-Dhando
   Chaitya.
2-pokhari
3-chaitya

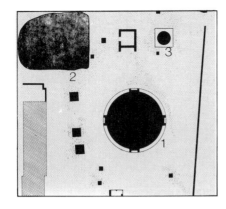

Rhapsody in blue at Chabahil.

emptied of their Buddha images, and some other classical Buddhist stone pieces. The most magnificent, one of the great sculptures of the Valley, is a 9th Century statue of a free-standing *bodhisattva* cut in black stone about one meter high, with smooth limbs and the tightly curled hair often seen on late Licchavi images.

Tastes of Tibet

With a community of Tibetan exiles estimated at about 12,000, the Kathman-

du Valley is fast becoming one of the principal centers of Tibetan culture outside of Tibet. Several Buddhist monasteries have sprung up recently in the immediate vicinities of Bodhnath and Swayambhunath. Near Pharping, just outside the Valley southeast of Patan, Tibetans have built a white, castle-like monastery on a forested slope at the entrance to the **Gorakhnath Cave,** formerly a hermit's refuge now turned into a thriving center of Tibetan worship.

This cave bears the name of one of the ancient sages who meditated here. On the platform in front of the cave are his footprints, which according to the inscription were carved in 1390. Tibetan Buddhists consider this site sacred to Padma Sambhava, the "second Buddha" who introduced Buddhism to Tibet. His image and those of other deities inside the cave date from the 18th Century.

Nearby, at the shrine of **Sekh Narayan,** sacred to Hindus (see page 124), Tibetans have raised a monastery to commemorate the visit of the great Tibetan saint, Guru Padma Sambhava. Legend says he came here to meditate and to vanquish hordes of troublesome demons.

VISHNU SHRINES: THE WIDE-STRIDER

Between the 5th and 15th centuries, Hinduism expanded around the trinity of Brahma, Vishnu and Shiva. Vishnu was originally a minor Vedic deity. In the *Vedas,* he allied himself with Indra to conquer demons. He fooled a demon by changing from dwarf to giant, encompassing in three strides the earth, the air and heaven, a scene often depicted in stone or bronze imagery.

By the time the *Mahabharata* epic was composed, the "wide-strider" had become "The One Being of All." In the epic poem, he helped out the five Pandava brothers, assuming two incarnations as the black Krishna and his white brother, Balarama. As the flute-playing man-god who frolicked with the *gopis* (cowgirls), Krishna was a most popular figure.

A god with a thousand names, Vishnu comes in various forms or incarnations. In the earliest texts, he is identified with the lion, his vehicle. As the god Narayan, Vishnu is most often depicted lying on the cosmic ocean.

In the Kathmandu Valley, King Hari Datta established Narayan shrines not only as a means of veneration of Vishnu but also perhaps as a placement of political structure, a way to delimit his own kingdom. Later, however, the cult of Shiva predominated among the people. Later still, during the early Mallas, around 1390, King Jayasthiti Malla revived the Vishnu cult of the Vishnava sect, claiming to be an incarnation of Vishnu, a claim maintained until today by successive rulers. Since that time, one simple Vishnu shrine has stood in front of each former royal palace in the Valley. There are other important Vishnu temples and shrines within towns, and half a dozen more sacred shrines dedicated to the god scattered in the Valley. None is more impressive than Budhanilkantha.

The Reclining Vishnu

In dreamless sleep, Vishnu as Narayan floated partly submerged in the primeval ocean, Nara, like a fetus in its maternal womb. A lotus grew out of his navel, issuing Brahma who then proceeded to create the world. This Indian tale of the world's origin is Hinduism's most famous cosmic

The famous reclining Vishnu.

BUDHANIL-
KANTHA.
1-Narayan
image
2-east
entrance
3-south
entrance

myth, a source of great inspiration for artists in the subcontinent. But nowhere else have sculptors translated it into stone so powerfully and so literally, as the Neaplis did at **Budhanilantha**, a small hamlet nine kilometers (5½ miles) north of Kathmandu.

Some 1,400 years ago, a five-meter (16-foot) stone image of Narayan, the ultimate source and creator of life, was placed in a small pond at the foot of the Shivapuri Hills. Man had apparently dragged the huge black stone a long way, probably from outside the Valley, to this spot at the Valley's edge, where a small settlement had grown up by Licchavi times. This hamlet may have been a satellite of the famous nearby Licchavi town called Thatungri Dranga. In time, that town died and today only old bricks mark the site where it stood, a little northeast of Budhanilkantha.

Vishnu, as Narayan, reclines serene upon a bed made from the coils of a huge snake, Ananta. Eleven of Ananta's hoods rise up to form an elaborate oval-shaped outer crown encircling the god's diademed head. Even while he sleeps, Vishnu opens

Budhanil-
kantha water
festival.

his eyes to the sky above. He is placid and comfortable: his legs are crossed at the ankles and, aside from some large ornaments, he wears only a loose *dhoti*. His four arms hold four attributes: the discus (symbol of the mind) in the upper right hand, the mace (primeval knowledge) in the upper left hand, a conch (the five elements) in the lower left hand, and a lotus seed (the moving universe) in the lower right hand.

Worshippers descend a small stone walkway to the recessed water tank and

perform their rituals from a wooden platform near the reclining figure. Every morning at about 9 o'clock, a priest goes into the basin to wash the god's face and make similar offerings while attendants ring bells.

The Festival of Budhanilkantha is one of the big events in the Valley. But even on ordinary days, pilgrims abound. *Paths* (shelters) and *dharmasalas* (rest houses) have been built for them nearby. These structures mar the overall effect, which is rather pleasant with a huge tree reflected in the cosmic ocean of the pond, itself carpeted with shimmering ceramic tiles.

The Licchavis sculpted at least three of these almost-identical Vishnu images, all of them lost for centuries. The one at Budhanilkantha, which is the largest, was the first to be found. It may or may not be the oldest.

The second Vishnu image to be found was in **Balaju**. The third one, supposedly dug up near the central part of the Valley where the Licchavis once had their main settlement, was brought to the royal palace in Kathmandu for King Pratap Malla in the 1600s. This monarch had a small canal built in order to bring water in a constant flow from the natural spring at Budhanilkantha down to his palace.

A forecast of death forbids the kings of Nepal, themselves incarnations of Vishnu, from looking at the monumental image in Budhanilkantha. But the kings may view the other two Vishnu images, as they are believed — rightly or wrongly — to be only replicas of the Budhanilkantha original.

A beautiful pastoral walk leads through paddy fields from Budhanilkantha to Kathmandu (see page 111).

The Priceless Treasures of Changu Narayan

The temple of **Changu Narayan**, built on a hilltop some 12 kilometers (7½ miles) east of Kathmandu, was completely rebuilt after a fire destroyed it in 1702. But its origins go back to the 4th Century.

The best access starts from the Sankhu road and proceeds across the Manohara River. It is a good 40 minutes' walk up the hill to reach the large temple bathed in sunshine. As you walk through the main entrance, you are greeted by a couple of

Changu Narayan, left, and its ornate entrance.

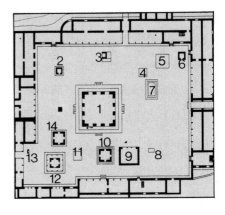

stone elephants. You pass some small temples, then encounter a twin-roofed pagoda and the main two-tiered temple.

To the right, another temple has two important stones. These are an allegoric version of a lion-headed Vishnu Narsingh, dismembering the king of the demons, who is stepping on his fallen crown; and Vishnu Vikrantha, a dwarf with six arms.

Behind these, on a small terrace, is erected a slab of flat black stone with its top right angle broken. At its bottom is Narayan reclining on Ananta; in the center is Vishnu, with 10 heads and 10 arms going through the different layers of the universe. This beautiful priceless piece of the 5th or 6th Century is surrounded by half a dozen more images dating back to the 9th Century.

There is an image of Garuda, the mythical bird that serves as Vishnu's heavenly vehicle, in front of the main temple; it also dates to the 5th or 6th Century. Beside it is one of the oldest and most important Licchavi inscriptions in the Valley.

Apart from various Vishnu and Garuda images, and graceful statues of Bupathindra Malla and his queen in a gilded cage, there is one more very interesting

feature here. This is the paving of the temple-wide platform. In the central part, triangular bricks are used; in the periphery, old bricks with completely rounded edges are employed. The vast courtyard is surrounded by various buildings which are used as resthouses for pilgrims.

From this sanctuary, there is a sweeping view over the surrounding countryside. To the east, a path slides down amid rice fields to **Changu**, which holds ruins of the Licchavi period. A very plea-

sant two-hour walk east along the ridge brings you to the Nagarkot road (see page 110). The old road from Kathmandu to Bhaktapur branches off to the right at the far side of the village.

The Cave Where Shiva Hid

Another spectacular view of the Valley is the main reason to visit the **Bishankhu Narayan**, which may be reached by a dirt road that branches off the Godavari road toward the east, beyond the village of Bandegaon. Although it is one of the most celebrated Vishnu shrines in the Valley, it is only a natural twisting rock cave, sitting in the saddle of a range that separates the Godavari area from the Valley proper. A steep, narrow stairway cut into the rock leads to a wooden platform in front of a tiny opening to the cave, where free-formed stones are usually protected by a lattice of metal links.

The connection to Vishnu is through a legend: Shiva once hid here from the demon Bhasmasur, who had obtained from him the power to turn all living things into ashes and dust by a touch of the hand. Vishnu convinced the demon to touch his own forehead, and the demon

turned himself to dust. The hillock adjacent to the cave is said to be made up of the ashes of Bhasmasur.

Laundry and Erotic Carvings

The rock temple of **Sekh Narayan** is located at the foot of the Gorakhnath hillock on the east side of the Pharping road, at the southern fringe of the Valley. At this point, the road twists at a sharp angle. There are four pools set at two different levels. By the bottom ones, women are forever washing themselves and their laundry, some of which is spread out to dry in an abstract composition.

In the waters of a pond green with algae, a 13th Century Surjya panel and an image of Surjya, the sun god often identified with Vishnu, are reflected half-submerged. Along the footpath, set into a wall, is a graceful early image of Shiva and Parvati.

Two stone stairways link the pool area with the Sekh Narayan temple, some 50 feet above the upper pool. It has been a place of pilgrimage since at least the early 15th Century. The temple sits snugly at the base of the ochre yellow overhanging cliff. It is a small, dark, single-story structure in wood and metal, with erotic carvings on its struts.

Vishnu's stone-carved figure is the main image within the shrine. The 14th Century bas-relief of Vishnu Vikrantha is the latest (and most inferior) of four sculptures found in the Valley depicting that particular incarnation of the god. Here, one of his feet is raised to heaven, the other planted on earth. More powerful, probably older, but unfortunately incomplete, is another stone sculpture of Vishnu next to the Vishnu Vikrantha. Vishnu's left leg is also raised, but his knee remains bent.

The religious shrines throughout this area are superbly integrated into exceptionally beautiful natural surroundings. Near the top of the same hillock is the cave of Gorakhnath (page 119), and above it is yet another temple, the **Bajra Jogini** (page 137). Nearby is the **Dakshinkali Shrine** (page 138) at the confluence of two streams.

A Fish in the Mustard Fields

Further west, in the immediate vicinity of **Machhegaon**, the neglected site of **Machhe Narayan** is reached from either

Submerged Surjya at Sekh Narayan.

Kirtipur or the Raj Path via a small footpath meandering through mustard fields, bamboo groves and clusters of rural houses. Every third year, thousands of people from all over the Valley come to this shrine, which celebrates Vishnu's incarnation as a fish.

The small stone temple occupies the center of a sacred stone-walled tank shaded by trees, with two simple public ponds flanking it. The gargoyles here are no longer spouting water, and the water in the ponds is stagnant and murky. But in the sanctum, among images of other gods, is a sculpture of Machhe Narayan standing up, emerging from the mouth of a fish.

Don't be surprised, however, if you are told — perhaps even by the priest himself — that "the priest is not here" to open the shrine.

Two Smaller Shrines

During the month of *Kartik* (October-November), thousands of worshippers begin a day's pilgrimage in **Ichangu Narayan**, then proceed to Changu Narayan, Bishankhu Narayan and Sekh Narayan. The **Ichangu Narayan** shrine is surrounded by clumps of trees and open fields at the foot of the Nagarjun peak north of Swayambhunath. The two-story temple was built in the 18th Century on a site where, according to legend, King Hari Datta installed an image of Narayan in the 6th Century. The usual attributes of Vishnu can be seen within the walled compound. The stone pillars and carved struts are of special interest. A Brahmin priest conducts daily worship. There is a lovely walk from here to Balaju (see page 110).

Dhum Varahi, on the northeastern outskirts of Kathmandu, offers a rather weird scene on a windy day when leaves are blown away. against a gray sky. On an open field overlooking the Dhobi Khola stand two huge trees, one of which — a pipal — crushes between its roots a brick shrine containing one of the most outstanding pieces of sculpture from the 6th Century Licchavi period. It is an almost life-sized stone sculpture of Vishnu's incarnation as a half-man, half-boar, rescuing the goddess Earth. A visit to this shrine can be incorporated in the walk from Budhanilkantha to Kathmandu (see page 111).

Ichangu Narayan.

SHIVA SHRINES:
THE GREAT GOD

Shiva is a composite god. He is both Destroyer and Creator, at once the end of things and the beginning of new ones. Terrible, he is Bhairav ("The Cruel") or Rudra or Ugra or Shava ("The Corpse"). Peaceful, he is Mahadeva ("The Great God") or Ishwara ("The Lord") or Pashupati ("The Lord of the Beasts").

Shiva is usually represented as a light-skinned man with a blue throat, five faces, four arms and three eyes. He holds a trident (the symbol of lightning), a sword, a bow, and a mace topped with a skull. Together with his son Ganesh, the elephant-headed god, he is the most helpful god in the Kathmandu Valley — if also the most awesome.

In other representations, he may be seen wrapped in three snakes, one of which is considered to be the sacred cord of Brahmins. As Bhuteshvara, "Lord of the Evil Spirits," he haunts cemeteries; in fact, there still exists one Shaivite sect that eats corpses.

Sometimes Shiva is seen as a disheveled, unkempt holy man, the shame of the pantheon. Today, many of his faithful *sanyasins* and *sadhus* forever on the same trip of dust, ashes and ganja, swarm from all over India and Nepal to celebrate the festival of Shivaratri at **Pashupatinath** in February or March. It is here, at this most sacred of all Nepalese Shiva shrines, that Shiva's dual aspects are best depicted.

The Shepherd of Fertility

Throughout the year, Shiva is worshipped at Pashupatinath as a *lingum,* or phallus. His vehicle, Nandi the bull, is regarded as an ancient symbol of fecundity. Indeed, Shiva as Pashupati displays only his sweeter side: a shepherd of animals and humans, and prime inheritor of original Vedic beliefs of fertility.

Perhaps the most interesting way to reach Pashupatinath, five kilometers (three miles) east of Kathmandu, is to follow the ancient route of pilgrims. This is a picturesque road which in ancient times was a symbolic link between the temporal power of the king and the

Pashupatinath, left; and below; Shiva and *lingum*, far right.

spiritual power of Shiva. King Pratap Malla had it built as a flagstone highway.

Today, the route crosses the Dhobi Khola river by a steel bridge. It traverses the Pashupatinath Plateau, the probable site of the former Licchavi capital of Deopatan, then reaches a crossroads. Here you'll see a large *dharmasala* (now being rebuilt) which opens onto an inner courtyard sheltering pilgrims and dying sacred cows. The road continues through a large expanse of brownish grass where monkeys prance through scattered trees. Eventually you pass through a hamlet. The approach to the temple is on the right-hand side of the road.

The main square in front of the temple is occupied by petty vendors and peddlers selling necklaces, rings, plastic bangles and toys, mirrors, small bowls full of tiny buttons, black stones inlaid with shells, tangerines and mangoes.

Entrance to the temple precinct is forbidden to non-Hindus. Notices on either side of the much-decorated gate make that abundantly clear, and policemen are there to remind you. But as you look from outside, you can catch a glimpse of the pigeons swarming on a huge structure of

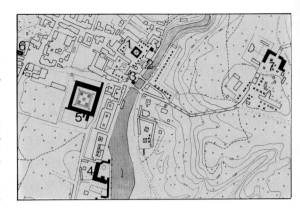

Nandi, and you'll also see a small Hanuman statue under its umbrella.

This large, gilded, triple-roofed temple was built in 1696. (Like many Valley temples, it has decorative roofs without corresponding floors.) Nearly 300 years earlier, there was a structure on this site, and its importance probably goes back long before that.

Immediately to the left of the temple, there is a ramp with a few steps of carved stone slabs, recycled from former Licchavi structures. The ramp leads to a small hill

Visitors at Pashupatinath: pilgrims, left, and yogi, right.

named after the famous Mount Kailash. From a grassy platform strewn with a few stone *lingas,* there is a good view of the whole Pashupatinath site.

The temple complex is a rather unhappy mixture of corrugated iron roofs clustered around the gilded triple roof of the temple. The sacred **Bagmati River,** which borders the complex, twists into a gorge on your left.

Two bridges span the river and lead from the main village street of Pashupatinath to a stairway climbing the wooded hill on the east bank. Before the bridges to your left are *ghats* reserved for the cremation of royalty. Those *ghats* to the right are for commoners and are popular spots for bathing.

The *ghats* are a popular place for celebrations at various times during the year. Saturdays are particularly busy days. On votive days, and at the end of their menstrual cycles, women come here to purify themselves, changing into new saris afterward.

This area is also noted for the local craft of block-printing textiles. In the hamlet, artisans dip their wooden blocks into green, black and red dye. They print square or lozenge patterns about 10 cen-

timeters (four inches) wide. Pools of white cotton are put out to dry on mats along the streets.

On the opposite bank, just in front of the temple, are 11 identical stone *chaityas* containing *lingas.* They are lined up at the foot of a terraced retaining wall stepping up toward the hill. Before the construction of the *chaityas,* there were hermits' and *sadhus'* caves here.

Along the road going around the grassy platform away from the river stands a small two-story 18th Century temple. It is dedicated to Pashupati's legendary teacher, Guru Dakshina Murti, and has erotic carvings on its struts.

Other erotic scenes and colorful Tantric representations can be found in the small two-roofed **Bachhareshwari Temple** of the 6th Century, located on the western *ghats.*

On the left bank of the river, near one of the bridges, is a beautiful Buddha bust probably dating to the 7th Century. Today it is half-buried, but is an important vestige of the past.

Further down the river, the **Ram Temple** with its extensive courtyard shelters yogis and *sadhus* during festivals — especially the Shivaratri celebration,

when tens of thousands of pilgrims flock to Pashupatinath. The government provides them with a free meal and firewood every day of the festival.

Pashupatinath is one of the four most important pilgrimage sites in Asia for Shiva devotees. It has been closely linked to orthodox south Indian Shaivism since the visit of Shankaracharya during the high tide of Buddhism in the Valley. This famous Brahmin cleaned up the Pashupatinath shrine, threw out the Buddhists, and established the strong rule of orthodox Shaivite belief.

Guhyeshwari and Gokarna's Mahadev

Friendly monkeys may escort you up the stepped path climbing the hill, which has many votive *shikharas* and shrines topped by Shiva *lingas*. Farther on, the path descends to the **Guhyeshwari Temple**. It first leads to the **Gorakhnath Shikhara**, a tall brick structure flanked by a large brass trident and surrounded by *paths* and *lingas* on a wide platform.

The paved track meandering down the hill through shady trees eventually leads you to the Guhyeshwari Temple. This is a shrine of Shiva's *shakti* in her manifestation as Kali. Again, its entrance is forbidden to non-Hindus. Some child will no doubt be quick to raise the alarm if you creep up the stairs to catch a glimpse of the beautiful gilded structure of the temple, ornamented with flags in front.

Beyond Pashupatinath and Bodhnath, a road branching off the main road to the northeast leads to Gokarna and the King's Forest. At Gokarna, on the banks of the Bagmati, sits another important Shiva shrine: the majestic, ochre-colored, three-roofed **Mahadev Temple.**

This shrine sits atop three sets of irregularly shaped stone stairways, following the natural contour of the river bank. Shiva lies on a stone bed of cobras just above where the steps enter the water.

The temple was built in 1582. It is surrounded by a sort of outdoor "sculpture garden," featuring a multitude of gods and goddesses. Its upper gilt roof — which boasts a finial, trident, bells, pots and birds as decorations — glistens against a backdrop of green hillsides, fringed on top with tall trees. The inner sanctum houses a much-venerated *lingum.*

On the approach steps is a small single-story prayer hall, the Vishnu Paduka, built

Guhyeshwari in the 19th Century.

GOKARNA
MAHADEV
1-Mahadev
2-Vishnu
  Paduka
3-Parvati

during the 19th Century. It contains 16 metal plaques and displays Vishnu's footprint embedded in the stone floor. This is an important place for after-death ceremonies.

None has the aesthetic power of Parvati, the finest and oldest image at Gokarna, standing inside a small isolated shrine between the temple and the main road. Sculpted in the 8th Century, Parvati holds in her left hand the stem of a lotus. Her figure, beautifully modeled with round, full, high breasts, slim waist and long limbs, rises from the simple oval of a lotus pedestal. With a ring of flames around her, adorned by fine jewels and a tall crown, the transcendent lotus goddess embodies the heavenly female. You can walk from here to Bodhnath (see page 111).

The **Tika Bhairav** is a shrine of an altogether different register. It shows the darker side of Shiva as the terrible Bhairav.

To reach this shrine, you must travel outside the Kathmandu Valley to the Lele Valley, which adjoins it to the southeast. The shrine is situated on a peninsula made by the confluence of two rivers south of Chapagaon. Its site is marked by an enor-

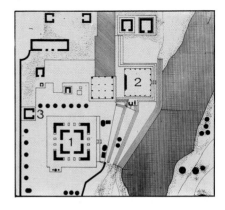

mous *sal* tree.

Don't look for a temple. Just walk past the few houses on the edge of the plateau, and continue to one of the most pleasant surprises in Nepal: a monumental, multicolored fresco showing a closeup of Bhairav's face in almost abstract design. The painting is on a three-by-six-meter (10-by-20 foot) brick wall. A simple brick platform constitutes the altar, and a dingy metal roof serves as shelter. Once a year, thousands of people come here to worship Bhairav.

Gokarna
Mahadev
Temple.

GANESH SHRINES: GOD OF LUCK

Ganesh, the elephant-headed god, is one of the most popular divinities in Hinduism, and is certainly the most popular in the Kathmandu Valley. Regarded as a god of good luck who casts obstacles aside, he is consulted by one and all before any task is undertaken — be it a journey, the building of a house, or even the writing of a letter. Ganesh must be invoked early every morning. Tuesdays and Saturdays are particularly propitious days to honor him.

There are differing legends as to his ascendency. He is commonly believed to be the son of Shiva and Parvati. Ganesh is usually represented as a white-skinned deity with a fat, round belly. His elephant head has only one tusk, the other having been broken. His four arms hold a conch, a discus, a mace or goad, and a lotus or water lily. He travels on a shrew and is greedy for offerings of food, especially fruit. He has two wives, Siddhi and Buddhi.

Ganesh shrines are numerous in all Newar settlements in the Valley. Four shrines are particularly sacred: Chandra Binayak in Chabahil, Surjya Binayak near Bhaktapur, Karya Binayak near Bungamati, and Jal Binayak near Chobar.

Shrines for Disease Cures And Marriage Picnics

Two hundred meters (650 feet) west of the Chabahil stupa, in the middle of the village, is the **Chandra Binayak**. This double-tiered, brass-roofed temple houses a tiny Ganesh. The god sits on a golden tympanum, with twin flags and bells in front of him on either side. A brass shrew waits for Ganesh atop a big pillar in front of the shrine. Struts depict the eight forms of Bhairav and the eight mother goddesses.

People of all creeds come to this shrine to worship Ganesh. It is believed he can cure diseases and external bodily injuries.

South of Bhaktapur, halfway up the foothills in the southeastern part of the valley, is the **Surjya Binayak.** The Ganesh image here, merely a stone in the shape of the god, has been traced to the 17th Century. It is considered able to give the

Classic Ganesh image.

SURJYA
BINAYAK
1-sanctum
2-Ganesh
 shikhara
3-entrance gate

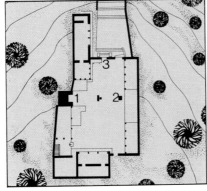

also a *hiti* with a carved stone tap. Figures of devotees kneel nearby.

This is a favorite spot among Nepalese for marriage picnics. If you encounter one here, you may be invited to join the guests for a hearty meal and heartier drinks. The bride and groom will be watching over the gathering from the first floor of the *pati*, on one side of the rocky precinct.

Shrines for Completing Tasks And Strengthening Character

In a forest preserve between the villages of Bungamati and Khokana, south of Kathmandu, lies the **Karya Binayak**. From the road linking the hamlets, a path leads uphill to a beautiful clearing and a small walled compound with a single-roofed shrine. Families often come here to ask Ganesh for help in completing difficult tasks.

In the shrine's altar is a free-shaped stone that takes significance in Ganesh cults as a symbol of the god.

A little below the shrine, and off to one side, is a brick building with a vaulted roof. Pilgrims are sheltered in the three arcades here.

Shrine at
Surjya
Binayak.

power of speech to children who are slow to talk; this makes it a popular spot for family visits. The image is flanked by a pillar with representations of a shrew (Ganesh's vehicle) and a bell.

The path to the shrine starts from a bridge across the Hanumante River. It heads uphill, passes through a large gateway constructed by the Ranas, and leads up an open stone-paved stairway into a small enclosed space in the middle of dense forest. A tall brick and plaster structure marks the main sanctuary. There is

From this tranquil compound, where the only sounds are the babble of a nearby brook and the cries of crows in surrounding trees, there is a splendid view of the Bagmati Valley and the western foothills.

Jal Binayak

Those persons seeking strength of character go to worship Ganesh at **Jal Binayak**, situated just beyond Chobar Gorge.

Whole Newar families, dressed in bright saris and smart suits, wearing perfume and jewelry, often make pilgrimages here. You may see them carrying small trays with offerings like flowers, eggs, powders or incense.

Pilgrims such as these may have been coming here for centuries before the present temple, with its three tiers of roofs, was constructed in 1602. A worn sculpture of Uma Maheshwar, carved about 500 years before the shrine was erected, can still be seen on the square base platform of the Jal Binayak.

The main image of the shrine is a massive rock. It extends outside the temple at the back; only a small part in front

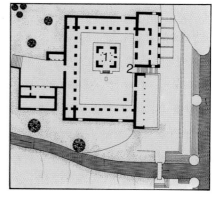

JAL BINAYA
1-sanctum
2-main entran

vaguely resembles an elephant tusk. Devotees apparently built the temple to shelter this object of devotion.

On the struts are carved eight Bhairavs and the eight mother goddesses, or Ashta Matrikas. Ganesh always appears together with these goddesses. Half of the struts on the lower roof depict Ganesh himself flanked by a beautiful damsel; lush branches above her figure suggest this may be a tree goddess. There are tiny erotic carvings below both Ganesh and the female.

Ganesh's shrew at Jal Binayak.

SHRINES FOR FEMALE DEITIES

Hindu mythology has no lack of female deities. But auspicious forms of goddesses are relatively few, and these inevitably take on ferocious, fierce, bloodthirsty appearances.

The most important of all these goddesses is **Devi** or **Maha Devi**, "The Great Goddess." As Parvati, Shiva's *shakti*, she follows the moods and forms of her male counterpart. But more than this, she actually dominates him.

Shiva is often represented as being at peace with himself, totally passive. His *shakti* is the dynamic element of the relationship. When they engage in sexual intercourse, Shiva is at ease while Parvati is extremely energetic. When Shiva is depicted in his corpse form as Shava, his *shakti* is attempting to arouse him sexually. The image of the goddess as the active element has taken over in popular belief.

Shaktism as a cult devoted to the female is a return to the primitive cult of the cosmic mother goddess. When the Aryans conquered India, they overturned these phallic cults, reversing the female-male order with Vedic and Brahmin gods. But when the *Upanishads* were composed about 600 B.C., the neolithic Bronze Age goddess was depicted as having far greater wisdom than the patriarchal Aryan gods themselves.

Maha Devi the Terrible

The innermost shrine of a mother-goddess temple has a form symbolic of the female organ. There are many examples of this throughout the Valley. Even Buddhism, in its Tantric form, is not immune from the mood: "Buddhahood abides in the female organ," states one of its late aphorisms. Placing the human female in the center of the symbolic system, the Tantric Shakti cult makes each living couple a symbol — and hence, an incarnation — of Shiva and Parvati, thus justifying sexual coupling as a ritual to reach the divine.

Just as Shiva has thousands of names and incarnations, so does Maha Devi, his *shakti*. She is the black goddess Kali, "The Dark One," and Durga, "The Terrible of Many Names." From her womb, she is

Malla Kings and Queens.

forever giving birth to all things.

But Maha Devi's stomach is a void which can never be filled. She craves for the ambrosia of blood — blood of demons, of animals, of human beings. In centuries past, human sacrifices were universally characteristic of cults of worship for the goddess. They were officially banned in Nepal in 1780 and in India in 1835.

There are many shrines in the Valley dedicated to the cult of female deities. Many more contain decorations or statues of such deities.

There are four principal shrines for *joginis*, or mystical goddesses. These are located in or near Sankhu, Guhyeshwari, Pharping and Vijeshwari.

Varahis — *shaktis* in the form of she-boars — portray the female aspect of the ultimate principal. They also have four main shrines scattered through the valley.

Various other sites are consecrated to the Ashta Matrikas, the divine mother goddesses who attend both Shiva and Skanda, the god of war. They are frequently sculpted on the struts of temples, and are generally associated with the violent forms of Tantric gods and goddesses.

Sankhu's Bajra Jogini

Hills encircle the ancient settlement of Sankhu in the northeastern part of the Valley. They are covered with dense forests which hide a temple to a secret goddess, the **Bajra Jogini**. Halfway up the hillside, tucked away among tall, dark pines, her shrine is in a secluded spot fit for a Tantric deity.

Nepalese legend says the goddess has resided here from primeval history. She is credited with having persuaded Manjushri to drain the waters of the lake which once occupied the Valley floor.

To reach the shrine, follow a wide path, paved with stone, north from Sankhu for about 600 meters (0.4 mile). Then climb up a steep flight of steps to the temple. Along the stairway you will note a sanctum of Bhairav; it is marked by a large triangular stone with a gross Ganesh image on one side. Animal sacrifices are often made here.

The central temple is located amid a series of stupas containing four directional Buddhas. Its platform appears to have been cut from rock. Built in the 17th Century, it has three roofs, struts with figures

Goddess paraded to Sankhu Bajra Jogini.

SANKHU BAJRA
JOGINI

1-temple
2-chaitya
3-Mhasukhwa
  Maju

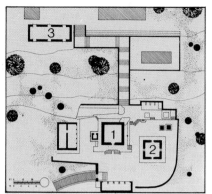

Dyochhen. Locked inside the nondescript building are some of Nepal's most ancient and valuable sculptures, the most prized of which is a 7th Century head of the Buddha. On the way to the *dyochhen*, you will pass a 10th Century water tank with a stone spout and a recessed, carved stone fountain at its center.

A chariot procession from Sankhu to the quiet site of this temple has been performed every year since the end of the 16th Century.

You can walk from this area to Nagarkot (see page 110).

Sacrificial
party at
Sankhu.

of various deities, and a golden *torana* (crest over the door) portraying the Bajra Jogini as an unusually pleasant female figure. Within the temple sanctum, the goddess is flanked by her two traditional Nepalese companions, Simhini the lion son and Byaghrini the tigress daughter.

There is no god sheltered in the neighboring 16th Century, twin-roofed **Gunvihar Temple**, but there is a Swayambhu *chaitya*. Behind this temple, a stone-paved path leads uphill to the **Bajra Jogini**

The Temple at Pharping

Another temple of the same name and of the same period, a 17th Century **Bajra Jogini**, stands on a green hillside above Pharping, south of Kathmandu on the way to Dakshinkali.

A steep stone path from the village of Pharping merges into a stairway leading to the temple. Images of Bajra Jogini occupy two separate sanctums on the upper floor. She is also the central figure in *toranas* above her sanctums.

The Tantric goddess is identified by her awesome implements — the chopper with a *vajra* handle and a skull cap. In all four representations here, her left leg is raised high, as if the artists who created her had been influenced by the much older Vishnu Vikrantha sculpture at the nearby Sekh Narayan Temple. Here again, against all "rules," Bajra Jogini has a pleasant face, pretty clothes, and as much heavy jewelry as any rich Nepali bride could want.

A path to the west leads to a small meditation cell. Above, the **Gorakhnath Cave** is marked by prayer flags hung from trees. In former times, this location was considered an ideal stopover place for pilgrims following a two or three-day walk from the Terai. From this hill, there is a fine view of the Tibetan ranges; below is Pharping, nestled on a plateau, and further away is the Kathmandu Valley.

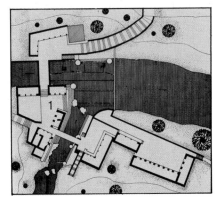

DAKSHINKAL
1-Kali shrine

The Sacrifices of Dakshinkali

The most spectacular, regular, open religious worship performed in the Valley takes place where the main road south ends. Fittingly, this is at a shrine to the Dakshin, or "southern" Kali.

More animals are brought for sacrifice at the pit of Kali, situated at the bottom of a long stone stairway, than to any other shrine. Twice a week, a large-scale massacre is staged; an even more incredible annual ritual is held during *Dasain*, with the image of Kali being bathed in blood. The men who kill the buffaloes, goats, pigs, lambs, ducks, chickens and other animals — invariably uncastrated males — stand ankle deep in their blood after slicing their throats or severing their

Dakshinkali sacrifice, below, gets a fearful glance from a Chhetri girl, right.

heads. It is a gruesome scene to which pilgrims and tourists flock, packing the rest houses, shops and *paths*.

But the guided-tour atmosphere cannot break the spell created by the mystery of this dark spot. Situated in a natural recess between two mountains, at the spot where two streams unite between forested hillsides, it is a place of considerable beauty. Legends say that Kali herself commanded a 14th Century Malla king to build her this shrine here.

Now walled, it is decorated with brass tridents and a canopy adorned with snakes. Inside, the main Kali statue is of black stone. The six-armed goddess, trampling a male human, stands in the company of Ganesh, seven Ashta Matrikas, and a free-shaped stone of Bhairav.

The phenomenon of a "mother-daughter" shrine is notable at Dakshinkali. The path passing the lower shrine of Kali winds up a steep cone-shaped hill to the simpler shrine of her mother.

The eastern and northern slopes of the hillside on which the shrines rest have grassy lawns, where worshippers often picnic — cooking and eating the sacrificed animals. Nearby, at the top of the stairs, where cars and buses are parked, the inevitable curio vendors do a thriving business. Peacock feather fans, bracelets, bangles and other trinkets are sold here, as are *khukris* and, occasionally, hashish.

Of greater scenic, if not religious, interest is the **Vajra Varahi Temple.** This site, one of the most important of Tantric origin in the Valley, is located in a sacred grove of trees east of Chapagaon.

The paths to the temple lead from Chapagaon through an interesting network of canals — some of them underground — with little round bridges, an exceptional indication of a sophisticated but long-forgotten irrigation and drainage system. Beyond the canals are bright, open fields; you then pass through the dense cover of tall trees before reaching the temple.

The recently renovated Vajra Varahi was built in 1665, but the site existed long before that time. Various natural stones here are regarded as images of Ganesh, Bhairav and the Ashta Matrikas. On the fringe of the forest are eight cremation grounds amidst vegetable patches and mustard fields.

Shrine to a Demon Slayer

Outside the valley to the southeast is the **Chandeshwari Shrine**. From Banepa, the biggest settlement in the area, a path leads into a vale northeast of the hamlet. As you approach, you can see the shrine sitting on the right bank of a steeply sloping gorge. An annual chariot procession follows this route.

Legend says this entire valley was once crowded with wild beasts that the local folk regarded as demons. They called upon Parvati to rid them of Chand, a demon whom they particularly feared. When the goddess succeeded in her quest, she became known as Chandeshwari, "The Slayer of Chand."

In thanks, this shrine was built to her. It is a three-tiered temple in a wide precinct, with a lion and peacock on columns in front of the main altar. The *torana* and struts are richly carved with the customary eight Ashta Matrikas and eight Bhairavs. In the sanctum is a free-standing image of the goddess Chandeshwar, ("The Master of the Slayer of Chand."), wearing rich silver ornaments. A multicolored fresco of Bhairav, painted on the western wall of the temple, is sometimes regarded as the shrine's main attraction.

Next to the temple is a brick shrine housing a Shiva *lingum* which is recognizable by the image of Nandi the bull, Shiva's vehicle, facing the entrance. To complete the family gathering, Ganesh sits between the temple and Shiva's shrine.

Outside, just below the temple precinct, people come to wash and bathe in a pond by the brook. Three round *ghats* are located within a flight of five stairs near here; this is a place where the sick and the aged come to die. Local folk look after them, and when the last moment nears, they prop the body up on an inclined plane between two of the *ghats*, so that the dying person's feet touch the sacred water of the stream and the head rests next to a tiny carving of Vishnu. Some of the holy water is given the dying person for a last drink, and he thus goes to a dignified death.

A bizarre fresco of Bhairav adorns the western wall of the Chandeshwari Shrine near Banepa.

THE VALLEY'S NATURE SITES

The Kathmandu Valley's first religious rites were associated with tangible natural landmarks, such as rivers and mountains, rocks and forests. The Valley's earliest inhabitants established their spiritual and ritual domain through this natural network. Each important site of worship is located on a propitious, if not grandiose, site. Swayambhunath, for example, is perched on a hilltop; Pashupatinath is hidden away in a gorge. Many other sites, no less sacred, are tucked into the lace of hills and forests surrounding the Valley.

Traditionally, it was the highest landmarks that became the most important centers of meditation and spiritual focus. Places that had remained above the waters of the primeval lake of Kathmandu were considered especially sacred. The smallest cave and the tiniest spring attracted meditating sages and legendary Buddhas. More prosaically, these summits, draped in pine and fir, are tranquil scenic sites. Whether or not adorned by a stupa or a Hindu shrine, they are ideal for a stroll or a picnic.

The Legendary Gorge of Chobar

Your exploration of nature sites should begin with a visit to **Chobar Gorge**, through which — legend tells us — the waters of the lake of Kathmandu escaped after being released by Manjushri. This natural wonder is located southwest of the city, where Chobar Hill, the highest point in a range of gentle hills, is sliced in two by the muddy waters of the Bagmati River.

The path to the top of this hill starts near the bank of the Bagmati at the hill's base. An impressive example of natural engineering and skillful design, the wide stone-paved track adjusts beautifully to the contour of the slope. After a series of steps and a pair of gates, it enters the courtyard of a Buddhist temple known as **Adinath Lokeswar.**

The most remarkable features of this triple-roofed structure — built in the 15th Century and reconstructed in 1640 — are the numerous water vessels, pots and pans nailed to boards all along the building. Below the golden *torana* depicting six Buddhas, the masked face of the Red Machhendra stares out from the main sanctum.

Facing the shrine, a stone *shikhara* is believed to be the entrance to a stone cave that cuts through the hill, emerging at the **Chobar Cave** below.

A suspension bridge, imported from Scotland and erected in 1903, spans the gorge. From halfway across, the view is impressive. On one side is the deep scar in Chobar Hill which legend says was cut by Manjusri's sword; probably, he had considerable help from an earthquake. Just to the south is the Jal Binayak shrine of Ganesh (page 134). Far below it, women can be seen washing and bathing on a flight of stone steps linking two round cremation platforms.

Adventurous walkers can stop at Chobar en route from Kirtipur to Patan (see page 111).

Beyond the Chobar Gorge, the main road changes from bitumen to dust. It soon passes a small pond set scenically within open fields with small clusters of farmhouses scattered about. This is **Taudaha Lake**, which legend says was created by Manjushri himself so that the *nagas* (serpents) which had lived in the great Valley lake could survive after he had drained it. Local folk believe the *nagas* still live here, and leave the pond's

The Jal Binayak temple at Chobar Gorge, left, is a short walk from the mirror image at Adinath Lokeswar, right.

stagnant water to the wild ducks and lotuses.

A beautiful mountain known as **Dinacho** ("Meditation Point") or **Champa Devi** rises here beyond the patchwork of terraced fields. A single large tree crowns its summit; once there were a pair of trees at the top, and the peak still bears the nickname "Two Trees."

The Machhe Narayan temple complex (page 124) is not far to the west. It can be reached down the forested slopes of **Chandragiri**, "The Mountain of the Moon," capped by a small *chaitya* of Lord Buddha.

The road continues to the east, following the twists and turns of the Bagmati River from the heights. Contrasting panoramas unfold before it. In the foreground, sunshine brightens the ochre shades of a few houses resting in a fluctuating wave of green and mustard-yellow fields. In the distance, mist blurs the features of the Valley and the light blue peaks beyond.

Northeast of Kathmandu, the pilgrims' route that winds past Pashupatinath, Chabahil and Bodhnath soon skirts a forest grove preserved since before the time of the Licchavi monarchs. This grove, bordered by the holy Bagmati, was held sacred and spared from axe and hoe. It is said to be the place where Shiva himself once wandered, disguised as a beautiful golden deer under cover of the low forested hills.

Local people built a fine shrine, the Gokarna Mahadev temple (page 130), on the river bank opposite the forest. Toward the end of the 19th Century, the grove was walled in and a deer park created. Today, Gokarna Forest it is known as **The King's Forest**. Visitors pay a fee to wander the roads and footpaths threading through the two-square-mile reserve, which contains a safari park and other facilities. Many species of deer roam here, as well as pheasants and peacocks, which may welcome you with a show of bright feathers. Elephants and ponies are available for adventurous riders.

Several miles north of Gokarna, the Bagmati's nascent waters rush down the foothills above **Sundarijal** to be captured in a century-old reservoir encased by forested slopes and terraced, cultivated fields. This is one of the Valley's main water supplies. The approach road is particularly picturesque.

The Royal Botanical Garden, left, and Godavari Kunda, right.

PHULCHOKI
MAI

1-temple
2-Bhairav
    Shrine
3-Nau Dhara
    (tank).

Where the road forks before the reservoir, the smaller trail leads east to a tiny rock cave. Inside is a 13th Century stone image of Maha Devi, as well as free-shaped stones worshipped as **Sundara Mai** and the Ashta Matrikas. A later shrine housing a Shiva *lingum* honors Shiva and Parvati as deities of beauty; it is said they once rested in this simple cave when descending from their Himalayan abode on Mount Kailash-Meru.

Phulchoki and Godavari

Tallest of the foothills that encircle the Valley is **Phulchoki**, 20 kilometers (12½ miles) southeast of Kathmandu, beyond Godavari. A triple-peaked mountain culminating at 2,762 meters (9,062 feet), its name means "flower-covered hill." This it is, especially in spring, when pilgrims climb high to fetch blossoms — orchids, clematis vines and rhododendrons — for offerings to the mother of the forest, **Phulchoki Mai**, to whom two shrines have been built on the mountain.

One of these shrines is at the base of Phulchoki, not far from a roadside marble quarry. Built on a platform surrounded by dense forest, this three-roofed temple

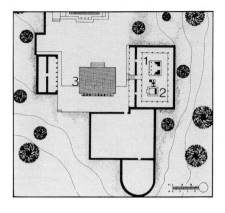

wears a dilapidated but attractive look. It is flanked by a single-story Ganesh temple and a grand 17th Century *hiti* with nine spouts. The main icon within the shrine representing the goddess is only a free-shaped stone. As usual in a Tantric temple, the struts are carved with figures of the eight Ashta Matrikas.

This shrine is considered no more than a lower-elevation substitute for the true **Phulchoki Shrine** above, at the apex of the mountain's central and highest peak. In this open shrine, the goddess is wor-

Doorway and stone image at Phulchoki Mai.

shipped not only as mother of forests, but also as Lakshmi and Vasundhara, two goddesses of wealth, and as Varada, goddess of blessings.

The view from Phulchoki's summit can only be termed phenomenal. To the north, the whole Kathmandu Valley lies at your feet. Beyond, the snow-clad Himalayan range provides an incomparable backdrop. To the south, you gaze across the valleys of the lower hill ranges that lead into the Terai and India.

At the foot of Phulchoki, in the **Godavari** area, are located **St. Xavier's College**, one of two schools run by the Jesuits; the **Royal Botanical Garden**; the **Royal Department of Medicinal Plants**; and a fish farm. The botanical garden, entered upon payment of a small fee, has thatched-roof picnic shelters, lily ponds, rushing streams, and beds of seasonal flowers. Kept in greenhouses on the slope of the hill just above is a notable collection of orchids, ferns and cacti.

The path to the fish farm leads by a quiet spot with a *kunda*, a clear-water spring that emerges from a natural cave. Water collects in a pool at the bottom of a stepped brick wall, then flows through a series of carved stone taps into a pond in the outer courtyard. None of the images at this **Godavari Kunda** are especially old, but this natural site — where the sacred waters of the Godavari river pour from the mountains, is revered by Hindus as having magical power. Every 12 years, hundreds of thousands of pilgrims come here to bathe. To them, a dip in the Godavari Kunda is equal in merit to distributing six million cows to Brahmins.

The Lele and Matatirtha Kundas

Two other important *kundas* are situated in the southern hills. The first of these is in the tiny, dusty Lele Valley, a bumpy trip south from Kathmandu. The track winds its way steeply downhill through terraced fields, reddish-brown soil and a few green plots to Lele village, where the arrival of a taxi is a major event for local children.

East of the village, a tiny, four-faced Shiva *lingum* stands in the wide expanse of a pond overshadowed by foliage. Past a small bridge, a storehouse bulges with dozens of bags of tea leaves to be carried by porters to Kathmandu.

A lane leads to two temples in the midst of a lovely grove. The small structure on

Festival at Matatirtha.

the east is the **Saraswati Kunda**. Its entrance is marked by a single-roofed Muktinath shrine built in 1668. The shrine contains a number of 16th to 18th Century sculptures.

Farther on, adjacent to the main **Lele Kunda**, stands the 16th Century *shikhara*-style **Tileshwar Mahadev**. On the temple platform is an interesting carved-stone panel of Kailash Parivar, representing Shiva and Parvati surrounded by their entire family, dating to the 12th Century.

If Lele Kunda gives an impression of an almost hidden, intimate beauty, the wide-open spaces of **Matatirtha Kunda**, in the southwestern foothills of the Valley, give the opposite effect. There is nothing here of great historical interest, but the site has a wild charm of its own.

A wide, flagstoned pilgrimage track leads from the Raj Path near the village of **Kisipidi**, and opens onto a spacious open courtyard where grass grows over the flagstones. In the center is a recessed water tank with carved stone spouts, from which clear spring water flows. The main *kunda* is in one corner of the courtyard, flanked by a small stone shrine containing a Shiva *lingum*. The site was established in the first part of the 18th Century; now,

devotees of all religions come here once a year to honor their deceased mothers.

The Images of Balaju

Is the reclining Vishnu in **Balaju** — Kathmandu's "industrial estate" a few kilometers north of the city center — older than the one in Budhanilkantha? That question has always been open to controversy. But one thing is not disputed: this fine sculpture, set in a secluded tank and shaded by the sacred forested hill above it, enjoys a tranquility missing from its more celebrated counterpart.

The Balaju tank is adjoined by a 14th Century **Shitala Mai** image, housed in a 19th Century twin-roofed temple. The area surrounding this small temple to Shitala, the goddess of smallpox, is a sort of outdoor sculpture garden. Many stone images are displayed here, including a 16th Century Harihari, a composite half-Shiva, half-Vishnu god.

At a lower level, a large open water tank displays 22 stone water spouts in a row, more than any other *hiti* in Nepal.

The wooded part of the hill behind Balaju, called **Nagarjun**, is a fine, walled

The Tika
Bhairav at
Lele.

forest reserve administered by the Royal Palace. Pheasants, deer, leopards and other wild animals live here amidst a great variety of trees.

The eastern slope of Nagarjun has two caves, about a kilometer apart. A small image of the Buddha is kept in the lower one, while the upper cave, though smaller, has two Buddha images and a figure of Nagarjuna, a famed philosopher who lived in south India not long after the birth of Christ.

The top of the wooded hill can be reached in two hours by a footpath through the **Jamacho** forest reserve. At the summit is a Buddhist *chaitya*. Tibetans believe the Buddha preached a sermon here centuries ago. It is now possible to drive to the top of this hill; on a fine day, the view of the Himalayas is quite spectacular.

Koteshwar's Sacred Confluence

If springs are holy places in Nepal, so too are the confluences of rivers. They are considered ideal places for worshipping, and hence for living.

At the spot where the three sacred rivers — the Bagmati, the Manohara and the Rudramati — meet, legend tells that Maha Devi once appeared to the demon

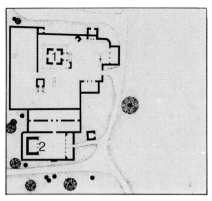

KOTESHWAR
MAHADEV
1-Mahadev
2-Bhagvati

king Shankhasur in the form of a Vishwarup Shiva with innumerable faces. Today, the **Koteshwar Mahadev** shrine commemorates this event. The worship of Koteshwar (*koti* means "millions" and *eshwar* means "gods") as the most powerful form of Shiva has traditionally been associated with having difficult prayers fulfilled.

The temple, a dome-roofed brick building, lies on a small plateau east of Patan near the rivers' confluence. It is marked by a few tall trees. Inside the shrine is a Shiva *lingum* said to date from the 8th Century. In adjoining courtyards are shrines to Bhagvati and to Gaganeshwar Mahadev. Further south, the **Kuti Bahal**, with its 15th Century *chaitya*, stands at the place where relatives and friends gathered to bid farewell to Patan citizens traveling to Tibet.

Another confluence of streams in the western part of the Valley is the site of a double shrine. Here, where two rivulets join near **Naikap** village, a footpath between rice fields leads to a sunken altar. A 300-year-old stone tympanum and a *path* stand in front of it.

The open Mahadev shrine on the platform opposite the *path* is dedicated to Shiva. Two tridents are set beside a primitively cut, four-faced 6th Century *lingum*. A standing 8th Century Mahagauri is imbedded in a wall nearby the shrine; Mahagauri is armless, and the head set on top of the broken neck is probably not hers. Among the various stone images on the grass is a superb but headless 10th Century Saraswati, carved from a large broken slab of stone. Her right arm and hand are mutilated; the absence of a head somehow adds to the aesthetic power of this masterpiece.

A carved *lingum* at Lele, and a pastoral scene near Bisankhu.

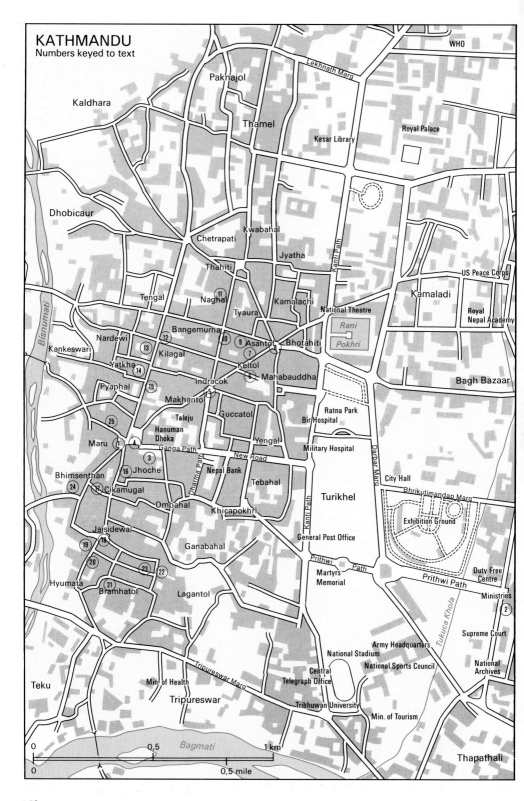

KATHMANDU
Numbers keyed to text

WHO

Lekhnath Marg

Paknajol

Kaldhara

Thamel

Kesar Library

Royal Palace

Dhobicaur

Kwabahal

Chetrapati

Jyatha

Thahiti

US Peace Corps

Tengal

⑪ Naghal

Kamalachi

Kamaladi

Tyaura

Bangemurha

National Theatre

Royal
Nepal Academy

Nardewi

⑫

⑩

⑨ Asantol

Rani

Bhotahiti

Pokhri

Kankeswari

⑬ Kilagal

⑦

Bagh Bazaar

Yatkha ⑭

Keltol

Pyaphal

⑮

⑥ Mahabauddha

Indracok

Makhantol

Taleju

Guccatol

Ratna Park

Bir Hospital

⑤ Maru

① Ⓐ

Hanuman
Dhoka

Yengal

Military Hospital

Ganga Path

New Road

③

City Hall

Bhimsenthan

⑯ Jhoche

Nepal Bank

Tebahal

Turikhel

Exhibition Ground

⑫ Cikamugal

⑳ ④ Cikamugal

Ombahal

Khicapokhri

Jaisidewal

Ganabahal

General Post Office

⑲ ⑱

Prithwi
Path

Duty Free
Centre

⑳

Martyrs
Memorial

Prithwi Path

Ministries

Hyumata

㉑ Bramhatol

㉓ ㉒

Lagantol

②

Supreme Court

Tripureswar Marg

Army Headquarters

National
Archives

Teku

Min. of Health

National Stadium

National Sports Council

Central
Telegraph Office

Min. of Tourism

Tripureswar

Tribhuwan University

Thapathali

0   0,5   Bagmati   1 km

0   0,5 mile

Bisnumati

Darbar Marg

Kanti Path

Dharma Path

Bhrikutimandap Marg

Tukuca Khola

TIMELESS KATHMANDU

The founding of Kathmandu city is usually said to have taken place during the "Dark Ages" at the end of the Licchavi period and the time of the ascendancy of the Mallas. But it is almost certain that a conglomeration of small settlements existing prior to that time eventually united as one city.

One of the first known areas of settlement was at Deopatan, just northwest of Pashupatinath. A further settlement must have developed in the southwestern part of present-day Kathmandu, at the confluence of the Valley's two main rivers, the Bagmati and Bishnumati; river confluences have always been considered spiritually auspicious locations. In addition, several important Licchavi ruins are scattered about the Valley.

The hub of the city in medieval times, as today, was the area around the **Kasthamandap** (1). From this point, it was said, the city of Kathmandu spread in the shape of a sword, its handle to the south and its blade to the north. There is no way to trace this shape in the late 20th Century layout of the city, however.

According to legend, the Kasthamandap, "The House of Wood" (see History section), was erected at the crossroads of two important trade routes. This sizeable structure was used as a community center for trade and barter. It probably functioned very much as it does today. The name "Kathmandu" is a derivative of "Kasthamandap," giving certain proof that this building must have been its original center.

Kathmandu city developed radially from this point, the Royal Palace and the Durbar Square being constructed soon after. Some theorize that the palace marked the northeastern boundary of the Old City.

Urban explorers who search the old and narrow streets leading toward the rivers inevitably discover buildings of great stature and quality that may have been past palaces. Along the river bank, one can find remains of early temples and shrines. A great deal of history still lies buried.

When the Valley was first unified by King Jayasthiti Malla in the 14th Century,

Kathmandu became his administrative capital. Considerable expansion took place from this time, with the fulcrum of activity shifting slightly toward the palace complex itself. Nevertheless, the old trade routes — particularly the diagonal road running from the Kasthamandap through Asan Tole — were thoroughly maintained and are still very much in evidence today.

The Ranas' Legacy

Architectural styles generally changed very little for centuries. Only a trained eye can differentiate between earlier and later artistry in traditional Newari buildings. It wasn't until the mid-19th Century, with the Ranas in power, that dramatic changes in architecture occurred. The leaders' travels in the outside world, from which the rest of the country was isolated, led to the introduction of many Western-influenced styles.

In Europe at this time, a great neo-classical revival was in full blossom. Jung Bahadur Rana returned from an 1850 visit to England and France with visions of grandeur in his head. The Western-style palaces he built as copies of Euro-

Preceding pages, a rainy day street scene; right, a resident of Kathmandu.

pean structures are in sharp contrast to the indigenous Nepali architecture of the time.

The culmination of this architectural style was the Ranas' palace, **Singha Durbar** (2). A building of gigantic proportion and size, it consisted of 17 courtyards and as many as 1,700 rooms, and was reputed to be the largest private dwelling in Asia, if not in the world. It took only 11 months to construct in 1901.

Sadly, all but the main wing containing the state rooms was damaged by fire in 1973. By that time, the place was being used as the government secretariat. An ambitious plan of renovation and repair of the main courtyard has been completed; it now houses the Prime Minister's offices and the National Planning Commission.

The Singha Durbar was only one of several hundred palaces that sprang up around Patan and Kathmandu during the Ranas' reign. With their decline in political power and the reemergence of the royal family, however, the Rana palaces have all become tarnished. Many of these sumptuous buildings have been taken over by government or private organizations, stripped of their internal grandeur. Today, they are mere shells of their former splendor.

Also under the Ranas, Kathmandu's suburbs started to grow and expand. The traditional concept of the tightly knit Newar city, designed to preserve every square meter of arable land outside the city, was broken. Western-style dwellings were built on the outskirts of the city, particularly to the northeast.

Recently, a second period of Westernization has caused Kathmandu new growing pains. The gardens of the old palaces have been sold and subdivided, and a spate of new modern architecture has sprung up. Nevertheless, it is still surprising to find in the center of the city sizeable cultivated areas, strongholds of the Newar tradition.

New City and Old City

Because of the two markedly different styles of architecture, there are today two quite distinct parts of Kathmandu. There is the western "Old City," flanked to the east by the **Tundhikhel,** a long open expanse used as a parade ground; and the ex-

Kathmandu city from the air.

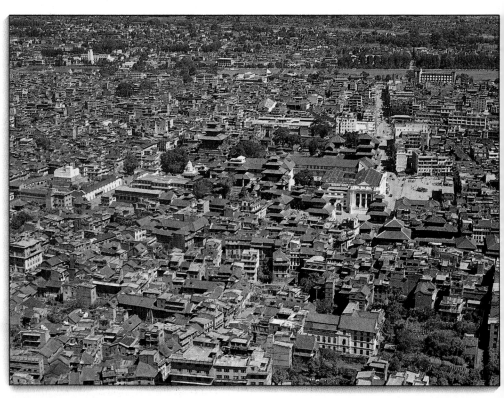

panding eastern area of mixed Western and traditional styles.

The two parts of town are basically divided by the north-south **Kanti Path**, or **King's Way**. This main artery skirts the Royal Palace, cuts across the **Lazimpat** district of embassies, and continues north as far as the reclining Vishnu of Budhanilkantha. On the outskirts of both Kathmandu and Patan, houses and buildings of various styles are beginning to join the two ancient cities into a single metropolis. Patan today has about 100,000 inhabitants, and Kathmandu at least three times that many.

The Old City has remained intact through the centuries, with the exception of one modification: after a major earthquake in 1934, **New Road** was constructed over the ruins. Running west from the Tundhikhel, it ends at Basantapur and the Durbar Square in front of the old palace. This wide street is the most vital commercial axis of the city today. The diagonal cross street that in medieval times was the main route to Tibet today has kept its role as a center for traditional petty trade.

Old New Road

New Road — properly called Juddha Sadak — is the paradise of the new consumer society that has rapidly emerged in the Valley since Nepal was opened to the West. You will find everything here, from the latest gadgets to antiques no older but certainly no cheaper than anywhere else. Moneyed people come here window-shopping, parading in their latest Western outfits, buying French face cream, imported tinned food, Japanese stereo equipment, films, drugs, jewels, cigarettes, local and foreign magazines.

The road opens on a plain, daubed stucco portico. About halfway down, a big pipal tree shades a small square with many *chaityas* where newsboys sell local papers. Intellectuals like to gather here and debate. At the end of New Road, facing the Crystal Hotel at the corner, a large new supermarket has been built. Its bulk isolates a small, active, recessed shrine.

The street going north to meet the diagonal axis of the Old City can boast the first commercial arcade in town. Behind a door, you find yourself in Hong Kong, Singapore or Bangkok, only to jump back

Salute to the King on the Tundhikhel.

Where Have All the Hippies Gone?

Hardly had the Flower Children blossomed in San Francisco's Haight-Ashbury in the mid-1960s than they began taking seed in Nepal. The climate was perfect, cool and enchanted; the soil was rich, warm and understanding; and everywhere was the fertility of Shaivist Hinduism and Mahayana Buddhism, the mystic and the sublime, the indulgence of lotus eating (if also acid-eating), and the acceptance of a friendly people. Besides, hashish was growing wild and was sold in licensed shops, and harder stuff was readily available.

So while the Beatles and Jimi Hendrix sang of love with a whiff of smoke about it, while *maharishis* and newly discovered *rimpoches* gathered followings of the tuned-in and turned-on and the words "love" and "peace" took on a new connotation, Kathmandu experienced an invasion the likes of which it had never seen before — and will almost certainly never see again.

They came bearded or shining-shaved, in boots or bare feet, heavily costumed or nearly naked, wearing beads or pierced-nose jewels, filthy or scrubbed clean, undernourished or well-fed, drug-dumb or highly articulate, wearing Buddhist saffron or Hindu white, locust people who settled where

they found their green and stayed until tolerance ran out.

Their monument remains: Freak Street, a lane within the long shadow of Basantapur, King Prithvi Narayan Shah's victory tower. The street is still gaudy if faded, and is trying hard to make a comeback. The velvet, satin, silk and Nepalese homespun fabrics still hang in shops. The well-thumbed second-hand books are there too, with the shoulder bags, the used shoes, the paper prints of gods and innocent erotica.

In the perfumed shadows of evening, ghosts of days not long past linger at their old haunts. The music has gone, the heavy beat and blare of acid rock pouring from smoky caverns named "Don't Pass Me By," "Yes Yes," "Hungry Eye," "The August Moon." Their signs are down. They no longer exist.

On the trail of the hippies came Indian filmmakers. One movie became a contemporary Indian classic: *Hare Rama Hare Krishna*, featuring a song called "Dum Maro Dum," or "Smoke, smoke, smoke."

All that is gone now. It went so suddenly, almost as if it had never happened. Some say King Birendra's 1975 coronation took them like an epidemic. Or perhaps official tolerance waned with the prohibition of hashish and other drugs. Visas were refused and canceled. Free transport out of the country was provided for those without means. But there was no mass exodus, and no one remembers seeing them go. They just seemed to vanish in the smoky mist.

When the penniless hippies departed, their more well-to-do peers remained for awhile: artists, dancers, writers, poets who published with the likes of Archibald Macleish and Allen Ginsburg. And there were the mystics, those who could tell the future from the stars, from your palms, from the vibrations of the earth. Then most of them, too, with their capes and earrings and felt hats, left the Valley.

More startlingly, perhaps, the familiar psychedelically painted coaches, vast in size and sometimes even double-decked, suddenly drove away. No more do buses carry labels like "London," "Paris," "Frankfurt," "Tehran," "Khajaraho" or "Goa," always Goa. Where is the Chapati Express now?

The young people in Nepal today are primarily international budget travelers known as "Trippies." They are highly respectable compared to their predecessors: rarely a whiff of illicit smoke, and not a bare breast to be seen in public. Their haven is Thamel, at the north end of Kathmandu's Old City.

But even here, where colorfully named restaurants outnumber colorfully named lodges, and together they nearly outnumber nameless trekking-gear shops, the hippies' legacy can be seen. There are the pie shops, the print shops, the second-hand book shops with names like "The Tamang Tantric," "High" and "The Kathmandu Trade Post." The restaurants and lodges, many of which still offer rooms for next to nothing, rest on foundations established in the hippy era.

Cat Stevens sang a song about Kathmandu when it was one of the world's most famous hippie paradises, and Goa was at the other end of the rainbow. Today, Joan Baez's civil-rights era song would be a more appropriate theme: "Where Have All the Flowers Gone?"

10 centuries when you step out. Narrow, paved side lanes thrust between rows of wall-to-wall traditional houses. Here and there are a few modest restaurants, shady hotels and tiny, dimly lit tea houses. A whole population wanders about or exchanges news to the whine of transistor radios. These alleys culminate in squares with corner *patis,* central *chaityas* and occasional temples.

Behind the Crystal Hotel, you can see the silhouettes of several temples. In the background is the Swayambhunath stupa on its hilltop, and the girdle of mountains in the far distance. At the crossing, pigeons copiously anoint the statue of Juddha Shamsher Rana (prime minister from 1932 to 1945), under whose direction New Road was built.

Forgotten Freak Street

As you walk further west, you soon come to a large open space known as **Basantapur** (3). It derives its name from the biggest tower looming over the massive palace structure on the right. This square was once a courtyard where the royal elephants were kept. After the 1934

earthquake, when New Road was opened, new buildings were erected and the square turned into a marketplace. When the nation was preparing for King Birendra's coronation in 1975, the market was phased out and a brick platform erected.

People loiter here, talking in small groups, eager to warm themselves in the sun. Rickshaws cycle past, and street peddlers display assortments of local trinkets, bracelets, bangles, religious images, swords and knives. They sell their wares all over the square, as well as on temple platforms beneath the struts of the Hanuman Dhoka Palace.

Immediately to the left of Basantapur starts the famous **Freak Street**, once a favored hangout of long-haired travelers, today more often visited by tourists in search of the "hippies" who have long since moved to other less conspicuous locales. Freak Street is a narrow lane with cheap hotels, dim taverns and a variety of shops.

The Living Goddess

Farther on, near a couple of modern schools, you'll note a white stuccoed

Bustling New Road.

facade with intricately carved windows. This is the house of the living goddess, the **Kumari Bahal** (a). This monastic court-yard was built in the mid-18th Century. Two painted lion statues guard the en-trance steps, which have lintels carved with laughing skulls. Carved deities, peacocks and doves adorn the balcony windows.

But there are even more attractive sights to be seen inside the small court-yard, where the woodwork on all four walls is truly remarkable. After one rupee per visitor has been collected, the *kumari* or living goddess appears at a window, either the one on the third floor opposite the entrance, or the second or third-floor window above the entrance. Taking pic-tures of the *kumari* is strictly forbidden, but you may freely photograph when she is out of sight.

Some consider the *kumari* to be the in-carnation of the "virgin goddess" Kanya Kumari, one of the 62 names given to Par-vati, Shiva's *shakti*. Others consider her a personification of Durga, another form of the same Parvati. Yet others say she is one of the eight Ashta Matrikas, or mother goddesses. This particular *kumari* is called the Royal Kumari, to distinguish her from past *kumaris* who live or have lived in Kathmandu, and scores of others who are worshipped throughout the Valley.

One legend tells of a girl of the Sakya clan in the 8th Century who claimed to be an incarnation of Kumari. She was exiled by the king, but when his queen became enraged, the repentent ruler brought the "goddess" back and locked her in a tem-ple. Another legend says that a Malla king used to play dice with the goddess Taleju, who appeared to him in human form. One night he lusted for Taleju, and the goddess in great wrath told him she would never return. The king pleaded with her, and finally Taleju promised to return as an in-violable young virgin.

The living goddess is always chosen from a selection of girls four or five years of age, all belonging to the Sakya clan of goldsmiths and silversmiths. The *kumari's* body must be flawless and must satisfy 32 specified, distinctive signs. The final phase of the selection process is a ter-rifying ordeal in the hall of the temple: men masked as demons try to scare the girls, and bloody buffalo heads are placed around them in the darkness. The girl who remains calm throughout this ordeal,

reason the Nepalese, cannot be other than the goddess herself. She confirms her selection by choosing the clothing and or-naments of the previous *kumari* from among a large collection of similar items.

Once astrologers have assured that the girl's horoscope is in harmony with the King's, she is settled in the *bahal*, which becomes her home until she reaches puberty or otherwise loses blood, as from a small wound. She is allowed to leave on-ly for various religious festivals, and then she must be carried, as her feet must not touch the ground. During the Indrajatra festival in August-September, men drag her flower-bedecked chariot through the city on three separate days. (See feature article on festivals.)

When her term as *kumari* has ended, the girl leaves the temple richly endowed and free to marry. But many would-be candidates are deterred by the prospect of a beautiful child, accustomed to years of utter idleness and adulation, being sud-denly released to become a housewife and mother. Besides, some say, an ex-goddess brings bad luck to the household and early death to her husband.

Durbar's Forest of Temples

As you leave the *bahal* of the *kumari*, the **Temple of Narayan** (b) a three-roofed structure built about 1670 on a five-tiered plinth, is to your immediate left. You are now entering the **Durbar Square** (4). This wide area has less charm and less spatial cohesion than its counterpart in Patan. But it contains more than 50 important temples and monuments, dominated by the impressive bulk of the **Taleju Temple** (v), which houses the titulary divinity of the Royal Family.

The plinth of the Narayan temple and other surrounding stepped platforms are entirely covered by people during festivals. On ordinary days, curio or vegetable sellers requisition the first steps for their spreads of cheap goods. On the brick-paved square, farmers carry huge burdens on their backs or on shoulder poles, while rickshaws and taxis honk their horns impatiently to penetrate the throng. Bicycle bells, children's shrill cries and hawkers' shouts add a dense bazaar atmosphere to the scene.

In the chilly hours of dawn, however, the Durbar Square and its neighboring streets wake up to black and white-clad men who silently hurry to temples for

The Kumari.

early-morning devotions, and to traders unlocking their antique padlocks, removing their wooden blinds and unloading surplus goods into the streets from their crammed shops. Pigeons swoop to snatch the rice of offerings, and the most sacred temples become aviaries.

Soon the flux and tide of human commerce sets alive the chiseled gods in this forest of temples that is the Durbar. Here in the square, and all along the ancient road to Tibet, is the heart of old Kathmandu. The lane slashes through the Old City in a diagonal southwest-northeast direction, following the course of the sun which casts raw blocks of deep shadow in the transparent atmosphere.

Although the lane will draw you eastward, reverse your direction. The best complete view of the Durbar Square is from its western end. Walk past a small stone Vishnu temple flanked by a beautiful statue of Garuda, and enter an area called **Maru Tole.**

The main feature here is the famed **Kasthamandap** (c) or "House of Wood," built about the 12th Century at the crossroads of the trade routes around which the city of Kathmandu grew.

Originally a community center where people gathered for ceremonies and other events, it later was turned into a temple dedicated to Gorakhnath. The god sits in the center of the platform in a little wooden enclosure. There are several other shrines for different gods in the building. Small carved figures around the first-floor cornice illustrate Hindu epics, and a pair of bronze lions guard the entrance.

Early morning is a good time to visit the Kasthamandap, which squats at the center of a rectangular open space. Porters, dressed in various earthy tones, sit here awaiting customers. Nearby, between the arcades of a rather low, two-tiered structure, petty vendors sell betel nuts, chilies, ginger, potatoes, onions, peanuts, dried fish, sweets, silver coins, votive powders and tressed wicks of incense.

Hidden behind the Kasthamandap is the small but very important golden **Ashok Binayak** shrine (d) of the Kathmandu Ganesh. Commonly called the Maru Ganesh, there is a constant flow of worshippers here; in particular, people who are leaving on journeys will pay a visit to ensure their safety.

KATHMANDU
DURBAR
SQUARE
Letters keyed
to text.

a–Kumari Bahal
b–Temple of Naray.
c–Kasthamandap
d–Ashok Binayak
e–Shiva Temple
f–Shiva-Parvati
  Temple House
g–King Pratap Mal
  statue
h–Degu Taleju
  Temple
i–Krishna Mandir
j–Hanuman Dhoka
k–Nasal Chowk
l–Mohan Chowk
m–Sundari Chowk
n–Basantapur Tow
o–Kirtipur Tower
p–Lalitpur Tower
q–Bhaktapur Towe
r–Lohan Chowk
s–Pancha Mukhi
  Hanuman
t–Jagannath Temp
u–Gopinath Mand
v–Taleju Temple
w–Tarana Devi
  Mandir

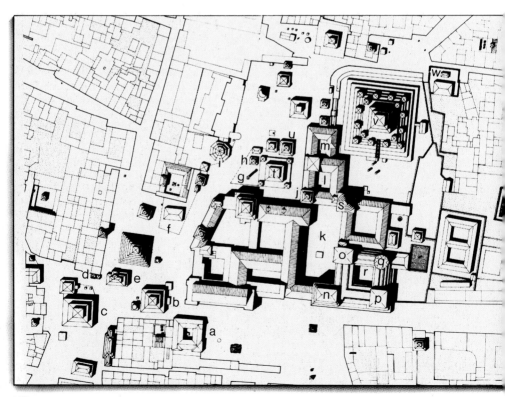

160

Returning to the square, there is a **Shiva Temple** (e) on the left, with three roofs on a nine-step plinth.

Continue into a second square on the right. Just before entering this courtyard, note the **Shiva-Parvati Temple House** (f) on the left. The deified couple, carved in wood and crudely painted, looks benignly down from the center window of the upper balcony.

Set on a pillar at the entrance to this second part of Dunbar Square is a statue of **King Pratap Malla** (g), who was responsible for the construction of many of the surrounding structures. He and his consorts were set up on a stone column facing the inner sanctum of his private prayer room, on the third floor of the **Degu Taleju Temple** (h). The northeastern corner of the square is taken up by post-1934 earthquake construction.

Opposite the entrance to the Hanuman Dhcka stands the **Krishna Mandir** (i) one of the few octagonal temples in Nepal. On the right-hand corner, a large wooden lattice screen hides an enormous gilded face of the **Seto Bhairav**, a fascinating masterpiece of popular art. The screen is removed only during the Indrajatra festival, when the fierce figure is showered with flowers and rice. Beer flows through his hideous mouth from a tank above him, and hordes of men jostle to drink this holy nectar.

Nasal, 'The Dancing One'

Leaving aside, for the time being, the temples in the outer Durbar Square, you come to the entrance of the **Hanuman Dhoka** (j) the Royal Palace. On one side of it, a 1672 statue of the monkey-god Hanuman stands under a small umbrella. The deified animal is wrapped in a red cloak and his face is covered with a thick layer of *sindur*, red dust mixed with mustard oil. Hanuman, a hero of the epic *Ramayana*, is a congenial character reputed to bring success to military pursuits. Every morning, devotees bring him grains of rice, coins, burning incense, and sometimes errands written on small pieces of paper.

The palace gate, a surprising mixture of blue, green and gold, is flanked by two stone lions. The animal on the right is mounted by Shiva, the one on the left by his *shakti*, Parvati. Note the highly colored group of characters in a niche above the gate: the Tantric Krishna of fierce

aspect is in the center, flanked by Krishna the god of love and two of his favorite *gopis*, and by King Pratap Malla and his queen. The King and Krishna are both regarded as incarnations of Vishnu.

The gate opens upon the **Nasal Chowk** (k). Of 14 courtyards here, this is the one in which the actual royal coronation ceremony takes place. *Nasal* means "the dancing one;" the square owes its name to a small figure of the dancing Shiva placed on the eastern side of the square. Here is the entrance to the museum dedicated largely to the memory of King Tribhuvan.

The founding of the Royal Palace dates back to late Licchavi times. The Ranas made considerable improvements during their reign, but most of the structure dates from the Malla times. The construction was accomplished progressively over many centuries by successive additions — beginning in the north with the small **Mohan Chowk** (l) and **Sundari Chowk** (m), built for Pratap Malla in the 16th Century, and continuing to the south.

After his conquest of the Valley in 1768, Prithvi Narayan Shah oversaw the renovation and completion of buildings around and to the east of Nasal Chowk.

These included the nine-story **Basantapur Tower** (n) and the smaller towers of **Kirtipur** (o), **Lalitpur** (p) and **Bhaktapur** (q). All four are set in a square around and above **Lohan Chowk** (r). In this work, Prithvi Narayan Shah introduced the Valley to the concept of the fortified tower, such as he had previously built at Gorkha and Nuwakhot.

Later rulers made several additions and restorations. The area west of Nasal Chowk was constructed in the mid to late 19th Century by the Ranas, while the golden gate as it now stands was restored during the early modern Shah period. Nasal Chowk and all four main towers were extensively restored prior to King Birendra's coronation, and work still continues.

Immediately to the left of the gate is a stele representing Narsingh: Vishnu as a man-lion tearing apart his arch-enemy, the demon Hiranya-Kashipu. This image is followed by a gallery with a row of portraits of the present Shah dynasty rulers in full regalia. In the corner, the five round roofs of the five-faced **Pancha Mukhi Hanuman** (s) pile up high into the sky; this is one of only two such structures in Nepal, the other being in Pashupatinath.

Towers of Nasal Chowk.

After admiring the erotic carvings on the struts along the facade of Basantapur Tower, you can climb to its top through a maze of steep staircases and balconies. From here, you can peek into the Lohan Chowk to view its remarkable wood-carvings.

A Garland of Skulls

Leave the palace grounds and return to the central part of Durbar Square. You can see more erotic carvings, almost at head level, on the struts of the two-tiered 17th Century **Jagannath Temple** (t), the oldest structure in this area. Next to the Jagannath is the **Gopinath Mandir** (u), with three roofs and a three-stepped plinth; and a composite structure dedicated to Shiva, a white *shikhara* above a Newar-style temple.

Then you'll encounter a masterpiece: an oversized relief of the fierce-looking Kal Bhairav. Highly admired and revered, this **Black Bhairav** is indeed fearsome. The black-skinned god wears red and yellow ornaments, plus a tiara and garland of skulls. His eyes and fangs protrude, and three pairs of arms are each armed with a sword, a severed head, a hat-

chet and a shield — all attributes of Shiva in his fierce form. Bhairav tramples on a corpse, symbol of human ignorance, and carries a ritual skull bowl into which believers put offerings.

The Black Bhairav, brought here in the second half of the 18th Century, is said to have been found in a field north of the city. People believe that the god punishes those who lie in front of him by causing them to instantly bleed to death. Many an argument is resolved with a challenge to "go and tell it to Kal Bhairav."

This northeastern end of the Durbar Square is dominated by the magnificent three-tiered **Taleju Temple** (v), built on a huge stepped platform amid a number of smaller temples opposite the main Hanuman Dhoka gate. Everything here is gilded, and thus is particularly resplendent at sunset. The walled precinct is off-limits to all but the King and certain priests, although Hindus are allowed access during the Durga Puja festival.

The goddess **Taleju Bhawani**, originally a South Indian deity, was brought to Nepal in the 14th Century and was enshrined as the ruling family's deity. She

anuman
hoka
alace.

became a symbol of legitimacy for the sovereign; the rulers of Bhaktapur and Patan, in turn, set up their own shrines to Taleju in front of their palaces.

The present temple was restored in 1562 by King Mahendra Malla. Human sacrifices were performed here until, according to legend, the goddess became displeased when the usurper Prithvi Narayan Shah attempted to celebrate his victory with the customary slaughter of a conquered foe.

Nearby, protected by a fence along the white wall of the palace precinct, there is a long inscription in honor of the goddess Kalika. It is written in no fewer than 15 different alphabets and languages. Its text notes that it was carved on January 14, 1664, by King Pratap Malla, who prided himself on being an accomplished linguist and poet.

Massacre and Sacrifice

At the northwestern end of Durbar Square is an open courtyard called **Kot**, or "armory." It is surrounded by army and police quarters and barracks. While it is of little artistic appeal, it has great historical significance. Here, in 1846, Jung Bahadur Rana, the forefather of the Rana dynasty, perpetrated the "Kot Massacre," eliminating all the promising scions of the Nepalese aristocracy and paving the way for his seizure of power a few weeks later.

There is another mass blood-letting here every year during the Durga Puja festival, when hundreds of buffaloes and goats are sacrificed by young soldiers who must attempt to cut off the head of each animal with a single stroke.

At the entrance of **Makhan Tole**, a Garuda statue lies half buried in the ground. It must have once faced a temple that was destroyed long ago. As you pass to the right of the Taleju, cast a glance at the **Tarana Devi Mandir** (w). This low brick structure has three carved doorways, over-painted struts representing the multiple-armed Ashta Matrika mother goddesses, and a festoon of colored skulls.

There are other important structures nearby. The **Makhan Bahil**, a great monastery in late Malla times, features the remains of eight votive *chaityas* and a shrine with a *torana*, of Manjushri. The **Mahendreswar Mahadev** was built in the early 1960s and named after the late King Mahendra. It is dedicated to Shiva in his phallic form.

Hanuman statue, left; a curious Nepali, below; and the Taleju Temple, right.

Centers of Commerce

The Makhan Tole is about six meters (20 feet) wide, flanked by facades of various colors, with wooden balconies and columns defining *patis* and shops. It leads into the **Indra Chowk**, an open space from which six streets radiate in all directions.

This area, traditionally dedicated to the sale of blankets and textiles, including soft woolen shawls known as *pashmina*, is particularly picturesque and animated. Crowds collect around cloth and flower sellers. A man selling flutes, which are inserted in a pole like the branches of a tree, strolls past a wayside dried-fish market. Tucked behind is the glittering magic of the bead market, where lengths of varied color combinations can be made up while you wait.

To the west stand three temples, all at street corners. The most important is the one on the south, a three-story house containing a highly revered shrine to Akash Bhairav on the first floor. The facade stands out with its white, purplish-red and green ceramic tiles. The house has yellow windows and two balconies, the lower one with four gilded griffins rearing onto the

street. The shrine is active during major festivals, including Indrajatra, when the large image of Bhairav is displayed in the square. During the same festival, a huge *lingum* pole is erected in the center of the square in place of the stones which normally occupy that position.

There are other important buildings in the vicinity. In a niche just before the house containing the **Akash Bhairav** shrine (5) is a tiny but highly venerated all-brass **Ganesh Shrine**. Sellers and buyers of bundled cloth crowd the stepped plinth of the **Mahadev Mandir**. Women selling bracelets and cotton-cord ornaments for the hair squat at the foot of the **Shiva Mandir**. The latter, a simplified version of Patan's Krishna temple, is a thick-set stone structure above a four-stepped plinth where carpets are displayed. Vines grow over the arches and pillars of the first level.

Beyond Indra Chowk, and as far as the oblong open space known as **Khel Tole**, is the most typical, oldest trading segment of the diagonal street. There is a constant coming-and-going of farmers, strollers, rickshaws, even cars forcing through the narrow lane. From the upper floors of

Textiles for sale at Indra Chowk

traditional houses, women and girls watch the crowd scene below. At ground level are shops selling all manner of goods, though each seems to specialize: floor mats, warm blankets, shawls, saris, cloth, huge copper jars for ceremonies and festivals. Popular among visitors are Tibetan-made carpets in various designs and colors.

The White Machhendranath

Past a small shrine smeared with fresh blood, turn left and enter one of the most venerated temples in the whole Kingdom. This superb construction, standing freely in the center of a monastic courtyard, is the **Seto Machhendranath** (6).

Two magnificent brass lions guard the entrance. Under the porch leading to the courtyard, musicians assemble in the evening to chant sacred songs. Take a few more steps into a splendid sight. Behind various steles, *chaityas* and pillars carved with deities and animals stands the famous temple. Note the gilt-copper roofs, the ornamental banners, the tympanum, the struts depicting the various forms of Avalokiteshwara, the girdle of prayer wheels around the pedestal, the lions and griffins guarding the approach steps to the shrine doorway.

The god within the shrine is Padmapani Avalokiteshwara, the most compassionate divinity in the Valley. Buddhist, but also worshipped by Hindus, this deity is known by the people as Jammadyo or Machhendra. The white *(seto)* god is taken out of its shrine once a year during the lively Seto Machhendra festival in March-April for chariot processions across the city.

The date of construction of this temple is unknown. It was restored in the early 17th Century. Its well-paved courtyard contains a variety of shops selling cloth, wool, string, pottery, Nepali caps, ribbons and beads, curios and paper prints.

Leaving the temple, you come immediately to the **Lunchun Lunbun Ajima** at the next street corner on the left. This well proportioned, small Tantric temple has three roofs, white ceramic tiles, a recessed altar, and portraits of the King and Queen between erotic carvings.

Proceed to the northeast. Somewhere to your left is the polygonal **Krishna Temple** (7). squeezed between private houses.

ruit vendor
t Indra
Chowk.

Under its three roofs, the whole elevated ground floor is a *pati* where people sell ginger and potatoes.

Houses along this street have three, four, even five stories. One of them on the left is the first house to have glass windows in Kathmandu. Atop two shops, one selling vegetables, the other pipes and tobacco, it is adorned with an interesting plaster frieze depicting a general riding in a column of riflemen, cavalry, dancing girls and color bearers.

All along the street, the tiny ground-floor shops overflow with goods. There is a whole shopping mall selling household utensils, then a stall specializing in Gurkha *khukris*. From cages in some of the shops, the songs of canaries filter through the lane.

Classical Asan Tole

Then you emerge on **Asan Tole**, the real heart of the Old City. This large open space features three temples, of which the all-metal **Annapurna Temple** (8), with its three levels of gilded roofs with upturned corners, holds a special fascination. Many passers-by ring its bell and pay homage at its shrine, containing no statue or stone image but a fine *kalasha*, or pot. Nearby is a smaller temple to a four-armed Ganesh, and a tiny Narayan shrine stands nearer the center of the square.

Asan Tole, besides being an important crossroads, is the traditional rice marketplace and a center for hiring porters. The crowd here is dense. If you continue down the diagonal axis, you will find the street less congested as the buildings become less typical, some of rather recent style. There is an area of bicycle repair and hire shops, then another area where rickshaw drivers traditionally congregate.

Finally, you come out at the asphalted Kantipath, the main north-south axis. In front of you is a large water basin, the **Rani Pokhari**. In the 16th Century, the wife of Pratap Malla had a temple built at its center in memory of her son who died young. The temple later collapsed, and a new shrine was erected. Beyond the fenced-in lake, you can see the clock tower of the **Trichandra College** built by the Ranas, and to your right, the wide expanse of the Tundhikhel and the landmark column of the **Bhimsen Tower**.

To see more of the northern part of the Old City, turn northwest from Asan Tole along a wider extension of the morning vegetable and fruit market. The street gets narrower as you proceed west, and is made even further congested by various food stalls.

To the left, an anonymous door opens into the **Haku Bahal** courtyard. An interesting projecting window balcony is supported by six small carved struts and an elaborately carved door frame, the *torana* of which was dedicated in the mid-17th Century. At the center of the courtyard is a stucco *chaitya* which looks like an overbaked meringue pie. Houses in this area are compactly built, but many are in various stages of decay.

A few steps farther on the same side of the road, facing a lane heading north, is a three-roofed temple of **Ugratara** (9), worshipped for relief of eye sores. Glasses, donated to the temple, have been placed on the walls.

The God of Toothache

Rickshaw drivers wait by the **Ikha Narayan** (10), a small two-roofed temple to

your right. Its shrine houses a beautiful 10th or 11th Century four-armed Sridhara Vishnu, flanked by Lakshmi and Garuda.

Opposite, under a roof, a piece of wood is punctured with thousands of nails around a tiny gilded image of **Vaisha Dev**, the god of toothache. To plant a nail here is to get rid of pain by pinning down all evil spirits and influences. In case the nail doesn't do its job, a nearby lane is filled with dentists' parlors left and right. Some of them are open to the road, so all who wish can watch a tooth being filled or an extraction being performed.

Beyond, past a 400-year-old **Narayan Temple** on the north side of the square, is a remarkable 5th Century image of the Buddha carved in a slab of black stone. Further north is a fine bas-relief of Shiva-Parvati as **Uma Maheshwar** set in a brick case. This stone image represents Shiva holding the left knee of his *shakti* while sitting on Mount Kailash.

A short distance on the left, a lion-guarded passage leads to a monastery courtyard. In its center stands the famous **Srigha Chaitya** (11), commonly known as the Kathe Shimbhu, a smaller replica of the

Swayambhunath stupa. Those too old or too ill to make the climb to Swayambhunath can earn the same merit by taking a pilgrimage here.

Return to the westward-leading street and pass a bicycle shop plastered with posters of Nepali and Indian singers and movie stars. If you continue, you'll cross the Bishnumati River and be on your way to Swayambhunath. Instead, turn south (left) into the lane returning to Durbar Square. You'll traverse an area of degenerating temples and *bahals*. People of mixed origins live in the area.

Crocodile Guardians

A variety of shops selling brassware, tin trunks, salt, *ghee* and cooking oil occupy the ground floors of houses as you head south. At the first crossing is the **Nara Devi** (12), a popular three-tiered temple dedicated to one of the Ashta Matrikas. Red and white lions guard the entrance to a spacious altar where women prostrate themselves. Colored ceramic tiles and paintings under the roofs are entrancing.

Across the square to your right, you can seen the three roofs of the enclosed

If the god of toothache doesn't help below, perhaps a dentist will, right.

Narsingh Temple (13). To visit, you must walk through a gate, under a board reading "Deluxe Painters," and weave through several courtyards to a small platform over the street facing the temple. Inside the shrine is an image of Vishnu with a lion's head.

Further down the main street, on the left, is the **Yatkha Bahal** (14), a Swayambhunath-like stupa sitting in a spacious courtyard. A *bahal* behind the stupa is considerably older than the recently constructed buildings around it. A *torana* over the doorway is wrought in the design of two crocodiles with upturned snouts forming an arch. The woodwork is excellent and well preserved, and the four 14th Century female figures carved on the window balcony are exceptionally seductive.

Across the street is a metallic door painted with two figures. One stares at you with four eyes. Above its gilded tympanum, depicting the Ashta Matrika Chamunda, a pretty face pops out of an intricate woodwork window frame. This is a god-house to **Kanga Ajima** (15); it houses *jyapus,* or farmers.

Return to the Durbar Square, again passing the Kot. If you travel south from here, you can tour Kathmandu's most congested and rural-looking sector.

An Erotic Nucleus

Turn left and head south from the Kasthamandap, crossing an open space where peasants sell vegetables in the morning. The first building on your right, with its row of shops, was built to be used as a shopping center. Immediately after it on the left is the ceramic-tiled, three-roofed **Adko Narayan** (16), considered one of the four main Vishnu temples in Kathmandu. Vishnu's image is carved over erotic scenes on the struts below the second roof. The temple has a Garuda statue in front, lions in the corners, and small *chaityas* with images of the Buddha and Vishnu on *yonis.*

The street here is straight and fairly wide. Two and three-storied houses face an enormous building in mixed Nepali and Indian Muslim style; this is a private residence. Where vegetable and *chapati* sellers squat in the sun, the small **Hari Shankar Temple** (17) dedicated to Shiva is on your right.

Here you can taste the flavor of everyday life for many of Kathmandu's poorer residents. The street is busy with women wrapped in shawls, children and adults on bicycles, porters carrying wood. Small shops selling tea and biscuits do a roaring trade. One shop sells aquariums, another hundreds of bangles, and flies blacken a butcher's shop.

At a crossing, the three roofs of the **Jaisi Dewal** (18), a Shiva temple of the 17th Century, are piled atop a seven-stepped pyramid. Its struts have rather well executed erotic carvings. Behind it, set in a *yoni*, is a huge *lingum* made from a free-shaped, erect slab of stone. This area is believed to have been the nucleus of the Valley during Licchavi times. Next to the temple, the roots of a tree hold together a small *chaitya*.

The composite structure of the **Ram Chandra Mandir** (19), in its own courtyard to the right, contains on its highly colored struts the tiniest erotic carvings to be seen anywhere in the Valley.

Further down the street, within the **Takan Bahal** (20), is an unusual stupa in ruinous condition dating from the 14th Century. It is a round stucco mound with a brick structure over it; the intricacy of a tree's roots have pushed the crown up.

As you approach the southern end of the city, you pass through an area occupied by the lower castes. To your right, a bridge spans the Bishnumati. Take the lane to your left, walking past an open courtyard where a Narayan *shikhara*, currently turned into a billboard, stands behind heavy *chaityas* and a fountain with a Ganesh shrine in the corner.

Past here, the street narrows and twists past run-down houses covered with painted stucco. A small lane to your right leads into **Musum Bahal** (21). This is an old and plain structure with four Licchavi *chaityas* and a well, protected by a cement enclosure with iron bars. Local legend maintains that a famous Tantric pundit, Juman Gubhaju, once entered this well to end a drought in the Valley. A ceremony is held here every 12 years in remembrance.

Take a turn to the north, and you will emerge at an open crossroads, the **Lagan Khel**, where another **Machhendra Temple** (22) stands. This is a solid *chaitya* structure not more than 10 meters (33 feet) high. The popular god is covered with a red mantle within this shrine. During the Seto Machhendranath festival, the god's

chariot must be driven three times around this temple as part of the final ceremony. The chariot is then dismantled here, after the deity has been returned to its principal temple near Asan Tole, borne in a colorful palanquin.

God of Traders and Artisans

To the west, half a dozen *bahals* can be visited in succession. With the possible exception of the **Lagan Bahal** (23), they have little appeal. Continue west, past traditional four-story houses where dyers once lived. Past the pyramid of Jaisi Dewal, the road descends. In a small walled compound on the left, behind and below the *path*, a deepwater conduit built at the end of the 18th Century was recently fixed up. *Lingas* in *yonis* and cacti in boxes beautify this active fountain.

A bumpy lane goes down to the river; you must turn right to return to Durbar Square. Past the Hotel Snug on the left, look downhill to a bulky, pale green school building. Take a few steps past a small recessed Ganesh shrine, next to a small fountain in an open courtyard, and you are back on the diagonal axis road. This is where the old trade route left the city, via the Bishnumati bridge to the left and on toward Pokhara.

At this strategic location is found the **Bhimsen Temple** (24), an important and prosperous shrine dedicated to Bhimsen, the god of traders and artisans. It is a large, rectangular, three-tiered structure. The ground floor is occupied by shops. The wooden lattices of the shrine on the first floor are built at the same angle as the struts.

Bhimsen, a form of Shiva, has been popular in the Valley since the 17th Century. When there was active trade with Tibet, this image of Bhimsen was carried to Lhasa on the trade route every 12 years. Devotees come here to worship every morning. Curiously, the priest of this traders' temple is a member of the farmer caste.

Next to the temple are several four-faced Buddhist stupas and a small sunken *hiti* (water conduit) in a poor state of preservation. Quite different is **Maru Hiti** (25), one of Kathmandu's four primary conduits. It may be reached by crossing Maru Hiti Tole and proceeding through a narrow lane northwest of the Kasthamandap, not far from Durbar Square.

Erotic carvings on a strut of Basantapur Temple, Hanuman Dhoka.

WESTERN SETTLEMENTS

When the old trade route between India and Tibet meandered through the western part of the Kathmandu Valley, settlements like Satungal, Balambu, Kisipidi and Thankot were common stops on that road. Today, as there is a motorable road where before there were only footpaths, these interesting communities are readily accessible from Kathmandu via the Raj Path.

The first three villages lie within a kilometer of one another, about six kilometers (3½ miles) west of the city. **Satungal**, with a population of slightly more than 1,000, is the first you encounter. It lies just to the south of the Raj Path. Satungal is believed to have been established and fortified in the early 16th Century as a bulwark against hordes of northern invaders. A rather poor village of mixed castes, some of its landless peasants go to Kathmandu to find employment.

The main square of Satungal village is surrounded by *patis*. At its center is a two-

meter (6½-foot) stone Buddha sitting on a free-standing platform. To the north, through a vaulted gate structure with two *patis*, and down several steps, you will find the **Vishnu Devi Temple**. It is of little artistic merit, but it nonetheless a much frequented site.

Balambu, which lies north of the Raj Path, has more than 2,000 inhabitants. Several inscriptions found in and around the village attest that it was established during the Licchavi period, and later also fortified. Girdled by a row of trees, this community is even more rural-looking than Satungal. Its main temples, notably the double-roofed **Mahalakshmi Temple**, are located in the central square. The square is lined with a row of three-story residences, among which the **Ajima Devi** god-house, with a beautifully carved *torana*, stands out.

A kilometer east of here is the religious site of Naikap, where two rivers converge. To the south, a lane runs toward the Machhe Narayan shrine (page 124).

The hamlet of **Kisipidi**, with perhaps 650 residents, is a pleasant stop near Matatirtha (page 147). Lush green trees and small gardens are enclosed by stone

Taking a rest along the trail at Kisipidi.

walls, while traditional three-story houses are found on its eastern slopes. Kisipidi's main deity is **Kalika Mai**, who is honored with a twin-tiered temple in the village center.

The Village of Thankot

About two kilometers further along the Raj Path lies the sizable village of **Thankot**. This settlement is located to the southwest of the main road on an elevated sloping site surrounded by terraced fields. It was started under the Mallas, and turned into a military station by Prithvi Narayan Shah; hence its name, which means "military area." Thankot has about 3,500 inhabitants belonging to four different castes.

An uneven stone path leads uphill from here to the **Mahalakshmi Temple**, an impressive structure with two roofs, carved tympanum and columns, well-done erotic carvings, an open shrine, and kneeling devotees in petrified prayer facing it. There used to be a huge pipal tree in front of the temple; it was cut down to give way to a rather ugly L-shaped building.

From Thankot, a trail leads four kilometers (2½ miles) southwest to **Chandragiri,** "The Mountain of the Moon." A climb through a dense mixed forest of bamboo, pine and *sal* trees leads to the crest of the peak, where there is a small Buddhist *chaitya*. The view from the top of the 2,423-meter (7,950-foot) peak is impressive.

As you continue west along the Raj Path, you will approach a monument to King Tribhuvan on your left. This black statue, built to commemorate the reestablishment of royalty after the Rana regime, raises a hand against a background of dark green hills.

A panel by the roadside informs you that the Raj Path was built "by Indian engineers," and perhaps also by Nepali laborers, between 1953 and 1956. It was financed by India under the Colombo Plan. Before it existed, a triple relay of railway, ropeway and Tamang porters plied this route.

You can continue on the Raj Path to the pass at the entrance to the Valley. From here, the road winds down towards the Terai and India. Trucks trundle past, carrying loads of workers or goods, while overloaded buses painfully make their ways up the winding road.

A statue of King Tribhuvan, left, salutes travelers on the Raj Path.

PATAN OF THE GOLDEN ROOFS

The city of Patan is located on a high plateau above the course of the Bagmati River, just south of Kathmandu. Sometimes called "the town with a thousand golden roofs" or "the city of fine arts," most local people know it as Lalitpur: *Lalita Pura*, "the beautiful city."

An essentially Buddhist city, Patan was built in concentric circles around its royal palace. Four main roads radiate from the palace to four directional stupas, earth and brick mounds said to have been erected by Emperor Ashoka himself. If true, this would make Patan the oldest Buddhist city in the world.

Whether or not this is so, Patan has been an important town since very early times. Inscriptions from the 5th Century refer to King Manadeva's palace, the Managriha or "House of Mana," which might have been located in the area now called **Mangal Bazaar**, adjoining Patan Durbar Square. The city's great building period took place under the Mallas, particularly from the 16th to 18th centuries. Most of today's leading monuments were built or rebuilt at that time.

With no fewer than 136 classified *bahals* and 55 major multi-roofed temples, Patan is really the cradle of arts and architecture of the Valley, a great center both of the Newari Buddhist religion and of traditional arts and crafts.

The town has only recently developed beyond the limits marked by its stupas. It is at once more rural and more industrialized than Kathmandu. More than a third of its 100,000 inhabitants are farmers, and a substantial proportion of its population engages in small-scale home industries. The **Patan Industrial Center** has attracted some of the qualified manpower, contributing to the expansion of local craftsmanship. The town also acts as a reservoir of labor, especially in the public and commercial sectors, for the ever-growing capital to the north.

The Royal Palace Complex

The north-south and east-west axis roads divide Patan into four geographic sectors, which meet at the **Durbar Square** and **Royal Palace** complex. This oblong space constitutes perhaps the most spectacular example of Newari architecture in

Preceding pages, the Tusa Hiti; left, a Kathak dancer in Mul Chowk.

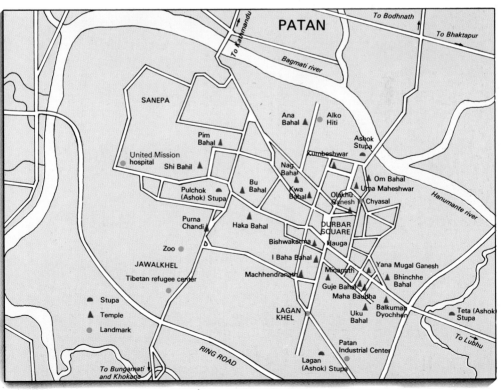

any urban context. To the west, a dozen free-standing temples of various sizes and styles occupy a square framed on three sides by multi-story residences. To the east is the Royal Palace and its walled gardens.

The palace consists of three main *chowks*, or courtyards. The central **Mul Chowk** (a), built in 1666 for Srinivasa Malla, is the oldest. Two stone lions guard its entrance. The low two-story former residence of the Patan royal family, complete with *agam* house and king's prayer room, encloses a large square courtyard with a small gilded shrine, the **Bidya Mandir**, at its center.

Two tall, beautiful repousse brass images of Ganga on a tortoise and Jamuna on a *makara*, or mythical crocodile, flank the doorway of the **Shrine of Taleju**. The gilded *torana* depicts the Ashta Matrikas. On the roof over the shrine is a three-tiered square structure. Towering over this part of the palace, in the northeastern corner of the courtyard, is the triple-roofed octagonal tower of the **Taleju Bhawani Temple** (b), built for Srinivasa Malla about 1666.

The smaller southern courtyard, the **Sundari Chowk** (c), holds in its center a masterpiece of stone architecture, the

sunken royal bath called **Tusha Hiti**. The walls of the bath, created around 1670 and renovated about 1960, are decorated with a double row of statuettes representing the eight Ashta Matrikas, the eight Bhairavs, and the eight Nagas. Several of these statues are missing, perhaps stolen.

Two wriggling *nagas* girdle the top of the basin into which the water flows through a conch-shaped stone spout covered with gilded metal. Hanuman and the Buddha sit in front of this beautiful *yoni* basin while a live armed soldier stands guard.

The three-story buildings around the *chowk*, surmounted by the three roofs of a corner temple, offer fine woodcarvings, especially on the upper-floor window grilles. Stone images of Ganesh, Hanuman and Narsingh flank the outside entrance to this *chowk*. The central window above the entrance is of gilded metal, and those flanking it of carved ivory.

Shiva and Parvati, encased in a *torana*, crown the much-admired **"Golden Gate"** gilded doorway leading to the third courtyard, the **Mani Keshab Narayan Chowk** (d). This northern *chowk* was completed in 1734 after 60 years of construction.

Between it and the central *chowk* is the

Patan's Durbar Square shows little change between the 19th Century, below, and today, right.

180

temple of **Degu Talle** (e), the personal deity of the Mallas. Built for Siddhi Narsingh Malla in 1640, and rebuilt after its destruction by fire in 1662, this three-story building is crowned by a hefty four-roofed tower. The kings performed their sacred Tantric rites here in special ceremonial rooms. Beyond, in a small open space, dances and plays were performed.

Moghul Architecture

Facing the Sundari Chowk is the large, octagonal **Krishna Temple** (f), a stone *shikhara*-style building with a stairway guarded by two lions. To the west of this *shikhara* squats the ugly **Bhai Dega** (g), redeemed by a Shiva *lingum* within. To the north, an enormous bell hangs between two thick pillars; you may see porters, their baskets full of wood, resting on its sunny platform. Nearby, women crouch on the stepped base of the three-roofed 17th Century **Hari Shankar** (h), all carved struts and *toranas* on arches and pillars.

Immediately to the north of this temple, **King Siddhi Narsingh** (i), has been praying for more than 300 years, golden on his robust pillar. The *shikhara* behind him dates from 1590. On the other side of a small 17th Century Narayan temple is probably the oldest surviving temple in the square — a two-tiered brick structure built in 1565 for the god **Char Narayan** (j), with struts depicting the *avatars* of Vishnu.

Facing the northern *chowk* of the palace is the **Krishna Mandir** (k), probably the most remarkable stone building ever raised in the Valley. It betrays influence of Moghul architecture from India. The first and second stories are made up of a line of pavilions in smooth black stone. A slender *shikhara* emerges from the second floor. On horizontal beams, episodes of the great Indian epics, the *Ramayana* and *Mahabharata*, are depicted with explanations in Newari. On the first floor, where the main divinity was installed in 1637, old people can enjoy music-making while watching the square below.

In front of the Krishna Mandir is a statue of Garuda on a high pole. The next temple, the **Bishwa Nath Mandir** (l), is of the same age and style as the Hari Shankar, and is profusely decorated. Its elephants are bigger than those of its counterpart,

but it has only two roofs.

Ending the long row of temples is one of the most venerated and prosperous-looking temples, the **Bhimsen Mandir** (m), dedicated to Bhimsen, the god of traders. This three-roofed brick building with artificial marble facade from Rana times was erected in the late 17th Century. Its tympanums and struts are partially painted in silver, while the central body is gilded.

At the corner of the northern *chowk* of the palace, the lotus-shaped, deeply recessed **Manga Hiti** (n) has three beautifully carved spouts in the shape of crocodile heads. At certain hours, men and women queue up to refresh themselves with its clear water. Adjoining *patis* have old struts carved with mildly erotic scenes.

Rural Northern Patan

Leaving the Durbar Square in an easterly direction, you first come to a small square, framed with traditional town houses containing shops on their ground floors. Here stands a small three-story **Olakhu Ganesh** with funny erotic carvings. Most of the people here are Hindu, mainly of the *jyapu* (farmer) caste. Far-

ther to the north, a small lane opens on a large open space where women are weaving cloth on a row of bamboo poles.

The **Bhimsen Dyochhen**, an ordinary-looking god-house, faces a larger open square with a pond and a well. The street to the west leads past a small stupa to the **Unmatta Bhairav Temple**, flanked by a rice mill.

The eastern road leads into open fields and on toward the **Balkumari Temple**. You can turn north here in front of the **Naya Hiti**, an 8th Century sunken fountain with two spouts. Immediately to your right is another larger, newer fountain, the **Chyasal Hiti**. On its top is a painted statue of the goddess Saraswati as a green-and-yellow woman riding a goose. This popular fountain also has many beautifully carved ancient stone images of the late Licchavi period.

A bit further is the small **Chyasal Ganesh Temple**. The path then narrows through rows of three and four-story houses. It turns twice, then enters a small square with an old stone *chaitya* in its center, the **Om Bahal**.

The path leads north, then west, to join the main northern axis of the city. To the north, three adjacent *bahals* face the

PATAN DURBAR SQUARE

Letters keyed to text.

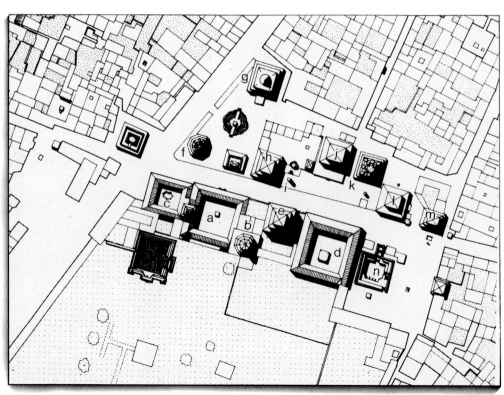

Ashok Stupa, a white plastered dome with a yellow top. Well preserved, it is surrounded by smaller *chaityas*. Beyond the precinct wall stretches a splendid view of the countryside, with mustard fields and patches of vegetables at your feet, an open field by the Bagmati River, and the city of Kathmandu slightly to the west in the distance. Prominent on the skyline is the Everest Sheraton Hotel on the airport road.

The Kumbeshwar Temple

To the south of the Ashok Stupa is the towering **Kumbeshwar Temple,** which dominates this whole area of rural streets and houses. It and the Nyatapola Temple in Bhaktapur are the only temples in the Valley with five roofs, with the exception of the round, five-tiered Panch Mukhi Hanuman of Kathmandu's Hanuman Dhoka Palace.

Founded in 1392, the Kumbeshwar is also the oldest existing temple in Patan. Its struts, cornices and door frame are finely carved. Elegantly proportioned, it stands in a spacious courtyard surrounded by various Licchavi, Thakuri and Malla sculptures and steles. Notable is a figure of

Char Narayan, left, and Krishna Mandir.

Ganesh that Giacometti would have been proud to have created. Like most Shaivite temples, the Kumbeshwar has a piece of grassy land adjoining its precinct: it is a grazing ground for the bull Nandi, Shiva's vehicle.

The platform also has two ponds, both filled with clear water during the Kumbeswar Mela in August. This water comes from a spring issuing from a sunken shrine within the compound; it is thought to originate from Gosaikund Lake, several days' walk north of Kathmandu. Persons who take an annual ritual bath here earn the same amount of merit as those who bathe in the lake.

During the Janai Purnima, in July-August, thousands of colorful pilgrims gather to brave a narrow catwalk and a possible dipping in the pond, to pay homage to a beautifully decorated silver and gold *lingum* that is placed on a specially constructed shrine set in the middle of the tank. Rice, coins and flower petals are thrown to the image. Men in loin cloths, boys in singlets, and women in dripping saris swim around the tank.

Brahmans and Chhetris, meanwhile, renew their *munja*, or sacred thread, which they wear around their left

shoulder from the time of their initiation rite until death. Here and in other Shaivite temples, Brahmin priests — in exchange for rice and coins — tie a golden thread *(rikhi doro)* around the wrists of the faithful to protect them against diseases and evil spirits. During the Mela, drum-bearing sorcerers, or *jhankris,* wearing plumed headgear and white flared skirts, dance around the temple, working themselves into a trance to the increasingly frenetic rhythm of drums.

In the southern part of the Kumbeshwar precinct, the **Ulmanta Bhairav**, a particularly important shrine for the Newar community, contains a four-faced brass Shiva *lingum.* Its sanctum is chiseled in silver. Bells and a blue, white and red garland decorate its black tympanum.

Pigs and Pastels

Outside the Kumbeshwar platform, past the large **Konti Hiti** where women often gather, beyond the **Konti Bahal** and the shock of huge Big Brother eyes in the inner courtyard, you enter an old section of Patan. Hindus and Buddhists live together here in more widely spaced

houses and *bahals.* The atmosphere is definitely rural: a small cobble-and-earth lane, where pigs wallow in the mud and cakes of cow dung are stuck. on house walls, wends downhill to the end of town.

urther to the northwest, the **Ana Bahal** has a naive facade of ceramic tiles in pastel colors and two stucco images in blue and orange representing the sun over the mountains. A few steps farther is one of the most beautiful water conduits still in use in the Valley, the **Alko Hiti**. Surmounted by five Licchavi *chaityas,* this conduit holds various other Buddhist and Hindu sculptures.

According to legend, this *hiti,* which has three spouts shaped like crocodile heads, was built with the blessings of the serpent king.

Return to the towering Kumbeshwar and head east, where you get lovely glimpses of brick bathed in sunshine, birds in vines, and small stupas in inner courtyards. The next major crossing has a fine **Krishna Temple**, two stone square-column stories on a stepped platform topped by an unfortunate brick and stucco dome of recent vintage. East of this, the **Dhum Bahal** is a fine old house in ochre and violet, with prayer wheels on either

The gods never sleep.

side of its main door, struts carved in 1685, and a few statues of devotees. It serves members of the ironsmith caste who live nearby.

From the Krishna Temple, the main axis road returns south to the Durbar Square. The road is flanked by houses of fine quality with well-executed carvings. Keep an eye peeled for an opening to the left containing a small two-tiered shrine: known as the **Uma Maheswar**, it contains a beautiful Licchavi stone carving of Shiva and Parvati. Closer to the Durbar Square, on the left, is a two-tiered temple with a fine image of Garuda dated to 1706, a *naga* set into the paving, and a stone image of Vishnu with four hands. At the entrance to the Durbar Square, there are several shops selling curios and hawkers selling fruit.

Patan's Southern Sector

Return to the crossroads in Mangal Bazaar. The main southern axis road leads from here to the Lagan Stupa. Starting from the **Lakshmi Narayan Temple** built above shops, you first enter an area called **Hauga** which has several shops and workshops dealing in brassware. A side lane to the west leads to the **Bishwakarma Temple**, whose entire facade is embossed in copper. Above the *torana* crowning this shrine to the god of carpenters and masons is a fixed window, which shows a solar disc intersecting triangles. The brass and copper craftsmen living in this area keep it resounding with the clang of hammers.

About 200 meters south, at a crossing to the right, stands a *chaitya*-shaped shrine of Lakshmi-Narayan in ruins, and a dome-shaped Shiva temple of little appeal. Opposite them to the left is the famous **I Baha Bahil**, one of the oldest monasteries in Patan. It was built in 1427. Part of it is now in ruins; the rest houses a school.

The next small open space to the east has a sunken fountain, **Chakba Lunhiti**, with three spouts and an inscription dating it to the mid-11th Century. Restored in the mid-1960s, it is an important focal point of life in this area.

Behind it, two huge statues guard the entrance to the beautiful 16th Century **Minanath Temple**, which is set in its own enclosure. A double-roofed shrine decorated in yellow and black brass, it has a huge prayer wheel in a cage to one side. Struts display multiple-armed goddesses.

A basket seller and his wares.

The divinity of this temple is closely connected with the adjacent Rato Machhendranath, and accompanies the Machhendra chariot in a much smaller chariot during the annual festival.

The Red Machhendranath

You will reach the **Rato Machhendranath** temple by turning west into the first lane from the main axis. The S-shaped paved path leads to a large, walled open space. Here is the three-story Patan home of the Red *(rato)* Machhendra.

Machhendra is the popular Tantric expression of the god Avalokiteshwara as well as of Lokeshwar. Venerated as Shiva by Hindus, he is worshipped by all as a god of rain and plenty.

A temple may have been built on this site as early as the 15th Century. The present structure dates from 1673. Pairs of lions guard the entrances to its four intricately carved doorways, while various animals on pillars face the main altar. Under the metal roofs, the struts depict Avalokiteshwara above the various tortures of condemned souls in hell. A row of prayer wheels underline the base.

The piece of dark red wood representing Machhendra is taken out of the shrine every year and paraded about on a chariot for several weeks of processions during the Rato Machhendra celebration which begins in May. This is Patan's biggest annual festival. The celebration concludes when the chariot is taken to **Jawalkhel** at the southwestern entrance to Patan and dismantled.

But every 12 years — the next occasion will be in 1991 — the chariot is dragged to **Bungamati,** five kilometers (three miles) south of Patan. There, Rato Machhendra has a second residence in a temple in the center of the village where it resides for six months every year. The route from Patan to Bungamati is quite rugged, with a bumpy road surface and long uphill stretches; taking the chariot this way is a difficult undertaking. There is a saying that if the chariot fails to reach Bungamati within a certain time period, the god will be taken to Bhaktapur.

Ganesh and Narayan

The main road continues to the **Lagan Stupa,** the southern Ashok stupa in Lagan Khel, through poorly constructed houses inhabited mainly by butchers and sweepers. Turning back north again, along a road parallel to that main axis, you go through an area flanked on the west by open countryside, and on the east by houses of *malis* (gardeners), who take care of the flowers needed for daily worship.

Soon you come to an open space with an interesting collection of buildings: a stone Ganesh Temple, a well-proportioned three-tiered **Bhairav Shrine** with rows of bells under metal roofs, and a 16th Century **Narayan Mandir** in brick with nicely carved struts and a Garuda squatting in front of it. Craftsmen in the vicinity originally worked in ivory; some are now merchants and traders.

A few steps farther on, two huge stone "sofas" mark the entrance to the 17th Century **Nayakan Bahil.** The shrine's blue, white and green glazed tiles, added in 1940, are eye-catching.

Where the street meets the main east-west axis, a small, low **Mahapal Ganesh Shrine** juts out. Sticks of incense are kept burning in the empty shrine. This is a predominantly Buddhist sector where artisans produce woven items, mats, baskets, porter belts, and cane trays or *nanglo,* all sold with gypsum stones in nearby shops.

Returning by the same route, you go back through Mangal Bazaar, skirt the Durbar Square and the palace garden walls, and enter the eastern sector of Patan.

Powdered Lions and Prayer Wheels

Through the open air bazaar, the road east leads to the grassy mound of the **Teta Stupa.** As the pavement narrows, note a brick platform similar to that at Basantapur. It used to be a vegetable market; now it houses shops in rows. Further along, three and four-story houses flank the route. They contain the workshops of silversmiths, goldsmiths and diamond cutters. Their craftsmanship is worth an extra look. Many people here smoke the *hookah* even while working.

The herring-boned road soon leads past a workshop of artisans making *tablas,* traditional hand drums. In the open space facing a fountain are a couple of small temples. One of them, the recently renovated **Hari Shankar,** exhibits corner struts with leaping griffins in green and violet; an important sculpture of Surjya, dated 1083, beside the door; and a kneel-

The Red
Machhen-
dranath.

ing Garuda in front. Siddhi Narasingh Malla is said to have had his residence in this *tole*.

Continue down the road, keeping an eye out for a lane which leads south to the **Guje Bahal**. The lions at the entrance, their heads copiously smeared with red and yellow powder, are linked by a flowery wrought-metal arch. Reconstructed in the mid-17th Century, this monastery has a fine-looking facade: a row of meditating Buddhas and a painted panel of Buddhist divinities decorate the upper stories. Behind the temple are a well and the **Guje Chaitya** stupa.

The lane to the left leads to the slender three-story **Yana Mugal Ganesh** built in the mid-16th Century. Its Ganesh image is painted in flashy orange. However, the metal *torana* pediment, a recent addition, depicts Bhairav.

Sundhara and Shikhara

An **Uma Maheshwar** *shikhara*-style temple is on the right as you continue. The main road opens into a square with various pleasant if slightly decaying temples, monuments and *bahals*. To the right, at road level, is a *sundhara*, a

sunken fountain with a beautiful gilded water spout. This is an important local watering hole. Beyond it is another tall, thin *shikhara* dedicated to Uma Maheshwar; in the corner of the square stands a fine house with a wooden trellis on the ground floor and a completely carved facade. This square is important during the Rato Machhendra festival. It is the easternmost point of the Machhendra chariot's journey; from here, the god is carried south.

Leave the square and follow the road east through rural village houses. Note a fine three-roofed Ganesh shrine on your left. Opposite is the **Balkumari Dyochhen,** with circular latticed grilles on the ground-floor window frames. This part of Patan is inhabited by members of the sweeper caste. These low-caste people act shy compared to other Nepalis: they hide when drawing on their *hookahs,* do not smile freely, and rarely answer the customary *"Namaste"* greeting.

Four hundred meters (a quarter-mile) away, past a deep sunken fountain and a little bridge, stands the eastern Ashok stupa, the **Teta Stupa**. It stands amidst a landscape of mustard fields spiked with brick and tile kilns. This stupa is smaller

The naked horse.

188

in circumference than either its western or southern counterparts. The Buddhist niches were added in the 19th Century.

The Thousand Buddhas

If you continue east, you will soon come to a *jyapu* area. Turn left, off the main road, to find the large **Bhinchhe Bahal.** This monastery features a large, rectangular three-story shrine. You are likely to find men embossing *mantras* on a piece of brass to be rounded into a prayer wheel.

Of the various monuments at the northern limit of town, a three-roofed construction holds the visitor's attention because of a series of flaking paintings under its first roof. These depict a variety of weird scenes, perhaps taken from the *Ramayana.* One in particular is striking: it represents the silhouette of a horse made out of a jumble of naked human bodies.

Return south and west down an uneven village street full of cats. It is unusual to find the animals in the numbers they exist here: cats are not at all popular with Nepalis, who believe they are the embodiment of evil spirits. Turn through the Sun-dhara square into an adjacent commercial street and head towards a much-visited architectural masterpiece: the **Maha Baudha**, or "Temple of the Thousand Buddhas."

Although the temple is not visible from the street, you cannot miss it. An arrow to your right points to a short lane overflowing with curio shops. Here, in a cramped courtyard, stands the tall structure entirely covered by terra-cotta plaques depicting the Buddha.

The temple is intended to be a copy of the Mahabodhi Temple at Bodhgaya in India's Bihar state. But if the construction principle is the same, the structure and details are substantially different — all the more so because this *shikhara*, built at the end of the 16th Century, was renovated after suffering severe damage in the 1934 earthquake. After the renovation, there were many "spare parts" left over, due to a reduction in the temple's original height. With this leftover material, a smaller *shikhara* was constructed adjacent to its parent temple.

From the roof terrace of one of the surrounding shop-houses, you can get a plunging view of the monument and its surrounding rooftops. Various craftsmen

Wary boy, left, eyes a bronze beast near the Maha Baudha, right.

working in precious metals live in the neighborhood.

Farther south is one of the most famous Buddhist monasteries in Patan, the **Uku Bahal**. This *bahal*, a large rectangular structure with two gilded roofs, has recently undergone a major restoration. As you enter, look on the right-hand side to see carved wooden struts of great artistic simplicity. These masterpieces, one of the earliest known works of this type, were in fact moved from the back of the *bahal* to their present "safer" location.

Chaityas and Bajracharyas

In front of the Uku Bahal are several *chaityas*, guardian lions and several other rather true-to-life animals, and a statue of a Rana maharaja in military uniform. The latter stands on a pillar like a displaced Napoleon III in this 17th Century compound. Behind the *bahal*, in the center of an open square with grass and trees, is the stone **Yatalibi Chaitya** stupa.

Return to the Patan Durbar Square and head west from the Bhai Dega Shrine. The main axis road is asphalted. It goes through two and three-story residential houses inhabited mostly by *bajracharyas*,

the traditional Buddhist priest caste. The *kumari* or living goddess of Patan is chosen from among the daughters of the priests of **Haka Bahal**, a popular monastery which may have originally been located on the site of the Keshab Narayan Chowk in the Durbar Square. On the facade of the shrine is a row of 10 Buddhas set amid green, yellow, brown and white ceramic tiles.

Farther on, a small opening to the right leads to a large, noisy, open courtyard with the free-standing **Bu Bahal** looking over it like a temple. The beautiful facade of ceramics and gilded metal is marred by the proximity of a small, brick-yellow plastered building.

The lane south passes a two-story **Krishna Mandir** and skirts an oblong green-water pond to reach the interesting 17th Century **Purna Chandi**. This shrine to Durga has three roofs and three *torana*-crowned doorways, and is painted red with yellow and black spots. It holds only free-shaped stones. The struts depict Bhairav and the Ashta Matrikas.

Wander through a rural district, then leave the main east-west road to wander northward and glance at various interesting *bahals* and temples. First, you

Western Ashok Stupa provides grandstand for parade spectators.

will see the highly adorned **Shi Bahil** with its three roofs, pinkish facade and boards of ceramic tiles.

A Squinting Stupa

In an area called **Shiba Tole** is the beautiful little stupa of **Pim Bahal** a brick-and-stucco replica of Swayambhunath, overlooking a large pond. In popular belief, this is the fifth Ashok stupa. But the earliest record is a 1357 inscription mentioning the restoration of the stupa after its complete destruction at the hands of Bengal Muslims seven years earlier. Note the stupa's painted eyes: they are definitely squinting.

Toward the northern end of a pond stands a three-roofed **Chandeshwari Temple** with well-carved struts and crudely painted lions at the entrance. Follow the pond's longest side north, and come to the ancient looking, simple and beautiful wood structure of the **Joshi Agam**. This faces the 16th Century **Mahadev Temple**, a small, two-roofed brick-and-wood shrine on a platform by a well.

Return eastward along the main road. Pass through a tall, arched gate and turn past a movie house; here, you are sur-rounded by houses of mixed styles with occasional shops. There are various monasteries on either side of the road, including one with mural paintings representing death in the form of a phallic skeleton.

The houses become higher, finer and more compact, separated by narrow side lanes. One of these lanes on the north side leads to the enormous **Nag Bahal**, an open space which focuses on the life of 20 or more families. Half of the buildings around it have been rebuilt, and do not mix well with the older houses. Some have Western-style windows. In a corner, a sunken well is decorated with a statue of the Buddha. The building in the middle of the open space is used as a school. There is a special festival in this precinct every fifth and twelfth year.

You must return to the main road to reach the next courtyard, called **Ela Nani** from the name of its associated shrine, located to the left as you enter. Immediately to your right, the **Michhu Bahal** faces the same courtyard. Although both shrines have fine woodwork, they do not compare with the wonders of the adjoining inner squares to the east.

Here is the peaceful, vine-covered

Smile from a young visitor at the Kwa Bahal.

Saraswati Nani. This stocky single-story shrine is dedicated to Manjushri, the Buddhist god of learning, rather than his Hindu counterpart, the goddess Saraswati; the two are often confused in popular religion.

Next to it is the marvelous "Golden Temple," otherwise known as the **Kwa Bahal** or **Hirana Varna Mahavihar.** This Buddhist monastery is a large, rectangular building with three roofs and a facade richly embossed with gilded copper. The entrance is guarded by a pair of temple lions. Within the shrine are many images, including some early bronzes of Gautama Buddha and Avalokiteshwara. The metal-work, especially that of the *toranas,* shows great detail and craftsmanship.

You must take off your shoes to step into the lower courtyard. In its center is a small shrine, lavishly embellished with silver doors and images — many of them with a strong Hindu influence. The *gajur* which crowns the shrine is overly ornate, but a masterpiece nevertheless. A gilded frieze depicting the life of the Buddha is situated immediately in front of the main shrine.

This is an ancient sanctuary. Legend connects its origin with a 12th Century queen named Pingala of Marwar, although the earliest available records date from 1409. It is still actively patronized by Buddhist communities. Various groups stay at the monastery for a month at a time, observing very strict rules as they look after its maintenance.

A staircase leads to a Lamaist *gompa* on the first floor. If you ask one of the novice monks to guide you, he'll be happy to point out the interesting frescoes and other images of the Buddha within.

At the southwestern edge of Patan is **Jawalkhel**, site of the Valley's largest Tibetan refugee camp. This area is popular with visitors as a center of typical Tibetan handicrafts. In two large buildings, a couple of hundred men and women are always busy carding wool and weaving carpets. In the first building, five rows of women in traditional costume sit on the floor, one to three on a carpet, weaving traditional patterns, chatting and singing. In the next building, old men and women comb the wool and loom it into threads. Shops display these handicrafts for sale. Portraits of the King and Queen of Nepal and the Dalai Lama look down from the walls on a maze of carpets, blankets, woven bags and small coats.

Tibetan at Jawalkhel, below; and the Golden Temple's courtyard.

SOUTHERN SETTLEMENTS

South of Patan, various vehicle and walking tracks link settlements and sacred sites to the one-time capital. West of the Bagmati River are Kirtipur and its satellite hamlets, Panga and Nagaon. The twin settlements of Bungamati and Khokana lie on either side of the sacred Karya Binayak site. There is a road leading to the Lele Valley, and a trail to Godavari and Phulchoki, passing through Harisiddhi, Thaibo and Bandegaon. And an eastern lane takes travelers to Sanagaon and Lubhu. The history of all these villages is linked to that of Patan.

Rocky, Neglected Kirtipur

Almost all Newar settlements in the Valley are on plateaus. **Kirtipur**, perched on a twin hillock about five kilometers (three miles) southwest of Kathmandu, is a magnificent exception. First established as a kind of outpost of Patan in the 12th Century, it later became an independent kingdom and the last stronghold of the Mallas which fell, after a prolonged siege, to Prithvi Narayan Shah in 1769-70. It is said the Malla soldiers taunted the Gorkha forces as they struggled up the fortress-like hill. After the conquest was complete, the vengeful Gorkha ruler had the noses and lips of all of Kirtipur's male inhabitants cut off — with the exception of those who could play wind instruments.

Remains of the original fortification wall can still be seen. The earlier fortified city had 12 gates, one for each ward. Beyond and below the fortifications live low-caste people. A majority of the 8,000-plus inhabitants are *jyapus* (farmers), and most others are *shresthas* (merchants). The nearby **Tribhuvan University** occupies portions of Kirtipur's former farmlands; as a result, some farmers have had to seek jobs as bricklayers, carpenters or laborers.

Besides farming, traditional occupations are spinning and weaving. The 900 handlooms of Kirtipur's **Cottage Industry Center** spin cloth for Kathmandu.

Kirtipur is neglected. Resting on a rocky saddle, it withstood the series of earthquakes that so damaged several other Valley settlements. But age has gnawed at buildings, and decay enhances

A Thecho woman, left, and children of Kirtipur.

a feeling of walking back into Nepal's past. Some of the multi-storied houses still have exquisite carved windows; all the homes are laid out on stepped terraces linked by ramps and sloping paths.

One of the approaches from Kathmandu is up a long flight of steps. It enters the town near a huge pond, settled on the saddle between the two hills. The southern hill is surmounted by the **Chilanchu Vihar**, a central stupa surrounded by eight small shrines, all with stone images set at the cardinal directions. Around it are several Buddhist monasteries. The higher northern hill is inhabited by Hindus who have settled around the **Kvath**, a recently restored temple dedicated to Uma Maheshwar.

Where the two hills meet north of the central tank stands the famous **Bagh Bhairav Temple**, a place of worship for Hindus and Buddhists alike. This three-roofed temple, heavy within its enclosed courtyard of uninteresting facades, has a veranda on its ground floor and trellised balconies on its upper floors. The temple is decorated with swords and shields presented by the Newar troops after Prithvi Narayan Shah's 18th Century conquest. Within the temple is a famous

image of Bhairav in his tiger form. Of particular interest is the upper *torana* above the main sanctum; it shows Vishnu riding Garuda above, and below, Bhairav flanked by Ganesh and Kumar. There are also some interesting if rather indistinct early wall paintings under the arcade, around the base of the temple.

The Kvath's setting and approach, up a long flight of stone steps flanked by stone elephants, is more striking than the temple building itself. It commands a view of the Valley and the agricultural patchwork of green and yellow terraced fields.

From the Kvath, you can see in the southeast the two small villages of Panga and Nagaon. A path from the rice fields of Kirtipur leads into **Panga**, the larger of the two. Founded and fortified to cope with northern invaders during Malla times, it is an oblong settlement of about 600 houses. Most of its residents are Newari Buddhists, primarily farmers with some carpenters and bricklayers. There are a half-dozen or so temples in the village, but none is particularly outstanding or older than the 19th Century.

The hill opposite Panga is capped by a large, rounded, earthen mound called **Mazadega**. This was planned as a stupa,

but was never completed.

A path from Panga continues to **Nagaon**, which it enters between a small pond and a water tank. This settlement, whose name means "newly settled village," has about 200 mainly Buddhist households.

Machhendra and Karya Binayak

The twin settlements of Bungamati and Khokana date from the 16th Century. The Malla ruler of Patan at that time wanted to control his land while preventing people from moving too far away from the city. He decided on two sites near the Karya Binayak shrine, amid particularly fertile fields.

But the area had to be sanctified. Legend says that at the time of a big drought, the king — accompanied by a Tantric priest — went to visit Machhendra in the rain god's temple in India, and invited the god to settle with his people in the Valley. A shrine for Machhendra was established at the place where the village of **Bungamati** now lies. As early as 1593, the custom was established of leaving the Rato Machhendra in Bungamati during the winter months. The rest of the time he

The streets of Kirtipur, left, and Bungamati, right.

stays in his shrine in Patan; a palanquin carries him to and fro.

The approach road from Patan to Bungamati is dotted with small votive *chaityas*, appropriate for an ancient processionary path. The village of over 2,000 people is tightly clustered against a hilly riverside slope, surrounded by terraced rice fields and clumps of trees. Open ponds flank the paved path as it enters the village.

Past a Ganesh temple, a series of steps leads to a gate guarded by two lions and the head of a third one, which juts from a ramp obviously built around the animal. Here is the powerful, *shikhara*-style **Rato Machhendranath** temple, with heavy columns and beautiful supports in its lower part. In the courtyard, cows, buffaloes and goats lie amid several *chaityas*. Through the grille of the wooden door of the nearby **Lokeshwar Shrine**, you may catch a glimpse of the huge head of Bhairav, with crooked nose, greedy lips and globelike eyes.

Ten minutes' walk away, past the important Karya Binayak shrine on a tree-covered hillock (see page 133), is the village of **Khokana**. Slightly bigger than Bungamati, with a population of about 3,000 Newari Buddhists, Khokana is famous for its mustard-oil manufacturing. It is worthwhile to seek out one of the village's oil presses, located in poorly lit factories with medieval atmospheres.

Khokana's streets are brick and stone-paved with central gutters. They are flanked by plain brick facades with no frills. The main street is remarkably wide; it was built after the 1934 earthquake. The village's main temple is dedicated to the goddess **Shekali Mai**, also known as Rudrayani, one of the Valley's nature goddesses.

The Lele Valley Road

The road to Chapagaon and Lele, two villages which have greatly declined in importance since Licchavi times, is not often plied by casual visitors to Nepal. But this enchanting route unfolds picturesque scenes: black-and-white-clad civil servants going miles on foot every morning to their offices in Kathmandu; stands of bamboo drenched in sunshine; yellow mustard fields, green rice fields, misty blue hills, and a neat background of white snow-capped peaks.

On a high, flat plateau on the verge of

the next valley, **Sunaguthi** sits by the roadside. This settlement, founded in 1512, numbers about 2,000 people of various castes. The main shrine here, consecrated to the god **Bringareshwar Mahadev**, is not particularly beautiful, but it houses one of the 64 most sacred *lingas* in the Valley. On the same village square is a small two-roofed temple devoted to the Indian god **Jagannath**.

Gently winding its way uphill amid terraced fields, the path soon reaches **Thecho**, a larger settlement of more than 4,000 inhabitants of different castes. You may be inclined to stay awhile in this friendly town, watching the women washing clothes, scraping jugs and pots, or soaping their hair around greenish ponds.

Thecho's Balkumari Temple

In an open space surrounded by *patis*, a peacock stands on a column in front of the gaudily colored **Balkumari Temple**. On the square below, grain and chilies are scattered on mats and dried. In the northern part of the settlement is the second main temple, this one consecrated to

Brahmayani. Its two-roofed structure, guarded by familiar lions and a less familiar duck (the vehicle of Brahmayani) on a column, overlooks another square. Framed Indian religious pictures hang below the first roof, and King Birendra watches the temple from a poster on a nearby communal house.

Two kilometers past Thecho, **Chapagaon** stretches along the main road. According to legend, a Malla king exiled one of his own sons here for siring a caste of his own, called *babu*. At the entrance to the village is a metal Ganesh shrine smeared with dry blood and a statue of Brahma beside a huge *yoni*. In the central square, beside two double-roofed temples to Narayan and Krishna, one of which has fine erotic carvings on its struts, is the **Bhairav Shrine**, a sacred single-roofed structure dedicated to the main deity of Chapagaon. Overall, this settlement of some 2,500 people looks fairly prosperous with a variety of shops and an effective drainage system. East of here is the fine Vajra Varahi Temple (page 139).

Immediately to the south of Chapagaon lie the two small satellite hamlets of **Bulu** and **Pyangaon**, peaceful rural settlements near the Valley's southern foothills.

Thecho, below, and landscape near Lubhu, right.

BHAKTAPUR: CITY OF DEVOTEES

Seen from a distance in the early morning light, the long stretch of ochre brickwork blends perfectly with the landscape of gentle hills. Roofs are a double line of gray, and a single temple rises into the sky like a beacon. At the foot of the hill, the sacred Hanumante River draws the southern border of the city of Bhaktapur.

Bhaktapur — which is almost as well known by its alternate name of Bhadgaon — is said to have been designed sometime in the 9th Century in the shape of Vishnu's conch by its legendary founder, King Ananda Malla. In fact, the backbone of the city is a double S-shape, directed east-west, opening here and there on squares with temples, shrines and sunken fountains.

These open spaces were old village centers established along the ancient trade route to Tibet. Chroniclers of the time recall locations like Khopo, Khuprinibruma and Bhaktagrama, the latter name implying village *(grama)* status. After the

8th Century, these villages joined and grew into a town. This urban growth was the result of an evolutionary process rather than voluntary planning, or so legend would have us believe. Certainly, a concentric growth pattern, such as that of Patan, is absent in Bhaktapur.

The original center of Bhaktapur was the eastern square around the Dattatraya Temple. When the city became the capital of the whole Kathmandu Valley between the 14th and 16th centuries, there was a shift from east to west with the development of a new palace area. There are indications that the town was fortified by the mid-15th Century, as the new focus of the city moved to Taumadi Tole with its Bhairav and Nyatapola temples.

A Medieval Showcase

Bhaktapur has preserved its character and identity better than the Valley's other two major cities. There are three main reasons for this: its independent development until the Valley was reunified by Gorkha invaders in 1768; its subsequent isolation and stagnation; and the greater attraction of Kathmandu for hill-tribe im-

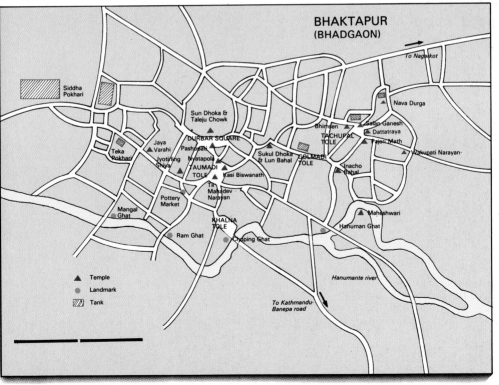

BHAKTAPUR
(BHADGAON)

To Nagarkot

Siddha Pokhari

Nava Durga

Sun Dhoka & Taleju Chowk

Bhimsen
TACHUPAL TOLE
Salan Ganesh
Dattatraya
Pujari Math

DURBAR SQUARE
Jaya Varahi
Pashupati
Teka Pokhari
Jyotirling Shiva
Nyatapola
Sukul Dhoka & Lun Bahal
GOLMADI TOLE
Wakupati Narayan
TAUMADI TOLE
Inacho Bahal
Kasi Biswanath

Til Mahadev Narayan
Pottery Market

Mangal Ghat

Maheshwari

KHALNA TOLE
Hanuman Ghat

Ram Ghat
Chuping Ghat

Hanumante river

▲ Temple
● Landmark
▨ Tank

To Kathmandu-Banepa road

migrants and 20th Century visitors. Indeed, with its 50,000 inhabitants, Bhaktapur is regarded as a showcase of "medieval" Nepalese town life.

It is also the most self-contained and self-sufficient of the Valley's major settlements. Bhaktapur's own farmers grow its food. The city's own craftsmen build and decorate its houses, make its pottery and adorn its temple. Its traders serve its commercial needs, and its people generally have preserved original traditions. The women's white shawls, and their red-edged black sari-like dresses *(patasi)*, blend with the yellow and ochre of brick and wood. Streets are not crowded; life is unhurried but still purposeful.

The traditional approach road from Kathmandu passes through a grove of pine trees on a hillock, skirting the **Tundhikhel**, a large open field. It then passes alongside two reservoirs. The *pokhari* or tank on the northern side is the **Siddha Pokhari**. It was properly excavated about four centuries ago, and is said to have been the largest clean water reservoir for Bhaktapur. Today it is far from clean, but it is nevertheless sacred to people of all creeds: Shiva and Vishnu shrines and a small Buddhist stupa group around it.

There is a legend that a large serpent has taken up residence in this tank; to this day, people are fearful of draining the tank for fear that they will expose the monster.

The Center of Bhaktapur

At this point, the road forks. The left-hand fork leads into the **Durbar Square**, which originally was outside the city proper. The square only became integrated during the reign of King Bupathindra Malla around the beginning of the 17th Century, and it was then linked to a lower square, Taumadi Tole, where the spire-like Nyatapola Temple stands.

If you were to take the right-hand fork, this would take you along the old east-west route through Bhaktapur. The street is lined with fine traditional houses, a scattering of roadside shrines, important temples and water taps. It eventually leads into the Taumadi Tole.

But for now, keep to the left. Entering the Durbar Square through the royal gate, you immediately become aware of the sparseness of temples, compared to the Durbar Squares in Kathmandu and Patan. In old prints and etchings,

Bhaktapur Durbar Square in the 19th Century.

Bhaktapur Durbar Square was overcrowded with highly decorated buildings of all shapes and sizes. Today, by contrast, it is a vast open brick square.

The 1934 earthquake caused considerable damage here, entirely destroying two large temples which formed the focal point at the end of the square. The square, in fact, consisted of two smaller areas divided by a wing of barracks or *patis*. The buildings that remain, however, can impart a tribute to the former splendor of the Durbar Square. It is said that Bhaktapur Durbar Square once contained at least 19 different courtyards. Legend claims there were, in fact, 99 — though this is hard to believe.

A Walk Through Durbar Square

As you walk through the main entrance to the square, on either side of a small gateway (a) leading to the police headquarters are a pair of very fine stone statues. These represent the goddess **Ugrachandi Durga** with 18 arms and **Bhairav** with 12. Both wear necklaces of severed heads. Legend has it that their anonymous sculptor had both his hands cut off so that he could not copy these masterpieces elsewhere.

To the left, on the northern side of the square, are the remains of what was once a palace with multiple courtyards. Opposite the palace, on your right, are a series of minor temples: to Jagannath and Bhadri, to Vishnu, and a Rameshwar temple dedicated to Shiva (b). Adjacent to these is an interesting brick *shikhara*-style temple dedicated to Durga (c); it is decorated with sculptured images of Hanuman and Narsingh.

As you move into the Durbar Square, the most striking feature immediately ahead of you is a life-sized gilded statue of **Bupathindra Malla** (d) seated on a tall pillar of stone. He is facing toward the **Sun Dhoka** or "Golden Gate" (e) leading through to the Taleju Chowk and the Kumari Chowk.

The Sun Dhoka is generally held to be the single most precious masterpiece of art in the Valley. Often equated with Ghiberti's famous Baptistery doors in Florence, Italy, this gilded copper gate was erected in 1753 by Jaya Ranjit Malla. It is a monument to the skill of the craftsman who produced it. The door frame itself illustrates many divinities. The *torana* exhibits a very fine example of Mahavaishnavi, and at its head is an excellent Garuda. The gate itself, set into glazed brickwork, is capped with a gilded roof, which has finials of elephants and lions over it.

Standing back from the gate, what remains of the former **Royal Palace** (f) can be seen on the right. The first important addition in the early 18th Century was the so-called "Palace of 55 Windows," painted black and red. In the 1934 earthquake, this palace was practically razed to the ground, and much of its artistry was lost.

To the left stands a "modernized" section of the old palace. It is still possible to make out some of the original Malla architectural features. The gateway, flanked by Hanuman the monkey god and Narsingh the man-lion, is the entrance to what is now the **National Art Gallery** (g). Within is a remarkable collection of *thangka* painting. This was no doubt the original entrance to the palace.

The Golden Gate, through which you now pass, leads to the religious and ritual courtyards. As you go through the gate, note a very small courtyard leading through an impressive guarded gateway.

BHAKTAPUR DURBAR SQUARE
Letters keyed to text.

The present guard is a local bull who has adopted the guardhouse as his personal stable.

Two Holy Chowks

Pass another small courtyard whose entrance is guarded by two beautiful Malla stone figures. Wind your way around to the back of the courtyard, where the opening to the **Taleju Chowk** (h) is found to the left. This small entrance, adorned with a magnificent woodcarving, is as far as a non-Hindu visitor may go: the two courtyards of the Taleju and Kumari *chowks* are sacrosanct.

But the military guards at the doorway can usually be persuaded to let you get a glimpse of the courtyard. In particular, try to look at the **Taleju God-house** on the southern side. Squinting through the doorway you can see, on the protective roof above, two dragons about to grab tiny elephants. A couple of lizards enhance the pointed roof, and a five-tiered umbrella crowns the whole. At the center of the *torana* over the entrance to the shrine, barely visible from the doorway, is an image of Taleju with four heads and eight arms. The doorway itself is flanked by two helpers of Ganga, and Jamuna on her tortoise.

Cast your eyes around the courtyard and see the richness of the carving and decoration. In the far right-hand corner is another small doorway that leads through to the **Kumari Chowk** (i). These two courtyards can perhaps be singled out as those most endowed with rare and beautiful artistic masterpieces, as well as representing two of the most holy shrines to be found anywhere in the Valley.

Before leaving this part of the palace, it is worth trying to get into the area known as the **Sundari Chowk** (j), the ritual bathing courtyard of the Bhaktapur King. Unlike other bathing courtyards, this one is no longer surrounded by buildings. However, the tank itself is lined with stone divinities and is much larger than the one in Patan. From the center of the tank rises a magnificent *naga* or serpent, facing east toward another equally beautiful specimen. The water is supposedly piped from the hills beyond Bhaktapur through a lead-lined conduit.

Today, the Bhaktapur palace is still a place in which one should linger awhile: a place to contemplate the beauties con- The "Golden Gate."

tained in what may once have been the most impressive of all Durbar Squares.

Plinths and Pillars

Return to the bustle of the Durbar Square and turn east to reach the smaller of the two enclosed plazas that make up the square. Past the plinths of what was once an octagonal temple, you will see on your left a fine stone *shikhara* dedicated to Durga (k). Interesting animal guardians line the steps of the entrance to the shrine.

The square itself is framed on two sides by an L-shaped, two-story *dharmasala* (l), and on the north by the multi-level platforms of several temples ruined in the 1934 earthquake. In a corner beneath them, curio shops sell all kinds of traditional tourist trinkets, masks and puppets on strings. To the east, opening onto the street just beyond the square, is an unusual Buddhist monastery called **Tadhunchen Bahal** (m). It has retained the authentic look of a medieval *bahal*. According to an inscription, the cult of a human *kumari* was instituted here.

Reorient yourself to the praying king's pillar opposite the Sun Dhoka in the Dur-

bar Square. Next to the pillar is a big stone bell that was erected in the 18th Century to call the faithful to morning prayer at the Taleju Shrine. Behind the bell, the stone *shikhara* of **Batsala Durga** (n) looks like the Krishna Mandir in Patan's Durbar. Many divinities are represented in stone carvings around the *shikhara*, as well as copper pinnacles and wind bells.

Farther on is a two-roofed shrine Known as the **Pashupati Temple** (o). It is apparently a replica of the Pashupatinath in Deopatan, but is much less impressive because of the less striking setting. However, it is one of the oldest temples in the Valley, having been constructed toward the end of the 15th Century. Its black, carved woodwork depicts common men, elephants, lions, *shardulas* or griffins, and finally two minor deities, Simhini and Byaghrini. Beyond this temple, a short street running east leads down to the lower **Taumadi Tole**.

Two Great Mystical Shrines

Here, the **Nyatapola Temple**, Nepal's tallest, stands more than 30 meters (98 feet) high. Carved wooden columns support five roofs and form a balcony around

Malla King Bupathindra and Queen.

the sanctum. The temple is balanced superbly upon five receding square plinths. A steep central stairway is flanked by huge guardians on each of the plinths. Each pair of guardians is believed to have 10 times the strength of the pair on the plinth immediately above them. Thus, the two famous Malla wrestlers at the bottom are 10 times stronger than the dragons on the next plinth.

Power culminates in the Nyatapola's main deity, Siddhi Lakshmi, a mysterious Tantric goddess to whom the patron-king Bupathindra Malla dedicated the temple in 1702. The image of the goddess can only be seen in the dark of night by the temple's Brahmin priests. Exactly 108 colorfully painted wooden struts show the goddess in her manifold forms; other minor divinities are also depicted.

The Balance of Terror

On the surrounding brick platforms, there is a permanent fair. Farmers bring baskets full of vegetables, and chickens and goats to be sold for sacrifices. Curio sellers unfold treasures like knives, *saranghis, thangkas,* precious stone objects, masks, prayer wheels, and other things.

The **Kasi Bishwanath Temple**, with its rectangular base resting directly on the square, is set at right angles to the Nyatapola. This three-tiered structure was completely rebuilt after 1934, using many parts of the previous temple. That in turn had been built in the early 18th Century on the foundation of what was probably an earlier structure yet.

This massive building is a perfect architectural foil to the spire-like, vertical Nyatapola. Both temples show the Nepalese version of the balance of terror: the Tantric goddess in her sacred shrine is counterbalanced by the awesome powers of Bhairav, to whom this temple is dedicated.

Paradoxically, the image of Bhairav, which is taken out for chariot processions across town during the Bisket festival, is hardly a foot high. It usually rests in a niche about one meter from the ground. A horizontal brass ledge cuts the central door in two; above it is a small hole through which offerings are thrust into the temple's mysterious inner space.

The real entrance to the Kasi Bishwanath is from behind, through the

Buildings restored, left, to dignity displayed in 19th Century painting, right.

small **Betal Temple**. Betal, enshrined as a human figure in metal, accompanies Bhairav on all his journeys in Bhaktapur.

The tile-roofed, three-story brick houses on the west side of Bhaktapur Durbar Square still have fine woodcarvings. The south side, by contrast, is mobbed with plain, post-earthquake houses. But behind them, a plastered-over, arched passage yields entry to the **Til Mahadev Narayan Temple**, one of the oldest temple sites in the city and an important place of pilgrimage in Nepal. An inscription attests to the fact that these premises have been sacred ground since 1080. The temple enshrines a 12th to 14th Century sculpture of Vishnu.

Near the shrine is a four-faced *linga* in a *yoni* under a cage. A jar is suspended over the *lingum*; water is supposed to fall drop by drop on the symbolic phallus. Many old women come to this compound to pay homage to the various stone sculptures.

The Other Approach

If you return to the Siddha Pokhari tank where the road forks at the western entrance to Bhaktapur, and this time take the right or southern fork, you will soon walk under the city gate guarded by two stone lions. Three and four-story brick houses line the street, which slopes downhill, then uphill again. Attached to the houses are *patis* with carved wooden pillars that jut into the road. Radios echo each other along this rather narrow asphalted road, where city life and rural scenes alternate. This main axis of Bhaktapur winds its way in an east-west direction, roughly following the course of the sun.

Past a large open space on the right, you will come to another walled water tank, the **Teka Pokhari**. The painted murals of a low doorway to your left indicate a *bahal* within; this is the rather primitive-looking **Ni Bahal**. Its central image is Maitreya, the Buddha of the future.

A side lane to the right, brick-paved but muddy because of regular rainfalls and an almost constant lack of sunshine, leads to one of the western *ghats*, the **Mangal Ghat**.

Ahead, on the left-hand side of the main road, a structure protrudes from the building line. Its facade looks like an *agam* house, with intricately carved woodwork, overpainted figure struts of the eight Ashta Matrikas, and a row of small bells

on the eaves. In fact, it is a temple consecrated to **Jaya Varahi**, Vishnu's *shakti* in his incarnation as a boar. Jaya Varahi's image can be seen on the *torana* above the middle window on the second story.

A small, tiled Ganesh shrine juts into the road almost next door; it has a beautifully worked bronze *torana*. On down the road are brass shops, several more *patis*, and another, smaller Ganesh shrine. Glancing down the lanes to the south, you can catch glimpses of ascending hills on the other side of the Hanumante River.

Pass a small brick-paved square, now almost a ruin, and a hodgepodge of various shrines. Soon you come to another square, this one dedicated to Shiva. The complex boasts a sunken *hiti* decorated with a 5th Century stone relief of Shiva caressing his *shakti* Parvati. The water tank behind the *hiti* is a lovely pool used for bathing, swimming and laundry. Most interesting is the *shikhara* devoted to **Jyotirlingeshwar Shiva**. It has two separate sanctums. On the ground level is an ancient free-shaped stone considered to be one of the Valley's 64 sacred *lingas*; and hidden in the inner sanctum is an image of Nriteswar, the god of dance.

The Pottery Market

At the next crossing, the lane to the left goes directly uphill into the Durbar Square in front of the palace. The side lane to the right, paved with bricks, slopes gently downhill and merges with an open plaza. At the corner of the lane and the main road, a steep stone stairway leads up to a hill. There is a small Ganesh shrine here, a large pipal tree, and a lovely vista of the southern hills.

Take another set of steps on the other side of the hillock, and descend into one of the most fascinating corners in all of Bhaktapur: the **Pottery Market**. Thousands of pots dry in the open square. The huge potters' wheels, set up all around the plaza, are spinning all day long. As the men make pottery, their women pound grain, and children swarm about them all.

A small shrine, with several images of Vishnu, occupies one side of the market square. Ganesh, the elephant-headed patron of potters, presides from his more showy double-roofed temple, the **Jeth Ganesh**. Its priest, quite aptly, is a potter. What's more, it was a local potter who donated this temple in 1646.

Potters at work.

210

From the pottery bazaar, the nearest lane south goes straight to the **Hanumante River**. Here is **Ram Ghat**, one of the bathing and cremation places serving the western part of the city. The lane across the river leads to the **Surjya Binayak Shrine.**

The Eastern Ghats

The eastern *ghats* are well worth a detour. Just before entering the Nyatapola square is a small brick-paved plaza leading into a steep flagstoned lane. It continues south as a neat path with multi-purpose drains: these are used as a kind of railroad track for the religious chariots that are guided in an often uncontrolled manner down this street at Bisket time. This is the processional route followed by the goddess Bhadrakali and her spouse Bhairav once a year, symbolically joining the upper and lower parts of the city.

This path merges into the **Khalna Tole**. Unpaved except for one traversing road, this open space has three free-standing structures and one octagonal *pati* which shelters the Bhairav image during Bisket. From here, the **Chuping Ghat** along the banks of the river can be seen.

Every year the Bisket festival brings tens of thousands of people from far and near to Khalna Tole. Bhadrakali and Bhairav are there too, ensconced on a huge triple-roofed chariot to witness the extraordinary spectacle, with Betal hoisted prow-like in front. A 25-meter (82-foot) *lingum* pole is erected in a circular stone *yoni* base. The *lingum* is hung with greenery and two large banners. When it is later pulled down, it marks the start of the New Year in the Valley.

The open shrine to the left along the river is dedicated to the Tantric goddess Bhadrakali. She is represented here by plain stones. When her image is brought here for the Bisket festival, it reveals only a headless standing female figurine.

To the right, just before the Hanumante bridge, is a large complex of temples, small shrines and *patis* by the riverside. Across the bridge, the stone-paved road continues as a wide track. This was Nepal's traditional main route to Tibet and the East. It's a short country stroll upstream to the **Hanuman Ghat**, a favorite bathing place for local people. Two arms of the Hanumante River come together here.

The Peacock Window.

Past the next bridge, you come to two huge *linga-yoni* structures on raised platforms surrounded by other *lingas* and shrines. Here Hanuman, who usually serves as a mere gatekeeper in Nepal, is elevated to the role of principal god. An image of the monkey god in his red hood and cape stands beside a modern shrine dedicated to his master, Rama. The corrugated tin roof extends beyond the sanctum to form a porch supported by wooden columns and girdled by vines.

In the southern corner of the complex, Ganesh and the Buddha guard the entrance to a small, pleasant stone platform behind a riverside *dharmasala*. The recessed pit on this platform holds a sacred silver-plated *lingum*. Women beggars here benefit from the generosity of the many visitors who throw them rice. The old and the ill await death in *dharmasalas*; when the last moment nears, their feet are submerged in the sacred waters, and they are subsequently cremated on a small hill on the opposite bank.

Further upstream, animal sacrifices are regularly performed at the **Maheshwari Temple** facing the *ghat* dedicated to the goddess with that same name.

The Old and the New

The lanes going north from the Hanuman and Maheshwari *ghats* enter the oldest part of Bhaktapur, known as **Tachupal Tole**. You go through a maze of tiny lanes, zigzagging passages, inner courtyards with chilies on mats, and corner *patis*, stepping over dozing men.

But suddenly you feel like pinching yourself. The pavement and the buildings around you are of the same old style, but somehow appear brand new. The ground, nicely bricked in a V-pattern, is so clean that even the women do not use mats to spread their grains for drying. Indeed, this whole area is being restored to its medieval elegance by the West German-assisted Bhaktapur Development Project.

The square of Tachupal Tole slopes slightly upward to the east. There, standing on higher ground, is the *tole's* main attraction: the **Dattatraya Temple** (a), tall and square, facing the rectangular and squat **Bhimsen Temple** (b) from across the whole length of the square.

The two-story Bhimsen, erected in 1605, has a simple *pati* for a ground floor. The austere image of the god, kept above, was molded from the earth. Behind the temple is a deeply recessed *hiti*. Facing the temple, a stone pillar supporting a brass lion shares a platform with a small double-roofed Vishnu temple. Roads shoot off in all directions from here: this area was indeed the original site of Bhaktapur, and the square was its main open space.

Syncretistic Shrine

The Dattatraya Temple is probably the earliest structure on this site, dating from 1427. This is the only temple in the Valley dedicated to the syncretistic Dattatraya, a deity whose cult originated in southern India. Worshippers of Vishnu number Dattatraya as one of their Lord's incarnations. Devotees of Shiva, particularly during the Shivaratri festival, venerate Dattatraya as Shiva's teacher. Local Buddhists, not to be outdone, consider Dattatraya to be Devadatta, a cousin of the Buddha, and they, too, offer gifts here to the deity.

The Dattatraya Temple is reminiscent of the Kasthamandap in Kathmandu, and like it must have served as a community hall for local citizens. Later a front section was added, accounting for its rather unusual form. Guarding the entrance are

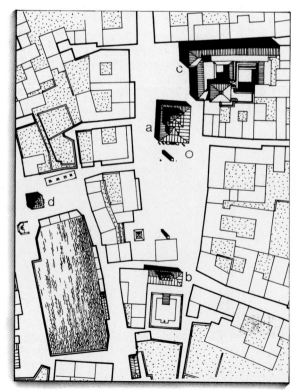

DATTATRAYA SQUARE. Letters keyed to text.

212

the same two Malla wrestlers found at the Nyatapola Temple; these are much larger in size, however. A few erotic scenes are carved around the base of the temple.

Priests' Houses And A Peacock Window

Within Tachupal Tole are 10 buildings which were formerly used as *maths* or Hindu priests' houses. The most famous, the **Pujari Math** (c) is located toward the south of the Dattatraya Temple. Built in 1763, it became so renowned that until this century, the government of Tibet annually sent a caravan laden with rich gifts. Today, this old house with excellent woodwork is used by the Bhaktapur Development Project; it is earmarked as a museum.

Many windows inside the *math*, especially those on the balcony of the ground floor of the central courtyard, are just as beautiful as the famed **Peacock Window** on the exterior, down a side alley; the *math* is best known for this work of art.

Within the Pujari Math, a Development Project map shows visitors that Bhaktapur's best-preserved houses line the main east-west axis on the north side of the city, and are also to be found around the Royal Palace. The highest density of population, more than 500 persons per hectare, is concentrated mainly on a vertical strip at the center of Bhaktapur, and in the whole newer eastern section of the city.

Standing in an open space north of the Tachupal Tole, the **Salan Ganesh** (d), erected in 1654, is a small but well proportioned and complete temple, lavishly decorated. Its sanctum has no icon, only a rock said to be a natural representation of the head of an elephant. Its struts depict Ganesh, Bhairav and the Ashta Matrikas, the mother goddesses.

Beyond, rural life takes over abruptly as the lane leads uphill to the **Nava Durga Dyochhen**. Inside, extraordinary, mysterious rites are performed. Tantric in origin, they are believed to be even more gruesome than ceremonial sacrifices frequently carried out in the square in front of the shrine.

The Commercial Artery

A quiet brick-paved lane goes in a southeasterly direction from here and

Dattatraya Square.

soon meets the main east-west axis of the town. At the corner stands a double-roofed, gilded temple dedicated to Vishnu as **Wakupati Narayan**. In the merry month of *Magha* (February-March), which is propitious for weddings and ritual bathing, large groups of Newars pass here en route to the *ghats* — singing sacred songs, blowing conches, and waving large flags with images of Vishnu. A 1408 chronicle mentions a Garuda pillar that was erected here by one of these families of bathers.

East along the main road is the **Brahmayani Mandir**, which marks the easternmost *ghat* of the same name. The landscape becomes progressively more rural, with a few potters' workshops, a loom, a fountain and a sawmill. The small brick temple of the *ghat* is built on a stone base and is flanked by two huge pipal trees, dwellings for crows eyeing worshippers' offerings.

Return to the main Dattatraya square and exit via its southwestern corner, heading toward the Taumadhi Tole. Here the road is quite wide and runs downhill. Ground-floor shops sell groceries, bread,

nails, tumblers, doorknobs, peacock feathers and temple offerings. This is, indeed, the commercial artery of the old town, winding gently to find itself again in the course of the sun.

Flying Angel Facade

At a crossing where two side lanes go down to the *ghats*, the small **Inacho Bahal** shows flying angels on a whitewashed facade. Then the main road skirts a large open space of the **Jaur Bahi**, a small single-roofed shrine which houses a Buddha in meditation. Although the shrine is modern, the elaborate doorway was taken from an old temple. A little further away is an ancient *dyochhen*-style building with a ground-floor shop selling brass and tin utensils.

At **Golmadi Tole**, the square is surrounded by several *patis* and is occupied by a plastered Buddhist stupa, shrines to Shiva and Vishnu, and a deep sunken *hiti*. There is also the triple-roofed, three-century-old **Gol Madi Ganesh**. Its 32 struts depict Bhairav Ganesh, a popular guardian of the Valley. Across the street, a charming miniature spire-like roof is perched atop a *dyochhen*.

Poetry in Colors

The dim road beyond here is lined with more shops displaying pottery, brass and other wares. Follow the elegantly dressed local women, clad in shiny red, green or blue dresses with white scarves tied around their waists, into the interesting **Lun Bahal** to the left. Although rather dilapidated, it has a certain poetic air about it, and an unusual feature. This structure of Buddhist origin, built in the 16th Century, was later appropriated by Hindus. They placed a stone statue of Bhimsen, consecrated in 1592, within the sanctum. The god is seen here with brass ornaments and a brass mask of fierce expression.

Almost next door is a *math* with beautiful woodcarving, both on its facade and inside. This **Sukul Dhoka** has been recently renovated.

There are two routes you can take from here. The street going straight ahead leads, within 200 meters, to the eastern square of the Royal Palace. The main road turns south, passes more shops and a vegetable market, and returns to the Nyatapola square.

Nava Durga, left; and right, father and son.

TOWNS WEST
OF BHAKTAPUR

Set upon a high plateau in the center of the Valley, about three kilometers (1.9 miles) west of Bhaktapur, **Thimi** — with 12,000 inhabitants — is the fourth largest settlement in the Valley. The history of this town goes back at least to the time of the independent Malla kingdom. Its name derives from *chhemi*, meaning "capable people," and was given by the Bhaktapur rulers to its farmers eager to help fight aggressors from Kathmandu and Patan.

Today, Thimi is renowned as the home of the Valley's most capable potters. Men and boys hammer and shape the smooth, moist and highly malleable reddish clay from the neighboring fields. They create cooking pots, water jugs and elaborate vessels for their favorite rice wine. Besides these practical items, they produce charming and unique miniature elephants and peacocks for use as flower pots. Thimi is also known for its traditional painted masks.

Thimi's one main road runs from north to south, at right angles to the old road

from Bhaktapur. It crosses several open spaces along the way. In the center of the southernmost square is the town's chief temple, a kaleidoscope of colors. Founded in the 16th Century, it is dedicated to Balkumari, one of the many consorts of Bhairav, who in turn is represented by a brass image inside his own small domed shrine near his *shakti's* much more imposing temple.

Near the northern boundary of Thimi is **Nade**, a compact settlement of fewer than 3,000 people. From the south, the stone-paved path leads uphill through a magnificent high-arched opening in the **Ganesh Dyochhen**. In an open space nearby is a locally famous temple of Ganesh. Small and well-kept, it has three roofs and an elaborate, colorful facade.

A large path from the old Bhaktapur road meanders through rice fields into **Bode**. You will be greeted by strong smells of manure as you cross two large open spaces; the second contains a pond, a paunchy *shikhara* and a stone *lingum*. Durga dances are performed once a year on the round stone platform here.

Straight on to the northern edge of town, you reach the **Mahalakshmi Temple** overlooking the Valley. This temple, of great local significance, has two roofs, the upper one of which is collapsing. Legend says that Bode was founded in 1512 after Mahalakshmi, who had a shrine at the site of the present village, appeared in a dream to the Malla king of Bhaktapur. The present temple was built in the 17th Century.

These three settlements are interdependent in their proper fulfilment of New Year's ceremonies. Every year on New Year's Day, the square around the Balkumari Temple in Thimi witnesses a spectacular gathering of 32 deities carried in elaborate multi-roofed palanquins under the shade of ceremonial umbrellas. During the journey, men throw vermilion powder — a sign of respect — over everyone and everything in their path. When several hundred men from Nade arrive with a palanquin bearing Ganesh, excitement reaches fever pitch. Later in the morning, many people rush to the Mahalakshmi Temple in Bode to see a similar but smaller procession.

Between Thimi and Bhaktapur is the small potters village of **Nikosera**, also known as **Sano Thimi** or "Little Thimi." Only a few families live here, but they create delightful objects of pottery.

Shaping clay in Thimi, left; and separating paddy from chaff near Bode, right.

EASTERN SETTLEMENTS

According to legend, the founder of the Bhaktapur dynasty, King Ananda Malla, created seven major settlements on the eastern side of the Valley in order to strengthen his new kingdom. Three of them pre-existed: these were Banepa, Nala and Dhulikhel. The other four, which he established, were Panauti, Khadpu, Chaukot and Sanga. Most of these settlements in fact lie outside of the Valley proper. Banepa and Dhulikhel took on increased importance with Ananda Malla's action, as they were located on the major trade route between the Valley and Tibet.

The trade route used to cut through the village of **Sanga**, which stands on top of the pass leading into the Valley from the east, five kilometers (three miles) east of Bhaktapur. The modern highway now bypasses it. After skirting Bhaktapur, the road climbs steadily past this community, then winds down rather steeply into the next valley. A small lane to the north leads into Sanga, which is more scattered than most Newar settlements but enjoys a lovely setting. A little further to the east, a small, rocky boulder crowned by a patch of rubble offers a comprehensive viewpoint over the Kathmandu Valley.

The village of Sanga itself has no important religious or cultural buildings, but contains a historically interesting small shrine of Bhimsen. Legend has it that when the Valley was a lake, the god Bhimsen crossed it by boat, rowing from Tankhot in the west to Sanga in the east. A shrine to commemorate his voyage was erected in each settlement.

The Banepa Valley

After leaving Sanga, you pass through part of the lush Banepa Valley to reach the relatively large trading post of **Banepa**. This village also extends north of the highway, at the foot of a forested hill. A major fire some 25 years ago destroyed many of its buildings, but it remains an economically important headquarters for the distribution of goods to the surrounding hill areas.

The main Chandeshwari Shrine (page 140) looks over the Banepa Valley from a hill on the northeast side of the town. To the northwest, a bumpy track cut by several brooks runs through terraced rice fields to **Nala**. It is said that one of the ancient Buddhas stopped here for his annual four-month meditation, as he was traveling from a visit with the Adhi Buddha at Swayambhunath to the home of the Nama Buddha at Namara. The latter meditation site is atop a hill three hours' walk to the south of Panauti; it is also possible to drive there from Dhulikhel.

The Buddhist shrine of Lokeshwar, called **Karunamaya**, is located about 100 meters west of Nala by the old Bhaktapur road. The temple is surrounded by buildings for pilgrims, and is marked by a water tank in front of it. Uphill from here, in the center of the village, a steep stone alley leads to a square dominated by the splendid four-tiered **Nala Bhagvati Temple**. Several processions take place around these two shrines during their colorful annual festivals.

From Banepa, the tarmac highway proceeds eastward to **Dhulikhel**. This village sits on a hilltop and is visible from a long distance away. On the main square is a **Narayan Shrine** and a pleasant **Harisiddhi Temple**. Many of the houses in Dhulikhel have beautifully carved wooden struc-

A mother at home, left, and a father in the fields, right.

tures around their doors and windows.

As you climb a hillock on the north side of the village, you come to an open space. Here, a stone ramp and an arch mark the entrance to Dhulikhel's **Bhagvati Temple**, a three-roofed structure built on a heavy stone platform with ceramic tiles on its facade. Various attributes of Shiva are depicted nearby. From the temple, there is a fine view of the Banepa Valley and the Himalayan Range. The thatched roofs and mud houses at your feet are a precinct of low-caste people living on the fringe of the Valley.

Dhulikhel is the center of one of the major sub-sections of trade between the Kathmandu Valley, eastern Nepal and Tibet. More than 4,000 people live in the village, as many as in Banepa.

The Newars' Panauti

Fewer than 3,000 reside in **Panauti**, one of the finest all-Newar settlements in the region. The village is built at the confluence of two rivers in a small valley surrounded by mountains south of Banepa. It is predominantly agricultural and self-contained. Before the development of Banepa it was an important trade center,

but today it has little trade. Nevertheless, shops do a thriving trade in food stuffs, electric goods and ritual paraphernalia.

The main village square, now often occupied by ducks, chickens and cows, used to contain a king's palace. A street branching to the south offers a view of the Roshi Khola river. Inside a walled open space are good examples of early temple architecture: a three-tiered **Indreshwar Mahadev Temple** built at the beginning of the 15th Century, and a **Narayan Shrine**. Both are being restored.

The Indreshwar Mahadev Temple is architecturally and historically one of the most important temples associated with the Newari culture of the Kathmandu Valley. Although the temple is said to have been founded as early as the 11th or 12th centuries, the present building dates from the early 15th Century, still making it one of the earliest extant structures. It is certainly a temple of fine proportions and exquisite carving, simple yet beautiful — a fine example of early Newar architectural style. The roof struts, showing incarnations of Shiva, are matchless in their serenity.

Shrines and Ghats

Outside the courtyard, you go past two shrines — one to Bhairav, the other containing a free-shaped stone representing one of the original nature goddesses. At the point where the two rivers meet, on a peninsula, is a temple dedicated to Krishna. Several Shiva *lingas* sprout nearby. Adjacent to the temple is an important cremation *ghat*.

Across the **Pungamati River** stands the famous 17th Century **Brahmayani Temple**, which has undergone a major renovation. Brahmayani is the chief goddess of Panauti after Indreshwar Mahadev. An important chariot festival is held each year in her honor.

Archaeological findings may reveal the existence of a pre-Licchavi settlement in or around Panauti. This is the opinion of several specialists in regional prehistory; it is backed by a legend which mentions the existence of an old kingdom near the site of modern Panauti. Perhaps it is here, on the outer fringe of the Kathmandu Valley, that some of the missing clues will be found about this fascinating civilization's earliest aspects and antecedents.

Indeshwar Mahadev, left; and Panauti's Brahmayani, right.

BEYOND THE VALLEY

Astride the long frontier between Nepal and the People's Republic of China lies the greatest concentration of high mountains on earth. Considered the consummate climbing challenge, the peaks of giants such as Mount Everest, Annapurna, Dhaulagiri, Makalu and Cho Oyu have long stirred the imagination of travelers and adventurers.

Rising from the glaciers on the flanks of these great mountains, a multitude of rivers plunge south to feed the holy Ganges. Cutting deep gorges, these torrential waters course through beautiful and enthralling country — verdant landscapes, thick stands of virgin forests, and villages steeped in ancient religions and cultures. Finally slowing as the waters meet the lowlands of the Terai, barely above sea level with still hundreds of miles to go before meeting the sea, the rivers meander quietly through the plains and dense jungles rich in birds and wildlife.

Fascinating glimpses of these wild regions are accessible to those willing to exert a little extra physical energy. One of the great charms of Nepal is that it is still largely without roads. Access to its interior — its villages and valleys, its mountains and hills — is by ancient foot trails and trade routes interlaced across the country. Only on foot can the traveler discover Nepal's true personality.

Outside of the Kathmandu Valley, there are four principal regions of interest to the visitor. From Pokhara, an important crossroads town west of the capital, one can explore the terrain of the Annapurna Massif or venture further west to Jumla and Lake Rara. Directly north of Kathmandu are the spectacular Langtang Valley and other isolated regions near the Tibetan boundary. East is the greatest of all mountains, Everest, and the homeland of the Sherpa people. South in all directions, abutting the Indian frontier, is the Terai with its bustling border towns, its great national parks teeming with tropical wildlife, and its pilgrimage sites like Lumbini, the birthplace of the Buddha.

About five percent of Nepal's total land area has been set aside as national parks or wildlife reserves, and these spots should be high on the list of priorities for explorers of inner Nepal. Tourism is encouraged in most of these sanctuaries, but a great emphasis is placed on its being compatible with conservation ideals, and in some cases, on its being economically beneficial to the local populations.

Nepal's National Parks and Wildlife Conservation Department of the Ministry of Forests administers six national parks and three wildlife reserves, with more on the drawing board. King Birendra has assigned his brother, Prince Gyanendra, to take an active role in the wildlife conservation movement; under this royal patronage, Nepal's park system is an example to the rest of Asia.

Nepal lies in the overlapping zones of Oriental fauna to the south and Palearctic fauna to the north. This factor, coupled with its dramatic altitudinal and climatic variation, has contributed to the kingdom's great variety of wildlife forms. For example, although the country contains only a fraction of 1 percent of the earth's land mass, about 10 percent of the planet's birds — roughly 800 species — can be found in Nepal. Its national parks, which represent three principal zones of terrain, trans-Himalayan, Himalayan and tropical, are set up to protect a representative cross-section of the land.

An increasing number of visitors to Nepal are now walking — or "trekking," as it is called here — into the interior. The word *trek* is Afrikaans in origin; South African Dutch pioneers used it to describe a long journey by ox-wagon in search of a new home. But words change meaning when they travel, and in Nepal, where no ox-wagons could possibly traverse the rugged mountains, officialdom defines trekking as "a journey undertaken on foot for seeing natural and cultural scenes in areas where normally modern transport system is not available."

In late 20th Century Nepal, trekking is one of the most popular activities for visitors. By trekking, you will discover many new horizons: the haunting beauty of the Himalayan reaches and the peculiar warmth of the mountain peoples, far from the feverish pace of Western civilization. To trek in Nepal is to undergo an almost spiritual experience. It is to walk in communication with nature and man, beneath the world's most exalted mountains.

Preceding pages, Dharma Gurgu, a Newar Tantric Priest, dramatizes the life story of the Buddha; left, trekking in the Kali Gandaki Valley

Trekking in Nepal, as it is known today, was established by a British citizen named Jimmy Roberts. A veteran of numerous first ascents of Himalayan peaks in Nepal and Pakistan, as well as a provider of logistical support for other major climbing expeditions, Roberts founded Nepal's first trekking agency — Mountain Travel — in 1965. In doing so, he created an industry which has benefited the mountain people and has since grown to become one of Nepal's major foreign exchange earners. There are dozens of trekking agencies active in Nepal today.

Trekking need not be especially demanding physically. There are treks for every level of fitness, from short walks on relatively level terrain to rugged, demanding expeditions. Treks can last for a few days to a month or more. They can take the traveler to regions of anthropological or cultural interest, to areas of exceptional mountain scenery, into the jungle, over high snowy passes, or to expedition base camps on the lower levels of the highest peaks.

Whatever the trek, good health, appropriate fitness, proper planning, good equipment and clothing, and detailed knowledge of the trekking route are necessary. Given these prerequisites, trekking can be a wonderful never-to-be-forgotten experience. (See Guide in Brief for the essentials of trekking.)

The best time for a trek depends upon the region to be visited. There are excellent treks in Nepal for nearly all months of the year. Generally, the summer monsoon gives way to clear skies at higher elevations in early October. By mid-October, the rains are over in the middle hills and jungles, and the crisp clear days of autumn fill the country.

In November and December, the weather remains predominantly clear. Higher elevations begin to get colder, but the days are normally quite sunny and pleasant.

In January and February, the Himalayan heights are quite cold. But the middle hills, lowlands and jungles are beautiful. Snow comes to elevations above 3,350 meters (11,000 feet) and the land takes on a new enchantment.

March and April are excellent months for trekking throughout Nepal, although certain high passes are not safely open until mid-April.

May can be beautiful. It is one of the finest months to trek at higher elevations.

While the weather may be hot below 1,200 meters (4,000 feet), it is generally clear and the hills a brilliant green.

With the onset of the monsoon in June, periods of rain are intermittent with bright, blue skies. Trekking through the so-called "monsoon curtain" of main valleys cutting through the Himalayan backbone can be unpleasant.

Trekking is allowed nearly everywhere in Nepal. Certain regions along the Chinese border are closed, but other accessible areas — such as Everest base camp, the Rolwaling Valley and Langtang National Park — are only a single kilometer (as the crow flies) from the Tibetan frontier.

All treks require a permit, valid for one specific trek, to be produced at all police outposts along your route. Trekking permits can be obtained through any trekking agency, or directly from the Central Immigration Department in Kathmandu. They can also be obtained from the Immigration Department in Pokhara for Pokhara-based treks only.

Treks organized by agencies are highly recommended, especially if you are trekking in Nepal for the first time. Agents can tailor treks to your own pace, ambitions and interests. What's more, they can provide services to help you get the most out of your limited time. Arranging itineraries, permits, transportation and food, hiring reliable Sherpas and porters, and arranging porter insurance (a government regulation) can be a frustrating and time-consuming experience — and sometimes a disappointing one — for the independent trekker.

The cost of treks is about US$50 to $60 per day, per person, for the best services and Sherpas. Treks priced at less than US$30 per day are available, but they inevitably sacrifice certain essentials to bring costs down.

Agencies normally provide tents, kitchen crew and food, porters for all gear, and a *sirdar* — a group leader, guide and interpreter, almost always a Sherpa. Some agencies will also rent out equipment to their clients and to trekkers who want to travel on their own.

Independent trekkers will find specific and valuable information in Stephen Bezruchka's *Guide to Trekking in Nepal*. This book, written by a Canadian physician who favors the individual approach, is detailed and informative, and contains many useful maps.

Campsite en route to Khumbu.

POKHARA AND WESTERN NEPAL

Two hundred kilometers (124 miles) west of Kathmandu, nestled in a valley beneath the Annapurna Massif, the town of **Pokhara** has quietly won the hearts of travelers from around the world. Many visitors find their most lasting impression of Nepal comes not from the Kathmandu Valley's Durbar Squares, but from the awesome "fish-tail" of majestic **Macchapucchare** reflected in the still waters of Pokhara's **Phewa Lake.**

In the not-too-distant past, when even Kathmandu was a forbidden city to foreigners, Pokhara's seclusion made it a place of mystery. Early hearsay accounts gave it a mythical air: certainly, novelist Han Suyin — in her book *The Mountain Is Young* — based the "Bongsor Valley" on Pokhara.

Today, if the proximity of this sub-tropical valley to the great Himalayan peaks keeps its mythical feeling alive, it is far from unknown. A tourist trade thrives here, feeding on trekkers going to and from the mountains, and on visitors merely passing through by road or air.

Pokhara is virtually in the geographical center of Nepal. Located on the main road between Kathmandu and Bhairawa, there may be no other place in the world from which the great Himalayan peaks can be admired from such a close distance. **Annapurna I** (8,091 meters or 26,545 feet) and its panoply of peaks lie only 50 kilometers (31 miles) away. Macchapuchhare (6,994 meters or 22,946 feet) shoots straight up, without a single intervening ridge between it and Pokhara, 30 kilometers (19 miles) distant. The horizon extends 140 kilometers (87 miles) from **Dhaulagiri** (8,167 meters or 26,795 feet) to **Himalchuli** (7,893 meters or 25,896 feet).

The valley of Pokhara itself lies at about 900 meters (3,000 feet), significantly lower than Kathmandu. With a subtropical climate and a heavy monsoonal rainfall (4,000 millimeters, or 157 inches, annually), the land is lush with vegetation. Citrus trees, bananas and cacti dot rice and mustard fields. There are low walls laced with ficus and hedges of thorny spurge spiked with red blossoms.

The valley floor is marked by intricate terraces and gorges cut by the Seti River, as well as a half-dozen lakes of varying

Preceding pages, a young lady of Larjung, a Thakali village near Dhaulagiri; below, the "fishtail" mountain.

sizes. Beyond, to the south, are lower hills of extensive cultivation. These are the contact zone of two cultures, the Hindu caste groups from the Terai plains and the Lamaistic tribal groups from the flanks of Annapurna. The ochre, thatch-roofed houses of the former and the white, slate-roofed homes of the latter add variety to the landscape.

The 20th Century Arrives

Until two decades ago, Pokhara was a small town of Newari and Gurung brick-and-tile shops that came alive only during the winter months, when mule caravans from Mustang and heavily laden porters from Butwal congregated to exchange goods. Even the primitive bullock cart was unknown here until 1961 — introduced, ironically, by the airplane, which made its first visit to Pokhara in 1952. The first motor vehicle, a Jeep, was taken to this valley by plane in 1958.

The eradication of malaria in the late 1950s, the commissioning of hydroelectric power in 1968, and the completion of the Kathmandu — Pokhara and Pokhara-Sunauli highways in the early 1970s have had a far-reaching impact on the growth of the town. Pokhara today is one of the fastest growing towns in Nepal: the present population of nearly 50,000 is more that double what it was 10 years ago.

An unstructured town, Pokhara is strung out for several kilometers along the main road. It gives a general impression of recent, hasty and anarchical growth, except for its trading heart, which is a cluster of multi-level brick houses. Nevertheless, the town has become a regional center for administration, commerce and cottage industry. The native peoples have been almost overwhelmed by Tibetan settlers, Manang traders and Gurkha soldiers, all of them involved in a lively jostle for new urban space. There are a bus station and post office in the lower part of town, a bank and even a movie house in the upper part. The **Bindhyavasini Temple**, on its shady and well-kept platform, overlooks a modest amusement park.

Phewa Lake, skirted by a large number of unpretentious lodges and simple restaurants, is the most congenial spot for visitors. Many former denizens of Kathmandu's "Freak Street" have migrated here. The placid surface may hide a more violent past: local legend claims the lake covers an ancient settle-

Pokhara's Phewa Lake.

ment erased by an earthquake.

A small golden temple to Varahi nests in foliage on an island in the center of the lake. Many fishermen and other pilgrims take their long canoes, carved from tree trunks, to the island to visit the shrine. On the nearby shore, King Birendra maintains a three-story villa as a winter residence.

Trekking Around Pokhara

There is a wide choice of trails in the mountains around Pokhara for trekkers. Some of the more scenic excursions include the drive to Sisuwa, east of Pokhara, and from there the climb up **Pachbhaiya Ridge** for a view of the lakes of Begnas and Rupa on either side; and the drive west to **Kubhinde Pass** on the Siddhartha Rajmarg to view the grand sunrise over the Annapurna Massif. Fifteen kilometers (9½ miles) south of Pokhara is **Nuwakot**, with a medieval fortress and sweeping views of Dhaulagiri, Annapurna and **Manaslu** (8,156 meters or 26,758 feet). And a few days' trek through rhododendron and oak forests are **Siklis** in the Madi Valley and **Ghandrung** in the Modi Valley.

The best of all possible treks in the Pokhara region, however, is the walk around Annapurna. This requires time — a minimum of 22 days — but many people consider it the classic trek in all of Nepal. It offers some of the most breathtaking Himalayan scenery, and at the same time gives the traveler a cross-section of Nepali culture, from the lush irrigated valleys of the south to the high arid country north of the massif.

An around-Annapurna trip can begin or end in Pokhara. Most trekkers choose to begin their walk from **Dumre**, a village midway between Kathmandu and Pokhara on the main road, and proceed through the **Marsyangdi Valley**, nestled in the watershed dividing the Annapurna Massif from the Manaslu Himal.

The trail up the Marsyangdi Valley affords excellent and ever-changing views of the high Himalaya. On the north and west, you can see Macchapucchare, **Lamjung Himal** (6,983 meters or 22,910 feet), **Annapurna II** (7,937 meters or 26,040 feet), **Annapurna IV** (7,525 meters or 24,688 feet), **Annapurna III** (7,555 meters or 24,787 feet) and **Gangapurna** (7,455 meters or 24,458 feet). Dominating the eastern skyline are Manaslu, Himalchuli,

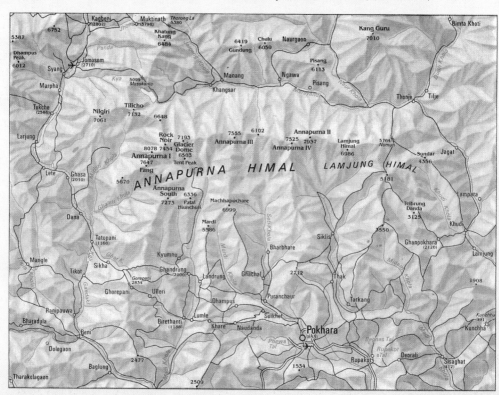

Peak 29 (7,835 meters or 25,705 feet) and **Baudha Himal** (6,672 meters or 21,889 feet).

Leaving Dumre, the trail meanders through the broad terraces of the lower Marsyangdi Valley. This river bed is extremely fertile and is heavily cultivated with rice. Millet, corn and buckwheat terraces scale the side hills. The farmers of this region are primarily Brahmins and Chhetris, with some communities of Gurungs and Magars in the foothills. In this part of Nepal, huge shady banyan trees shelter scattered villages, and mangoes and bananas flourish. Two-storied houses are brightly painted with red ochre or whitewash, and are usually surrounded by the scarlet and orange blossoms of poinsettias and marigolds.

The Manang Valley

At the bazaar town of **Bagarchap**, the Marsyangdi Khola river swerves due west to enter the long **Manang Valley**, until recently closed to foreigners. The canyon becomes much narrower at this point, and the trail frequently drops 150 meters (500 feet) to cross suspension bridges over the river before regaining elevation on the op-

A Gurung village west of Phewa Lake.

posite bank. The region becomes increasingly forested with pines and firs.

Between **Chame** and **Pisang** the effect of the Himalayan rainshadow can be observed. Though the forests do not disappear entirely as they do in the upper Kali Gandaki river region, they do become generally more sparse, with a greater amount of juniper. The fields are sown with barley, buckwheat and potatoes — hardy crops which can thrive in cold, semi-dry regions.

The Manang Valley is surrounded on all sides by major Himalayan peaks. The southern end is guarded by Annapurnas II, III and IV, while Gangapurna, **Glacier Dome** (7,193 meters or 23,599 feet) and **Tilicho Peak** (7,134 meters or 23,405 feet) loom to the west. Lesser known mountains stand to the north and east, including **Chulu Himal** (6,630 meters or 21,751 feet) and **Pisang Peak** (6,091 meters or 19,983 feet), both of which have been opened for non-expeditionary ascents.

The people of the Manang Valley are similar to Tibetans in culture and in dress, though their historic origins are unknown. For centuries they have monopolized trade in the upper Mar-

syangdi region. They are also notorious for international trading schemes which often take the Manang men as far from home as Singapore, Hong Kong and Bangkok.

The main villages in the Manang Valley — Pisang, **Braga** and **Manang** — are reminiscent of American Hopi Indian communities. Tight clusters of flat-roofed stone buildings, these villages huddle against eroding sandstone cliffs for defense purposes as well as for protection against the weather. One of the most interesting cultural sites in the valley is the **Braga Gompa**, which dates back 400 to 500 years and belongs to the Kagyu-pa Lamaist sect.

There are several spectacular day hikes within reach of Braga and Manang. The climb up **Braga Hill** provides excellent vistas of the Annapurna group. And across the river from Manang lies a shimmering glacial lake fed by a tremendous icefall on Gangapurna. It is possible to walk up beyond the lake and safely observe the caving waterfall of ice from a forested plateau at about 4,000 meters (13,100 feet).

Crossing **Thorong La** (5,416 meters or 17,769 feet) from Manang requires a long but gradual climb through grassy meadows and high yak pastures. From the top, there are unmatched views of the northern faces of Annapurna and her satellite peaks. As the trail descends into **Muktinath**, the symmetrical summit of Dhaulagiri appears on the southern horizon.

Muktinath lies at 3,810 meters (12,500 feet). Hindus and Buddhists alike consider it a holy pilgrimage site for the eternal flame burning here. Pilgrims also come to this region seeking black ammonite fossils from the Kali Gandaki gorge. Known as *sholigrams*, these fossils are considered to be the embodiment of Vishnu. Beyond lies the fascinating ancient city of **Kagbeni**.

Into the Kali Gandaki

The descent into the Kali Gandaki basin from Muktinath begins with a drop into the vast alluvial fan of the upper **Thak Khola** river, home of the Thakali people. The Thakalis are prosperous traders who hold a monopoly in Nepal on the Tibetan salt trade. Colorfully decorated mule caravans are frequently seen on the Kali Gandaki route; they carry loads of sugar, kerosene and rice up

Annapurna Two.

the trail, and tote salt and barley down to Pokhara. For agricultural subsistence, the Thakalis grow potatoes and barley, their towns reflecting this with their flat roofs for grain drying and a few elaborate irrigation systems.

The location of the Kali Gandaki gorge between Tibet and India, and its lack of high-altitude passes, have made it one of the most important trade routes through the Himalaya. From its origin, a tiny spring in forbidden **Mustang** on the Tibetan plateau of northern Nepal, the river flows south to India, carving its way through the towering massifs of Dhaulagiri and Annapurna. Only 35 kilometers (22 miles) apart, the summits of these two great mountains tower some 6,600 meters (22,000 feet) above the Kali Gandaki at the village of **Tatopani**, elevation 1,189 meters (3,900 feet). This is the deepest gorge on earth.

There are a number of interesting side trips off the main Kali Gandaki route. Two of the most spectacular for mountain scenery are the day hike to the **Dhaulagiri Icefall** and the three-day trek up **White Peak** (5,261 meters or 17,260 feet).

The icefall is an impressive mass of overflowing snow and ice tumbling off the steep slopes of Dhaulagiri. In 1969, it swallowed seven members of an American expedition attempting to climb the mountain. From the icefall's vantage point, there are excellent vistas of the Annapurna Massif, the Niligiri peaks, and Tilicho and Tukche peaks. The climb up to **Meso Kanto Pass** (5,099 meters or 16,729 feet) to see the famous lake at the foot of Tilicho Peak is a difficult but very worthwhile trip.

Emerging From the Rainshadow

Just before **Ghasa**, the landscape transforms into coniferous forest as the trail gradually emerges from the Himalayan rainshadow. The pine forests in turn become more deciduous, filled with rhododendron, azalea and eventually bamboo. Tatopani marks the transition in agriculture from the fields of hardy grains suitable for the arid Thak Khola to the much moister terraces of rice and millet. Water buffaloes, banyan trees and poinsettias also reappear as the trail travels through **Sikha** to **Ghorapani Pass** (2,880 meters or 9,449 feet).

The lowland areas are populated primarily by Gurungs, Magars, Brahmins

Annapurna South.

and Chhetris — people who share similar lifestyles, though they speak different languages and have varying histories and cultural backgrounds. Most of them are Hindus, but some in the more isolated villages still worship the older local gods and practice Bon and Tantric Buddhism.

An hour above Ghorapani Pass, **Pun Hill** (3,030 meters or 9,940 feet) has spectacular views of Dhaulagiri, Annapurna and the magnificent Kali Gandaki gorge slicing between them.

From Ghorapani, there are two possible return routes to Pokhara. Both climb southeasterly over subsidiary ridges of Macchapucchare and **Annapurna South,** with incredible views of these mountains. One route includes the prosperous Gurung village of **Ghandrung**, while the other follows the ancient trade route through the bazaar town of **Birethanti**. Both variations join in the fertile **Yangdi River Valley** and end the trek in the lush, heavily farmed vale of Pokhara.

Jumla and West Nepal

There is yet another region in the far west whose historic and scenic grandeur approaches that of Kathmandu and Pokhara. This is the **Jumla** region, 360 kilometers (224 miles) west of Kathmandu and 150 kilometers (93 miles) north of Nepalganj.

This remote land of elevated open valleys and long ridges, clothed in temperate forests and alpine meadows, once nurtured a great kingdom. The Khasa Mallas' reign reached its zenith in the 14th Century. They had a summer capital at **Sinja** and a winter capital at **Dullu**, and their territory extended from the Kali Gandaki to Kumaon, and from the Terai to Taklakhar in western Tibet. The remnants of this greatness are still evident in Jumla in the form of sculptured temples, stone pillars and folk songs.

Jumla is accessible by scheduled flights on Royal Nepal Airlines. Weather and distance often cause delays or cancellations of these flights.

From Jumla, elevation 2,340 meters (7,677 feet), you can trek west along the broad valley of **Tila Nadi** down the ancient highway marked by old milestones. The hot springs of **Tatopani** are about two days' walk west of Jumla town.

Another short trek is about three days' walk east to the valley of **Gothichaur** (2,750 meters or 9,022 feet). This

Sacred Muktinath, left; and a Manang man with a prayer wheel.

delightful valley is surrounded on all sides by grassy slopes and pine forests. A stone shrine adorns a water spout from the Malla days. The northern rim of the grassy bowl provides good views of the Chyakhure Lekh to the south and Patrasi Himal to the east.

Four days north of Jumla, through **Padmara**, **Bumra**, **Ghurchi Pass** (3,457 meters or 11,341 feet) and **Pina**, is the idyllic site of **Lake Rara National Park** in the remote northwest Karnali Zone. Lake Rara itself is 10 square kilometers of crystal blue waters at 2,980 meters (9,777 feet) elevation. Pine-clad green ridges and snowfalls which linger into May make it a place of serene scenic beauty. The national park, which consists of 106 square kilometers (41 square miles), is a focus of bird migration. Common visiting species during the winter months are mallards, teals, grebes and pochards.

Two other national parks in Nepal's west are the **Shey-Phuksundo National Park** and the proposed **Khaptad National Park**, both in the mountains of the Dolpo and Doti districts. Shey-Phuksundo contains 2,500 square kilometers (965 square miles) set aside to protect a trans-Himalayan ecosystem representing the

flora and fauna typical of the arid high-altitude desert of the Tibetan plateau. Snow leopards, blue sheep, great Tibetan sheep, musk deer and Tibetan hares have been seen here. The people of Shey Gompa and the spectacular scenery of **Lake Phuksundo** are within the park, which at the moment is off-limits to foreign visitors. This region and its fabled **Crystal Mountain** were the focus of Peter Matthiessen's *The Snow Leopard*.

Khaptad National Park will include 187 square kilometers (72 square miles) of forest land between 2,200 meters (7,218 feet) and 3,200 meters (10,499 feet). The flora consists mainly of high-altitude conifers, oaks and rhododendrons, interspersed with open pastures. This beautiful area is being set aside at the request of a royal guru, and like Shey-Phuksundo is inaccessible to foreign visitors.

Longer treks from Jumla head northwest into the Kanjiroba Himal, characterized by their wild remoteness and lack of human habitation. The highest peak in this region is **Kanjiroba South,** 6,883 meters (22,582 feet). Go well prepared if you plan to trek here; the terrain is rugged, food is scarce, and porters can be hard to find.

Highland village typical of Jumla area.

TREKKING INTO CENTRAL NEPAL

North of the Kathmandu Valley, between the Himalayan foothills and the Tibetan frontier, are several regions popular with trekkers. These include the Langtang Valley, the Helambu district, and the high country above Gatlang.

The **Langtang Valley** is located some 30 kilometers (19 miles) directly north of Kathmandu, close to the boundary with Tibet. Extending in an east-west direction, it is bordered on the north by the main crest of the Himalaya, dominated by **Langtang Lirung** (7,245 meters or 26,769 feet), the highest peak in the area. To the south are the **Chimse Danda** ridge, crossed by the **Ganja La** pass (5,122 meters or 16,804 feet), and the Jugal Himal, culminating in **Dorje Lakpa** (6,989 meters or 22,930 feet).

Glaciers spawned by the slopes of Dorje Lakpa, Langtang Lirung and other peaks feed the Langtang Khola river. This stream winds its way through the high, gentle Langtang Valley before emptying in a raging torrent into the Bhote Kosi river through a long, narrow defile at the west end of the valley.

Remote and until recently practically unknown, the Langtang area was not penetrated by a Westerner until the ubiquitous H.W. Tilman visited there in 1949. The next European visitor was Swiss Tony Hagen, who did geological surveys there in 1952. His exciting descriptions of the area aroused the interest of Warner Schulthess, a Swiss agricultural adviser for the United Nations; Schulthess subsequently established a Swiss cheese factory in the valley.

In 1976, Langtang became Nepal's second largest national park with approximately 1,710 square kilometers (660 square miles) of land. Within this area are about 16 villages — plus 1,000 plant, 160 bird and 30 mammal species.

The main approach to Langtang from Kathmandu is via the gorge of the Trisuli River (or the Bhote Kosi, as it is known above Dhunche). The spectacular track up this gorge once formed an important trade route to the Tibetan fort at Kyirong, just over the Chinese border at Rashwa Garhi.

The track turns east up the gorge of the Langtang Khola where this stream joins the Bhote Kosi. The trail passes through a dense forest of oak, birch and pine, hung with Spanish moss and hosting delicate orchids. Further on, the valley opens out into alpine meadows and yak pastures.

The inhabitants of the Langtang Valley live mainly in Langtang village itself. They are thought to be descendants of Tibetans from Kyirong who intermingled

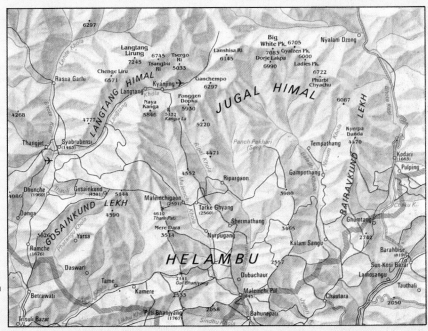

Preceding pages, a Gurung hunter at the Annapurna Massif; left, the Langtang Valley.

with Tamangs from the Helambu area. Their dialect resembles that spoken by Tibetans in Sikkim. They are mainly sheep and yak herders, but grow some hardy grains and vegetables.

The Swiss cheese factory is located at Kyangjin Gompa, just beyond Langtang village. There is also a small airstrip nearby.

Just north of the *gompa* is the high camp of **Yala Peak** (4,800 meters or 15,748 feet). The mountain scenery at the *gompa* is breathtaking.

Langtang National Park also includes the sacred Gosainkund Lakes and the Helambu district at the head of the Melamchi Khola river. Gosainkund is a pilgrimage site for thousands of Shiva devotees in July and August. They come to bathe in the lakes' holy waters in praise of their god. According to legend, Shiva formed the lakes by thrusting his trident into the mountainside, creating three gushing springs. They lie on the trail connecting Sing Gompa, in Langtang, with upper Helambu.

Lying immediately northeast of Kathmandu, Helambu, also known as Helmu, is bounded on the north by a wall of 5,000-meter (16,400-foot) peaks. The difficult Ganja La pass provides access to the Langtang Valley. The region is corrugated by a jumble of valleys and ridges running north-south, through which run the headwaters of the Sun Kosi river, of which the Melamchi Khola is the westernmost tributary.

Helambu's population is predominantly Sherpa — though of a type distinct from those of Khumbu. Even the dialect spoken here is different. There are several Sherpa villages and Buddhist monasteries scattered around the Melamchi Khola. The largest village and the nearest to Kathmandu is Tarkeghyang, with a fine *gompa*; there are beautiful views from Yangri Danda, north of the community. Other major villages are Melamchigaon and Sermathang.

Helambu is easily accessible, and is an ideal area for those with limited time to trek. In the spring, when the rhododendrons are in bloom, a visit here is particularly worthwhile. The region does not have the enormous peaks of the Khumbu and Annapurna regions, but the mountains of 5,000 to 6,000 meters (16,400 to 20,000 feet) elevation are wild and beautiful.

Helambu chorten.

242

RAFTING NEPAL'S RIVERS

Rising from the glaciers of the world's highest mountains and from the high plateau of Tibet, the rivers of Nepal plunge through the gorges of the Himalayas and traverse their rugged foothills. Before the melted snows reach the peaceful waters of the Ganges in India, the rivers course through tropical forest and meander through the plains of the Terai.

Rafting the rivers of Nepal is one of the best and most exciting ways to abandon the cities. Adventurers can closely examine the countryside, the rural villages and the native people without investing the time and energy required for a long trekking trip.

Tranquility and Excitement

Some rafting trips require you to paddle your own way. Others, under the direction of more professional companies, employ guides trained to international standards of rowing and controlling the craft. Either way, rafting can be a combination of introspective tranquility and tremendous excitement. But choose your trip organizer carefully: many of Nepal's rivers are remote and unpredictable, and a responsible river company with a good reputation is a necessity to ensure your safety.

For centuries, the rivers of Nepal have been considered sacred. Ashes of the cremated dead are still scattered into the country's rivers and carried to the holy Ganges. But if the waters are revered, they are also feared. The ability to swim is restricted to those who live along rivers, or the wealthy few living in cities. Others — where bridges are absent — still cross rivers in dugout canoes powered by a single paddle or pole. When bridges were built, they often collapsed, and ferries frequently capsized, always causing terror and often bringing death.

Whitewater Pioneers

Foreigners ventured onto the rivers soon after Nepal's borders were opened in the early 1950s. Sir Edmund Hillary attempted to ascend the Sun Kosi in eastern Nepal in 1968. Terry and Cheri Bech descended much of the Sun Kosi in a small raft in the early 1970s. Various sections of other rivers were kayaked by occasional visiting experts, including Michel Peissel, who tried to drive up the Kali Gandaki in a hovercraft in 1973.

It was not until 1976, when American Al Read started systematically exploring and charting the rapids of the Trisuli and upper Sun Kosi rivers, that river running began in earnest. Read formed Nepal's first river company, Himalayan River Exploration, and began taking visitors down the wild stretches of the Seti and Trisuli rivers to Tiger Tops in Royal Chitwan National Park.

Soon, the challenge of Nepal's rivers began attracting expert guides from the West. Native Nepali guides were also trained to international standards. Today, river guides are not only capable of operating a raft in complete safety, supervising camping and cooking fine meals. Many are well-educated college graduates, able to interpret flora, fauna and geology for the visitor's added understanding of his river journey.

River rafting is an exceptional experience anywhere — but in Nepal's unique terrain, it is somehow all the more fascinating.

Rafting on the Marsyangdi River.

EVEREST AND EASTERN NEPAL

Perhaps every Nepal visitor dreams of trekking to the foot of the world's greatest peak, **Mount Everest,** and camping among the hardy Sherpa people who live in its shadow.

The route followed by trekkers to this **Khumbu** region, which contains three of the world's seven highest mountains (including Lhotse and Cho Oyu), is certainly a well-trodden one. Since an American expedition in 1950 and a British party in 1951 first explored the region, and bridges and trails were subsequently improved, countless climbers and trekkers have ascended the track to the Everest base camp. The exploits and writings of some, like Eric Shipton, Sir Edmund Hillary, Chris Bonington and Reinhold Messner, have made the Khumbu famous. It is hardly surprising that the "roof of the world" would be the scene of some of mountaineering's most significant accomplishments and a favored haven for alpine enthusiasts.

As great an attraction as the mountains are the Sherpas, who rank among the hardiest and most egalitarian people in the world. Though best known for their accomplishments as high-altitude porters and mountain guides, the Sherpa people have traditionally been traders, herders and subsistence farmers. A deep adherence to the Tibetan Buddhist religion dominates their home lives, and their biggest festival — the dance-drama known as Mani Rimdu — depicts the victory of Buddhism over the ancient Bon faith. See it at Thyangboche in November-December or at Thami monastery, a short day's walk west of Namche Bazaar, in May.

Much of this area is contained within the bounds of **Sagarmatha National Park,** established in 1976 with help from the government of New Zealand, Hillary's native country. There is a visitor center at Namche Bazaar, and the **Everest View Hotel** is just above the Syangboche airstrip. A small hospital at Kunde has been developed with the assistance of Hillary's Himalayan Trust, along with schools, bridges and water pipelines in the area. The Himalayan Rescue Association mans an aid post at Pheriche during the

trekking season, to provide treatment for sufferers of altitude sickness and other ailments.

Trekking in the Khumbu

The Khumbu is too beautiful and too friendly a place to hurry. What's more, because of its high elevation, it is potentially very dangerous for those who try to trek too high too fast. Attempting to hike from Lukla to Everest base camp in less than a week is foolish; even a week may be too short for those who are slow to acclimatize. Adjustment to elevation has nothing to do with physical fitness. Trekkers should be aware of the early symptoms of mountain sickness — headache, nausea, breathlessness, etc. — and heed them by stopping or descending until the symptoms disappear. (See the Guide in Brief for full medical information.)

For persons with limited time, the best way to approach the Khumbu is to fly from Kathmandu to the precipitous airstrip at **Lukla**, 2,866 meters (9,403 feet) above sea level. The airstrip is perched high above the gorge of the boiling **Dudh Kosi** river. The flight takes only 40 minutes, but it saves up to 12 days of strenuous up-and-down walking from the nearest road.

From Lukla, the trail climbs gradually up the Dudh Kosi canyon, crossing from side to side and passing through forests of blue pine, fir and juniper. Between 3,600 and 4,200 meters (11,800 to 13,800 feet), birch and rhododendron predominate. Solid villages with rambling stone walls and tiny fields are interspersed among high meadows. Often, stones and even huge boulders lining the path are seen carved with the Buddhist *mantra: Om mani padme hum.*

The village of **Jorsale** is the location of the national park entrance post. All trekkers must register here and pay the applicable park entry fee. The entry ticket must again be produced at the Namche checkpost.

The View From Namche Bazaar

Above Jorsale, the **Bhote Kosi** river forks off from the Dudh Kosi, leading toward Thami and the **Nangpa La** pass, at 5,716 meters (18,753 feet) the passage to Tibet. From here, the Everest base camp trail climbs steeply up to **Namche Bazaar**. On the way, you'll get your first views of

Everest (8,848 meters or 29,028 feet) and **Lhotse** (8,511 meters or 27,923 feet).

Namche is a prosperous market town with two-story, glass-windowed wood houses, a bank and a number of stores selling everything from Tibetan artifacts to Star Beer and ice screws. The sacred Sherpa mountain of **Khumbila** (5,761 meters or 18,900 feet) towers to the north, while **Thamserku** (6,608 meters or 21,680 feet) and **Kwangde Ri** (6,187 meters or 20,298 feet) loom to the east and west, respectively.

Above Namche are two other major towns of the Khumbu, **Kunde** and **Khumjung**. More spread out than Namche, with rock walls dividing stony fields, these two towns have beautiful vistas on all sides. You can look across to **Nuptse** (7,879 meters or 25,850 feet), Everest, Lhotse, **Ama Dablam** (6,856 meters or 22,493 feet) and **Kang Taiga** (6,809 meters).

Across the canyon from Kunde, and opposite the confluence of the Dudh Kosi and Imja Khola rivers, the **Thyangboche Monastery** is perched on a high ridge at 3,876 meters (12,716 feet) elevation. This is the leading Buddhist center in the Khumbu, and its location is one of the most scenic. Pines, azaleas and colorful

mountain rhododendrons surround the attractive *gompa,* which rests amid stunning views of Everest, Lhotse and Ama Dablam.

It is a four-hour walk from Namche to Thyangboche. Halfway, where the trail crosses the Dudh Kosi, there is a settlement called **Phunki,** notable for its water-driven prayer wheels. Thyangboche itself features a rest house and a small restaurant run by the monks.

If you wish to visit with the abbot of the *gompa,* be sure to offer him a *kata,* or ceremonial scarf. One of the other monks at the monastery should be able to obtain one for you. It will be appreciated if you leave a small donation when you depart.

After Thyangboche, the trail crosses the **Imja Khola** and climbs to **Pangboche,** site of another large and ancient *gompa* amid the last scattered trees below timberline. Here the canyon begins to widen into high alpine meadows, with **Tawoche** (6,542 feet or 21,463 feet) and Ama Dablam sweeping upward to each side. The trail climbs gradually to **Pheriche,** a small hamlet with tea shops and stores, as well as the trekkers' medical post. Even those who feel in excellent condition are well advised to spend a day here

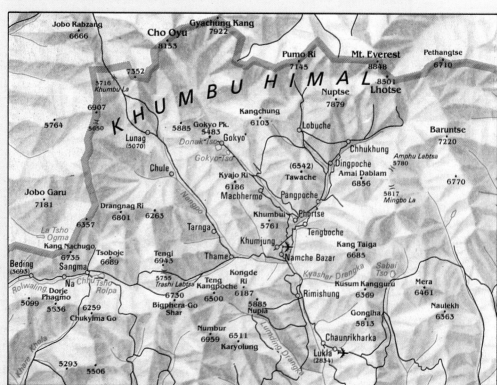

to acclimatize, perhaps making a side trip to the neighboring villages of **Dingboche** and **Chukung** at the base of Lhotse's great south wall.

The Final Climb to Base Camp

From Pheriche, a reasonably strenuous walk leads up around the terminal moraine of the huge **Khumbu Glacier** to **Lobuje**. This community is a collection of huts tucked in a narrow meadow between the glacier and **Lobuje Peak** (6,119 meters or 20,075 feet). The views of Tawoche and Nuptse, towering almost two kilometers directly ahead, are particularly spectacular from Lobuje.

It's another day's walk through jumbled moraine and grass-shattered rock to the foot of **Kala Pattar** ("Black Hill") and the tiny, sporadically occupied hamlet of **Gorakshep.** From here, the site of Everest base camp is easily accessible, as is the summit of Kala Pattar (5,545 meters or 18,192 feet), from which much of Mount Everest is clearly visible. On all sides loom the giants of the earth — Everest, with its savage Khumbu Icefall; **Pumori** (7,145 meters or 23,442 feet); Lhotse; the Tibetan peak **Changtse** (7,553 meters or

24,780 feet); Nuptse; Tawoche; and countless other needles and snow-fluted ridges.

The return trip to Lukla can be accomplished more quickly than the ascent. The trail down can be the same as the way up, or there are numerous variations possible. One alternative is a side trip to **Gokyo**; another is a detour from Pangboche through **Phortse**, bypassing Thyangboche on the opposite side of the canyon and proceeding directly to Khumjung. This latter trail is narrow and slightly precipitous, with more ups and downs than the main route. From Namche down, there is only one trail, though one must take care at the top of the grade, below **Phakding**, not to miss the turnoff to the Lukla airstrip on the east.

The trekker in the Khumbu may not see a yeti, regardless of how many stories he might hear from Sherpas. But there are many more common mammals he might encounter, including the musk deer, the Himalayan tahr, the ghoral, the serow, the wolf and the Himalayan black bear. Endangered species sometimes seen include the snow leopard, the red panda, and two dazzling pheasants — the crimson-horned and the impeyan. The lat-

Khumbu's beast of burden: the yak.

ter is Nepal's national bird. Smaller animals like marmots, pikas and martens are also found here.

The Side Trip to Gokyo

Filled with glaciers, turquoise lakes and savage mountain scenery, the Gokyo Valley north of Khumjung offers an exciting excursion from the main Everest base camp trek. The huge massifs of **Cho Oyu** (8,153 meters or 26,748 feet) and **Gyachung Kang** (7,922 meters or 25,991 feet) dominate the head of this rugged canyon. Countless other summits loom to either side. Though sparsely populated, the lower part of the valley shelters several interesting communities occupied by herders every summer.

The easiest route into Gokyo begins at the large *chorten* below Khumjung. After ascending a small pass above Phortse on the opposite canyon wall, the trail plummets down to the Dudh Kosi river, then climbs rapidly again up the west bank through scrub poplar forests to **Dole**. From here, there are dramatic views of sacred Khumbila, as well as of Kang Taiga and Thamserku. Above Dole, the canyon walls fold into a long system of meadows

as the trail climbs through the scattered pastoral hamlets of **Lhabarma**, **Luza**, **Maccherma** and **Pangka**.

The huge terminal moraine of **Ngozumpa Glacier** towers above Pangka. The trail passes it to the west, winding up through talus and detritus to another meadow squeezed between the glacier and the westward peaks. Three large lakes huddle one above the other in this tiny sanctuary. Most trekkers choose to tarry at least one day at the middle one, **Dudh Pokhari**, near the huts of Gokyo (4,750 meters or 15,580 feet) itself.

Above the lake rises an easily climbable peak called **Gokyo Ri** (5,483 meters or 17,984 feet). From here, an entire panorama of summits looms over the great glaciers below. These include Cho Oyu, Gyachung Kang, Pumori, Changtse, Everest, Nuptse, **Makalu** (8,481 feet or 27,825 feet), Ama Dablam, Kang Taiga, Thamserku, Khumbila, Tawoche, **Cholatse** (also called Jobo Lhaptshan, 6,440 meters or 21,128 feet) and more.

The return trek to the main Everest trail follows an alternate route through **Na, Thare** and **Konar** on the precipitous east canyon wall. From the larger village of Phortse it is an easy though occasional-

Himalayan panorama: Everest, left, and Lhotse.

ly precarious walk back to the main trail in Pangboche.

It is also possible to trek from Gokyo over the **Cho La** pass (5,420 meters or 17,782 feet) to **Dzongla**, **Duglha** and Pheriche. This pass requires only basic mountaineering skills, but is subject to the serious weather hazards of any high pass crossing. The route on the east side of the pass skirts magnificent **Tshola Tsho** lake and crosses the moraines beneath the incredible north faces of Cholatse and Tawoche.

The Hongu Basin

Except for the cliffs and summits of the great peaks themselves, it is a rare place in the Nepal Himalaya that can be termed "wilderness." Almost everywhere that goats, yaks or people can walk, there are huts, trails and travelers. The wild and rugged **Hongu Basin** of the Khumbu is an exception.

This huge glacial cirque, approachable only by precipitous high-altitude routes, is seldom explored. Five small lakes, known as **Panch Pokhari**, rest in the heart of the basin, surrounded by tumbling glaciers and great moraines. Overlooking it are the

beautiful summits of Ama Dablam, **Baruntse** (7,220 meters or 23,682 feet), **Hongu South** (6,057 meters or 19,872 feet), Chamlang (7,310 meters or 23,983 feet) and a number of unnamed pyramids of fluted ice, all over 6,000 meters (20,000 feet). **Chamlang** (7,310 meters or 23,983 clumps of grass. It is, indeed, a region fórbidding in appearance.

The elevations around Panch Pokhari are well above 5,000 meters (16,500 feet), too high for long-term human habitation. A trek to the Hongu is a difficult, serious journey and should be attempted only by persons experienced in mountaineering and properly equipped. Helicopter rescues are not possible because of the high elevation and terrain.

One way to approach the Hongu is up the Imja Khola valley east of Dingboche and Pheriche. Beyond the herders' huts of **Chukung**, the path nestles at the foot of the immense **Lhotse Wall**; here it requires careful route-finding along the south side of the valley between the **Imja Glacier** and the foot of **Kang Leom** (6,246 meters or 20,492 feet).

Where the glacier divides south of **Island Peak,** the route bears due south and ascends the steep **Amphu Glacier** to

the **Amphu Labtsa** pass at 5,780 meters (18,963 feet). Portions of this route, especially the very top, usually require technical climbing. The Amphu Labtsa presents spectacular views to both the north and south, including Everest, **Lhotse Shar** (8,383 meters or 27,503) and Lhotse's gigantic south face.

Other Routes to Panch Pokhari

The Hongu Basin side of the pass falls more gradually down to Panch Pokhari. There are excellent campsites where the southwest face of Baruntse towers above the amphitheater. Within the basin itself, there are a number of exploratory possibilities, including several small peaks, a climb of the West Col, and a crossing of the **Hongu Nup Glacier** to the top of the **Mingbo La** pass (5,817 meters or 19,084 feet).

An alternate approach to the Hongu, rather than the avalanche-prone Amphu Labtsa, is via the Mingbo La. This pass is reached from the Everest base camp trail by crossing the Imja Khola at Pangboche and climbing to the high uplands of **Mingbo**, directly beneath the incredible obelisk of Ama Dablam. Here are the re-

mains of an airfield used during Sir Edmund Hillary's Himalayan Scientific and Mountaineering Expedition of 1960-61.

East of Mingbo is a moraine and a small glacier leading to steel flutings beneath the Mingbo La. Several hundred feet of steep but straight-forward ice climbing gain the top of the pass. Panch Pokhari can be reached by a long descent eastward down the Hongu Nup glacier.

The Hongu Basin can be entered from the south by the high but gentle **Mera La** pass (5,415 meters or 17,766 feet). This pass is usually approached from Lukla by crossing a 4,943-meter (16,217 foot) ridge and continuing up the beautiful **Hinku Khola** river to the base of the Mera La.

The only way to enter the Hongu without crossing an excessively high pass is via the **Kemba La** (3,913 meters or 12,838 feet), a pass at the very southern end of the Chamlang Massif on the east rim of the Hongu Gorge. The Kemba La can be reached in several days from Lukla via the Sherpa village of **Pangkongma** and the Rai community of **Chemsing**. The pass can also be gained from the **Arun River** by an obscure and difficult route.

From the Kemba La, the route generally follows the **Kal Pokhari Danda** ridge

Tshola Tsho in the Khumbu Himal.

252

directly north to about 4,500 meters (15,000 feet), then descends gradually to the edge of the impassable Hongu Gorge. The route then climbs through thick bamboo and rhododendron forest to emerge finally at the grazing meadows of **Urpa** at the southern end of the Hongu Basin.

The Mysterious Rolwaling Valley

A few miles south of the Tibetan frontier, on the east side of the jungled banks of the Bhote Kosi, is an enormous rock precipice. From a narrow defile in the wall, perhaps only 10 meters (33 feet) wide and appearing as if split with a giant axe, there issues a raging torrent, its source hidden somewhere thousands upon thousands of feet above, lost among the great peaks and the mists surrounding them.

This is the **Rolwaling Khola**, the source of the Rolwaling Valley, one of the most remote and beautiful areas in all Nepal.

The Rolwaling, literally "The Furrow" in the Sherpa language, has always held a mysterious fascination. Not only is it wild and little known; it is here that repeated tales of the yeti, the elusive "Abominable Snowman," have poured from the mouths of the handful of Sherpas living and working in the valley's confines.

In 1951, British mountaineer Eric Shipton observed and photographed a yeti track on the upper **Menlung Glacier**, a section of the Rolwaling that is now Tibet. In 1960, Hillary led an expedition into the Rolwaling whose object was, in part, to search for the yeti. Results were inconclusive, but a number of scientists are convinced that the yeti does exist. (See feature article on The Yeti.)

The only easy way to enter the Rolwaling is from the west, through the village of **Simigaon**. Populated mostly by Sherpas and Tamangs, with a smattering of Brahmins, Thakuris, Gurungs and Kamis, this hamlet is perched above a line of cliffs which drop vertically to the Bhote Kosi. The cliffs themselves are covered with vegetation and are usually frequented by hoards of long-tailed gray langurs.

Above Simigaon, the trail climbs steeply up the **Sambur Danda** to a pass at the foot of the Mahalangur Himal, a rocky mass of peaks south of the Rolwaling. From this pass is an astonishing view of **Gauri Shankar** (7,145 meters or 23,442 feet), the Rolwaling's most famous peak. From the depths of the gorge below, a

Crossing Mera La on the way to Hongu.

series of cliffs and jumbled rock escarpments sweep upwards into knife-edged and corniced ice ridges which finally merge at Gauri Shankar's double summit.

So prominent is Gauri Shankar from Kathmandu and the Ganges Plain to the south that local legends long claimed it to be the highest mountain in the world. Its frightening appearance from most angles led to its taking on great significance in both the Hindu and Buddhist religions. To Hindus, the north summit represents the god Shiva, the south summits his consort Gauri. The Buddhist Sherpas of Rolwaling call the mountain "Jomo Tsheringma" and consider it holy, as do Sherpas throughout the region. Gauri Shankar resisted all mountaineering attempts until 1979, when its west face was finally scaled by a joint Nepalese-American expedition. A Sherpa who had been born in its shadow on a ridge north of Jiri was one of the two men to reach the summit.

The Sherpa village of **Beding** is the only settlement in the upper Rolwaling. It is a small village of perhaps 200 families living in stone houses with carved and painted trim. There is a small monastery here, and 150 meters above is a hermitage set in a cliff. Here the mystic Tantric saint, Guru Padma Sambhava, is said to have meditated 2,000 years ago.

Above Beding, the river dwindles to a stream and the gorge narrows. The forests give way to shrubs, which soon yield to rocks and scrub grass. Along the trail are *mani* walls and huge rocks carved with Buddhist prayers. Further east, where the valley broadens, is the summer settlement of **Na**, used by yak herders but abandoned at the first snow. Above is a stark moraine and a confusing tangle of ice peaks, obscure and little-used passes. Along the ridge just to the north is the Tibetan border.

The Panorama Above Na

Beyond Na to the east rises **Chobutse** (6,660 meters or 21,850 feet), a beautiful fluted-ice peak. Just south of Na there are reasonable climbing possibilities on smaller peaks — surprisingly, perhaps, given the precipitous nature of the Rolwaling.

One of the more enjoyable routes is on **Ramdung** (5,928 meters of 19,249 feet), recently opened for non-expeditionary climbs. Although the peak is technically easy and may be done in one or two days

Gauri Shankar from the Bhote Kosi.

254

from Na, any Himalayan ascent is a serious matter and no climb should taken lightly or without careful preparation. A magnificent panorama is seen from this summit, especially north up the **Ripimo Shar** and **Drolambao** glaciers descending from Tibet, and to the ice peaks of Bigphera-go Shar, Bigphera-go Nup and Tengi Ragi Tau.

Adjacent to Ramdung are several rugged passes which, though subject to avalanches most of the year, can be safely crossed in summer. These tracks lead south through a complex maze of rock escarpments to the **Khare Khola** and eventually west to meet the Bhote Kosi at the village of **Suri Dhoban.** From here, the hamlets of **Barabise** or **Jiri** can be reached in a few days.

East of Na, the country takes on the stark, silent beauty of gray moraine and ice. The grass is left for dust and boulders beneath the **Tashi Lapcha** pass. Two miles from Na is the **Tsho Rolpa**, a large glacial lake at the snout of the **Trakarding Glacier**, dammed by the terminal moraine of the Ripimo Shar glacier. During much of the year the lake is frozen, and the groaning of the moving ice in the remote silence echoes menacingly from the mountain walls on both sides of the valley.

The crossing of the 5,753-meter (18,875-foot) Tashi Lapcha to the Khumbu is demanding. Although the pass is not technical, crampons and ice axes are useful for all and a necessity for some. The crossing is extremely rugged, and the position and elevation of the pass make it subject to vicious storms. On the steep Rolwaling side, there are occasional dangerous rock falls, and climbers must be especially cautious.

It is prudent to begin the ascent of the Tashi Lapcha from a high camp above the Tsho Rolpa as early in the day as possible. This allows you to cross the moraines and the crevassed glacier at the foot of the pass before surface melting and the loosening of rocks begins. **Pharchamo** (6,272 meters of 20,575 feet), an easy but beautiful peak to the south, can be climbed in three to four hours from the pass.

From the top of the Tashi Lapcha, there are fantastic views of the huge peaks of the Khumbu and Rolwaling, the highest on earth. Here can be felt the enormity and impact of the great mountain wilderness that is the Himalaya.

Tibet's Menlungtse from the Rolwaling Valley.

Towns and Tigers of the Terai

At 7:30 every morning, the shrill hoot of a siren at the nearby distillery sends the 15,000-odd inhabitants of Bhairawa to work. Already the smell of the smoking chimney is overwhelming. From the surrounding countryside, long files of bullock carts full of sugar cane are converging on the mill in trails of brown dust. All around them stretches a patchwork of rice fields, dotted here and there with clumps of bamboo or huge, placid banyan and pipal trees sheltering a few huts with thatched roofs.

This is February, and the earth of the fields is cracked and dry. In a month or so, the torrid desert wind that the Indians call *loo* will raise temperatures to 50°C (112°F) until the monsoon rains arrive in late June. Then swollen torrents tumbling down the Himalaya will join forces, rush through the heavily deforested hills, and rage through the northern edge of the Terai — flooding crops, tearing away whole chunks of road, uprooting huts.

But here, at the edge of the vast Ganges plain, the alluvial soil is rich and bountiful. In some areas, peasants manage up to three crops a year — rice, wheat, jute, tobacco, and a variety of beans and lentils. Generally, however, farmers are content with a single annual harvest.

An occasional *topi*, the formal Nepali hat, on a *dhoti*-clad passer-by reminds you that this *is* Nepal, even if the Indian border post is only two kilometers south.

Pilgrimage to Sita's Janakpur

Bhairawa is typical of the main towns of the Terai belt. Like **Nepalganj** to the west and **Birgunj**, **Janakpur** and **Biratnagar** to the east, Bhairawa's fortunes are built on the trade filtering between Nepal and India. Each of these towns consists of a collection of ramshackle concrete and wooden houses, a few factories, and a handful of rundown hotels. Their streets are left to fleets of often idle rickshaws.

Soon a major thoroughfare, the East-West Highway, will link all these lowland towns and provide a continuity to Nepal's Terai settlements. The eastern end of the highway has been completed, but in the west Terai, although towns are linked by road with India, they are connected only by rough tracks or air within Nepal.

The Terai's largest town is Biratnagar

Preceding pages: a Royal Chitwan tiger; below, the Buddha's Lumbini birthplace.

on Nepal's southeastern frontier. Its population is about 90,000. It is notable for a major sugar refinery and a nearby hydro-electric project.

Far more interesting, however, is Janakpur, 128 kilometers (80 miles) southeast of Kathmandu and about the same distance west of Biratnagar. Hindu legend holds that in the mythical past, Janakpur was the capital of ancient Mithila and the birthplace of Sita, consort of Rama, hero of the *Ramayana*. Today, the **Janaki Temple** in the center of the town is dedicated to Sita, and is a site of pilgrimage for Hindus from all over the subcontinent. Built by a queen of Tikamagarh in 1910, the marble edifice is a replica of 17th Century Moghul architecture.

Within the eight-kilometer (five-mile) brick-paved ring road that encloses the town of Janakpur are 24 large tanks, 21 ponds and numerous Hindu shrines. These give credence to the claim that this was a well-planned city and once a major center of learning. There are numerous religious fairs and festivals here, and market days are held twice a week.

Birthplace of the Buddha

It is not only Hindus who find pilgrimage sites in the Terai. Buddhists find it important as well: 21 kilometers (13 miles) west of Bhairawa via a recently improved road is **Lumbini**, where the Gautama Buddha himself was born over 2,500 years ago.

Located some 250 kilometers (155 miles) west of Kathmandu, Lumbini rests on the plains of Kapilvastu. In the 6th Century B.C., when the Buddha lived, a confederacy of Sakya clan people was situated here. There are numerous buildings of religious significance in Lumbini, the most important of which is a massive stone pillar erected by the Mauryan Emperor Ashoka in 250 B.C. It was discovered only in 1895.

Nearby is the shrine of **Maya Devi**, undergoing a restoration. Said to be located at the exact place where the Buddha was born in a palace garden, it contains a stone relief depicting Gautama's nativity scene. There is also a rectangular pond said to be the remains of a sacred pool; the brick foundations of a ruined monastery; some small votive stupas; and several large plinths. In the area are modern Buddhist shrines and an older

Lamaist *gompa*.

About 27 kilometers (17 miles) west of Lumbini is **Tilaurakot**. Archaeologists have established this as the actual capital of Kapilvastu and the home of King Suddhodhan, father of Siddhartha Gautama, the Buddha. Chinese travelers who visited this place 2,500 years ago reported seeing numerous stupas, monasteries and palaces.

Marshes and Jungles

The higher part of the Terai belt, on either side of the first pre-Himalayan hills (known as the Siwalik Hills or the Churia Range), is an expanse of marshes, thick jungles and tropical forests slowly eaten away by logging and cropping. For a very long time, it was an unhealthy, dangerous, impassable zone. The abutment of hills — and even moreso, the scourge of malaria and the wild beasts roaming this region — provided an effective southern barrier against potential invaders.

Today, things have changed. Highways and air travel have made the hills less imposing. Malaria has been controlled with modern medicine. And the wild beasts, if much fewer in number than centuries ago,

Tharu girls bound for the village well.

are the Terai's No. 1 visitor attraction.

Those sections of the Terai not already cultivated have been secured by Nepal's parks department. Indeed, the preserves of the Terai constitute by far the richest wildlife zone of Nepal, and one of the best natural areas in Asia. Once the private hunting grounds of Nepal's ruling families and their guests, these areas were the sites of royal tiger and rhinoceros hunts organized every few years, with hundreds of elephants bearing the royalty of Europe and India.

Tiger Tops and Rhino Horns

Nepal's best-known and most accessible national park, **Royal Chitwan**, was also its first. Established in 1962 by the late King Mahendra as a rhinoceros preserve, and officially gazetted in 1973 to enforce laws against poaching, it is situated in the Rapti Valley about 120 kilometers (75 miles) southwest of Kathmandu. It covers an area of 932 square kilometers (360 square miles) of floodplain jungle and elephant grass at an elevation of about 150 meters (492 feet) above sea level.

In the heart of Royal Chitwan is the rustic **Tiger Tops Jungle Lodge**.

Elephants greet those who fly into Meghauli airstrip and carry them to their accommodation. Trained naturalists lead visitors on safaris (by foot, elephant, Land Rover or boat) to search for tigers, rhinos, crocodiles, and colorful bird life.

The Bengal tiger and the great one-horned rhino, both of them endangered species, are the "stars of the show" at Tiger Tops.

It is estimated that the tiger population of the entire Indian subcontinent has dwindled from 40,000 to a little over 2,000 in the past 50 years. About 200 tigers live in Nepal, and of those, about 40 are within the precincts of Royal Chitwan.

The tiger by nature is a solitary, shy animal. By night it hunts, and by day it hides in thick undergrowth to avoid disturbances. Tiger Tops visitors consider themselves fortunate to spot one of these big cats in the dawn or twilight hours.

There are only about 1,000 great one-horned rhinos left in existence. Many of them live in Indian Assam; an estimated 300 are resident in Royal Chitwan's tall-grass swamplands. As with the tiger, widespread cultivation of Terai grasslands by immigrant hill people in the 1950s

Boarding elephants at Tiger Tops, left, to search for rhinos, right.

shrank the animal's habitat and led it to the brink of extinction.

Another rare animal is the gharial, a fish-eating crocodile. A breeding center has been established near park headquarters to ensure its survival.

There are other animals in Royal Chitwan that visitors are likely to see. These include leopards, gaurs, buffaloes, sloth bears, wild boars, various species of deer, and marsh mugger crocodiles. Smaller mammals include langur and rhesus monkeys, jungle and civet cats, mongooses, jackals, otters, martens, porcupines and squirrels. River dwellers include the Gangetic dolphin. Other species are the pangolin, rattel, python, king cobra and Bengal florican. More than 400 species of birds have been identified, making Chitwan a paradise for bird-watchers.

Tiger Tops is a half-hour flight or a six-hour drive from Kathmandu. Alternately, it is three days by river through the Himalayan foothills. Accommodation is at the lodge on the Reu River, in a tented camp on an island in the Narayani River, or — for those preferring cultural experience to nature study — in a village of Tharu people on the edge of the park.

There are various more modest camps in Royal Chitwan. At **Saurah**, six hours by bus from Kathmandu via Bharatpur, are located the majority of these. Best known are **Gaida Camp**, **Hotel Elephant Camp** and **Jungle Safari Camp**.

Scattered east and west of Royal Chitwan, all along Nepal's Terai frontier, are other government wildlife reserves. The **Koshi Tappu** reserve, in the Koshi flood plain of the eastern Terai, is home to a rare herd of 65 wild buffaloes and thousands of migratory birds. The **Royal Suklaphanta** reserve in the southwest, on the Mahakali River plain, was established as a grassland reserve for 1,500 endangered swamp deer.

The **Royal Bardia** reserve, also in the west, comprises 368 square kilometers (142 square miles) of riverine terrain at the foot of the *sal*-forested Siwalik Hills. Thirty-two species of mammals, including Nepal's second largest tiger population, and 250 varieties of birds are found here.

Tiger Tops is pioneering tourism in Royal Bardia, and plans to open a tented camp for wildlife viewing and sport-fishing the noted *masheer* in the great Karnali River.

A LAND OF FESTIVALS

There are few places so designed for festivals as Nepal. Here in the shadow of the mountain gods, celebrations are so frequent that they often overlap each other. There are more than 50 such occasions a year, with as many as 120 days set aside to celebrate.

Thousands of gods and goddesses, demons and ogres, restless spirits and the family dead must be appeased and remembered. The various seasons must be honored, and there are appropriate rites for the blessing of seeds to be planted and of crops newly harvested. As the lunar calendar dictates, the gaiety of processions and the somber symbolism of incense find their way into the peoples' lives.

Some of Nepal's festivals are ancient indeed, having their origins in animism or legend. Others are more recent, the direct result of a monarch's command. The majority are tied to one or both of the two great religions of the land, Hinduism and Buddhism. Devotees of one religion take part in the others' festivals, adapting some of the rites of the other faith to their own festivals. Collective fun, a sense of accomplishment, and communion with the gods are of the essence.

The major festivals of the Nepalese year are discussed in this section. For a full listing, see the Guide in Brief.

The New Year

The Nepalese mark their New Year on the first day of the month of *Baisakh*, normally in mid-April by the Western calendar. At this time, Tamang hill people come by the thousands to light lamps in honor of their dead at the two great Buddhist stupas of Bodhnath and Swayambhunath. Vast throngs bathe at the fountains of Balaju, below the sacred Buddhist hill of Jamacho, for this is thought to be the most important time for ritual bathing.

At Bhaktapur is held one of the most exciting of all major festivals in the Valley, the week-long **Bisket** festival. Ceremonies start around dusk in the Taumadhi Tole in front of the Nyatapola Temple. A large four-wheeled chariot containing the deities Bhairav and Bhadrakali becomes the prize of a mammoth tug-of-war between the eastern and western halves of the town. The winning side is entitled to play host to the divinities for the next seven

Preceding pages, New Year procession at Thimi; left, carrying the Bisket chariot through Bhaktapur; and right, Tibetan dancers.

days. The deities are paraded throughout Bhaktapur and down a steep, twisting passage to the banks of the Hanumante River, where an enormous pole is raised — and the next day felled to signify the beginning of the new year.

Legend tells of an insatiable princess of Bhaktapur who demanded a new lover each night, for every morning, her prior night's lover was found dead in her bedroom. With the number of eligible men waning, a cunning royal prince offered himself to the lady. After a torrid session of lovemaking, the princess fell

asleep, and the prince hid in a corner of her room. Soon two venomous serpents emerged from the sleeping lady's nostrils. The prince drew his sword and severed their heads. The following morning, the city rejoiced to find the prince alive and the princess in love. This festival is the result of their joy. The pole erected is symbolic of *lingum*, or phallus; two banners hung from it represent the snakes.

Another New Year's celebration, known as **Balkumari Jatra**, is held in Thimi, a village between Bhaktapur and Tribhuvan Airport. Amid torch-lit processions, celebrants sprinkle one another with ochre powder in honor of the goddess Balkumari, one of Bhairav's consorts.

Homage is also paid to Ganesh.

Patan sees one of its biggest annual festivals in late April, the **Rato Machhendranath Jatra**. A chariot festival similar to Kathmandu's Rath festival of a month previous, this features a much larger chariot and takes a month to complete. The Rato (or red) Machhendra, considered by some to be the same god as the Seto (white) Machhendra of Kathmandu, is patron deity of the Kathmandu Valley and is equally venerated by Hindus and Buddhists.

The festival begins in Pulchok, where the chariot is built. For about a month, it wends its way through the streets of Patan. Because of its immense size, members of the Nepalese army are called upon to assist in pulling it. The festival culminates at Jawalkhel when a be-

jeweled tunic, supposedly belonging to the serpent king, is publicly displayed on an auspicious day in front of the King. The festival is designed to ensure a satisfactory monsoon rainfall for the rice crop in the paddy fields.

The Rato Machhendra deity is shared by Patan with the neighboring village of Bungamati, and spends three months of every year in a temple there. Every twelfth year, the huge Machhendra chariot must be pulled all the way from Patan to Bungamati, a distance of about six kilometers (four miles) over a dirt road that is hilly and far from smooth. It is a major undertaking, and progress is slow, punctuated with ritual, prayers and offerings.

The epic love of a king for his queen is remembered at **Gaijatra**, the festival of cows held in and around the Durbar Squares of Kathmandu, Patan and Bhaktapur during *Bhadra* (August-September). An eight-day carnival, it starts the day after Janai Purnima and honors those who have died during the past year. Dances and music accompany the frolicking of children who disguise themselves as cows and grotesque figures.

Legend tells of a queen who was inconsolable after the death of her most dearly loved son. The king ordered every family which had lost a member during the past year to drive cows through the street, so the queen could see she was not alone in her suffering. When this failed to move the queen, the king offered a reward to anyone who could make her laugh. As fantastic costumes and satire blossomed in the streets, the queen finally smiled. Thereafter, the king ordered an annual festival. Bereaved families still parade their decorated cows, bovine or human, through the streets in bursts of color and sound.

Eight Days for Indra

The most spectacular of all Valley festivals is the eight-day **Indrajatra**, celebrated at the beginning of September by Hindus and Buddhists alike.

Legend holds that Indra, the lord of heaven and god of rain, once came to steal flowers from a garden in the Valley. Unrecognized, he was caught and kept captive as a common thief, while his mount — the sacred elephant — searched the streets of Kathmandu for days and nights, looking for its master. In time, Indra's distraught mother descended from heaven to reveal her son's and her own identity. She granted two boons, taking with her to heaven the souls of all those who had died in the past year, and promising heavy dew and morning mists to ripen the autumn and winter harvests. This was a cause for great rejoicing and feasting among the people of the Valley, who proclaimed a festival.

Today, the festival begins with the torchlight dance of Indra's elephant, now a clothed and human-legged beast who prances through the streets. On the first day, a long pole is erected close to Hanuman Dhoka to propitiate Indra, and masked dancers stage a colorful display of classical dancing.

On the third day, the Kumari, or living goddess, is paid homage by the entire Valley, including the King — himself regarded as an in-

Newar priest, left, and drummers, right, are an integral part of most festivals: where there is religion, there is often music.

carnation of the god Vishnu. The Kumari (see Kathmandu city chapter) is seen to exemplify the harmony of Hinduism and Buddhism in Nepal. Chosen from the Buddhist Sakya clan of goldsmiths, she represents the royal Hindu goddess Taleju Bhawani, and is selected for 32 mystic virtues and a horoscope which exactly complements that of the King. On this day, she emerges from her home painted like a hummingbird, and is carried through the streets in a special chariot, accompanied by her attendants, Ganesh and Bhairav, represented by two young boys.

Along with Indra and the Kumari, the god Bhairav is honored during this festival. Innumerable masks of Bhairav are exhibited everywhere, including a gold mask exposed to

residence, and every person is expected to take ritual dawn baths at special sacred *ghats*.

On the first day of the festival, Brahmins plant barley seeds which will be distributed on the last day. On the fifth day, there are kite competitions. On the seventh day, known as Phulpati, offerings of flowers and leaves are made to Durga. The eighth day is Armed Forces Day; there are military parades at the Tundhikhel parade ground and a procession from Hanuman Dhoka to Trichandra College, in front of the clock tower.

Animal sacrifices highlight events of the ninth day. They are especially notable around the Taleju Chowk. Every household and institution offers buffaloes, male goats, ducks and fowl to the demanding goddess Durga. Im-

the public only on this one annual occasion. At certain times of the day, beer pours forth from its mouth through a spout; local revelers cheerfully battle for a drink. In the beer is a fish, and he who gets it is particularly blessed.

Festival of Dasain

The festival of **Dasain**, also known as **Durga Puja**, is held throughout Nepal. For 10 days of intense, sacrificial and joyous worship in mid-September, it celebrates fertility and the victory of good over evil, as represented by the goddess Durga Bhawani and the various gods who battle demons. Every house becomes a shrine in which the goddess is asked to take up

ages, shrines and temples are bathed in blood.

The final day of Dasain, known as Vijaya Dashami, sees the opening of the Royal Palace to one and all. Even the most poverty-stricken subject may receive a *tika* from the hands of the King or Queen. A *phulpati*, or votive offering of flowers and leaves, carried by runners from Gorkha, the ancestral home of the Shah kings of Nepal, is received by the King as a royal salute booms out over the land.

Maha Shivaratri

Also colorful is **Maha Shivaratri**, observed during *Falgun* (February-March) in all temples dedicated to Shiva, the Hindu god of destruction and rebirth. It is the greatest festival of the year at Pashupatinath, regarded as one of Shiva's holiest abodes. Thousands of pilgrims converge on the temple, many having walked all the way from India, to make reverent offerings and take ritual baths. Ablutions are also made to Lord Pashupati, the protector of animals and guardian of the Kathmandu Valley.

This Nepalese "Benares" is most impressive. Tousled Indian *sadhus* are conspicuous, many of them performing feats of yoga on the *ghats* by the river. Pilgrims keep votive oil lamps burning all night along the banks of the Bagmati as they sing and beat drums until dawn.

Elsewhere in the Valley, children burn bonfires at key crossroads to ward off evil spirits. At the Tundhikhel parade ground, the Royal

Nepalese Army stages a military display with an impressive volley of gunfire witnessed by the King.

The Festival of Lights

Tihar, also known as **Diwali** or the **Festival of Lights,** is held in late October throughout the Indian subcontinent to honor animals over a five-day period. On the first day, crows — the "messengers of death" sent by Yama, lord of the underworld — are fed rice. On the second day, dogs — who guide souls across the river of the dead — are honored with garlands of flowers and *tikas*. Cows are praised on the third day, bulls on the fourth.

Lakshmi, the goddess of wealth, is believed to visit every home which has been suitably lit and decorated on the evening of the third day, to ensure prosperity throughout the year.

The fourth day, Moh Puja, coincides with the Newari New Year, so there is a great deal of ceremonial feasting.

Tibetan Rites

One of the most beautiful festivals is held on **Tibetan New Year** in February, below the towering gold spire of the great white stupa of Bodhnath. Processions of colorfully clad *lamas*, carrying banners and a portrait of the Dalai Lama under a brocade ceremonial umbrella, snake through throngs of Tibetan people from the distant mountains. There is one moment when everyone present throws a fistful of flour in the air to the chant of "Sho, sho." As evening falls, the monasteries surrounding the stupa blaze with votive oil lamps.

The week-long **Festival of Color**, known as **Holi**, is a frolicking, joyous occasion. On the first day, a three-tiered umbrella is erected in front of the throne room at Basantapur Tower in Kathmandu, amidst the sprinkling of colored powder and water. The umbrella is burned on the eighth day, which precedes the full moon.

Dedicated to Krishna and Vishnu, the festival is a variation on the annual water festivals held elsewhere in Buddhist Asia. Throughout the week, every person is a target of young people who throw multicolored powder and water balloons.

The separate festivals of **Chaitra Dasain** and **Seto Machhendranath** occur simultaneously in the third week of March. Ritual offerings are made to Durga at midday on Chaitra Dasain, exactly six months before an equivalent day during the festival of Dasain. These offerings also mark the start of Kathmandu's four-day **Rath** festival.

The Seto Machhendra image is taken from its shrine near Asan Tole and is placed in a towering chariot. Hundreds of young boys tow the vehicle, which stands on wheels 1.8 meters (six feet) in diameter, through the streets of Kathmandu in the early evening hours for four days. The chariot's size dwarfs the buildings it passes. Each night, it stops at specific places; residents of the locality workship and care for the image. On the final day, the chariot is dragged around a tree in Lagan Khel. Then Machhendra is transported back to his temple on a small palanquin.

A Shiva devotee during Shivaratri, left; and the Machhendra chariot in Patan, right. Following pages, a visiting *sadhu* at Pashupatinath.

HAVILDAR MAJOR, GURKHA RIFLES

BRAVEST OF THE BRAVE

As I write these last words, my thoughts return to you who are my comrades, the stubborn and indomitable peasants of Nepal. Once more I hear the laughter with which you greeted every hardship. Once more I see you in your bivouacs or about your fires, on forced march or in the trenches, now shivering with wet and cold, now scorched by a pitiless and burning sun. Uncomplaining you endure hunger and thirst and wounds; and at the last your unwavering lines disappear into the smoke and wrath of battle. Bravest of the brave, most generous of the generous, never had country more faithful friends than you.

— Bishop Stortford, 1930, as quoted in the introduction to Ralph Lilley Turner's Nepali Dictionary

Rare is the person today who has not heard of the Gurkha soldiers, the brave troops from Nepal's isolated hills who bolster the forces of the British and Indian armies.

Famed for their tenacity and loyalty in warfare since the late 18th Century, these *khukri*-wielding soldiers underscored their fame by playing a key role in the 1982 Falkland Islands (Islas Malvinas) crisis.

The original Gurkha troops were Gorkhalis from Gorkha, the small principality in central Nepal from which Prithvi Narayan Shah conquered the Kathmandu Valley in 1768 and unified the land of Nepal. Composed largely of Thakuri, Magar and Gurung men, these forces by 1814 had swept their long curved *khukris* across the central Himalaya.

The first two regular Gorkhali battalions were raised in 1763. Known as the Sri Nath and the Purano Gorakh, they fought together against the British in 1768, and saw separate action against Tibet and in the Anglo-Nepal war of 1814-16. It was the Anglo-Nepal war that first thrust the legend of Gurkha bravery into Western minds.

Impressed by what they had seen, the British East India Company began recruiting Gurkhas into their service. Gurkha recruitment was not formalized by the British until 1886, but by that time, India already had eight Gurkha Rifles units. Most of the men were drawn from the Magar and Gurung tribes, but others came from the Rais, Limbus and Sunuwars of the eastern hills and from the Khasas of the west.

At first, given their past hostilities, the relationship between the British and Nepalis was uneasy. By the time of the emergence of the Rana regime in 1846, and the subsequent visit to England of Jung Bahadur Rana, there was no question of the Gurkhas' allegiance. During the Indian mutiny of 1857, the British Gurkha regiments were joined by 12,000 of Jung Bahadur's own troops, with decisive results.

Over the next 50 years, the Gurkhas fought all over south Asia, from Afghanistan to Malaya, and even as far afield as African Somaliland in 1903. And when they weren't fighting, they were climbing mountains. Long before the Sherpas had achieved fame as porters and mountaineers, Gurkhas were climbing many western Himalayan peaks.

In the Alps of Europe in 1894, a pair of Gurkhas named Amar Singh Thapa and Karbir Burathoki traveled 1,600 kilometers (1,000 miles) in 86 days, crossing 39 passes and 21 peaks. They named a Swiss peak Piz Gurkha after being the first to scale its 3,063 meters (10,049 feet); a nearby col was named Gurkha Pass. In 1907, Burathoki and Englishman Tom Longstaff accomplished the first major ascent of a Himalayan peak, Trisul (7,120 meters or 23,360 feet). Gurkhas were involved in five Everest expeditions between 1921 and 1937.

The World Wars

But war beckoned the Gurkhas to new destinations. With the advent of the First World War, they were called on in even greater numbers. More than 114,000 Gurkhas were called into active service in Givenchy, Ypres, Gallipoli, Palestine, Mesopotamia, Suez, Persia and Waziristan. Another 200,000 men were mobilized in the Indian army. Two Gurkhas — Kulbir Thapa (France, 1915) and Karna Bahadur Rana (Palestine, 1918) were awarded the Victoria Cross for their gallantry.

In the Second World War, Gurkha strength was expanded to 45 battalions. Soldiers saw action in Iraq, Persia, Cyprus, Tunisia, Italy, Greece, Burma, Malaya and Indonesia; 10 Victoria crosses were awarded. Two of the battalions were paratroopers.

As the tale is told today, the British were seeking volunteers in a Gurkha regiment for a risky 1,000-foot airdrop behind enemy lines. About half of the troops stepped forward. The regiment leader proceeded to explain the troops' role in the drop, when a surprised voice queried: "Oh, you mean we can use parachutes?" Every remaining Gurkha promptly volunteered.

Two years after the Second World War ended, with the granting of independence to India, the Gurkha regiments were divided. Six of the 10 regiments became the Indian Gurkha Rifles; the remaining four — the 2nd, 6th, 7th and 10th — remaining the British Brigade of Gurkhas. In India, the troops plunged immediately into the India-Pakistan conflict over Kashmir; later came the Sino-Indian war of 1962 and further battles between India and Pakistan in 1965 and 1971.

The British Brigade served in Malaya, Indonesia, Brunei and Cyprus. Another Victoria cross, the 13th awarded to a Gurkha soldier, was presented to Lance Corporal Rambahadur

in fact, earns more. Gurkha salaries, pensions and related services provide about US$15 million a year for Nepal.

Gurkhas today man posts in Hong Kong, Singapore, Brunei and Belize in Central America. But it was the South Atlantic skirmish between Britain and Argentina that brought them back into the public eye.

Perhaps the Gurkhas' ire was raised by the Argentine press, which belittled them as a cross between dwarfs and mountain goats. Perhaps the long sea voyage from the British Isles made them anxious to expend extra energy ashore: Gurkhas are notoriously bad sailors, and rely heavily on seasickness pills for travel between ports. Or perhaps the curry-and-rice diet which provides their daily sustenance gave

Limbu for heroism in the face of overwhelming odds in Sarawak in 1965.

Gurkha soldiers are recruited as teenagers of 17 or 18 from their villages. There are recruiting depots at Pokhara in west central Nepal and at Dharan in the east. Strict medical tests limit enlistment; those who succeed are provided with uniforms and good food, and are flown to Hong Kong for 10 months of schooling and basic training. Then they have their first home leave, and their villages invariably treat them as heroes.

Many Nepalese spend their entire working careers in the Gurkhas. It is a position of great status, and an important earner of foreign exchange for the country of Nepal. Only tourism,

them an emotional lift. Whichever, their action in the Falklands added another chapter to their legend.

Argentine troops guarding Port Stanley may have heard rumors about *khukri* decapitations of troops opposing the Gurkhas in other campaigns. For as the Gurkhas advanced on Argentine positions, the South American troops "turned and fled," according to a British newspaper report. The British Broadcasting Corporation reported that "the Argentines dropped their rifles and abandoned mortars and machine guns."

A platoon of the 3rd Gurkhas in Waziristan in 1919, above. Of their weapons, right, the best known as the deadly *khukri* (top).

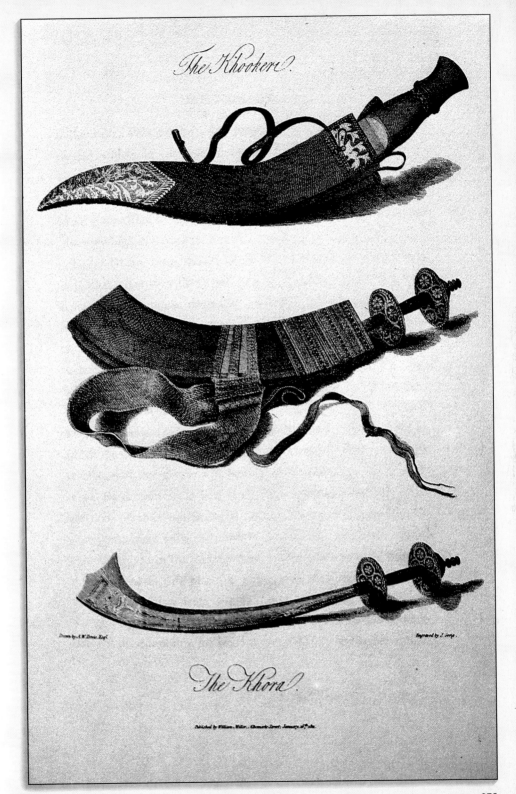

The Khookeri.

The Khora.

MAN AGAINST THE MOUNTAINS

We never achieve mastery over the mountains; the mountains are never conquered; they will always remain and sometimes they will take away our friends if not ourselves. The climbing game is a folly, taken more or less seriously, an indulgence in an activity which is of no demonstrable benefit to anyone. It used to be that mountaineers sought to give credence to their wish to climb mountains by concealing their aims behind a shield of scientific research. But no more. It is now accepted, though not understood, that people are going to climb for its own sake.
— *Joe Tasker,* Everest the Cruel Way, *1981*

Joe Tasker was a prophet. In that sense, perhaps many mountaineers are. He and his fellow British climbing mate Peter Boardman were killed on the northeast ridge of Mount Everest in May 1982.

They were not the first to die in the Himalaya, nor will they be the last. For as long as the remote, silent, majestic mountains tower into the heavens, there will be men who seek to climb them.

Eight of the world's 10 highest mountains are entirely within Nepal or fall on its borders with Tibet and India. A plethora of "lesser" peaks, most of them thousands of feet higher than any of the summits of Europe, Africa or the Americas, march range upon range across the northern reaches of this small nation.

Until 1949, Nepal's mountains were unapproachable for foreign climbers. Up to that time, the Nepalese government had a stringently enforced policy of excluding aliens, and Nepalis were not interested in scaling the peaks. So it has only been in the most recent decades that Nepal's Himalaya have been explored and many of the summits successfully climbed.

Even today, foreign mountaineers are not free to go off and climb any peak they choose. The Nepalese government regulates which mountains may be assaulted, when they may be climbed, by whom and by which climbing routes. Formal permission must be obtained from the proper authorities, and climbers must provide specified wages and equipment for Nepalis who assist them. At present, 122 Nepalese peaks are open to foreign alpinists.

Mountaineering History

A few explorer-climbers began coming to Nepal in 1949 and the early 1950s. The noted British mountain explorers H.W. Tilman and Eric Shipton penetrated unknown terrain in central Nepal and the Everest area. At the same time, a French party led by Maurice Herzog sought approaches to the 8,000-meter summits of Dhaulagiri and Annapurna. Herzog and climbing partner Louis Lachenal became the first men to scale any 8,000-meter peak

Preceding pages, Sir Edmund Hillary (left) and Reinhold Messner. At left, Mount Everest; and right, Tenzing Norgay Sherpa at the summit (1953).

CLIMBING TO THE ROOF OF THE WORLD

The massive rock of Mount Everest, 8,848 meters (29,028 feet) above sea level, bestrides Nepal's northern border with the Tibet Autonomous Region of China. It is named Everest after a British surveyor-general in late 19th Century India, George Everest. The Nepalese know it as Sagarmatha, and the Tibetans as Chomolungma.

A total of 191 persons — 185 men and six women — had attained its summit by all routes (from both the Nepal and Tibet sides) by December 1986. From the Nepalese side alone, 160 persons — 156 men and four women — from 22 nations had gone to the summit on a total of 34 expeditions. Another 35 expeditions were unsuccessful on this side of the giant mountain.

Important firsts in man's struggle to conquer Everest:

1922 — The first attempt to climb the mountain was made by Britons from the Chinese side. Seven Sherpas from India died in an avalanche, the first fatalities recorded on Everest.

1953 — Edmund Hillary of New Zealand and Tenzing Norgay Sherpa of India became the first mountaineers to reach the summit, climbing via the southeast ridge.

1963 — Two Americans, Willi Unsoeld and Tom Horbein, became the first climbers to ascend by one route (the west ridge and north face) and descend by another (the southeast ridge).

1965 — Nawang Gombu Sherpa of India became the first person to scale Everest twice, both times (in 1963 and 1965) by the southeast ridge.

1970 — Yuiichi Miura of Japan became the first person to descend a large part of Everest on skis.

1975 — Mrs. Junko Tabei of Japan became the first woman to reach the summit of Everest.

1978 — Everest was first scaled without the use of artificial oxygen by Reinhold Messner of Italy and Peter Habeler of Austria.

1979 — Ang Phu Sherpa of Nepal became the first person to scale the mountain by two different routes (southeast ridge in 1978, west ridge in 1979).

1979 — A West German expedition led by Gerhard Schmatz was the first to send all of its members to the summit. The leader's wife, Hannelore Schmatz, was the first woman to die on the mountain when she collapsed of exposure and exhaustion during her descent.

1980 — Leszek Cichy and Krzysztof Wielcki of Poland made the first winter ascent of Everest in February.

1980 — Messner made the first solo ascent of Everest (from the Chinese side, without the use of artificial oxygen).

1982 — Yasuo Kato of Japan became the first person to reach the summit in three different seasons (spring, autumn and winter). He died in a storm on his descent.

1985 — Sungdare Sherpa of Nepal became the first person to scale the mountain four times.

1985 — At age 55, an American, Dick Bass, became the oldest person ever to scale Everest.

1986 — Two Swiss, Erhard Loretan and Jean Troillet, made the fastest ascent ever in a two-day climb to the summit via the north face without artificial oxygen.

when they scaled Annapurna I (8,091 meters or 26,545 feet) on June 3, 1950.

The most historic climb of all was achieved on May 29, 1953, when Edmund Hillary of New Zealand and Tenzing Norgay Sherpa of India achieved the 8,848-meter (29,028-foot) crest of Everest, the world's highest peak. Within seven years thereafter, the remaining six 8,000-meter mountains in Nepal had all been scaled.

In 1950, when Herzog and Lachenal stood atop Annapurna after their north face ascent, they looked down the precipitous south face and judged it an impossible route for any man. But just 20 years later, two Britons — Don Whillans and Dougal Haston — surmounted the final rocks and ice of that "impossible" face. Their success signified enormous ad-

success on Kangchenjunga's north face in 1979, a climb up Dhaulagiri I's precipitous east face in 1980, and a solo ascent of Makalu's west face by Poland's Jerzy Kukuczka in 1981.

Women in the Himalaya

Women as well as men have made notable achievements in Nepal's Himalaya. An all-women's expedition from Japan put the first female mountaineer, Junko Tabei, atop Everest in May 1975. Other women have followed her to that lofty summit. American women have reached the peak of Annapurna I and another Japanese team successfully scaled Manaslu.

When Hillary and Tenzing prevailed on Everest, it was believed that humans could not

vances in mountaineering technique and equipment in the span of two decades.

The Whillans-Haston climb also typified the shift in emphasis in Himalayan mountaineering, parallel to what had happened in the European Alps a century earlier. Men first succeeded in scaling mountains by their easiest ridges or faces, then went on to attack ever more difficult features by ever more difficult methods, and in colder, windier seasons. Among the more notable ascents were a British climb of Everest's southwest face in 1975, a Japanese

Pertemba Sherpa is an outstanding young Sherpa climber of the 1980s, having twice achieved the apex of Everest. He has tried again and made his third ascent in April 1985.

survive at such a high altitude without the aid of artificial oxygen. But 25 years later, Italian mountaineer Reinhold Messner and his Austrain partner, Peter Habeler, proved the theory wrong when they dared to climb to the top of the world without oxygen. Other men have since duplicated this feat, and Messner himself repeated it in 1980 when he soloed Everest — with no oxygen, no companions, no fixed camps, no ropes or any other sophisticated mountaineering aid.

In recent years, teams of mountaineers have begun climbing Nepalese peaks in winter's bitterly cold, fiercely windy weather. A Polish expedition sent climbers Leszek Cichy and Krzysztof Wielcki to the summit of Everest in

February 1980, the first winter conquest of any 8,000-meter peak.

What challenges remain today? There are still many extremely difficult routes that have never been attempted. The next steps might be assaults on such routes in fierce winter weather, and ultimately, solo ascents of 8,000-meter mountains by the most difficult routes imaginable in winter. Challenges will always remain in the high peaks of the Nepalese Himalaya.

The Human Element

To be a successful climber in the Himalaya, a person must have skills beyond those normally required in the mountains of Europe

especially staggering to those visiting Nepal for the first time, often causing errors of misjudgment.

The most insidious problem of all is acclimation to altitude. It is one thing to make an extremely difficult climbing maneuver in the Alps or Rockies, but quite another to attempt the same move at 7,500 meters (24,600 feet). While some skilled rock and ice climbers may adapt to the altitude, many do not.

Altitude Adjustment

Modern medical science does not understand why some persons acclimatize more easily than others. All climbers are cautious about acclimation. The most experienced ones

or the Americas. Finely honed ability in rock climbing, ice climbing, bouldering and mountaineering — any one of which can be regarded as a sport in itself — must be blended to conquer the more difficult peaks anywhere. But here in Nepal, the peaks' enormous dimensions and their remote, isolated locations add new factors to the equation.

The time and effort expended just to reach the base camp at the foot of a mountain can be a complete lifetime adventure in itself. Nepal's base camps generally lie at about 5,500 meters (18,000 feet) elevation, higher than any mountain in Europe and higher than most in North America. Before the mountaineer even begins his actual climb, he is often intimidated by the sheer magnitude of the Himalaya. This is

measure their rate of acclimation by their comparative fatigue, normalization of heart rate after exertion, and breath rate; and by considering their appetite, the speed with which a scratch heals, and their general state of health. Mountaineering history is filled with early accounts of Himalayan climbers succumbing to pneumonia. Some of these deaths were no doubt that, but many other almost certainly were altitude sickness: pulmonary or cerebral edema.

The trip to base camp is more or less a trekking experience. Above base camp, the day-to-

An avalanche rumbles down a slope below Mount Everest, just above the Everest Base Camp at 18,000 feet.

day climbing is 80 percent boredom and back-breaking labor, 19 percent elation and fun, and one percent stark terror.

Intense Harmony

Himalayan peaks can take from a few days to seven weeks to climb. Many days can be spent sitting in a tent, waiting for a storm to abate. Condensation in the tent may leave everything wet in the morning, frozen when the sun disappears in the late afternoon. Snow must be melted to obtain the life-giving water. Loads of equipment must be carried to ever-higher camps; this includes stocks of fuel, food and equipment to meet any and every contingency. Meticulous planning is essential.

that took his life. The spectre of death is more real in the Himalaya than in any other mountain range on earth. Statistics suggest that one out of every 40 Himalayan climbers will not return from their expedition.

Advances in equipment, skills and technical knowledge have reduced the percentage of fatalities in recent years, with death or serious injury claiming relatively few members of the 90 or so annual expeditions to the Nepal Himalaya. Most fatalities are caused by objects falling on climbers — ice pinnacles toppling over, rocks coming loose, snow avalanches of varying sizes. Some persons are killed in falls, and as more and more difficult routes are attempted, these will increase in number.

Not surprisingly, the mountain that has

But the hardships are secondary to the experience. The views are astonishing, the situations amazing. To feel mind and body in total harmonious concentration on one of the highest mountains in the world is a unique and wonderful experience. The intensity of a single situation builds lifelong friendships among foreign climbers and Sherpa porters. Each day, each hour, each step will be remembered forever.

Real Adventure

Climbing is adventure — real adventure, as distinguished from mere sport or games. Here is the real risk that Tasker wrote about, the risk

taken the most lives is Everest. By December 1986, 57 lives were lost on Nepal's side of the mountain alone. But Everest has attracted by far the largest number of expeditions; in terms of percentages, only 2.1 percent of all climbers perished on the mountain between spring 1971 and December 1985.

After Everest, the most life-threatening peak is Annapurna I. By December 1985 it had claimed a total of 34 lives, just under one life for each of the 36 persons who have reached its summit.

The Langtang Himal, as seen from the slopes of the Ganesh Himal across the Trisuli River gorge. The high peak is Langtang Lirung.

A TALE OF TWO MOUNTAINEERS

The two best-known mountaineers in the world today are a one-time beekeeper and a former schoolteacher.

The beekeeper, who shot to world fame in 1953 when he became the first man to master Mount Everest, is New Zealander Sir Edmund Hillary. The schoolteacher, a man of the next generation of climbers who has scaled more of the world's giant 8,000-meter (26,250-foot) peaks than any other person, is Italian Reinhold Messner.

Hillary came late to the mountains. He was 16 years old before he even saw a real mountain, and 20 when he ventured into New Zealand's rugged Southern Alps in 1939. But once his interest in mountaineering had been sparked, there was no stopping him.

He began with climbs in New Zealand before and during the Second World War. After the war, during which he served as a navigator in the Royal New Zealand Air Force, Hillary spent more and more time in the mountains, less and less with his family's beekeeping business. Then he went to Europe to climb in the Alps, and found his way to the Himalaya in 1951.

In Nepal, Hillary met Eric Shipton, the famed British climber-explorer. Together they charted the most feasible route up Everest on the Nepalese side of the border. Hillary returned in 1953 with a large British expedition, and as every schoolchild knows, he and his Sherpa companion Tenzing Norgay succeeded in becoming the first men to ascend to the top of the world. "We knocked the bastard off," was Hillary's summary of the achievement.

As Hillary returned to climb in the Nepalese Himalaya in ensuing years, he became increasingly involved in the day-to-day problems of the Sherpa people. The Sherpas were illiterate and their health problems were acute, for there were no schools or hospitals in their remote region. The organization which Hillary founded to aid his friends — the Himalayan Trust — now supports 22 schools and two hospitals that he himself has taken a hand in building. He has now become New Zealand's ambassador to Nepal.

Hillary's adventures have not been restricted to the Himalaya. In 1957 and 1958, he and

several others raced by tractor across the Antarctic wastes to the South Pole. In 1977, he led a group of friends on a pilgrimage by jet-boat from the mouth of the holy Ganges River to one of its high-mountain sources. As late as 1981, he was back on Everest, accompanying an American mountaineering team on an east face attempt, by way of Tibet.

Messner, born in September 1944, grew up in a small village surrounded by the Dolomite Mountains in the Tirol of northern Italy.

Messner's first attempt to conquer a Himalayan peak was successful. He and his brother Guenther, members of a German expedition to Pakistan's Nanga Parbat (8,126 meters or 26,660 feet), made history's third ascent of the mountain and the first by its Rupal Face.

There are only 14 of these 8,000 meter-mountains on earth, and Messner soon set about scaling them all, one by one — or sometimes two by two. In 1972, he alone, among members of a large Austrian team, gained the summit of Nepal's Manaslu (8,163 meters or 26,781 feet), on a previously unclimbed route. In 1975, he and Austrian climbing partner Peter Habeler, working as a two-man team, ascended Gasherbrum I (Hidden Peak), 8,068 meters (26,470 feet) high in Pakistan's Karakoram Range. They did it without artificial oxygen.

In 1978, Messner achieved two milestones. In May, he and Habeler teamed to make the first ascent of Everest without artificial oxygen. In August, Messner made the first solo ascent of any 8,000-meter peak, this time on Nanga Parbat again. In 1979, he climbed the world's second highest mountain, K-2 (Mount Godwin-Austen) in Pakistan's Karakoram, 8,611 meters (28,253 feet).

Messner returned to Everest in 1980. For what many consider his greatest achievement: a solo ascent of the highest mountain on earth. In four days, he climbed from base camp to summit and back to camp, without fixed camps or companions or artificial oxygen.

On October 16, 1986, Messner became the first person to have scaled all 14 8,000-meter mountains when he made it to the summit of the world's fourth highest, Lhotse, 8,516 meters (27,940 feet), just 20 days after having been to the top of the fifth highest, Makalu, 8,463 meters (27,766 feet). Following his success on the world's third highest, Kangchenjunga, in May 1982, he had set the autumn of 1986 as the deadline for his completing all 14, and now on schedule he had achieved this formidable goal and without ever making it easier by taking bottled oxygen. He was three 8,000ers ahead of his closest rival, Jerzy Kukuczka of Poland.

A European climber and his Sherpa companion find a trail through an icefall on the ascent of Manaslu in central Nepal.

REINHOLD MESSNER: WHY DOES MAN CLIMB?

For years, I have had the feeling that if I go on an expedition, nothing will happen. I am prepared, and everything is ready. But in the same moment, I have exactly the opposite knowledge — that this time, maybe, I will die. And it seems a little bit impossible, but I feel it like this.

If a professional climber is going to spend his whole life doing hard things quite on the limit, the risk to die is quite high. It is almost exactly 50-50. Of the leading climbers, 50 percent are dying on the mountain and 50 percent are surviving to die in bed. It's not that the good ones are surviving and the not-so-good ones are dying. It's a question of luck. And if somebody is climbing his whole life, he has to know that maybe he's in the 50 percent that has to die.

And each top climber who is truthful to himself knows that sometime he has had great luck, in the Icefall of Everest or somewhere. A climber should know this; otherwise, he is not really aware of what he is doing.

Look back through the 100-plus years of climbing. The Matterhorn was climbed in 1865. Of the top climbers then, 50 percent died in the mountains. And you can go all through mountaineering history. It's a miracle that Hillary and Tenzing, the two people who first reached the summit of Everest, both were alive. Normally of two summiters like them, one is dead. Tenzing died in his bed in May at the age of 72.

So why do people climb if the hazard is so great?

There are studies showing that in very dangerous situations, to the very limit this side of death, the body is able to make something like heroin that helps to put down all pain, to take away fear. It helps to be very concentrated, to see everything. If a man, a climber, gets this often, he has to get it again, like a man who is addicted to drugs.

The farmers in my village say that a certain man will always climb. He has to do it — he is, addicted. They don't use the word "addicted" because they don't know what it is, but they say the same thing in simple words.

And there was a Swiss geologist who did a study in 1892 about the same thing. He studied maybe 80 people who fell while climbing, and they all said that after their falls they went to climb again; that with this fall, their real climbing began.

I am always surprised when relatively few people fall in the Himalaya each season. In recent years, quite a lot of the small expeditions have had accidents. I think many people know how to handle a big expedition, but it is much more dangerous if you have four members or two members only, and there is nothing between your first camp and your fifth bivouac.

I do not expect to see the number of accidents in the Himalayas go down in coming years. The experienced people are getting older and will be going out of the climbing scene. The young people coming will have to learn. You can learn only with activity, and that's risky. And it will always be that way. The high peaks are high peaks, and they are not changing.

I agree with Doug Scott, the British climber, that oxygen at high altitudes is not a big help. It does give some help, but it is not a big help if you learn to acclimatize, to know your body and everything about the mountains. But you need a long time to reach this point. The young climbers who are coming now say, "Okay, we will do all this without oxygen." But they don't have the experience, that is the problem. Especially, to combine this with small expeditions is not so easy.

I think only the British know how to do it right. Doug Scott, Joe Tasker, Peter Boardman, they know exactly how it works, and they haven't died. They didn't succeed on K-2, but they went very high and they survived. They did Kangchenjunga on a small expedition, and they survived Everest in the winter. They know how to do it. (Editor's note: Tasker and Boardman died on the northeast ridge of Everest almost as this interview was being conducted in late May 1982.)

John Roskelley (American climber) knows how to do it; he showed that on Makalu. Then Peter Habeler and I learned to do it, and we succeeded on Everest. There is nobody else who knows how to survive at high altitudes without (artificial) oxygen.

Mountain Motives

The motivations for climbing are as different as climbers are. There are many motivations. There is also the name — I will be the first to do this and the first to do that. That's also part of climbing. Nobody speaks about it, but it's there. On the other hand, I don't think it's the most important motivation; because if someone is in a difficult situation and needs help, it breaks down.

I have found that I cannot work for a whole year without using my body and going to the limit of my abilities. Finding out something about myself comes automatically now. In the last few years, I have got more experience in feeling my inner self and listening to it. I am quite sure that only in this way — under extreme conditions — can we go deeper into the self, as scientists are doing.

On my last expedition to Kangchenjunga (in May 1982), I found out two important things. First, I learned in dreams during the climb and afterwards — and this is true only for climbs of mountains higher than 8,000 meters — the whole dream world changes for awhile.

And second, I found that you see certain things between dreaming and not dreaming, because you don't really sleep. They reminded me of *mandalas*; you don't see totally different pictures, but things are round and in the same form. I'm quite sure that many *lamas* have visions from high altitudes, because the *mandala*

the time, I am quite free. Not so many climbers are free to do it.

I have a chance to climb all of the 14 8,000 meter mountains in the world. I always thought that if I succeeded on Kangchenjunga, as I did, the chances would be quite good. Had I failed, I would have forgotten the idea, because I could not go back a second time to Kangchenjunga or Makalu or Lhotse. I will never use oxygen; Kangchenjunga was the highest I had left to climb. Makalu is not so easy; I'm getting older, and it's high. Lhotse is not so difficult on the normal route. As for Dhaulagiri and Annapurna, it's no problem. They are lower, and I can do them later.

So I am thinking about it again. But I am not in a hurry. I would be very happy if I could finish in Pakistan, finish Broad Peak and

is a vision.

In the last camp near the summit, I had a very strange vision of all the human parts I am made of. It is very difficult to keep the vision, but I know that I could see a round picture with many pictures inside — not only of my body, but of my whole being. There was a lot of what my life has been, what I did these last years, like seeing my life and my body and my soul and my feelings inside a *mandala*. But I was not even sure if it was only mine or generally human, yours or anybody's, just a human being's. It was very, very strange.

So I will continue to subject myself to these extreme conditions. Maybe I have done more high-altitude expeditions than anybody else in the last 10 years because I can afford it, I have

Gasherbrum II. (He was successful on both in a period of 10 days in July and August 1982.) And then there is Cho Oyu in winter. Winter is harder and it is the only season I have no experience of in the Himalaya.

Cho Oyu is quite good because it's a south face, so the wind coming from the northwest should not hit us so hard. But from the technical side it is surely less difficult than Kangchenjunga.

Reinhold Messner, fourth from left, poses for a team portrait during the 1972 Austrian expedition to the summit of Manaslu.

SIR EDMUND HILLARY: MY LIFE WITH SHERPAS

I first met the Sherpas in 1951 when I was a member of a four-man expedition to the Gawhal Himalaya. All of us had read great stories about the Sherpas' prowess and loyalty on expeditions in the past, and now we had the opportunity to live and work with them ourselves.

Our four Sherpas joined us from Darjeeling. We were immediately struck by their small sinewy bodies and their ready smiles. While they were not outstanding mountaineers — just middle-of-the-road, able men — we quickly developed a warm affection for them.

By the end of that Gawhal expedition, we had successfully climbed a number of virgin peaks and learned something of the tough load-carrying ability of our Sherpas. Then two of us were invited to join the British Everest Reconnaissance to the south side of Mount Everest, led by the famous mountaineer Eric Shipton. We caught up to the British team inside a monsoon-drenched Nepal.

There I met one of the most redoubtable of all Sherpas, Sirdar Angtarkay — a cheerful, tough, brown man with tremendous vitality and strength. I admired him enormously and appreciated his kindness and friendliness. On this expedition I learned a lot about the Sherpa district of Khumbu and experienced the warm hospitality of the local inhabitants. Village elders would come out of their doors and literally drag us inside their homes, to ply us with their local raw spirits and hot tasty boiled potatoes.

First Meeting With Tenzing

In 1953, I became acquainted with a somewhat different type of Sherpa — Tenzing Norgay. Tenzing was very strong and vigorous, with a wide experience of climbing and load-carrying on many Himalayan peaks. But unlike many Sherpas, who largely climbed for the economic return it produced, Tenzing had a tremendous motivation to actually reach the summit of his mountains. This motivation — combined with his physical ability — made him formidable indeed, and resulted in his reaching the summit of Everest with me on May 29, 1953.

Over the next few years, I spent much time in the mountains and in the Sherpas' homes. I learned something of their culture and religion, and built up close friendships. It was impossible not to realize how many things they lacked:

education, medical care and a supply of good clean piped water. In 1961, I first made the effort to fill some of these needs with the construction of a school in Khumjung, the first in this area. Gradually, many more village schools, several hospitals, water pipelines, bridges and even airfields were built.

Meanwhile, the Sherpas were increasingly in demand for Himalayan expeditions. A wide variety of foreign expeditions kept pouring in: French, Japanese, Italian, Austrian, British, American and a dozen others. The toughness and reliability of the Sherpas and their tremendous skill at carrying loads at high altitudes made them extremely effective. And they were delightful people to work with — cheerful, hard-working, agreeable and lacking in any sense of inferiority.

'I Have Never Forgotten'

I had experienced these pleasant characteristics back in 1952, when George Lowe, myself and three Sherpas made the first crossing of the Nup La pass and descended down the West Rongbuk glacier to the north side of Everest. Then the monsoon broke. The result was warm conditions, heavy snow and concealed crevasses.

We struggled back over the Nup La and plunged down the steep crevassed slopes into Nepal. There was minimal visibility and avalanches were rumbling down from every direction. I led the way down, constantly breaking through the soft snow bridges into crevasses — but always being checked with a tight rope by George and the Sherpas. It seemed to go on forever and we thought we would never get out of danger.

Then we emerged onto the glacier below the icefall — still a wild and desolate place but now reasonably safe. George and I wearily started to pitch our tent but the Sherpas would have none of it. They gently sat us down on rocks, put the tents up themselves, and helped us into our warm sleeping bags. Soon we were being served tea and hot stew, and as I lay there in considerable comfort with great gusts of wind shaking the tent, I felt a tremendous sense of appreciation for the kindness and generosity of our hardy Sherpas. I have never forgotten their help on that occasion.

As the Sherpas became increasingly involved in expeditions, their exposure to mountaineering dangers grew. While foreign expedition members waited in their tents for the next thrust forward up the mountain, Sherpas were relaying loads backward and forward up the slopes. They were constantly in peril. Many died in crevasses, in avalanches and in tumbles down the mountainsides.

Trekking to New Lives

Soon a major change started taking place in the lives of the Sherpas. Increasing numbers of foreign visitors were coming to Nepal and lots of them wanted to trek into the mountains. The Sherpas were ideal people to conduct such journeys with their energy and cheerful temperament. Whereas opportunities for rewarding employment previously had been confined to mountaineering, there was now a

still climb as before and play a vital role in the success of great expeditions. But more are involved in trekking — in conducting visitors over the steep Nepalese countryside and up into the mountains. They have turned to other tasks, too — running small hotels and tea shops, working as traders and businessmen. Some Sherpas are even politicians and wardens of national parks.

Warmth and Hospitality

If you are a friend and visit their remote homes, you will find that many things have not changed over the years. The warmth and hospitality remain: you will be given the place of honor beside the fire and will be plied with

safer road to a comfortable lifestyle. Trekking agencies sprang up in Kathmandu, and trekking became big business.

Sherpa wives, who in the past had reluctantly accepted the mountaineering efforts of their husbands, with the potential of injury or death, now encouraged them to undertake trekking, with its similar opportunity for financial gain but a far better chance of survival. Education and the ability to speak English became of prime importance. It was easy to pick an ex-Khumjung student, with his bright eyes and ready grasp of the English language.

And so the lives of the Sherpas have changed. Renowned now throughout the world for their work on mountain peaks, many of them

chhang (beer) and arak (spirits). You may indeed be presented with Tibetan tea, a traditional mixture of tea, salt and yak butter. In the background you may hear the chanting of Tawas from the local gompa — maybe prayers for the ill or the dead, or just encouragement for the growth of a good crop of potatoes.

This is one of the greatest charms of the Sherpas. They introduce you so readily in to their culture and religion; they ask so little from you except politeness and friendship; they laugh so easily at your jokes and their own.

Sir Edmund Hillary carries planks for construction of a new schoolhouse in the Khumbu district. Hillary's Himalayan Trust finances these projects.

THE MOUNTAIN WORLD OF THE SHERPAS

When mountaineer A.M. Kellas used Sherpas as high-altitude porters in Sikkim in 1907, he was innocently enriching and glamorizing the future of a remote race of people.

In no time, Sherpas were on every Himalayan expedition. Some achieved the distinction of being called "Tigers of the Snow" by the Alpine Club. But they remained porters until the dramatic ascent of Mount Everest in 1953 by Edmund Hillary and Sherpa Tenzing Norgay.

Tenzing demonstrated to the world what Sherpas could achieve, given the opportunity. He became an instant folk hero in Nepal and India, and a popular subject of Nepalese troubador songs. Since his success, 30 other Sherpas have reached the summit of the world's highest mountain.

'People From the East'

The Sherpas are a Mongolian race who claim to have migrated to their present home from Minyak in eastern Tibet's Kham region. In the Sherpa language, the word *shar* means east, *pa* means people; so Sherpas are "the people from the east."

Early Sherpa history, etched in oral tradition, maintains that a Tibetan chief of Kham named Thakpa Tho — literally, "Great Leader Above All" — led his people south after being so instructed by visions and the pronouncements of oracles. Legend says this migration took place a somewhat mystical 1,008 years ago; it paused briefly at Tingri in southern Tibet, then continued through the Nangpa Pass to the high fertile valleys around Namche Bazaar in northeast Nepal.

In fact, the original Sherpa tribes were probably nomadic herders driven south by invading Mongol hordes, or perhaps forced to flee due to persecution by the warlike people of Kham, sometime between the 12th and 15th centuries. They were unwelcome in Tingri, and property disputes there led them to cross into Nepal, peacefully and unopposed.

To this day, the Sherpas of Khumbu and the Rolwaling Valley are seminomadic. They have permanent villages up to 4,200 meters (almost 14,000 feet), temporary summer settlements at altitudes between 4,600 and 4,900 meters (roughly 15,000 to 16,000 feet). Most Sherpas function as easily at 5,800 meters (19,000 feet) as the rest of the world does at sea level.

Traditionally, the Sherpas spent their summers in Tibet and their winters in Nepal. They traded, grazed cattle, and farmed in crude virgin-forest clearings. Then the Sherpas discovered the potato, and with its cultivation, they settled permanently in Nepal. Potatoes remain the principal crop of the high-altitude Sherpas; together with barley and wheat flour, they provide the staple diet.

The Sherpas' standard of living, high in comparison to other hill tribes, is a result of the trade that once flourished between Nepal and Tibet. Acting as middlemen, the Sherpas imported kerosene oil, cloth, dyestuffs and manufactured goods from Kathmandu and bartered them for Tibetan salt and wool. As there is no indigenous salt in Nepal, the Tibetan salt trade was a most profitable business.

After the Lhasa uprising of 1959, when the Dalai Lama fled Tibet, the border was closed by the Chinese and the lucrative trade through Khumbu came to an abrupt end. But trekking and climbing enterprises have amply compensated the loss of trade in the decades since.

Social Customs

There are 18 distinct Sherpa clans, each with its own traditions and taboos, living in northeast Nepal. In addition to Khumbu and the somewhat lower Solu region — complexes of valleys immediately south of the Everest massif — Sherpas inhabit the valleys of the Dudh Kosi and Rolwaling west of Solu-Khumbu; the Kulung area below Mount Makalu, east of Solu-Khumbu; and the Langtang-Helambu region directly north of Kathmandu.

These widespread Sherpa clans often speak in unique local dialects. But the Sherpa language is very similar to Tibetan and employs the Tibetan script, so there is no communication gap amongst Sherpas, or between them and Tibetans. The men and women even dress in Tibetan style — when they are not clad in modern climbing gear.

Rigid tribal law once prevented marriage between certain of the clans. Although this custom is rapidly dying out, marriage between members of the same clan is still not permissi-

This distinctive Sherpa painting shows Thyangboche Monastery above Namche Bazaar, and a yeti climbing the high mountains behind.

ble. This is an especially important restriction, as Sherpas already show certain signs of degeneration due to inbreeding.

Marriage and divorce are not complicated in Sherpa communities. Parents exchange bowls of *chhang*, a fermented barley beer, to signify acceptance of their children's marriage. This rite of engagement is more important than the wedding itself, which is marked by lavish ceremony and feasting. Divorce is settled either by a compensation payment or an amicable toast; in such a case, daughters normally stay with their mother, sons with their father.

Money lending is big business among Sherpas, as cash is not always readily available. Interest is excessively high: 25 percent is not considered outrageous. This helps to explain the

pare with that of their neighbors in Tibet, Bhutan and India; their architecture, though impressive in its solidness, cannot be accused of any real art. The beautiful silver drinking cups used in Sherpa country, as well as the silver and stone jewelry, the gay felts and brocades, are almost all imported from Tibet or India.

Image-making, rock-carving, and the painting of scrolls and murals are practiced by a few *lamas* and lay individuals. Skilled *lama* artists are still called upon to travel many miles to paint murals in monasteries throughout Sherpa country. Sherpa paintings of their Everest-area homeland, done in traditional Tibetan style, are colorful and attractive. The fine house built by one artist family in Khumjung is testimony to the profitable demand for this type of work.

great popularity of mountaineering expeditions that pay cash wages far in excess of anything the Sherpas could hope to earn elsewhere. This income is invested in loans, cattle, land, tradeable articles and jewelry — in that order of preference.

A large amount of Sherpa energy is expended in the tending of yaks and related breeds of cattle. These animals command a good price. Their butter is in huge demand for burning in votive lamps, both in monasteries and in private homes. Although often rancid, the butter is also an essential ingredient in the popular Tibetan tea drunk by the Sherpas.

There is little real handicraft among the Sherpa people. Their weaving does not com-

Rock-carving remains a flourishing business, even if the artistry is not as precise and beautiful as it once was. Sherpas commission artisans to carve religious texts or icons in large rocks in the vicinity of villages or along major tracks. Small tablets are also carved for offerings at roadside shrines.

Without exception, Sherpas are Buddhists of the Kar-gyud-pa sect, the oldest unreformed Tibetan sect. As recently as the turn of the 20th Century, Sherpas looked to Lhasa for spiritual and temporal leadership; even today, the Dalai Lama and certain other reincarnate

The bustling Sherpa village of Namche Bazaar, the largest town in the Khumbu region, is an important stop for trekkers and climbers.

lamas enjoy popularity equal to that of the King of Nepal. This is not suggestive of any political disrespect for the Nepalese monarch. It merely emphasizes the cultural heritage of the Sherpas, and the fact that — until quite recently — communication with Tibet was easier and more profitable than with distant Kathmandu.

Ritual and Sorcery

Religious practice and ritual are as natural to the Sherpas as growing potatoes and breeding yaks. *Gompas*, or monasteries, are the centers of their culture and learning. The greatest of these *gompas* is Thyangboche, the spiritual core of Sherpa country and the home of the

Just as Tenzing was a hero for the Sherpas three decades ago, another young man today is a model for Sherpa mountaineers. His name is Pertemba, and he is one of the rare breed of man who has stood atop Mount Everest on two separate occasions — in 1975 and in 1979 with West Germany's Gerhard Schmatz.

A dynamic yet personable man, Pertemba credits Sherpa climbing ability to living at high altitude, enduring extreme cold, coping with a difficult lifestyle — and being forced by weather into idleness for several months each year. Today, the Nepal Mountaineering Association school in Manang trains Nepalis in technical climbing skills, preparing them for acceptance of the good-money opportunities offered by expeditions.

first Sherpa reincarnate *lama*.

The Buddhism practised by the Sherpas has roots deep in the pre-Buddhist Bon faith and in indigenous animism. Sorcery, witchcraft and sacrifice have been adopted as ritualistic tools by *lamas*. Demons and gods are believed to inhabit every cave, forest, valley and mountaintop. Myth and fable have been given religious authority, written into sacred texts and otherwise encouraged. Indeed, Bon worship and Buddhism are almost indistinguishable.

But if the Sherpa touches his amulet and murmurs mystic phrases as he walks, he is entitled to these beliefs. After all, his mountaineering skills subject him to more perils than any other race in Nepal, perhaps in the world.

Pertemba, like Tenzing Norgay before him, is anxious to participate in an all-Sherpa assault on Everest. Mountain Travel, the climbing and trekking agency, is gathering the financial backing to support the expedition, which may take place later this decade.

In the meantime, Pertemba will be on Everest again with an American expedition in 1983. He looks forward to being one of the few to reach the summit three times by three different routes.

"My family is against it," he admits. "I suppose all our families are. But we are Sherpas."

Inside a typical Sherpa home, life centers around the kitchen — normally a simple wood fire. The staple food is potatoes.

THE YETI: FIENDS IN HIGH PLACES?

Of all the myths and legends of the high Himalayas of Nepal, perhaps the best known is that of the yeti or "abominable snowman."

But is it a myth? Or is there, in fact, a creature roaming the frozen wastes, preying on yaks and frightening human intruders?

Such a beast was first described to the West as a shaggy wild man by a European mercenary in Mongolia in the early 15th Century. Himalayan peoples who lived in remote areas below the snow line spoke of him as anything from ape to supernatural being. To the Sikkimese, for instance, he was the spirit of the hunt: he could be seen only by the devout, and votive offerings of any kill had to be made to him.

The British tended to dismiss, as colorful legend, native sightings of strange snow creatures. In 1899, however, Major L.A. Waddell, an authority on Tibet and Tibetan Buddhism, described finding mysterious footprints that "were alleged to be the trail of the hairy wild men who are believed to live among the eternal snows." In 1921, Colonel C.K. Howard-Bury, who led the reconnaissance on the north side of Everest through Tibet, saw dark figures moving across the snow and later came upon enormous footprints.

'The Abominable Snowman'

Stories continued to flow from Tibet and Sikkim, and the great snowman debate was on. It was given credence by a popular British columnist who mistranslated the beast's Tibetan name — *migyu* — as "the abominable snowman." The label stuck.

Years later, when Nepal's Rana government finally allowed foreigners to enter the country to attempt climbing Mount Everest from the south, the "snowman" became fixed in the imagination of the world. The Sherpas who assisted on those early expeditions told climbers a spate of stories about the *yeh-tch*, or yeti. Giant footprints were seen by such well-known mountaineers as Frank Smythe, H.W. Tilman and John Hunt.

On a November afternoon in 1951, climber Eric Shipton found a clear trail of naked human-looking footprints high up in the snow of the Menlungtse Glacier. He and his companion, Sherpa Sen Tenzing, following the trail for about a mile until it disappeared in moraine. Shipton took clear and well-defined photographs of the yeti footprints; they were

oval in shape, more than a foot long, and very wide, with a distinctive protruding big toe. Suddenly, all those mysterious sightings, the unknown yells and whistles, the stones and branches hurled at startled travelers at night, seemed to make sense. There was something out there.

Three Types of Yeti

According to the Sherpas, the *yeh-tch* — literally, "man of the rocky places" — is of three distinct types. There is the huge, cattle-

eating *dzu-tch* (or juti); this creature is about eight feet tall when standing on its hind legs, but is usually on all fours, and is almost certainly the blue bear of Tibet. There is the *thelma*, a small ape-like creature which walks on its hind legs, has long dangling arms and is covered in red or blond hair; this is probably the Assam gibbon strayed far from home. And there is the *mih-tch* (or miti), a man-sized ape, which but for its face and stomach is covered in shaggy red hair. By all accounts, it is an abominable creature, attacking on sight. Some say it is a man-eater.

A priest at the Pangboche monastery displays what he claims is a yeti scalp. Some say it is a fake, but others insist it is genuine.

The *mih-tch* is the true yeti for which there is no definite explanation. It is this anthropoid that is painted into monastery murals and religious scrolls. Sherpas single out the orangutan when shown photographs of known animals; fossils of long-extinct giant orangutans have been found in the Himalayan foothills. Could some have survived by taking refuge in the once-remote reaches below the snow line? Are they even now on the verge of extinction?

Some theorize this *mih-tch* could be a direct descendant of *Gigantopithecus* — Peking

Man of one million years B.C. This ape man, they say, could have evolved in obscurity, in inhospitable habitats.

In Search of the Yeti

Several expeditions have set out in search of the yeti. In 1954, London's *Daily Mail* fielded an impressive team of experts which, though it failed to find the yeti, returned with a bank of knowledge on the creature. Tom Slick, a Texas millionaire, sent several yeti expeditions to the Himalaya before diverting them to find the American Sasquatch. Mountaineer Norman Dyhrenfurth in 1958 found footprints similar to those previously photographed by Shipton. In 1960, Sir Edmund Hillary led an expedi-

tion to Shipton's yeti country, below the great peaks of Gauri Shankar and Menlungtse. The expedition was equipped with the latest scientific equipment and a signed-and-sealed order from the Nepalese government that the yeti, if fouund, was on no account to be killed or kept in captivity.

Hillary's expedition procured furs alleged to be those of yetis, and found endless suspicious tracks in the snow. It also borrowed the legendary "yeti scalp," a sacred relic, from the Sherpa monastery of Khumjung. This iron-hard dome of leather and red bristles had baffled climbers and other observers for years. But when taken for examination to Chicago, Paris and London, the "scalp" was declared to be a 200-year-old artifact made from the hide of a wild Himalayan goat, the serow. Hillary's furs, meanwhile, were discovered to be those of the Tibetan blue bear. Many of the footprints were those of foxes and ravens, whose tracks had melted in the sun and had taken on grotesque sizes and shapes. Western "experts" were quick to debunk the yeti legend.

The Legend Lives On

But the yeti refuses to be killed so easily. There are two other scalps in Sherpa country, in the monasteries of Pangboche and Namche Bazaar, and a skeletal yeti hand at Pangboche. One of these scalps was examined in Europe in the early 1970s; some declared it a blatant fake, but others, including a parapsychologist, said it was genuine.

A Sherpa girl was said to have been savaged by a large ape in 1974. Several yaks' necks were broken by something that grabbed them by the horns and twisted their heads. The high whistles have been heard again. Expedition camps — Japanese in 1974, Polish in 1980 — have been visited at night by a creature that left telltale footprints in the snow. When members began following and photographing, something screamed at them.

Ape, sub-human, wild man of the snows, or demon — the myth lives on. Perhaps someday the yeti will be found. It was not very long ago, after all, that China's giant panda and Africa's mountain gorilla were mere legends.

Sherpas not only talk about the yeti; they paint its picture. This is one artist's portrait of the Himalayan legend.

GUIDE IN BRIEF

Traveling to Nepal

By Air

More than 90 per cent of all non-Indian visitors to Nepal arrive by air at Tribhuvan International Airport, about eight kilometers (five miles) from Kathmandu.

Airlines serving the kingdom are the national flag carrier, Royal Nepal Airlines Corporation (RNAC); Bangladesh Biman; Burma Airways Corporation (BAC); Indian Airlines; Thai International Airlines and Pakistan International Airlines. There are daily round-trip flights — two to Delhi, and one to Varanasi (Benares) — as well as weekly round-trip flights — nine to Calcutta and Bangkok; two to Colombo, Singapore and Patna; four to Rangoon and Hong Kong; three to Karachi; 10 to Dhaka; and one to Dubai.

One-way fares for non-Indian foreigners aboard RNAC as of 1985 are: Bagdogra (near Siliguri) — Calcutta US $62 (by road, from Bogdogra to Kakar Bhitta takes half an hour, but passengers need Darjeeling Permit); Kathmandu — Delhi US $142; Kathmandu — Calcutta US$96; Kathmandu — Patna US$41; Kathmandu — Varanasi US$71; Kathmandu — Karachi US$200 with a special fare (SF) of US$160 (a round-trip costs US$300); Kathmandu — Dhaka US$90; Kathmandu — Rangoon US$190 (SF US$170); Kathmandu — Bangkok US$245 (SF US$200); Kathmandu — Colombo US$395 (SF US$190); Kathmandu — Hong Kong US$435 (SF US$290); Kathmandu — Singapore US$454 (SF US$285); Kathmandu — Dubai US$383 (SF US$240, and a round-trip costs US$450). All special fares are payable in foreign exchange only. Nepalese and Indian nationals are granted special reduced rates fares on flights between Nepal and India. These airfares fluctuate with the exchange rate.

In-flight Seating Arrangements

There is a Rs. 150 airport tax on departing international flights, payable on check-in.

When coming from the west to Kathmandu on a clear day, sit on the left side of the aircraft to gain a look at the western Himalaya. Close in succession, you will see Gurja Himal (7,193 meters), Dhaulagiri (8,167 meters), the dark, deep valley of the Kali Gandaki River leading north to Mustang, the six peaks of the Annapurna Range, the pointed Manaslu (8,163 meters), and the three lumps of Ganesh Himal (7,429 meters) which dominate the Kathmandu Valley.

Coming from the east, sit on the right side of the aircraft. You may gaze successively at the flat-topped Kangchenjunga (8,586 meters) on the border with Sikkim, Makalu (8,463 meters), Everest (8,848 meters), Cho Oyu (8,201 meters), Gauri Shankar (7,134 meters), and finally past Chhoba Bhamare, Dorje Lhakpa (6,966 meters), and Langtang Lirung (7,234 meters) standing above the Kathmandu Valley.

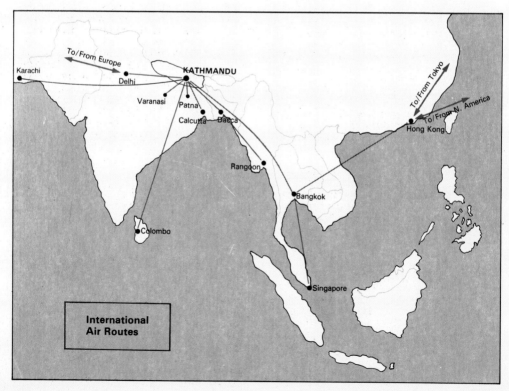

International Air Routes

Overland

Leisurely travelers have a vast choice of routes and means of transport by which to enter Nepal. In addition to Tribhuvan Airport, there are 11 official entry points:

Kakar Bhitta (Mechi zone), with connections to Darjeeling and Siliguri, India.

Rani Sikiyahi (Kosi zone), just south of Biratnagar.

Jaleswor (Janakpur zone).

Birganj (Narayani zone), near Raxaul, India, the most common point of entry for overland travelers.

Kodari (Bagmati zone), on the Chinese Tibetan border, open to tourists with Chinese visas providing access to Lhasa.

Sonauli (Lumbini zone), near Bhairawa on the road to Pokhara.

Kakarhawa (Lumbini zone), road unsuitable for motor vehicles.

Nepalganj (Bheri zone).

Koilabas (Rapti zone), road unsuitable for motor vehicles.

Dhangadi (Seti zone).

Mahendranagar (Mahakali zone), road unsuitable for motor vehicles.

Within India, trains are a convenient means of transportation, but there is no railway to speak of in Nepal. A 47-kilometer line was built in 1925 between Raxaul, India, and Amlekhganj, south of Kathmandu; and further east, a second line was built in 1940 between the Indian border and Janakpur, some 50 kilometers north. That's it.

Combining Indian rail with Indian and Nepalese roads, it takes about three days to travel from Delhi to Kathmandu via Agra, Varanasi and Patna, crossing the border at Birganj.

From Calcutta, rail and road will get you to Kathmandu in 1½ days via Bhagalpur and Muzaffarpur. Again, the border crossing is at Raxaul-Birganj. The journey between Muzaffarpur and Patna is by ferry across the Ganges and takes about one hour, 30 minutes; there is talk that a bridge may be built.

If you're coming from the Indian hill station of Darjeeling, you can take the train to Siliguri. From there, it's a one-hour taxi journey to Kakar Bhitta, a Nepalese border post. You can catch a bus from the Kanchanbari bus station there to Biratnagar. Another route, for those who like to do it the hard way, is to take bus, taxi or train to Siliguri, then another bus or Jeep to Badrapur.

If you're transiting India, an Indian visa is required when entering India at a border post. In addition, if you're planning to travel overland from Nepal to Darjeeling via Kakar Bhitta, a special Darjeeling permit is required for all passports, including Commonwealth. If you are planning to commute once or twice between Nepal and India, get an Indian multiple-entry visa.

If you're entering Nepal by private car, plan on at least two hours, often more, to get through any of the Indian border posts. A carnet de passage en douanes is required for cars and motorbikes. These exempt the owner of the vehicle from customs duty for three months. A driver's license, national or international, is also required. Motor vehicles in Nepal are driven on the left side of the road.

Travel Advisories

Immigration

Visitors should possess a valid passport and a health certificate of inoculation against cholera and yellow fever, if coming from an infected area. Checking of health certificates is haphazard.

All passport holders require a visa for Nepal. A tourist visa can be issued by a Nepalese embassy. This visa is valid for 30 days in the Kathmandu valley, Pokhara and other parts of Nepal linked by highway. A seven-day visa can be issued on arrival at Kathmandu's Tribhuvan Airport for 10 US Dollars. This can be extended to the full 30-day period at no additional cost. Persons intending to trek outside of the main highway areas must obtain a trekking permit (see "Trekking" section). Indian and Bhutanese citizens require no visas.

A single-entry visa to Nepal costs US$10 for 30 days. Visas can be extended for up to three months, at a rate of Rs. 75 a week for the second month and Rs. 150 a week for the third month. Longer stays require the recommendation of the Home Ministry.

Extensions are granted at the Central Immigration Office in Maiti Devi Tel: 412337, Kathmandu (open 10 a.m. to 4 p.m. except Saturdays and government holidays; bring your passport and two passport-size photos). If you've got a trekking permit in hand (they cost Rs. 65 a week), your visa can be extended at no additional cost. It is now required to show that you have changed money to obtain a visa extension.

Customs

On entry, the traveler may bring in 200 cigarettes, 20 cigars, one bottle of spirits and two bottles or 12 cans of beer duty-free. Also duty-free are the following personal effects: one pair of binoculars, a camera with a reasonable amount of film, a record player with 10 records, a tape recorder with 15 tapes, a musical instrument, a transistor radio, one video camera (without deck) and a fishing rod.

Controls are quite strict at Tribhuvan Airport, and customs officials must chalk up all your luggage before you leave. Prohibited are firearms and ammunition (unless an import license has been obtained in advance from the Ministry of Foreign Affairs, or the Home Ministry), radio transmitters, walkie-talkies and drugs. Special permits are required for 16 mm cameras. Customs are sensitive even about 8 mm movie cameras and may write them in your passport.

You also must clear customs when you are leaving the country. To avoid hassles, be aware of the following:

1) Souvenirs can be exported freely but antiques and art objects require a special certificate from the Department of Archaeology, National Archives Building, Ram Shah Path, Kathmandu. It takes at least two days to get it. It is forbidden to export any object more than 100 years old. If you are in doubt, obtain a certificate.

2) It is strictly forbidden to export precious stones, gold, silver, weapons and drugs. Animal hides, fangs or wild animals may not be exported either. Live pet animals such as Tibetan dogs may be taken out.

3) Have your currency card ready for inspection.

On entry, everyone is handed a currency card to be filled in with name, nationality and passport number but not the amount of currency imported. Every time you exchange foreign currency for Nepalese rupees, the transaction must be recorded on the card with the stamp of the bank or other authorized dealers. At the end of your stay, excess Nepalese rupees can be converted back into hard currency as long as what remains does not exceed 10 percent of the total amount changed.

Non-Indian visitors are not allowed to import or export Nepalese or Indian currency.

There is an exchange counter at Tribhuvan Airport.

The official rate of exchange fluctuates against all currencies. In early 1987, the rate was Rs 22 to US $1. Dollars are in high demand, and there is sometimes a black market in Kathmandu. Buyers should be cautious and keep in mind currency card requirements.

The official exchange rate for all currencies is published daily in *The Rising Nepal* newspaper and broadcast every day by Radio Nepal in the Nepali language.

There are banknotes in denominations of Nepalese Rupees 1,000, 500, 100, 50, 20, 10, 5, 2 and 1, and coins of Rs. 1.00 and of 50, 25, 10 and 5 *paisa*. There are 100 *paisa* to one rupee. Half a rupee (50 *paisa*) is called a *mohar*, while 25 paisa is referred to as a *sukaa*.

The foreign currency exchange counter at Tribhuvan Airport is open throughout the day, every day. The New Road Gate exchange counter of Rastriya Banijya Bank is open daily from 8 a.m. to 8 p.m. The Nepal Bank on New Road is open from 10 a.m. to 3 p.m. Sunday through Thursday, and from 10 a.m. to noon on Fridays.

Tips

Tipping has become a habit in hotels and restaurants patronized by foreigners. A hotel waiter or porter will expect a one or two rupee tip. Taxi drivers need not always be tipped but when they have been particularly helpful, about 10 percent of the fare is in order. A 10 percent tip is also customary in Westernized restaurants. Elsewhere, please do yourself and the country a favor: abstain from tipping.

Climate

From the eternal snow of the higher peaks to the tropical expanses of the lowlands, Nepal enjoys an extreme variety of climates. Altitude and exposure to sun and rain are the most influential factors.

Sitting at an elevation of about 1,350 meters (4,400 feet), the Kathmandu Valley knows three seasons. The cold season — from October to March — is the best time to visit the country. The night time temperatures may drop nearly to the freezing point, but the sun warms the atmosphere by day, so that the morning hours see the mercury climb from 10°C to 25°C (50°F to 77°F). The sky is generally clear and bright; the air is dry and warm. Nippy mornings and evenings are invigorating. In the winter, there is frequently an early-morning mist — a result of the rapid heating of the cold night air. October and February are particularly pleasant. The weather is noticeably warmer in the Pokhara valley, where temperatures rise to 30°C (86°F) at midday in the lower altitude.

In April, May and early June, the weather becomes hot and stuffy, with occasional evening thunderstorms. Nature is in full bloom but the brightly colored landscapes are often shrouded in heat mist. Daily temperatures in Kathmandu oscillate between 11°C and 28°C (52°F and 83°F) in April, and between 19°C and 30°C (66°F and 86°F) in June, with maximum temperatures of 36°C (97°F).

By the end of June the monsoon arrives, heralded by pre-monsoon rains which normally start in May. The rainy season lasts three months, during which time the Himalaya usually remain out of sight though the rains create some spectacular lighting effects. Violent downpours create some flooding but it is still possible to visit the Kathmandu Valley. Trekking stops with the proliferation of leeches (*jugas*), as the lowlands are cut off by swollen rivers and occasional landslides.

The monsoon ends around mid-September. Autumn brings clearer skies, cooler nights and a symphony of brown and gold to the land.

Clothing

Your wardrobe will depend upon when you are going to Nepal and what you intend to do there. Unless you are planning to meet Their Majesties, government or embassy officials, there is no need to bring anything but the most casual clothes.

From mid-September to March, light clothing is fine in the Kathmandu Valley. Avoid synthetic fibers which irritate the skin. For evenings and early mornings, a heavy woolen sweater or a padded anorak or jacket will be needed. Blue jeans, corduroy trousers or long skirts are in order and comfortable shoes are a must, even if you do not intend to go trekking. High-heeled shoes are out. Sneakers are ideal. Do not bother to bring a raincoat; it's too warm for it in the daytime, and a locally bought umbrella will suffice for sun as well as rain.

Special gear required for trekking can be hired or bought in Kathmandu or Pokhara, in standard Western sizes. The same applies for sweaters, ponchos, caps and other woolen or down clothing.

From April to September, only light clothes, preferably cotton, are needed in Nepal. That's true most of the year in the Terai, but cold lowland nights in December and January make a sweater and jacket essential.

Getting Acquainted

Hygiene and Medical

Although there is no more danger to health in Nepal than in many other Asian countries, elementary sanitary precautions are in order. Health control is lax on entry, but the traveler is advised to get the whole range of injections against typhoid, hepatitis, cholera and tetanus. Make sure children's immunizations are up to date.

Never drink unboiled and unfiltered water. Avoid eating raw vegetables and peel fruit before eating. Never walk barefoot. Do not trust ice cubes or water anywhere, except in the best hotels. Clean your hands often. If you follow these guidelines, you should thus avoid many intestinal disorders, known locally as the "Kathmandu Quickstep."

Nevertheless, it is common for minor problems to occur soon after arrival in the country, especially after long intercontinental flights. This is generally due to the change of diet and climate, and perhaps also to jet lag. Should trouble persist or develop into something more serious like amoebic or bacillary dysentery or giardia, get a stool test and medical assistance.

Readily available in Kathmandu pharmacies are medicines for diarrhea. Use Streptomagma (a composite of Streptomycin with Kaolin and Pectin) for traveler's tummy, Tiniba 500 (Tinidazole) for amoebic dysentery and giardia, and Septram (Sulfa and Trimethoprim) for bacilliary dysentery.

Malaria is on the increase elsewhere in the subcontinent, but the elevation of most of Kathmandu is too high for the kind of mosquito that carries it. If you are planning to visit lowland areas, however, a preventive treatment is advised. Take chloroquine pills, starting two weeks before you arrive in the Terai and continuing for six weeks after you leave. Bring a mosquito repellent during the warm months.

Your medical kit should also include a broad-spectrum antibiotic, aspirin, medication for throat infections, a sunburn ointment, antiseptic and plasters. A small pair of scissors and a pocket knife to peel fruit will come in handy.

Pharmacies in Kathmandu, mainly along New Road, offer a wide range of Western drugs for very low prices, as well as some traditional Indian remedies. For would-be trekkers, a more comprehensive medical arsenal is required (see "Trekking" section). For more serious problems there are doctors attached to the big hotels, and hospitals with English-speaking staff.

Major hospitals are:

Bir Hospital, Kantipath, Kathmandu (in front of the Tundhikhel parade ground), Tel: 221119.

Patan Hospital, Patan (with foreign staff). Tel: 521034, 521048, 522286, 522278.

Tribhuvan University Teaching Hospital, Maharajgunj. Tel: 412303, 412404, 412505.

Postal Services

The Central Post Office in Kathmandu has three sections. Fortunately, they are located close to one another at the junction of Kanti Path and Kicha-Pokhari Road.

The so-called Foreign Post Office Tel: 211760, deals only with parcels sent or received from abroad. Avoid sending or receiving any during your stay.

To buy stamps, send letters or receive them through Poste Restante, go to the General Post Office Tel: 211073, (open 10 a.m. to 5 p.m. daily except Saturdays and holidays). During the months of November to February, it is open only to 4 p.m.). Make sure that stamps on letters and post cards are franked in front of your eyes. If you use Poste Restante, ask your correspondents to either mention only your family name on the envelope, or to write it with a big initial. Main hotels will handle your mail; this is certainly easiest.

Telephone and Cables

The Telecommunication Office, Tripureshwar deals with telephone calls, cables and telexes. Its telex service is available only during government hours at the Central Telegraph Office. There are sometimes inexplainable delays in the delivery of incoming cables. International telephone connections are now excellent with the installation in late 1982 of the British earth satellite station. Dial 186 for the international operator. Dial 187 for calls to India. Dial 180 for internal trunk calls and 197 for enquiries.

Electricity

Major towns in Nepal have been electrified using 220-volt alternating current, though some fluctuation is normal. On festive occasions, Kathmandu is ablaze with lights at night. A few large hotels have their own power generators, as there are frequent power cuts. The rural electrification program has a long way to go before it can phase out the poetry of candles and firesides. A small flashlight is useful.

Weights and Measures

Nepalese use the decimal system, but for specific purposes stick to traditional measures. As elsewhere in the Indian subcontinent, they count in *lakh* (unit of 100,000) and *crore* (unit of 10 million). Heights are usually measured in meters but sometimes also in feet. (One foot equals 0.305 meters; one meter equals 3.28 feet). Distances are counted in kilometers.

Weights are measured in kilos (kilograms), with the following exceptions:

For rice and other cereals, milk and sugar: One *mana* equals a little less than half a liter; one *paathi*, about 3¾ liters, contains eight *manas*; 160 *manas* equal 20 *paathis* equal one *muri*, about 75 liters.

For vegetables and fruits: One *pau* equals 200 grams; one *ser* equals four *paus*, or one kilogram; one *dharni* equals three *sers*, or 2.40 kilograms.

For all metals: One *tola* equals 11.66 grams.

For precious stones: One carat equals 0.2 grams.

The term *muthi* means "handful," whether it be of vegetables or of firewood.

Cigarettes

Nepal produces four brands of cigarettes with lyrical names — Sayapatri (Marigold), Lali Guras (Rhododendron), Gaida (Rhinoceros), Naulo (New) and Yak. Little brown beedees are favored by locals. Imported cigarettes are available, but expensive.

Photography

As film is expensive in Nepal and available only in Kathmandu, you are advised to bring enough for your personal use. Photography shops in New Road can process black-and-white and color prints, as well do repairs and supply batteries. It is best to arrive self-sufficient with regard to all photographic equipment. Telephoto lenses are useful in photographing wildlife and distant mountains.

Business hours

Government offices are open from 10 a.m. to 5 p.m. Sunday through Friday for most of the year. They close an hour earlier in the winter. Saturday is the rest day in Nepal, Sunday being a full working day for offices and banks. Only embassies and international organizations take a two-day weekend; they are generally open from 9 or 9:30 a.m. to 5 or 5:30 p.m. during the remainder of the week. Shops, some of which remain open on Saturdays and holidays, seldom open before 10 a.m. but do not usually close until 7 or 8 p.m.

Time conversion

Nepal is 15 minutes ahead of Indian Standard Time and five hours, 45 minutes ahead of Greenwich Mean Time. Thus, international time differences are staggered as follows:

Kathmandu	12 noon today
New Delhi	11:45 a.m. today
Bonn	7:15 a.m. today
Paris	7:15 a.m. today
London	6:15 a.m. today
New York	1:15 a.m. today
San Francisco	10:15 p.m. yesterday
Hawaii	8:15 p.m. yesterday
Sydney	4:15 p.m. today
Tokyo	3:15 p.m. today
Hong Kong	2:15 p.m. today
Bangkok	1:15 p.m. today
Rangoon	12:45 p.m. today

Marking Time

Five different calendars are in simultaneous use in Nepal, including the Gregorian calendar familiar to the West and the Tibetan calendar. Traditional are the Sakya Era calendar, which began counting years in 108 A.D., and the Newari calendar, starting in 879–880 A.D.

The official calendar is the Vikram Sambat calendar, named after the legendary North Indian King Vikramaditya. Day One of Vikram Sambat was Feb. 23, 57 B.C. Hence, the year 1984 of the Christian era is 2040 of the Vikram era. This system is the only one you'll find in newspapers, public service and the world of government bureaucracy.

The Nepalese celebrate their New Year in mid-April, according to the Western calendar. The fiscal and budgetary year begins in mid-July. The Nepalese year is 365 days long, same as in the West, with 12 months ranging in length from 29 to 32 days. These months are called *Baishak* (31 days), *Jesth* (31 days), *Asadh* (32 days), *Srawan* (32 days), *Bhadra* (31 days), *Ashwin* (30 days), *Kartik* (30 days), *Marga* (29 days), *Poush* (30 days), *Magha* (29 days), *Falgun* (30 days) and *Chaitra* (30 days). The number of days in a month in a Nepalese calendar is never constant as it is dependant on the solar movement.

The seven days of the week have been named according to the planets. They are *Aityabar* (Sunday), the Sun day; *Somabar* (Monday), the moon day; *Mangalbar* (Tueday), Mars day; *Budhabar* (Wednesday), Mercury's day; *Brihaspatibar* or *Bihibar* (Thursday), Jupiter's day or the day of the lord; *Sukrabar* (Friday), Venus day; and *Shanisharbar* or *Shanibar* (Saturday), Saturn's day.

Transportation

Airport Buses and Taxis

For travel from Tribhuvan Airport to Kathmandu, a bus service is theoretically provided by RNAC and by Indian Airlines. Passengers arriving on other airlines are left at the mercy of taxis. The taxi ride from the airport should not cost more than Rs. 35 by meter. Taxis can accommodate three passengers. Often the driver is assisted by an "interpreter." When traveling from Kathmandu to the airport, buses depart from the RNAC building at the beginning of New Road.

Domestic Air Travel

Flying is the best way of moving around fast in Nepal. RNAC, the national airline, has monopoly on domestic flights and runs an extensive network using a fleet of 44-seat Avro 748s, 19-seat Twin Otters and five-seat Pilatus Porters. The airline spider-web spreads from Kathmandu to the west (Dang, Dhangadi, Jumla, Mahendranagar, Nepalganj, Rukumkot, Safi Bazar, Silgari Doti, Surkhet); to the center (Baglung, Bhairawa, Gorkha, Jomosom, Meghauly, Pokhara, Simra); and to the east (Bhadrapur, Biratnagar, Janakpur, Lukla, Lamidanda, Rajbiraj, Rumjatar Taplejung, Tumlingtar). Details can be obtained from the RNAC office in New Road.

Fares are reasonable. On some routes, there is one fare for foreigners and a lower one for Nepalese and Indian nationals. In 1987 these are the fares (payable in Rupees) for foreigners on selected routes:
From Kathmandu to Bhairawa, US$53; to Jomosom, US$58; to Biratnagar, US$60; to Lukla, US$55; to Pokhara US$40; to Meghauly (for Tiger Tops), US$45; to Nepalgunj (for Karnali Tented Camp), US$28.
From Pokhara to Jomosom, US$35.

On domestic and international flights, RNAC grants a 25 percent discount to card-holding students under 25 years.

An Avro takes visitors on a daily one-hour "Mountain Flight," leaving Kathmandu in the early morning to fly along the Himalaya for a view of Mount Everest. You can photograph from the cockpit; at US$65, it is a worthwhile trip. 3 daily flights.

There is a Rs. 30 airport tax on many domestic flights. Contrary to RNAC's generous international service, in-flight service is minimal: there are usually sweets and sometimes tea.

It is advisable to book ahead, especially to distant destinations where only the smaller aircraft operate. There are cancellation fees of 10 percent if you cancel 24 hours in advance, 33 percent if less than 24 hours in advance, and 100 percent if you fail to show up without informing the airline. If the flight is cancelled due to bad weather or other causes, your fare is refunded. Get a good travel agent to help you with the arrangements.

Small planes can occasionally be chartered; but with RNAC's aircraft heavily committed to scheduled flights, these are expensive and difficult to book. Pilatus Porters carrying up to five passengers cost US$550 per hour. Twin Otters cost US$735 per hour and Avros cost US$1710. It is advisable to book through a travel agent. Helicopters can be chartered in addition to emergency rescues from the Royal Nepal Army, though expensive. Alouettes cost about US$750 per hour and Pumas US$1300 per hour.

You need to produce a trekking permit at Tribhuvan Airport on departure from Kathmandu to restricted areas. You should always take your passport along, as there are occasional police checkpoints on all roads.

Road Links

In this mountainous country with deep valleys etched between peaks and ranges, roads are vital for bringing together the various communities. But until Nepal started opening to the outer world in the early 1950s, the kingdom had nothing except village trails and mountain paths. Cross-country trading was a tortuous affair measured in weeks and months. Since the '50s, there have been major efforts to construct roads. Foreign powers have lent a hand — none more so than Nepal's bigbrotherly neighbors, India and China, prompted by obvious strategic considerations.

There are presently six main road links:

Tribhuvan Raj Path, linking Kathmandu with Raxaul at the Indian border, 200 kilometers (124 miles) away, was opened in 1956 and built with Indian assistance.

The "Chinese Road" or Araniko Highway leads to the Tibetan border at Kodari. Some 110 kilometers (68 miles) long, it is a good road. Built with Chinese assistance, it opened in the mid-'60s.

Chinese engineers also helped build the Prithvi Raj Marg covering the 200 kilometers (124 miles) between Kathmandu and Pokhara; it opened in 1973. There are two recently opened extensions to the Pokhara road: Dumre to Gorkha and Mugling to Narayanghat. In 1970, Indian engineers completed the 188-kilometer (117-mile) extension from Pokhara to Sonauli on the Indian border; this road is called Siddhartha Raj Marg.

The most ambitious road is the result of the co-operation of the Soviet Union, the United States, Britain and India. An east-west lowland thoroughfare called Mahendra Raj Marg, this 1,000-kilometer (621-mile) route is part of the fabled Pan-Asian Highway linking the Bosphorus with the Far East. Popularly known as the East-West Highway. it has been completed east of Bhairawa.

China has completed a 32-kilometer (20 mile) long ring-road around Kathmandu, and Chinese technicians have also installed an efficient trolley-bus service between Kathmandu and Bhaktapur.

The newest highway 110-kilometer (69-mile) long stretching from Lamosangu to Jiri east of Kathmandu was begun in 1975 with Swiss technical assistance and was completed and inaugurated in September 1985.

During the rainy season, whole portions of existing roads are damaged and must be repaired. Inquire locally before setting off on a long-distance road trip.

Buses

All roads are plied by local bus services, with express coaches on the main routes. A bus ride in Nepal is a bumpy, noisy, smelly affair that can nevertheless be fun. Some of these antediluvian beasts are mere sheet-metal boxes on wheels, but they eventually arrive at their destinations, even if passengers have to occasionally alight on the steepest climbs. No matter what, they are a cheap, convenient way of going about inside and outside the Kathmandu Valley. They allow for a long, close look at the local folk inside the bus, if not always at the scenery outside.

There are minibuses on the same routes as the buses and coaches. They are less crowded, a bit faster, and more expensive.

It is recommended to book one day ahead. The main bus station Kathmandu is on one side of the Tundhikhel parade ground, opposite Kanti Path. Minibuses start from near the post office; those bound for Pokhara leave from in front of the Madras Coffee House (near the Bhimsen Tower). In Pokhara, the bus terminal is close to the post office. For details, see the following box.

Within the Kathmandu Valley, there is a comprehensive system of routes served by both buses and minibuses. See box.

Scooters

The three-wheel public scooters can carry up to six passengers. They always ply the same route within Kathmandu, starting from Rani Pokhari. Also available are black-and-yellow metered scooters for private hire.

Rickshaws

The gaudily painted, slow moving, honking rickshaws are part of the Kathmandu street scene. They are large tricyles with two seats in the back covered by a hood; a man pedals up front. Whatever the driver may demand, a ride in town should not cost more than Rs. 10: on average, Rs. 2.00 per kilometer. Make sure the driver understands where you are going and that the price is settled before you start. Remember, rickshaws should not cost more than taxis!

By the way, do not try to swap places with the driver; keeping control of the vehicle on Kathmandu's narrow streets is quite a feat. If you must, remember that a broken wheel costs around Rs. 75

Taxis and Hired Cars

Taxis are available to go most places in the Kathmandu Valley. They have black registration plates with white numbers; private cars have white numbers on red plates. Make sure their meters are working and, due to the rising gasoline costs, expect to pay a 10 percent surcharge. A short ride within the city will cost between Rs. 7-12. If you want to hire a taxi for half a day or a day trip within the Valley, negotiate a price before starting;

Buses

No.	Destination	Fare	Departure point	Time
1	Patan Gate, Jawalkhel, Lagankhel	Rs 0.75 1.00	Ratna Park (in front of Indian Airlines office)	7 a.m. to 7 p.m.
2	Bhaktapur	Rs 1.50 2.00	National Stadium (trolley bus) & Baghbazar (local bus)	7 a.m. to 8 p.m.
3	Pashupatinath, Bodhnath	Rs 1.00 1.25	Ratna Park	5:30 a.m. to 7 p.m.
4	Dhulikhel	Rs 5.25	Main Bus Station	6 a.m. to 6 p.m.
5	Barabise (Chinese Road)	Rs 17.00	Main Bus Station	5:40 a.m. 4:45 p.m.
6	Kodari (mail bus)	Rs 25.00	near Post Office	6 a.m.
7	Balaju	Rs 1.00	near Post Office & Rani Pokhari	7 a.m. to 7 p.m.
8	Trisuli	Rs 16.00	Pakanajol	7 a.m. and 12:30 p.m.
9	Pokhara & Jomosom (trekking)	minibus Rs 47.00 bus Rs 36	near Post Office Main Bus Station	5.30 a.m. to 9 a.m.
10	Birgunj (connections to Raxaul, India)	minibus Rs 46 bus Rs 39	near Post Office Main Bus Station	5.30 a.m. to 9 a.m.
11	Janakpur (connections to Indian border at Jaleswar)	bus Rs 65	Main Bus Station	5 a.m.
12	Biratnagar (connections with Jogbani, India)	minibus Rs 93 bus Rs 99	near Post Office	5 a.m.
13	Kakar Bhitta (connections to Siliguri and Darjeeling)	bus Rs 122.00	Main Bus Station	5 a.m.
14	Pokhara to Bhairawa (connections to Nautanwa, India)	minibus Rs 45 bus Rs 38	near Post Office in Pokhara town	6 a.m. to 9 a.m.

you should not pay more than Rs. 400 per day, gasoline included.

More reliable are private cars hired from any travel agency. They will cost between US $40 and $50 for the whole day but they are more comfortable and less likely to break down. The driver will wait until you have done you sightseeing and drivers normally speak at least a little English. A tip at the trip's conclusion will be welcome, but it is not mandatory, and should not be more than Rs. 50. A car holds three or four people; a metered taxi usually cannot hold more than two.

Avis is represented in Nepal by Yeti Travels, near the Annapurna Hotel; Hertz by Gorkha Travels, also on Durbar Marg.

Should you get stuck in the outskirts of Kathmandu when few cars are passing, you may try hitchhiking with passing trucks. It is polite to offer a rupee or two, or a few cigarettes, to the driver.

Bicycles

Cycling is one of the best ways of exploring the town and valley. Many shops in the old part of Kathmandu and near the main hotels have Indian and Chinese bicycles for hire at Rs. 10 for the whole day. There's no deposit; your hotel address is enough. Make sure that the bike's bell rings. This is the most important part of the vehicle — you will need it to weave your way through the throngs. Next in importance come the brakes. Lights are supposedly compulsory after sunset, but few bicycles have lights. The law is enforced, but a flashlight will suffice.

Near tourist spots, children will compete to be recognized as official caretaker of your bicycle, for a few coins and maybe a free ride on the sly. Elsewhere, it is quite safe to leave your bike unattended (but locked) while you visit a temple or go for a walk.

It is possible to hire Japanese motorbikes by the hour (Rs. 50) or the day (Rs. 500) from a garage. But these noisy, polluting nuisances are hardly suitable for the quiet stillness of the valley and its few roads and tracks.

On Foot

Be prepared for a lot of walking. Taxis and bicycles can only take you so far. Apart from a few well-trodden tourist spots, most of the interesting sites have to be reached on foot. Nepalese do not count distance by miles or kilometers, but by the number of walking hours. There's no need to compete with their often brisk pace. A leisurely stroll amid rice and mustard fields, across villages, up, down and around, is certainly the best way to "absorb" the valley, its people, their culture and way of life. Do not hesitate to venture off the tourist track. You will be safe everywhere, people will be even more friendly, and you will have the pleasure of discovery.

Accommodations

Kathmandu

Kathmandu has in the last decade seen a mushrooming of international class hotels. During the spring and fall seasons, the better hotels are working at almost full capacity; it is advisable to book well in advance. There are, however, plenty of less glamorous but still decent hotels to suit everyone's fancies and finances.

Most hotels offer a choice between three packages: bed and breakfast (CP); bed, breakfast and one other meal (MAP): or room and full board (AP). Rates listed overleaf, however, are for room only (EP), unless otherwise indicated. Where two prices are indicated, one is with and one without attached bathrooms. These are valid in 1986, add 10 percent to these quotes for service charge and 12-15 percent for government tax, depending on star rating. Rates are given in US dollars.

Besides these officially recognized hotels, there are a number of small lodges where amenities are minimal. Rates vary between US $2 and $5 a night depending on facilities; toilets and showers are generally communal and heating is extra. These small hostelries are located in the old part of Kathmandu, in the streets around the Durbar Square or in the Thamel district.

Pokhara

Hotels at Pokhara are either across the road from the airport or near Phewa Lake. While not famous for high quality lodging or food, they are generally comfortable.

The most charming place to stay in Pokhara is the **Fishtail Lodge** (tel. 71/72, cable: FISHTAIL). It stands on a rocky promontory at the eastern end of the lake, accessible only by raft from the opposite shore. It is an ideal place to rest after a trek or to admire the spectacular view. Rates are US$27 single, US$39 double; there are 35 rooms available and it is advisable to book well in advance.

Younger travelers may prefer to join the "hippie" crowd along the northern shore of Phewa Lake. A long string of lodges provides bed and breakfast for no more than US $6 a night. The general ambience and scenic surroundings are more pleasant than along the airport road, and from here one can hire boats and dugouts to travel on the lake.

The **Kantipur Hotel** opposite the Fishtail has 15 rooms in bungalows ranging from US$2.50-US$8 and an excellent restaurant. The **Kantipur Restaurant** has good food. For seclusion and peace, the **Gurkha Lodge** has three double rooms with bath at a cost of Rs. 135.

Midway between the airport and the lake is the **Dragon Hotel** (tel. 52), with 20 rooms at US$19 single, $28 double. Here the Mandala Folk Troupe performs a daily dance show.

Kathmandu Hotels

HOTEL	PHONE	CABLE	TELEX	ROOMS	DAILY RATES SINGLE	DAILY RATES DOUBLE	REMARKS
Soaltee Oberoi xxxxx	211211 211106 214213	SOALTEE	2203	300 10 suites	70	90	15 minutes from city centre. Casino, swimming, tennis, 4 restaurants.
Yak and Yeti xxxxx	412351 411436	YAKNYETI	2237	110+ 2 suites	59	81	Central. Swimming, tennis, shopping.
Everest Sheraton xxxxx	224960 220389	MALARI	2260	155	80	88	On aiport road, fine mountain views.
Annapurna xxxxx	221711 221552	ANNAPURNA	2205	150	59	72	Central. Swimming, tennis.
Kathmandu xxxx	413103 413082	RADIO SERVICE	2256	120 3 suites	58	71	Opened Nov 86. Opposite Royal Guest House, Maharajgunj.
Himalaya xxxx	521887 521888	FLORA	2566	100 3 suites	55	70	Opened Jan 87. PatanDhoka.
Malla xxxx	410320 410966 410968	MALLOTEL	2238	75	41	58	Near Royal Palace.
Shangrila xxxx	412999 4l0108	SHANGRILA	2276	50	44	55	Fine gardens, friendly service.
Shanker xxxx	412973 410538	SHANKER	2230	135	45	61	Former Rana palace. Huge gardens.
Dwarika's Kathmandu Village	414770 412328	KATHMANDAP	2239	19	30	40	Traditional bungalows with carvings and antiques. Rate charm, though not central.

Hotel	Phone					Description
Summit Hotel	521810 521894 522694	2342	30	23	38.50	Charming with good mountain view, traditional-style rooms, conference facilities, pool, craft shop.
Crystal xxx	223397 223611 223636		55	24	33	Central. Roof terrace with best view of old town.
Narayani xxx	521711/2 521442 521408	2262	88	38	45	In Patan. Good pool and garden.
Vajra	224545 224719	2309	40	14	17	More a cultural experience than a hotel. Near Swayambunath. Tibetan painted rooftop bar, October Gallery.
Woodlands xx	212683 216123 412351	2282	69	22 (B&B)	34	Near town center.
Ambassador xx	214432 410432 414432	2321	32	15	17	Lazimpath. Friendly and convenient. Same ownership as Kathmandu Guest House.
Nook xx	213627 216247		24	10	16	Good location, recently renovated.
Kathmandu Guest House x	213628 413632	80	6	8		Favorite with world travelers. Nice garden. Excellent value. In the heart of Thamel.
Star x	411004 216161		60	4.50	6.00	Thamel.
Blue Diamond x	213392 216320		29	5.60	7.25	Thamel Tole. Quiet.
Tibet Guest House x	214383 215893		32	11	12	Chetrapati, near to Thamel. Quiet, clean, Tibetan-run.

With only two flights a day arriving in Pokhara, airport activities are more entertaining than disturbing. Facing the airport are two good hotels:

New Crystal Hotel (***) (tel. 35/36, cable: NEWHOTEL) has 46 rooms at US$27 single, $39 double. The New Crystal also has an annex of 24 rooms for US$9 single, $14 double. The management is the same as Kathmandu's Crystal Hotel.

Hotel Mount Annapurna (**) (tel. 27/37, cable: MOUNTANNA) has 64 rooms at US$14 single, $21 double. Note the Tibetan murals in the dining room and bar, the management is Tibetan.

Also close to the airport is the **Himalayan Tibetan Hotel**, with cheap Tibetan and Nepali food in modest surroundings. Close by is **Pokhara Craft**, a shop specializing in local handicrafts and featuring nettle fabric (made from the stinging hill nettle) and woodcrafts. See craftsmen work here during the day.

Those not keen on walking can rent a pony from Pokhara Pony Trekking for US$15 a day.

Up-country lodging

Tiger Tops Jungle Lodge (P.O. Box 242, Kathmandu, Tel: 222706, 222958, cable: TIGERTOPS, telex: 2216 TIGTOP NP) is set in the heart of the Royal Chitwan National Park, 170 kilometers (106 miles) southwest of Kathmandu in the Terai jungle. Rates range from US$90 to US$165 a day. This includes full board, transportation by elephant or four-wheel-drive vehicle from Meghauly airfield, explorations by elephant of the surrounding jungle, boat trips, and guided walks with trained naturalists. There is also the Tiger Tops Tented Camp for those of more adventurous spirit.

Just outside the park is the new **Tharu Village**, with accommodation in the style of traditional Tharu tribal longhouses. Guests eat Nepali food, see Tharu dancing, and make visits to local villages.

For these highly recommended destinations, it is advisable to book well in advance. Contact the Tiger Tops office in Durbar Marg, Kathmandu, for further information.

Adjacent to Royal Chitwan National Park at Saurah, accessible by road via Bharatpur, are several lodges, camps and numerous teahouses. Best known are **Gaida Wildlife Camp**, and its satellite **Chitwan Jungle Lodge, Jungle Safari Lodge, National Park Cottages** and **Wendy's Lodge**.

For a more remote wildlife adventure in Far West Nepal, Tiger Tops is now operating **Karnali Tented Camp**, five hours drive from Nepalgunj, in the Royal Bardia Reserve. Accommodation is for 16 people at US$100 a day fully inclusive.

Lodges also exist in the mountains usually near airstrips, in addition to the teahouses found in every village on trekking routes. More comfortable accommodation can be found at Lukla, Phaphlu and Jumla.

More accessible (34 km east of Kathmandu) but with the atmosphere of the Himalaya is **Dhulikhel Mountain Resort**, an hour's drive past Bhaktapur toward the Chinese border. This establishment is perched high on a bluff and commands spectacular views of Himalaya. Recommended for sunrise breakfasts or sunset dinners, the food is good and reasonably priced, while the surroundings are congenial. Accommodation is in seven chalet-styled cottages with 12 rooms (tel. 213997, 216930); US$30 for a single and US$32 for a double. Booking office is in Durbar Marg. P.O. Box 3203, Cable: Resort.

Food and Dining

Despite centuries of isolation and a variety of vegetables and fruits, Nepal has failed to develop a distinctive style of cooking. An exception is Newari cooking, which can be very elaborate and spicy; but this is found only in private homes. Nepalese dishes are at best variations on Indian regional cuisines.

In most parts of Nepal, including the Kathmandu Valley, rice is the staple food. It is usually eaten boiled, supplemented with *dhal* (lentil soup), vegetables cooked with a few spices (notably ginger, garlic and chilies), and — in times of festivity — plenty of meat. There is a predilection for enormous radishes. Hill people eat *tsampa* — raw grain, ground and mixed with milk, tea or water or eaten dry — as a complement to, or substitute for, rice. *Chapatis* diversify the diet. Some castes eat pork. Goat, chicken and buffalo meat — or in the mountains, yak meat — is available to all, but beef is forbidden in this Hindu kingdom.

The Nepalis enjoy eating sweets and spicy snacks such as *jelebis* and *laddus*. These come in a variety of shapes, and wrappings, not to mention ingredients and tastes. Fruit from the lowlands can also be found in Kathmandu. Transportation costs have pushed prices up, so that fruit is often sold by the unit or even by the quarter-unit for a few rupees.

Buffalo milk is turned into clarified butter (*ghee*) or delicious curd sold in round earthenware pots. Curd is a good buy, but be sure to scrape off the top layer. Dairy products are rare elsewhere in Asia, but fresh milk, butter and cheese are plentiful in Kathmandu. The main dairy is at Balaju. Excellent cheese is available at the Nepal Dairy at Mahabouda, behind Bir Hospital.

Fresh bread can be found in food shops, and doughnuts are sold in the streets. The Annapurna and Nanglo cake shops (both in Durbar Marg) are good but best of all is The Bakery in Kanti Path.

Certain areas of Nepal have developed regional dishes. The introduction of a potato crop in Sherpa country has revolutionized eating habits there. Sherpas now survive on potatoes, eating them baked or boiled, dipped in salt or chilies. More elaborately, they enjoy *gurr* — raw potatoes peeled, pounded with spices, grilled like large pancakes on a hot flat stone, then eaten with fresh cheese. Tibetan cooking, including *Thukba* (thick soup) and *momos* (fried or boiled stuffed raviolis), — is widespread in the mountains and is also available in Kathmandu.

Drinks

The national drink, *chiya* (tea brewed together with milk, sugar and sometimes spices), is served in glasses, scalding hot. Up in the mountains, it is salted with yak butter and churned, Tibetan-style. Another popular mountain drink is *chhang*, powerful sort of beer made from fermented barley, maize, rye or millet. *Arak* (potato alcohol) and *rakshi* (wheat or rice alcohol) also have their enthusiasts.

Coca-cola is bottled in the Kathmandu Valley and Lemu (a lemon drink), Fanta orange and soda are also available. Restaurants serve good Nepalese beer, Star, Golden Eagle and Iceberg, as well as imported brews, while the classiest establishments in Kathmandu suggest bottles of imported wine at prohibitive prices. Good quality rum, vodka and gin are produced locally. If you are a whisky drinker, though, be warned against the local variety.

Where to Eat

Kathmandu restaurants have vastly improved in the last few years. Prices are low by Western standards. Indian, Chinese, Tibetan and even Japanese cuisine is found, as well as a variety of Western menus. The large international hotels have three or four restaurants each, some of them excellent.

Outside of Kathmandu, it is often difficult to find appealing food in the Valley, even for a snack. Travelers on day outings should carry their own food; snacks from the Annapurna or Nanglo bakeries and some fresh fruit will do for a midday picnic before repairing to the more substantial menus of Kathmandu.

Chimney Restaurant, Yak & Yeti Hotel. The original Boris' restaurant, this is one of the best in town for good Western cuisine. A meal of pâte maison, shrimp cocktail, chicken a la Kiev and vegetable au gratin costs Rs. 400 for two people, excluding drinks. The atmosphere of this former Rana palace is cozy and congenial, with a central fireplace blazing in winter.

Ghar e Kebab, Durbar Marg, serves wonderful *tandoori* and Indian cuisine in comfortable surroundings, accompanied by Indian classical music. It is excellent value at around Rs. 80 a head. It is advisable to book in advance as this is one of the most popular restaurants in town (Tel: 221711, 221552).

Al Fresco, at Hotel Soaltee Oberoi, offers Italian cooking in elegant surroundings at elegant prices.

Far Pavilion, Hotel Everest Sheraton, an elegant new Indian dining experience on the top floor next to Ropes for barbecues and the Bugles and Tigers bar for a drink before. Unrivaled views.

Garden Terrace, at Hotel Soaltee Oberoi. Dinner and dance with live band; offers continental cuisine. Open from 7a.m.–11p.m.

Gorkha Grill, at Hotel Soaltee Oberoi. Hot snacks, tempting pastries through the day and chinese cuisine in the evening. Open from 7a.m.–11p.m.

La Marmite, Durbar Marg. French cooking of an ambitious nature. Popular with local residents. Closed Mondays.

Kowloon, Lazimpat, offers delicious spicy Chinese cuisine in unpretentious surroundings for about Rs. 50 per person.

Old Vienna Inn, Thamel, has reasonable, hearty Austrian and German specialities. Try the Appel Strudel.

Zen, Thamel, good Mexican-style food in simplest surroundings.

Arirang Restaurant, Durbar Marg. The only Korean food in town.

Sun Kosi, Durbar Marg, next to Tiger Tops office. An excellent selection of traditional Nepalese and Tibetan food is offered in pleasant surroundings. This is the only real Nepalese cooking outside private homes. Service can be slow and prices run about Rs. 80 per person.

Utse, Thamel. Tasty Tibetan food and good value; but hygiene is not the restaurant's forte. (412747).

Mountain City Chinese Restaurant, Malla Hotel. Szechuan cuisine is prepared by Chinese cooks from Chengdu. A meal will cost about Rs. 150 per person.

Golden Gate, Durbar Marg. This Chinese restaurant is also run by the Malla Hotel, offers Peking and Canton specialities.

Tso-Ngon, Chetrapati. Tibetan and Chinese cuisine runs about Rs. 50 for two.

Fuji Restaurant, Kantipath, newly opened, Japanese food in an imaginatively converted Rana bungalow with a picturesque moat.

Nanglo Chinese, Durbar Marg. The Chinese food here is good, though the decor is rather dark. It is good value at Rs. 50 per person.

Nanglo Pub and Snack Bar, Durbar Marg. The same management offers good Western food and sandwiches for lunch, served in the courtyard or on the roof. Excellent value.

Rumdoodle, Thamel. Named after a climbing spoof, this fun restaurant caters to mountaineers and trekkers with hearty appetites. Select steaks and hamburgers from an amusing menu for about Rs. 45 per dish. Atmospheric bar.

K C's Restaurant, Thamel, is a favorite hangout for aging hippies and world travelers. This is "where the action is," and K C is an amiable host. Good Western food. Try the recently opened section upstairs.

Kushi Fuji, Durbar Marg. This Japanese restaurant can be found above Tiger Tops office. There is an open counter with good food for about Rs. 50 per person.

Sakura-Ya Restaurant, Lazimpat. Newly opened spectacular Japanese restaurant with beautiful garden, authentic cuisine. Menu from Rs. 65 to Rs. 350.

Aunt Jane's, Dharma Path off New Road, is a relic of the hippie days. It serves American food at Rs. 15 to 20 per dish.

Yin Yang, Basantapur, is of the same vintage and was a favorite of the flower children. Call in for a drink.

Media

Press

There are several newspapers published in English in Kathmandu, as well as dozens in Nepali. They are somewhat controlled, although Nepali dailies and weeklies — when read between the lines — express various shades of opinion. In English, *The Rising Nepal* has wider coverage of foreign news than the more parochial *Motherland*. Both dailies devote a lot of their front pages to the King's activities.

The International Herald Tribune can be found at newsstands and hotels. (It arrives one day late). Also available are *Time, Newsweek, The Far Eastern Economic Review, Asiaweek* and *India Today*. There are few other foreign news publications to be found in Nepal, except Indian newspapers which arrive daily on the morning flights.

Books and Maps

Kathmandu has many bookshops with very good selections of books about Nepal, written in several languages. The best ones include **Ratna Pustak Bhandar** near the French Cultural Center off Bag Bazar; **Himalayan Book Centre** in Bag Bazar; **Educational Enterprises** in Kanti Path opposite Bir Hospital; **Everest Book Service** beside Rani Pokhari and **Himalayan Booksellers** in Bhotahiti with a branch in Thamel.

The green map of Nepal and the orange street map of Kathmandu published by Himalayan Booksellers will complement the maps found in this *Insight Guide* Regional trekking maps are also available, though most are not entirely reliable. The best are those prepared by Erwin Schneider, though they cover only eastern Nepal and the Kathmandu Valley. *Apa Maps, Nepal,* covers the country from Dhaulagiri to the eastern border.

Radio

Two news bulletins in English are broadcast by Radio Nepal daily at 8 a.m. and 8.30 p.m. There is also a "tourist program" between 8.15 and 9 in the evening. Bring a short-wave radio if you are addicted to international news.

Entertainment

Early in 1986, television arrived in Kathmandu with NEPAL TV presenting three hours of programmes 6 p.m.–9 p.m. daily, they have plans for future expansion. Kathmandu, however, has a few movie houses featuring mainly Indian tear-jerkers; Western visitors may enjoy the reactions of the audience more than the action on the screen. For Western films, see the programs of the European and American cultural centers. Video is flourishing among more privileged Nepalis.

By 10 p.m., Kathmandu is nearly asleep. The only life centers around some temples, the restaurants and tourists hotels. There are no night clubs, no dance halls, no massage parlors to speak of. You can dance at the Soaltee Oberoi, Yak and Yeti and Everest Sheraton hotels; the Copper Floor disco at Hotel Lali Guras in Lazimpat is open Fridays and Saturdays. The only action late in the evening is to be found in Thamel where drinking centers around the Up and Down Bar or at Pumpkins in the Everest Sheraton.

There is a casino at the Soaltee Oberoi Hotel, where Indians toss small fortunes to the wind on baccarat, chemin-de-fer, roulette and other games. The chit value is counted in Indian rupees or foreign exchange; no Nepalis are permitted entry. Casino Nepal is one of the few international casinos between Malaysia and the Suez. If you decide to come, the casino will provide a free taxi ride back to your hotel.

Some hotels have folk dances and musical shows in their restaurants. The best is staged by the Everest Cultural Society, at Lal Durbar near the Yak and Yeti hotel. Folk dances are presented at 7 p.m. daily and, if specially ordered by your travel agent, an authentic Nepalese dinner can be arranged.

Another leading cultural dance group staging classical and folk dances together with songs and music is the New Himalchuli Cultural Group, which performs daily from 6:30 pm to 7:30 pm (Nov. — Feb.), 7:00 pm to 8:00 p.m. (Mar — Oct.). For more information, you can write to:

New Himalchuli Cultural Group, P.O. Box 3409, Lazimpat, Kathmandu, Nepal. Tel: 4-11825.

For excellent Indian classical music, go to the Ghar e Kebab restaurant in the Annapurna Hotel in Durbar Marg.

But the best show of all is in Bhaktapur: spectacular local dancing, *son et lumiere*, and a Nepalese dinner amidst ancient squares and courtyards lit by countless oil lamps. This must be specially arranged in advance, and then for groups only; ask your travel agent for details.

Festivals

Because of the differences in calendars, festival dates vary from year to year. The Department of Tourism in Kathmandu publishes an annual brochure indicating the specific dates of each festival during the coming year.

Baisakh (April-May)

Major New Year celebrations are **Bisket** at Bhaktapur and **Balkumari Jatra** at Thimi. The **Rato Machhendranath Jatra** in Patan also falls in **Baisakh**.

Later in the month is the **Matatirtha Snan**, highlighted by ritual baths at Matatirtha, near

Thankot, for persons whose mothers have died during the past year. Meanwhile, in the Naxal district, ritual sacrifices to insure a prosperous summer are staged as part of the **Astami** celebration.

Observances are held throughout Nepal in May to mark **Buddha Jayanthi,** the birthday of the Gautama Buddha, born in the Terai township of Lumbini in the 6th Century B.C. There are pilgrimages to Buddhist shrines, especially those at Swayambhunath and Bodhnath in the Kathmandu Valley. Pilgrims from all over Nepal make this a very colorful affair.

Jesth (May-June)

Domestic offerings are made throughout the Valley to Kumar, the "divine warrior," at **Sithinakha.** This is a time for wells to be cleaned. A procession in Kathmandu marks the end of the farmers' time of leisure and the beginning of the rainy season.

The Sherpa religious festival of **Mani Rimdu** is held at the Thamel monastery of Namche Bazaar and lasts three days. Monks seek to gain merit by performing masked dramas and dances. Festivities are repeated six months later at the Thyangboche monastery northeast of Namche Bazaar.

Asadh (June-July)

The national holiday of **Tribhuvan Jayanthi** honors the memory of his late majesty King Tribhuvan, the present King's grandfather. The ceremony is at Tripureshwar, where the former ruler's statue stands.

Srawan (July-August)

The festival of **Ghanta Karna,** a relic of the belief in demons, is held in all Newar settlements. It marks the completion of the paddy planting season in the Kathmandu Valley. Street crossings are embellished with three-legged structures of fresh green reeds, intended to ward off evil spirits threatening the rice crop.

Naga Panchhami honors *nagas,* the divine serpents. In Kathmandu and the rest of the Valley, particularly at Pashupatinath, propitiatory offerings are made and paintings depicting *nagas* are pinned on doors and blessed by priests. This is also the day for the start of *lakhe* (masked dancing) in Kathmandu.

In ceremonies at the Kumbeshwar temple in Patan and at Gosainkund Lake in the Himalayan foothills north of the Valley, Shiva Mahadev is honored in the festival of **Janai Purnima** or **Rakshya Vandhana.** Brahmans and Chhetris renew their *munja,* or sacred thread, while priests distribute yellow threads to people of other castes to protect them against disease and evil spirits. These *rikhi doro* are worn until the Diwali festival, when they are tied to the tails of cows. Of special note are the trances of *jhankris,* musician sorcerers.

Bhadra (August-September)

This is a great festival month, with **Gaijatra, Indrajatra** and **Dasain** all falling within 30 days of each other. And there are more:

The festival of **Krishnastami** takes place in 11 sanctuaries and temples dedicated to Krishna. The main focus is the Krishna Mandir in Patan's Durbar Square. Offerings of *tulsi* plant are made as women sings hymns to commemorate the Krishna's birth.

The "festival of the five summer gifts," **Pancha Dan** or **Banda Yatra,** is held at Swayambhunath and elsewhere in the Valley. Buddhist priests chant hymns while women, waiting in front of their houses, give the priests rice and grains as they pass.

Gokarna Aunshi or **Father's Day** is highlighted by ritual bathing in the Bagmati River at Gokarna for those whose fathers have died during the past year. Living fathers are presented with sweets and other gifts by their offsprings.

Modern transportation has altered some traditions, but most women still walk to Pashupatinath for the three-day **Teej Brata** festival. Married women wear scarlet and gold wedding saris, and the unmarried young go singing and dancing in their brightest clothes to pray to Shiva and his consort Parvati for a long happy conjugal life. Then they take a ceremonial bath in the Bagmati in honor of their husbands or husbands-to-be. This festival is celebrated throughout the Kathmandu Valley with feasting on the first day and fasting on the second and third.

Ashwin (September-October)

The **Ganesh Festival** at the September full moon honors the pot-bellied elephant god without whose blessings no religious ceremony, be it private or public, is ever begun. Nepalis believe that even Surya, the sun god, offers *puja* to Ganesh before he journeys across the heavens.

Kartik (October-November)

The highlight of this month is the celebration of **Tihar,** the Festival of Lights.

The **Haribodhani Ekadasi** pilgrimage in honor of Vishnu is made to Budhanilkantha later in *Kartik.* It is preceded by a day of fasting.

Marga (November-December)

Pilgrims from all over Nepal throng to Pashupatinath for **Bala Chaturdasi** and spend the first night burning oil lamps as an offering to the gods. They start the following morning with a holy bath in the Bagmati River and make further offerings to Lord Pashupati. Then worshipers follow the traditional pilgrimage route through the Mrigasthali Forest, scattering several varieties of seeds and sweets so that their dead relations may reap the benefits of these offerings in the next world.

In Janakpur in the eastern Terai, the **Vivaha Panchami** festival recalls Sita's marriage to Rama, hero of the great *Ramayana* epic.

Poush (December-January)

Constitution Day is commemorated in every town in Nepal with ceremonies recalling the 1962 Constitutional Act. Tribute is paid to the late King

Mahendra, father of the current monarch.

The **Birthday of His Majesty the King** also falls in this month. Throughout the Kingdom, there are ceremonies, processions and military parades. King Birendra Bir Bikram Shah Dev was born December 28, 1945.

Magha (January-February)

Magha Sankranti marks the transition from the winter to the warmer seasons. It is a day for ritual bathing and singing traditional religious songs. Soon after, on the new moon, the fair of **Tribeni Mela** is held on the banks of the Narayani River.

The spring season is ushered in by the **Basanta Panchami** festival. In a ceremony at Kathmandu's Hanuman Dhoka palace, the King receives a *tika* and slices of coconut during a 31 gun salute, then listens to poems and songs in honor of spring.

Temples and sanctuaries dedicated to Saraswati, the Hindu goddess of learning, wisdom and music, and to Manjushri, her Buddhist counterpart, are gaily decorated with flowers. Schoolchildren parade in the streets, carrying school gear to be blessed by Saraswati; on the following morning, young children will begin to learn how to read. Older students go to Swayambhunath or Chabahil to ask Saraswati for success in their exams. Farmers practice special *pujas* in their fields to obtain a good summer crop, this being the time of the first plowing.

On the final day of Magha — **Magha Purnima** — a procession of bathers walks from the Bagmati River *ghats,* where they have bathed every morning for a month, to various temples. They also visit Sankhu, where they take ritual baths in the Salinadi River.

Falgun (February-March)

On **Rashtriya Prajatantra Divas** or **Democracy Day,** parades and processions are held all over the kingdom to celebrate the 1951 overthrow of the autocratic Rana regime.

This is also the time of the joyous Tibetan New Year and the colourful **Maha Shivaratri** festival.

Chaitra (March-April)

Horse races and displays of gymnastics and horsemanship are held on the Tundhikhel for **Ghorajatra.** In Patan, celebrants watch the crazy dance of a drunken one-eyed horse and its rider. Sacrifices are made to temples of the Ashta Matrikas, or mother goddess. On the third and final day, in Asan Tole, there is a rowdy meeting of these goddesses, who bow comically to each other amidst fanfares and torch-bearing processions.

At the same time, the Newari festival of **Pasa Chare** takes place. This is a time of hospitality among the Newars, when friends and neighbors visit one another. On the same day as the horse show, the demon Gurumpa is carried to the Tundhikhel in a midnight procession. In the Asan Tole, divinities are brought together in a ceremonial meeting.

In the third week of March, the festivals of **Chaitra Dasain** and **Seto Machhendranath** occur simultaneously in Kathmandu.

Meanwhile in Janakpur in the eastern Terai, the birthday of Ram Chandra, son of King Dasarath of Ayuthaya, is celebrated in the **Ram Navami** festival at the Janaki Mandir.

Sports

Sports as a pastime or occupation is an alien concept. It has only recently been introduced into school curricula and military training programs. Football (soccer) and cricket have become popular, however, while cycling and jogging are attracting some enthusiasts.

Paradoxically, in this mountain land, skiing is out of the question, though a few mountaineering expeditions do try it. The steepness of slopes and the exceptionally high snow line (bringing with it attendant altitude problems) make skiing impractical.

Tourists and foreign residents, however, can enjoy fishing and swimming, golf, tennis, squash and hockey, though facilities are limited. Two new golf courses, one of them replacing the old Royal Golf Club, are under construction. Outsiders can use the tennis courts and swimming pools of the Soaltee Oberoi, Yak and Yeti, Everest Sheraton and Annapurna hotels for small entrance fees.

Prudence is needed when bathing in mountain torrents and rivers because of swift, treacherous currents. The larger rivers in the lowlands are safer, but keep an eye out for the occasional crocodile.

Terai rivers and valley lakes are often good fishing grounds. Besides the small fry, the two main catches are *asla,* a kind of snow trout, and the much larger *masheer,* which grows to as much as 80 pounds (36 kilograms). February, March, October and November are the best months for fishing. Permits are required from the National Parks and Wildlife Conservation Department in Baneswar, just off the airport road. Contact Tiger Tops and West Nepal Adventures in Durbar Marg for information on fishing in the Karnali, Babi and Narayani rivers. Bring your own tackle.

Shopping

Kathmandu is a treasure trove for the unwary. Children sell *khukris,* belts, coins. Traders appear wherever tourists stray. Merchants wait on temple steps. Junk, guaranteed fake antiques, souvenirs are everywhere. Peer into the shops, take your pick or take your leave; try the next boutique or the next mat.

There are good buys to be found here, too:

● Clothes are certainly good value, from lopsided *topis* (caps) to knitted mittens and woolen socks; from Tibetan dresses that button at the side to men's cotton shirts tied diagonally with ribbons across the chest. *Topis* come in two types: somber black ones and multicolor variations. They are like ties, a must for all Nepalis visiting the administration, but with a difference — their asymmetric shape is said to be a replica of Mount Kailash, the most sacred mountain for Buddhists and Hindus.

● Pieces of Nepalese cloth, red, black and orange, checkered with dots, that women wrap around their shoulders. Shawls are made with the same cotton cloth, but are covered on both sides with thin muslin that gives pastel overtones to the cloth.

● Wool and para wool blankets are a typical product of Nepal; made of the finest goat wool called *pashmina*, they are extremely soft, warm and strong.

● "Tibetan" multicolored wool jackets, shoulder bags and boots of geometrical designs. Most are made in India, and jackets sell for about Rs. 100. The "authentic" ones sewn in the Jawlakhel Tibetan camp are more expensive.

● Various Nepalese folk objects. Among them are the national knife, the *khukris*, worn at the belt and sometimes highly adorned; and the *saranghi*, a small four-stringed viola cut from a single piece of wood and played with a horse-hair bow by the *gaine* (begging minstrels).

● All kinds of copper or brass pots, jugs and jars, sold by their weight (but rather heavy to take home).

● Tibetan tea bowls made of wood and lined with silver.

● Embossed prayer wheels of all sizes.

● Hand-made paper beautifully tie dyed by the women of Bhaktapur or woodblock printed in traditional designs.

● Papier-maché dance masks and terra-cotta elephants used as flower pots, made by the hundreds in Thimi, a village close to Bhaktapur.

● Copper or bronze statuettes of the Buddha and of various Hindu deities, none of them too old. All are produced semi-industrially, together with filigreed brass animals or ashtrays inlaid with small pieces of colored stones, and dreadful copies of erotic sculptures that seem to excite tourists so much.

● Numerous Tibetan trinkets, to be found primarily around Bodhnath but also in Patan and Kathmandu. They include everything from human skulls and leg bones to *thangkas* (painted scrolls). There is silver-plated jewelry inlaid with coral and turquoise (earrings, necklaces, amulets, belt buckles, plaited silver belts and daggers), as well as bronze mandalas, charm boxes, pieces of furniture, musical instruments — gongs, oboes and *damarus* (small drums).

● Carpets, the production of which is now flourishing with substantial exports and sales from Hong Kong to New York. The new ones, made in private homes or refugee centers, are done in bright colors with chemical dyes, or with more subtle (and more expensive) vegetable dyes in traditional Tibetan designs. Older carpets, with intricate motifs and natural dye colors, are still available at higher prices.

● Bamboo flutes are also a good buy and make cheap gifts. You will find them in the main streets of old Kathmandu. Look for a couple of vendors who play while toting a tree of flutes on their shoulders. *Hookahs* (water pipes) are tempting, but you might have trouble getting them past suspicious customs officials.

● Beautiful marriage umbrellas in a variety of designs and colors can be bought in Bhaktapur, but these are for decoration and are not waterproof.

Before going on a buying spree, you should remember a few things:

● Genuine prayer wheels are supposed to hold a roll of parchment or paper bearing a *mantra* (prayer formula).

● An authentic *khukri* should have a small notch at the bottom of the blade to divert blood away from the handle. In the back of the scabard, there should be two small knives for skinning and sharpening.

● Gold jewelry should show a slight tooth mark when bitten.

● A fine sculpture will have the fingers of its subject's hand separately sculpted, not merely outlined. This qualification leaves out about 99 percent of the modern works to be seen in Kathmandu.

● Unless otherwise certified by specialists, consider "antique" pieces to have been made the week before you see them in the shop, and pay accordingly. Tibetans and Nepalis will not willingly part with their jewels and adornments; it is impolite to pressure them to sell their personal heirlooms.

To get an idea of the variety of things that can be purchased, and of the relative qualities and prices, visits are suggested to:

● **Jawalakhel**, near Patan, for the best Tibetan carpets, old and new. They are displayed in the Tibetan refugee center and also in the many shops in that area.

● **Cheez Beez Bhandar**, "the Nepalese Handicraft Center" near Jawalkhel. This shop has handicrafts for sale from all parts of Nepal.

● **Tibet Ritual Art Gallery**, Durbar Marg, above the Sun Kosi restaurant. Here are excellent quality antiques and rare art objects — it is worth paying for the expertise and taste of Karma and Margot, the proprietors.

● **Patan Industrial Estate,** to see woodcarving, metalwork and *thangka* painting. See also the **Bhaktapur Crafts Center** in Dattatraya Square.

The main shops in Kathmandu for imported articles are in and around New Road. Shops selling handicrafts to tourists are centered around Durbar Marg and the big hotels. You might find something interesting to buy anywhere in the Valley, however.

Remember, when buying, that old *thangkas* and bronzes are forbidden for export if they are more than 100 years old. Certificates are required to prove their younger age if there is any doubt. Shopkeepers are happy to help you.

Dialing Direct

Police

| Emergency service | 211999, 211162 |

Tourist information centers

Main office: Ganga Path, Basantapur (in front of Hanuman Dhoka palace; open 10 a.m. to 4 p.m. Sunday through Friday; English-language information)	215818
Tribhuvan Airport Exchange (other offices in airports at Pokhara, Bhairawa, Birganj and Kaka Bhitta)	211933
Department of Tourism (cable: TOURISTS, Kathmandu)	211293, 214519
Telephone enquiry, Tripureshwor	197

Airlines

Aeroflot Soviet Airlines, Kanti Path	212397
Air France, Durbar Marg	223339
Air India, Kanti Path	212335
Air Lanka, Kanti Path	212831
Bangladesh Biman, Durbar Marg	212544
British Airways, Durbar Marg	222266
Burma Airways Corporation, Durbar Marg	214839
Cathay Pacific, Kanti Path	214705
Indian Airlines, Durbar Marg	211198
Japan Air Lines, Durbar Marg	412138
K.L.M. Royal Dutch Airlines, Durbar Marg	214896
Lufthansa, Durbar Marg	213052
Northwest Airlines, Kanti Path	215855
Pakistan International, Durbar Marg	212102
Pan American World Airways, Durbar Marg	411824, 410564
Royal Nepal Airlines, Kanti Path	220757
Swissair, Durbar Marg	412455
Thai International, Durbar Marg	213565
Trans World Airlines, Kanti Path	214704
Shanker Travel and Tours, Shanker Hotel, Lazimpat	213494

Sherpa Travel Service	222489
Tiger Tops Durbar Marg	212706
Trans Himalayan Tours, Durbar Marg	213854
Universal Travel and Tours, Kanti Path	214192
World Travels, Durbar Marg	212810
Yeti Travel; Durbar Marg	211234

Trekking Agencies

Annapurna Mountaineering and Trekking, Durbar Marg	212736
Express Trekking, Naxal	213017
Gauri Shankar Trekking, Lazimpat	212112
Great Himalayan Adventure, Kanti Path	216144
Himal Trek, Maharajgunj	211561
Himalayan Adventures, Thamel	212496
Himalayan Journeys, Kanti Path	215855
Himalayan Rover Trek, Naxal	412667
International Trekkers, Durbar Marg	215594
Lama Excursions, Durbar Marg	410786
Manaslu Trekking, Durbar Marg	212422
Mountain Adventure Trekking	414910
Mountain Travel, Durbar Marg	412455
Mountain Travel, Naxal	414508
Natraj Trekking, Kanti Path	216644
Nepal Trekking, Thamel	214681
Nepal Trekking and Natural History Expeditions, New Road	212985
Sherpa Cooperative Trekking Kamal Pokhari	215887
Sherpa Trekking Service, Kamaladi	222489
Trans Himalayan Trekking, Durbar Marg	213854

Social Clubs

International Club, Tahachal	213605
Lions Club (weekly meetings at Blue Star Hotel, Tripureshwar)	214612
Rotary Club, Thapatali	212583

Religious services

Roman Catholic:
| Jesuit St. Xavier College, Jawalkhel | 521050 |
| Annapurna Hotel (Sunday mass) | 211711 |
Protestant:
| Church of Christ-Nepal, Ram Shah Path | |
| Blue Room, USIS, Rabi Bhawan | 213966 |
Jewish:
| Contact Israeli Embassy | 211251 |
Islam:
Main Mosque, Durbar Marg

Saudi Arabia: Embassy, P.O. Box 94384, Al-Morabba, Nasir Bin Saud Bin Farhan Street, Behind Capital Marriage Palace, Riyadh-11693.

Spain: Consulate, Finca Ca'n Martin, Son Sardinia, Carretera Vaudemossa, Palma de Mallorca, Tel: (71) 202604; Gran Vai de Les Corts, Catalanes, 1075-7e La, Barcelona-20.

Sri Lanka: Consulate, 290 R.A. de Mel Mawatha, Colombo-7.

South Korea: Consulate, 541 Namdaemoonro, Jung-Gu, Seoul-100. Tel: 22-9992, 771-91.

Sweden: Consulate, Karlavagen, 97 S – 115 22, Stockholm.

Switzerland: Consulate, Schanzengasse 22, P.O.

Box CH-8024, Zurich, Tel: 01475993.

Thailand: Embassy, 189 Soi – 71, Sukhamvit Road, Bangkok-10110, Tel: 391-7240, 390-2280.

Turkey: Consulate; Ramtas A.S., Y.K.B. Ishani Valikonagi Cad. 4/4 Nisantas, Istanbul.

U.S.S.R. Embassy, 2nd Neopolimovsky Pere look 14/7, Moscow, Tel: 2447356, & 2419311.

U.K. Embassy, 12A Kensington Palace Gardens, London W8 4QU. Tel: 229-1594, 229-6231.

United Nations: Permanent Mission 820 Second Avenue, Suite 1200, New York, NY 10017. Tel: (212) 370-4188. (212) 370-4189; 1 Rue Frederic Amiel, 1203 Geneva, Tel: (022) 44-44-41.

U.S.A. Embassy, 2131 Leroy Place N.W., Washington D.C.-20008, Tel: (202) 667-4550. Consulates, 473 Jackson Street, San Francisco, CA-94111 Tel: (415) 434-1111; 16250 Dallas Parkway, Suite 110, Dallas TX-75248, Tel: (214) 931-1212; 212, 15th Street N.E., Atlanta Georgia-30309, Tel: (404) 892-8152.

Foreign Missions in Kathmandu

Australia, Bhat Bhateni	411578
Bangladesh, Naxal	410012
Burma, Pulchok	521788
China, Baluwatar	412589
Egypt, Pulchok	521844
France, Lazimpat	412332
Germany (East), Tripureshwar	214801
Germany (West), Kanti Path	211730
India, Lainchaur	410900
Israel, Lazimpat	411811
Italy, Baluwatar	412743
Japan, Pani Pokhari	414083
Korea (North), Patan	521084
Korea (South), Tahachal	211172
Pakistan, Pani Pokhari	411421
Thailand, Thapathali	213910
U.S.S.R., Baluwatar	412155
United Kingdom, Lainchaur	410583
U.S.A., Pani Pokhari	411601

International organizations

Asian Development Bank, Babar Mahal	214217
International Monetary Fund,	410158
Nepal Rastriya Bank, Baluwatar	211225
United Nations agencies, Lainchaur	216444
World Bank, RNAC Building.	214792
U.S.A.I.D. Mission, Kalimati	211144

Cultural Centers

British Council, Kanti Path	221305
French Cultural Center, Bag Bazar	224326
Indian Cultural Center and Library, RNAC Building	211497
U.S.S.R. Cultural Center, Ram Shah Path	216248
Goethe Institute, Sundhara	220528
U.S. Information Service, New Road	221250, 223893

Diplomatic Missions

Nepalese Missions Overseas

Australia: Consulate, 870 Military Road, Suite 1 Strand Centre, Mosman, NSW 2088, Sydney. Tel 9603565; 6/204, The Avenue, Parkville 3052, Melbourne; House of Kathmandu, 66 High Street, Toowong 4066, Brisbane, Tel: (07) 3714228; 16 Robinson Street, Nadlands, Perth.

Austria: Consulate, A-1190 Vienna, Karpenfenwaldgasse 11.

Bangladesh: Embassy, Lake Road, No. 2, Baridhara Diplomatic Enclave, Baridhara, Dhaka, Tel: 601790, 601890.

Belgium: Consulate, Nepal House, 149 Lamorinierstraat, B-2018 Antwerp, Tel: 03-2308800.

Burma: Embassy, 16 Natmauk Yeiktha (Park Avenue), P.O. Box 84, Tamwe, Rangoon, Tel: 50633.

Canada: Consulate, 310 Dupont Street, Toronto, Ontario, Tel: (416)9687252.

China: Embassy, No. 1 Sanlitun Xiliujie, Beijing, Tel: 521795. Consulate, Norbulingka Road 13, Lhasa, Tel: 22880.

Denmark: Consulate, 36 Kronprinsessagade, DK 1006, Copenhagen K., Tel: 01-143175.

Egypt: Embassy, 9 Tiba Street, Dokki, Cairo, Tel: 704447, 704541.

Finland: Consulate, Parkgatan 9, Helsingfors 14, Tel: 90-626789.

France: Embassy, 7 Rue de Washington, 75008 Paris, Tel: 43592861, 43593123. Consulate, 10 Rue Claude Gonin, 31400 Toulouse, Tel: 348413.

Federal Republic Of Germany: Embassy, Im-Hag 15, D-5300 Bonn, Bad Godesberg 2, Tel: (0228) 343097. Consulates, Flinschstrasse 63, D-6000 Frankfurt am Main 60, Tel: 069-40871; Landsbergerstrasse 191, D-8000 Munich 21, Tel: 089-5704406; Busako Luyken G m b H, Postfach 080206, Handwerkstrasse 5-7 D-7000 Sttutgart, 80 (Vaihingen), Tel: 0711-7864-615.

Hong Kong: Liaison office, H.Q. Brigade of Gurkhas, Prince of Wales Building, British Forces Post Office, Tel: 5-28933255.

India: Embassy, Barakhamba Road, New Delhi-110001, Tel: 381484, 388191, 387361, 386592, 387594. Consulate, 19 Woodlands, Sterndale Road, Alipore, Calcutta-700027, Tel: 452024, 459027.

Italy: Consulate, Piazza Medaglie d'Oro 20, 00136 Rome, Tel: (06) 3451642, 348176, 341055.

Japan: Embassy, 16-23 Higashi-Gotanda, 3-chome, Shingawa-ku, Tokyo 141, Tel: 444-7303, 444-7305.

Lebanon: Consulate, Rue Spears, Beirut, Tel: 386690.

Mexico: Consulate, Avellanos, No. 24 Jardines de Sam Mateo, Naucalpan, Estado de Mexico.

Netherlands: Consulates, Lange Voorhut 16, NL-2514 EE Den Haa, Tel: 070-458882; Prinsengracht 687, Gelderland Bldg, NL-1017 JV Amsterdam, Tel: 020-25-0388, 020-24-1530.

Norway: Consulate, Haakon VIIs gt.-5 P.O. Box 1384 Vika, 0116 Oslo, Tel: (2) 414743.

Pakistan: Embassy, House 506, 84th Street, Attaturk Avenue, Ramna G-6/4 Islamabad, Tel: 823642, 823754. Consulate, 1st Floor Union Bank Building, Merewether Tower, Chundrigar Road, Karachi-2, Tel: 234458, 228947.

Philippines: Consulate, 1136-1138 United Nations Avenue, Paco 2803, Manila, Tel: 589393, 588855.

Coping With Culture

What is a foreigner? By definition, he or she is wealthy. Think of how many bags of rice the plane ticket that got you to Kathmandu is worth. The postulate of foreign wealth has been deeply ingrained in Nepalese minds. Its consequences can be a bit unsettling for the visitor: the corollary is that the Nepalese should try to get a little of that wealth. Foreigners have often been extremely generous with sweets, goods, clothing and cash. As a result, a little blackmail is not unusual from porters and guides on mountain treks for those who go it alone. One often gets requests for free medicine, or encounters beggars in the tourist-trodden parts of the Kathmandu valley.

Children frequently chant the magic words "Rupee! Paisa!" with palms extended. It is mostly a game. Ignore them and they will smile and romp away. Should they insist, grown-ups will shout and scatter them, for there is pride in the valley as in the hills.

On occasion, rowdy crowds of unruly children will throng you. Take care of your belongings, make sure your bag is zipped up, your camera equipment secure. Mostly, they will annoy you by popping up between your camera and the statues you want to photograph. Let them be: children can give a sense of proportion to a picture. Get a friend to distract their attention. Or else give up, or pretend to, until they are busy somewhere else.

One can go about almost everywhere in complete confidence. Women can walk on their own without being bothered.

A source of bad feeling may arise if you are asked not to enter a certain precinct or not to photograph a shrine. Comply with good grace. The reasons for enforcing a taboo are as evident to the local people as they are obscure to you.

Nobody will ask you to forgo your own values and standards as long as you don't expect them to be followed by everybody. Respect and open-mindedness are essential. The apparent familiarity with which the Nepalese behave toward idols should be no invitation for you to imitate them by riding on statues or other such nonsense. The Nepalese understand that Western values are different from theirs. Even if they are shocked or stunned by your behavior, they will explain it as primitive barbarianism, and will not pursue the matter as long as they don't think the gods are offended.

Customs and Traditions

In Nepal, superstition and religion merge and diverge until they become indistinguishable. But the beliefs, whether stemming from religious dogma or pure superstition, are deep-rooted and ever present. It would be impossible to fully comprehend and adapt to the implications of these beliefs without becoming a thorough initiate of the religions, customs, traditions and rituals of the Nepalese people. However, an attempt is made here to list some important ones which, if you remember and heed them, will help to establish a congenial rapport between the Nepalese and yourself.

First of all, know and accept the fact that you are a foreigner and therefore ritually "polluted." Thus, some seemingly innocent act on your part, which could have been tolerated of a Nepalese, might have unpleasant repercussions.

Stepping over the feet or the body of a person rather than walking around him is not done. Never make the mistake of offering to share "polluted" food, i.e. food which you have tasted or bitten into.

Lack of toilet paper has led to the custom (which has eventually become a ritual) of using water and the left hand to cleanse oneself after a bowel movement. Therefore, nothing should be accepted, and especially offered, with the left hand only. If you offer or accept anything then do so with both hands (if it is practical to do so). This will please your Sherpa, or some Nepali whom you have met, very much. Using both hands to give or receive signifies that you honor the offering and the recipient or giver.

You will notice that most Nepalese take off their shoes before they enter a house or a room. It would not be practical to suggest that you unlace and take off your hiking shoes/boots every time you enter a village house. It would be helpful, however, if you were to avoid entering a house unless you wished to spend some time in it (to eat a meal or drink some tea, for example).

The kitchen area or the cooking and eating area are to be treated with special respect. On no account should you go into the kitchen or cooking and eating areas with your shoes on. You should avoid intruding into these areas unless you are specifically invited there — the hearth in a home is sacred.

Nepalese often eat squatting on the ground. Please take care not to stand in front of a person who is eating, because your feet will be directly in front of his plate of food. If there is something you have to tell him then it is wiser to squat or sit by his side.

Trekking Courtesies

On your trek you will come across *chortens*, big and small. They are revered, regardless of their size, with great devotion. These *chortens* are built to pacify local demons, deities or the spirit of some dead person. It is always wise to pass the *chorten* from the left side in a clockwise direction. The prayer wheel of the *lama* whirls its prayers out to the universe in a clockwise direction. You should circumambulate a temple in this direction, because the earth and the universe revolve in that direction.

You will see, especially in the Khumbu, small flat stones with inscriptions on them placed along the sides of a *chorten*. These are prayers and supplications which have been artistically inscribed with great love, devotion and belief. Though the temptation is great, because of the size and aesthetic beauty of these inscribed stones, please do not take them as souvenirs. The removal of these stones from their place of offering is a sacrilege.

At some crossroads you might come across bits and pieces of colored cloth, a bamboo framework with colored threads woven in an intricate design, or dyed wheat-flour dumplings lying on the ground. You must be careful not to touch these or to step on them. These are offerings made to malignant demons or deities. These should also be passed from the left.

Avoid touching a Nepalese dressed all in white. His white cap, white shirt, white trousers and white shoes signify his state of pollution due to a death in the family.

Prayer-flags often look old, ragged and torn, but to the Nepalese, and especially the Sherpas, their significance and potential never fade away. These flags carry prayers of supplication and gratitude on the breeze to the Compassionate One. Respect for these religious symbols will help you exhibit your appreciation of the customs of the Nepalese culture and country.

There are many, many more customs and rituals that could be mentioned and discussed, but these few points should provide you with a general guide.

Trekking Tips

What to Bring

As you are going to walk four to eight hours a day, shoes are of paramount importance. They must be sturdy and comfortable with good tread on the soles: high tennis shoes or well-broken-in hiking boots will do. Most trekkers hike only in tennis or running shoes in low altitude though in snow and at higher elevations, good boots are essential. They must accommodate one or two layers of heavy wool or cotton (no nylon) socks, of which you should have a plentiful supply. Light tennis shoes will help you relax when the day's walking is over.

For women, wrap-around skirts are preferable to slacks; in deference to local sensitivities, shorts should not be worn. Men should wear either hiking shorts or loosely fitting trousers. For clothing, two light layers are better than a single thick one. If you get too hot, you can peel the top layer off. Thermal underwear can be useful in particularly cold months and at high altitudes. It's better to carry too many clothes than not enough. Drip-dry fabrics are best.

Ideally, your pack should be light, tough, easily opened, packed in an organized fashion, and as small as possible. For a week's trek below 4,500 meters, your equipment should include:

Two pairs of woolen or corduroy trousers or skirts; two warm sweaters; three drip-dry shirts or T-shirts; ski or thermal underwear (especially from November to February); a half-dozen pairs of woolen socks; one pair of walking shoes; one extra pair of sandals; light tennis shoes; a wool hat; a pair of gloves or mittens; a down (or warm synthetic-fill) sleeping bag, preferably with a hood; a thin layer of synthetic foam rubber to use as a mattress; a padded anorak or parka; a plastic raincoat which can also be used to protect your sleeping bag; sunglasses and sun lotion; toilet gear (kept to a minimum); a couple of towels; a medical kit; a small (one-liter) plastic water bottle; and a light day pack.

You will also need an electric flashlight, candles, a lighter, a pocket knife, a pair of scissors, spare shoelaces, some string, safety pins, toilet paper, and plastic bags to protect food or to wrap up wet or dirty clothes.

Down jackets, trousers and some of the rest of this gear can be bought or rented in Kathmandu. To this list must be added the cooking and eating utensils — normally provided by the trekking agency and carried by the expedition's porters — plus food, tents and photographic equipment.

Take the following special precautions: Carry your trekking permit in a plastic bag in your day pack; don't leave it in your luggage. Lock up your bag with a small padlock to prevent pilferage or accidental losses. Your medical kit and toilet gear should be in separate plastic boxes with lids. Take a handful of one-rupee notes for minor expenses along the way.

Getting Fit to Trek

Do as much walking and exercise as possible in the weeks prior to your trek, to prepare for the effort that will be required of you in Nepal. Anyone who is reasonably fit can trek, but the fitter you are, the more you will enjoy it.

A thorough medical check-up is recommended before you leave for Nepal. Inoculations against cholera, typhoid and paratyphoid, tetanus and polio are suggested. An injection of gamma globulin just before departure is the best protection against hepatitis, a serious and common complaint in this part of the world. Some of these shots cannot be given simultaneously with others; if you need them all, start at least six weeks ahead of time.

Local food can become tedious for variety-oriented Western stomachs after a few days. Bring your own high-energy goodies like chocolate, dried fruits and nuts, and spirits (whisky and brandy) for a sip on nippy evenings.

On the trail all water should be well boiled or treated with iodine, available in Kathmandu pharmacies (four drops per liter); allow 20 minutes before drinking). Water contamination is a problem; do not drink from streams however pure they may look. Chlorine is not effective against amoebic cysts.

Minor ailments are to be expected. On some organized group treks, a collective medical kit is provided, and the *sirdar* will occasionally have some knowledge of first aid. Some items might be in high demand, however, and it is best to bring your own first-aid kit. This should include:

Pain relief tablets with codeine (for high-altitude headaches); mild sleeping pills (for high-altitude insomnia); Streptomagna (for travelers diarrhea); Septram (for bacilliary dysentery); Tinidozole (for amoebic dysentery); throat lozenges and cough drops; ophthalmic ointment or drops; a broad spectrum antibiotic; alcohol (for massaging feet to prevent blisters); blister pads; bandages and elastic plasters; antiseptic and cotton; a good sun block; transparent lip salve (to prevent chapping).

Emergency evacuations are difficult to organize because of a scarcity of radio communications and lack of availability of helicopters. A rescue operation takes time, and will start only when some guarantee of payment has been made. A good trekking agent can arrange rescues for its trekkers where necessary; individual trekkers stand no chance of securing a helicopter.

On the Trail

The trekking day begins around 6 a.m. with a cup of tea. After packing, a breakfast of porridge and biscuits is served. Walking starts around 7 a.m. Late in the morning, trekkers halt for a substantial hot lunch, the cook having gone ahead to select the site and prepare the meal. As early as 3 or 4 p.m. the day's walking is over. A camp for the night is set up, dinner is cooked and served. By 8 p.m. everyone is thinking of sleep.

If you choose, you can hike alone the whole day long. While the cooking crew races ahead, Sherpa porters bracket the expedition at the front and rear. You can make endless stops to enjoy the beauty of a particular spot, to chat with passing locals, to photograph, or to sip tea in a wayside shop.

A few hints may help the daily routine and increase your enjoyment. First and foremost, do not try too much too soon. Walk at your own pace, no matter what others may say. Watch the way your porters walk, slowly and steadily. Go uphill in short steps, feet flat on the ground, weight forward. Go downhill with your knees bent, using your thigh muscles. Drink as much liquid as you can to compensate for the sweaty hours under the sun; at high altitudes, this also helps your body to acclimatize. Do not wait until blisters develop to take care of your tender feet. Be careful in the night, as thieves sometimes slit tents to steal cameras and other valuables.

Finally, add to your baggage a strong dose of patience, understanding and congenial curiosity for the values and ways of a world altogether different from, and, at times, better organized than your own.

Altitude Sickness

Altitude sickness, if not treated when symptoms first appear, can lead to death. Often known as AMS or Acute Mountain Sickness, it can ruin treks and should be treated very seriously. Nearly half of those persons who trek to Everest base camp, for instance, suffer mild AMS, and in some cases lives are endangered.

Even experienced mountaineers tend to forget that the Himalaya Mountains begin where other mountain ranges end. Everest base camp is some 1,000 meters (more than 3,000 feet) higher than the summit of the Matterhorn. As altitude increases, especially above 3,000 meters (9,842 feet), the air becomes thinner, creating certain difficulties for the human body. This is especially true when one is sleeping above 3,700 meters (12,139 feet).

Youth, strength and fitness make no difference here. The only prevention is to give one's body time to adjust to high altitude. Those who go too high too fast are liable to be victims of Acute Mountain Sickness.

To minimize the pitfalls of AMS during your trek, we recommend heeding the following advice:

• Drink adequate fluids. At 4,300 meters (14,108 feet), for example, the body requires three to four liters of liquid a day. At low altitude try to drink at least a liter a day.

• Accept the fact that you cannot go very high if your time is short.

• Plan for "rest days" at about 3,700 meters and 4,300 meters. This means sleeping at the same altitude for two nights. You can be as active as you wish during the day, and go as high as you like, but descend again to sleep.

• Once you have ascended above 3,700 meters, do not set up camp more than 450 meters (1,476 feet) higher in any one day, even if you feel fit enough for a climb of twice that length.

• Learn the symptoms of AMS (see below). If you begin to suffer early mountain sickness, do not go any higher until the symptoms have disappeared. Should any of the more serious symptoms of AMS appear, descend at once to a lower elevation. Mild symptoms typically clear up in 24 to 48 hours.

Recognizing the Symptoms

There are three main types of AMS. Early mountain sickness is the first, and acts as a warning. If unheeded, it can progress to pulmonary edema (waterlogged lungs) or cerebral edema (waterlogged brain).

AMS develops slowly, and usually will not affect a person until two to three days after reaching high altitude. Early mountain sickness will manifest itself in headache, nausea, loss of appetite, sleeplessness, fluid retention and/or swelling of the body. The cure, again, is to climb no higher until the symptoms have disappeared.

Pulmonary edema is characterized by breathlessness, even while resting, and by a persistent cough accompanied by congestion in the chest. Should these symptoms appear, descend at once.

Cerebral edema is less common. Its symptoms are extreme tiredness, vomiting, severe headache, difficulty in walking (as with drunken, uneven steps), abnormal speech and behavior, drowsiness, even unconsciousness. Victims must return to a lower altitude immediately and stay there, abandoning the trek.

In the event of an emergency descent, follow these steps:

• The patient can walk or be carried down on a porter's back or on a yak.

• Do not delay descent for any reason. Begin at night if necessary.

• Do not wait for helicopter or aircraft evacuation.

• The patient must be accompanied.

• A patient with AMS may not be capable of making correct decisions. You may need to insist that he/she go down, against their will.

• Medicine is no substitute for descent. If a doctor is available, he may give medicine and oxygen. However, the patient must go down, even if given treatment.

The Himalayan Rescue Association

The Himalayan Rescue Association (HRA) is a voluntary non-profit organization which strives to prevent casualties in the Nepal Himalaya. The HRA runs a Trekkers' Aid Post at a height of 4,200 meters in Pheriche. It is manned and equipped to treat AMS during spring and fall. A new post high up in Manang is now in operation. In order to maintain and develop their activities, donations are most welcome. Such contributions may be received by the HRA, Box 495, Kathmandu, or channeled through your local trekking agency.

The HRA, which provided this information in conjunction with Mountain Travel Nepal, does not recommend any medicine for preventing AMS.

The following additional precautions are suggested:

• You should not go to high altitudes if you have heart or lung disease. Check with your doctor if you have any doubt.

• Do not expect everyone in your party to acclimatize at the same rate. It is possible that you will need to divide the party so that people who acclimatize more slowly will camp lower than others. Plan for this.

• Take extra precautions when flying in to high altitude STOL airstrips like Syangboche (3,700 m). Take two "rest days" before proceeding.

When and Where to Trek

There are an overwhelming number of trekking trails to choose from in Nepal. Your choice depends upon the length of time you have available, as well as on the time of year you are trekking and on your personal interests. The following list, compiled by Mountain Travel, may give some guidelines:

January and February

Khumbu is okay for the hardy, who can either walk in to Lukla and fly out (a 25 to 30-day trip), or fly in and out of Lukla with 10 to 20 days left for walking between Sherpa villages. Temperatures are cold, but there is sensational scenery, with snow at upper altitudes. Some delays on Lukla flights must be expected in the event of a spell of bad weather.

North of Kathmandu, the eight-day Helambu trek and the 12 to 16-day Langtang trek are both good. Helambu is especially interesting, both ethnically and culturally; you may meet some snow above the Sherpa villages of Tarkegyang and Melamchegaon, but it should not hamper your progress. On the other hand, snow could be a problem high in the Langtang Valley. It is not normally possible to cross the Gosaikund pass linking Langtang with Helambu at this time of year.

This is an excellent time to trek (by foot or pony) the old trade route between Kathmandu and Pokhara, an eight to 10-day trip including a visit to Gorkha. An excursion into Manang can also be made from Dumre, although the likelihood of early snow can prevent visitors from reaching Manang village.

Three good treks are recommended from Pokhara. The so-called "Royal Trek" follows the footsteps of the Prince of Wales for three to five days in the Gurung and Gurkha country east of the Pokhara Valley. Great views of Annapurna, Macchapucchare and Dhaulagiri are highlights of the six to 10-day Ghandrung-Ghorapani trek. And the 17 to 19-day Kali Gandaki to Muktinath route is in excellent condition in the winter, although some snow is possible at Ghorapani.

In late February, spring arrives in the Kathmandu Valley, and rhododendrons begin to bloom at lower elevations (to 3,000 meters). Up to mid-March, this can be the best time of year for walks at elevation up to 4,000 meters (about 13,000 feet).

March

Although spring has arrived, high-altitude conditions can still be quite harsh. Do not plan on crossing high passes before mid-April.

March is a good time to start a 25 to 30-day trek into Khumbu. This is still a little early for Rolwaling. Further east, a mid-month start for an excursion to the Milke Danda botanical area is okay, with a flight from Lukla ending a trip of 25 to 30 days.

The eight to 16-day Helambu and Langtang trips are good at this time, but leave crossings of Gosainkund pass to the end of the month. By the end of March, you can start 12 to 16-day treks up the Trisuli river and west to Gatland; but Tiru Danda will still have a lot of snow at this time. Elsewhere between Kathmandu and Pokhara, Manang should be free of snow toward the end of the month.

All Pokhara-based treks are okay. Some mountain haze develops during the second half of the month, although the wide variety of wild flowers is a plus. The Dhorpatan and Dhaulagiri glacier areas still are not open.

April

In this high spring season, temperatures are warm in the Pokhara Valley, and there is a likelihood of afternoon clouds and showers in most locations. But this is the best spring month for rhododendrons in the mountains. It is also good for alpine treks and for climbing.

The lowest elevations of Dharan and Dhankuta, in East Nepal are getting hotter by the day. For treks starting there, leave as early as possible and come out via Lukla. These include the botanical treks to Milke Danda and alpine treks to the Makalu base camp.

It's all go for Khumbu, although the low-level walk in can be disappointing due to increasing haze. It is perhaps best to fly in for 10 to 25 days of alpine and climbing treks to Rolwaling or Hongu.

Treks of eight to 12 days into the Jugal Himal are fairly tough, but are rewarding for the off-the-beaten-track adventurer. Spring flowers are beautiful. Links to Helambu, Langtang or Gatlang can extend this trip to 25 to 30 days. Between Helambu and Langtang, visits to the Gosainkund Lakes are attractive.

En route to Gatlang, Trisuli Bazaar and the Trisuli river valley are hot, but are worth enduring to reach the beautiful higher-altitude forests and wild flowers. A return via Tiru Danda keeps the route at a high elevation until a quick drop into Trisuli Bazaar concludes the 12 to 15-day trek.

Short treks of two to five days in the Kathmandu Valley are popular now. West of the capital, this is a superb month to spend high in the mountains of Manang. The climate is hot for the first couple of days out of Dumre, but is worth it. Climbing is possible on Chulu and Pisang. After mid-April, the Thorong La pass is usually open to Muktinath; the route then continues to Pokhara down the Kali Gandaki river.

Pokhara is hot and hazy in April. Consider it only as a center for treks on the eight to 10-day day Ghorapani circuit, or better, the 14 to 16-day round-Annapurna trip — even though late snows can sometimes spell avalanche danger. West of Pokhara, the higher altitude Dhorpatan and south Dhaulagiri glacier regions are highly recommended for trips of 18 to 25 days.

In the far west of Nepal, Jumla-based treks are always a problem, because of difficult access to this remote region. But the spectacular scenery rewards the more persistent adventures. Rara Lake can be reached from Jumla. It is unwise to rely on flights to this region, and it's a long walk from Pokhara.

May and June

In these pre-monsoon months, there is haze and heat at all lower elevations. If you are trekking, aim to reach higher altitudes quickly. Some of the better areas at this time are Khumbu (fly in and out of Lukla), Rolwaling, Hongu, Gatlang, the Ganja La or Tilmans Col areas of Langtang, and the round-Annapurna trek for those with sufficient time. Kathmandu Valley walks are pleasurable.

July to mid-September

Mad botanists and students of leeches will enjoy this time of year. It is generally not recommended for trekking; but in the Muktinath-Manang rain-shadow region, the terrain is lovely. Trekkers must realize, however, that rain, slippery paths and leeches will hamper their coming and going. Various alpine wild flowers are at their zenith at this time.

September 15 to October 10

The monsoon tails off about this time, and the countryside is fresh, green and beautiful. Lukla flights are not reliable before Oct. 20, so the rule of thumb for excursions to Khumbu is to walk in and fly out. When the mountains are free of clouds, the views are crystal clear. There are still a lot of showers at lower elevations. Recommendations are much the same as for April.

October 10 to November 20

This is the "high season" for trekking, and with good reason. It is the classic time for high-altitude alpine and climbing treks. For those who do not want to go too high, but who still wish to get off the beaten track, trips to East Nepal, the Jugal Himal, Gatlang and Tiru Danda, or destinations between Kathmandu and Pokhara are suggested.

The more popular routes are congested at this time; these include the Khumbu and the Pokhara region: Ghandrung, Ghorapani and Annapurna. Human masses create almost inevitable flight delays to and from Lukla.

For botanists, November is the best time for seed collection. Throughout this autumn period, harvests are in progress in the fields and there are many festivals everywhere.

November 20 to December 31

Winter comes to Kathmandu about Nov. 15, and this period generally offers the most stable weather all year. There is very little rain, and the high mountains usually have minimal snowfall. Low-level treks, at elevations to about 3,700 meters (about 12,000 feet) are best at this time of year.

For hardier trekkers, the Khumbu is still excellent, and flights to and from Lukla are more reliable than during the high season. After Dec. 1, however, there are no crossings of high passes.

Short treks are good at this time. The Pokhara region is ideal (see January/February), as are Helambu and Langtang, and East Nepal. Lots of variety is available, with pleasant walking conditions. With crops harvested, the countryside lacks color, but the clarity of mountain views is superb.

Scaling Valley Peaks

Three sizeable hills surrounding the Valley are worthwhile hikes for the energetic. The six-kilometer trail to the top of **Phulchoki** (2,762 meters) begins behind St. Xavier's School at Godavari village. From Budhanilkantha, it is a steady 3½-hour climb to the top of **Shivapuri** (2,732 meters), capped by the remains of a fortified palace in a rhododendron forest. The summit of **Champa Devi** peak (see page 144), above Pharping, can be reached in only about an hour of easy climbing. There are fine views from all three peaks.

Government and Economy

Nepal is ruled by His Majesty King Birendra Bir Bikram Shah Dev who receives counsel from his Prime Minister, the Right Honourable Marich Man Singh Shrestha, a Council of Ministers, and the National Assembly ("Rastriya Panchayat") elected by universal adult suffrage. The King (born Dec. 28, 1945) and Queen Aishwarya Rajya Lakshmi Devi Shah (born Nov. 7, 1949) have three children; the older, His Royal Highness Crown Prince Dipendra (born June 27, 1971), is heir to the throne.

Nepal's population is about 17 million, 42 percent of it under the age of 15. The annual rate of population growth is 2.6 percent. Life expectancy is 51.1 years.

In terms of economy, Nepal has a per capita income of US$160 (1987). The consumer price index (1973 equals 100) was 205 in 1981, 230 in 1982, 260 in 1983, 271 in 1984 and 354.5 in 1985.

The gross domestic product for 1985/86 was US $2.3 billion. Government revenue in 1984/85 was US$178 million, expenditure for the same period was US$328 million. In the 1983/84 Nepalese fiscal year (July to July) Nepal exported US$141 million worth of goods and imported US$434 million.

Tourism benefits the economy greatly, with gross receipts of about US $50 million. Foreign aid commitments promised US$218 million to Nepal in 1983/84.

In 1983, Nepal had a labor force of about 7 million, 93 percent in agricultural, 5 percent in government and public service, 2 percent in industry.

The literacy rate is 39 percent male and 17 percent female.

Health statistics show 1 doctor per 20,250 population and 1 hospital bed per 5000 population.

Suggested Reading

General

Bernstein, Jeremy. The *Wildest Dreams of Kew: A Profile of Nepal*. New York: Simon and Schuster, 1970. Personal travelogue.

Fleming, Robert and Linda. *Kathmandu Valley*. Tokyo: Kodansha International, 1978.

Frank, Keitmar. *Dreamland Nepal*. New Delhi: S.Chand, 1978. Photographic book.

Gurung, Harka. *Vignettes of Nepal*. Kathmandu: Sajha Prakashan, 1980.

Haas, Ernst. *Himalayan Pilgrimage*. New York: Viking Press, 1978. Nice photographic book.

Hagen, Toni. *Nepal: The Kingdom in the Himalayas*. Berne: Kummerly and Frey, 1961. Second edition, 1971. Geographical study with many photos and tropical maps. Hagen spent eight years surveying Nepal by foot.

His Majesty's Government of Nepal. *Nepal*. Kathmandu: Ministry of Industry and Commerce, Department of Tourism, 1974. Pictorical survey.

Hoag, Katherine. *Exploring Mysterious Kathmandu*. Avalok, 1978. City guide.

Matthiessen, Peter. *The Snow Leopard*. London: Chatto and Windus, 1979. Journal of a journey to Dolpo.

Murphy. Dervla. *The Waiting Land: A spell in Nepal*. London: John Murray, 1967. Travelogue.

Peissel, Michel. *Tiger for Breakfast*. London: Hodder, 1966. The story of Kathmandu's legendary Boris Lissanevitch.

Ragam, V.R. *Pilgrim's Travel Guide: The Himalayan Region*. Gunter: 1963.

Raj, Prakash A. *Kathmandu and the Kingdom of Nepal*. South Yarra, Vic., Australia: Lonely Planet, 1980. A pocket guide.

Rieffel, Robert. *Nepal: Namaste*. Kathmandu: Sahayagi Prakashan, 1978. A thorough guidebook.

Shah, Rishikesh. *An Introduction to Nepal*. Kathmandu: Ratna Pustak Bhandar, 1976.

Suyin, Han. *The Mountain Is Young*. London: Jonathan Cape, 1958. Novel set in Nepal of the 1950s.

Historical

Fisher, Margaret W. *The Political History of Nepal*. Berkeley: University of California, Institute of International Studies, 1960.

Hamilton, Francis. *An Account of the Kingdom of Nepal, and of the Territories Annexed to This Dominion by House of Gurkha*. Edinburgh: Archibold Constable and Co., 1819. Early history of Himalaya region.

Hodgson, Brian H. *Essays on the Languages, Literature, and Religion of Nepal and Tibet; Together with Further Papers on the Geography, Ethnology, and Commerce of Those Countries*.

London: Trubner and Co., 1974. Reprinted by Bibliotheca Himalayica, New Delhi.

Hooker, Sir Joseph Dalton. *Himalayan Journals*. London: Ward, Lock, Bowden and Co., 1891.

Kirkpatrick, Col. F. *An Account of the Kingdom of Nepaul*. London: 1800. Reprinted by Bibliotheca Himalayica, New Delhi, 1969.

Landon, Percival. *Nepal*. Two volumes. London: Constable, 1928. Reprinted by Bibliotheca Himalayica, New Delhi. Popular historical account survives as the best overall early summary.

Oldfield, Henry Ambrose. *Views of Nepal, 1851–1864*. Kathmandu: Ratna Pustak Bhandar, 1975. Sketches and paintings.

Oldfield, Henry Ambrose. *Sketches from Nipal. Historical and Descriptive, with Anecdotes of the Court Life and Wild Sports of the Country in the Time of Maharaja Jang Bahadur, G.C.B., to Which Is Added an Essay on Nepalese Buddhism, and Illustrations of Religious Monuments, Architecture, and Scenery from the Author's Own Drawings*. Two volumes. London: W.H. Allen, 1880. Reprinted by Bibliotheca Himalayica, New Delhi.

Rana, Pudma Jung Bahadur. *Life of Maharaja Sir Jung Bahadur of Nepal*. Allahabad, India: Pioneer Press, 1909. Biography and description of 19th Century palace life.

Regmi, D.R. *Ancient Nepal*. Third Edition. Calcutta: Firma K.L. Mukhopadhyaya, 1969. Detailed historiography (to 740) from Nepalese religious viewpoint.

Regmi, D.R. *Medieval Nepal*. Three volumes. Calcutta: Firma K.L. Mukhopadhyaya, 1965. Definitive historiography covering period 740 to 1768, plus source material.

Regmi, D.R. *Modern Nepal: Rise and Growth in the Eighteenth Century*. Calcutta: Firma K.L. Mukhopadhyaya, 1961.

Stiller, Ludwig F. *The Rise of the House of Gorkha*. New Delhi: Manjusri, 1973.

Wright, Daniel, editor. *Vamsavali: History of Nepal, with an Introductory Sketch of the Country and People of Nepal*. Translated from the *Parbatiya* by Munshi Shew Shunker Singh and Pandit Shri Gunanand. Cambridge: University Press, 1877. Second edition, Calcutta: Susil Gupta, 1958. Thorough and reliable early history.

Peoples, Art and Culture

Anderson, Mary M. *Festivals of Nepal*. London: George Allen and Unwin, 1971.

Baidya, Karunakar. *Teach Yourself Nepali*. Kathmandu: Ratna Pustak Bhandar, 1982.

Brown, Percy. *Picturesque Nepal*. London: Adam and Charles Black, 1912.

Deep, Dhruba Krishna. *The Nepal Festivals*. Kathmandu: Ratna Pustak Bhandar, 1982.

Furer-Haimendorf, Christoph von. *The Inter-relation of Caste and Ethnic Groups in Nepal*. London: University of London, 1957.

Furer-Haimendorf, Christoph von. *The Sherpas of Nepal: Buddhist Highlanders*. Berkeley and Los Angeles: University of California Press, 1964. Intensive study of Sherpa society.

Haaland, Ane. *Bhaktapur: A Town Changing*. Bhaktapur Development Project, 1982.

Hosken, Fran P. *The Kathmandu Valley Towns: A Record of Life and Change in Nepal*. New York: Weatherhill, 1974. Pictorial survey.

Indra. *Joys of Nepalese Cooking*. New Delhi: 1982.

Jerstad, Luther G. *Mani-Rimdu: Sherpa Dance Drama*. Calcutta: International Book House, 1969.

Jest, Corneille. *Monuments of Northern Nepal*. Paris: UNESCO, 1981.

Kansakar, N.H. *Nepali Kitchens*. Kathmandu: 1978.

Korn, Wolfgang. *The Traditional Architecture of the Kathmandu Valley*. Kathmandu: Ratna Pustak Bhandar, 1977. Limited edition with many diagrams.

Kramrisch, Stella. *The Art of Nepal*. New York: 1964.

Lall, Kesar. *Lore and Legend of Nepal*. Kathmandu: Ratna Pustak Bhandar, 1976.

Lall, Kesar. *Nepalese Customs and Manners*. Kathmandu: Ratna Pustak Bhandar, 1976.

Macdonald, A.W., and Anne Vergati Stahl. *Newar Art*. New Delhi: Vikas, 1979.

McDougal, Charles. *The Kulunge Rai: A Study in Kinship and Marriage Exchange*. Kathmandu: Ratna Pustak Bhandar, 1979.

Nepali, Gopal Singh. *The Newars*. Bombay: United Asia Publications, 1965. Subtitled: "An Ethno-Sociological Study of a Himalayan Community."

Pal, Pratapaditya. *Nepal: Where the Gods Are Young*. Asia House Exhibition: 1975.

Pruscha, Carl. *Kathmandu Valley: The Preservation of Physical Environment and Cultural Heritage, A Protective Inventory*. Two volumes. Vienna: Anton Schroll, 1975. Prepared by His Majesty's Government of Nepal in collaboration with UNESCO and the United Nations.

Rubel, Mary. *The Gods of Nepal*. Kathmandu: Bhimratna Harsharatna, 1971.

Sanday, John. *The Hanuman Dhoka Royal Palace, Kathmandu: Building Conservation and Local Traditional Crafts*. London: AARP, 1974.

Sanday, John. *Monuments of the Kathmandu Valley*. Paris: UNESCO, 1979.

Singh, Madanjeet. *Himalayan Arts*. London: UNESCO, 1968.

Snellgrove, David L. *Buddhist Himalaya*. Oxford: Bruno Cassirer, 1957. Excellent survey.

Vaidya, Karunakar. *Folk Tales of Nepal*. Kathmandu: Ratna Pustak Bhandar, 1980.

Natural History

Fleming, R.L. Sr., R.L. Fleming Jr. and L.S.

Bangdel. *Birds of Nepal*. Kathmandu: Avalok, 1979. Definitive work with good illustrations.

Manandhar, N.P. *Medicinal Plants of Nepal Himalaya*. Kathmandu: Ratna Pustak Bhandar, 1980.

McDougal, Charles. *The Face of the Tiger*. London: Rivington Books and Andre Deutsch, 1977. The classic work on the Bengal tiger, by the director of Tiger Tops.

Mierow, D., and H. Mishra. *Wila Animals of Nepal*. Kathmandu: 1974.

Mierow, D., and T:B. Shrestha. *Himalayan Flowers and Trees*. Kathmandu: Sahayogi Prakashan, 1978. Good handbook.

Stainton, J.D.A. *Forests of Nepal*. London: Murray, 1972. Standard work on the flora of Nepal.

Mountains

Armington, Stan. *Trekking in the Himalayas*. South Yarra, Vic., Australia: Lonely Planet, 1979. Survey of and guide to trekking.

Bezruschka, Stephen. *A Guide to Trekking in Nepal*. Seattle: The Mountaineers, 1981. One of the best books on the subject.

Bonington, Chris. *Annapurna South Face*, London: Cassell, 1971.

Bonington, Chris. *Everest South West Face*. London: Hodder and Stoughton, 1973.

Bonington, Chris. *Everest the Hard Way*. London. Hodder and Stoughton, 1976.

Fantin, Mario. *Mani Rimdu Nepal*. Singapore: Toppon, 1976.

Fantin, Mario. *Sherpa Himalaya Nepal*. Bologne, Italy: Arti Grafiche, 1978.

Hackett, Peter. *Mountain Sickness*. American Alpine Club.

Herzog, Maurice. *Annapurna: First Conquest of an 8,000-Meter Peak (26,493 Feet)*. New York: E.P. Dutton, 1953.

Hillary, Edmund. *High Adventure*. New York: E.P. Dutton, 1955.

Hillary, Edmund. *Schoolhouse in the Clouds*. Garden City, N.Y.: Doubleday, 1964. Account of 1963 climbing expedition and assistance rendered to Sherpa communities.

Hillary, Edmund, and Desmond Doig. *High in the Thin Cold Air: The Story of the Himalayan Expedition Led by Sir Edmund Hillary*. Garden City, N.Y.: Doubleday, 1962.

Hillary, Edmund, and George Lowe. *East of Everest: An Account of the New Zealand Alpine Club Himalayan Expedition to the Barun Valley in 1954*. New York: E.P. Dutton, 1956.

Hornbein, Thomas F. *Everest, the West Ridge*. San Francisco: Sierra Club, 1965.

Houston, Charles S. *Going High: The Story of Man and Altitude*. American Alpine Club: 1980.

Hunt, John. *The Ascent of Everest*. London: Hodder and Stoughton, 1953. Also *The Conquest of Everest*. New York: E.P. Dutton, 1954.

Hunt, John. *The Conquest of Himalayas*. New York: E.P. Dutton, 1954.

Hunt, John. *Our Everest Adventure: The Pictorial History from Kathmandu to the Summit*. New York: E.P. Dutton, 1954.

Iozawa, Tomoya. *Trekking in the Himalayas*. Tokyo: Yama-Kei, 1980. Excellent maps.

Izzard, Ralph. *The Abominable Snowman Adventure*. London: Hodder and Stoughton, 1955. Also Garden City, N.Y.: Doubleday, 1955. Report of the 1954 Himalayan expedition, with a bibliography on the yeti.

Izzard, Ralph. *An Innocent on Everest*. New York: E.P. Dutton, 1954. Also London: Hodder and Stoughton, 1955. Account of a solo journey from Kathmandu to Everest, chasing the Hunt expedition.

Jones, Mike. *Canoeing Down Everest*. New Delhi: Vikas, 1979.

Kazami, Takehide. *The Himalayas*. Tokyo: Kodansha International, 1973.

McCallum, John D. *Everest Diary, Based on the Personal Diary of Lute Jerstad, One of the First Five Americans to Conquer Mount Everest*. New York: Fallet, 1966.

Messner, Reinhold. *Everest: Expedition to the Ultimate*. London: Kaye and Ward, 1979.

Nicholson, Nigel. *The Himalayas*. New York: Time-Life Books, 1978. Part of the "World's Wild Places" series.

Peissel, Michel. *Mustang, the Forbidden Kingdom: Exploring a Lost Himalayan Land*. New York: E.P. Dutton, 1967. Trekking travelogue.

Rowell, Galen. *Many People Come, Looking, Looking*. Seattle: The Mountaineers, 1980. Personal trekking travelogue with good photographs.

Schaller, George B. *Stones of Silence*. London: Andre Deutsch, 1980. Report of a naturalist's survey in Dolpo.

Shirakawa, Yoshikazu. *Himalayas*. Tokyo: Shogakukan, 1976. Also New York: Harry N. Abrams, 1977. Beautiful photographic book.

Tenzing Norgay and James Ramsey Ullman. *Man of Everest: The Autobiography of Tenzing*. London: George G. Harrap, 1955. Also *Tiger of the Snows*. New York: G.P. Putnam's Sons, 1955.

Tilman, W. *Nepal Himalaya*. Cambridge: Cambridge University Press, 1952. Mountaineer's reports of attacks on high peaks.

Tucci, Giuseppe. *Journey to Mustang*. Translated from Italian by Diana Fussell. Kathmandu: Ratna Pustak Bhandar, 1982.

Ullman, James Ramsey. *Americans on Everest: The Official Account Led by Norman G. Dyhrenfurth*. New York: J.B. Lippincott, 1964.

Ullman, James Ramsey. *Kingdom of Adventure: Everest*. New York: E.P. Dutton, 1947.

Unsworth, Walt. *Everest*. London: Allen Lane, 1981. Best history of world's highest peak.

Waddell, L.A. *Among the Himalayas*. Westminster, England: Archibold Constable and Co., 1899. Mountaineer's travelogue.

Language

There are as many tongues spoken in Nepal as there are races, and almost as many dialects as there are village communities. But just as centuries of intermarriage have left the nation without a pure tribe or race, neither is there any pure language. Throughout history, the main languages have intermingled and influenced one another.

The official language, Nepali, is derived from Pahori, a language of northern India related to Hindi. Nepali and Hindi use the same writing system, called Devagnagari. Nepali has also borrowed heavily from some local dialects as well as from Sanskrit, an ancient scholarly language which has survived (like Latin), as a religious medium. Nepali, Sanskrit and Newari — the language of the Newar people, predominant in the Kathmandu valley — each has its own distinctive literary traditions. Newari, which uses three different alphabets, has the newer and more abundant literature.

In northern Nepal, the Tibetan language — another traditional vehicle for religious teaching — remains widespread both in its pure, classical form and as derived dialects (including Sherpa and Thakali). In southern Nepal, the various peoples of the Terai speak their own Indo-European dialects. Three times more people speak Maithili, an eastern Terai dialect, than speak Newari, a reflection of the uneven distribution of population in Nepal.

English is widely spoken and understood in official and tourism-related circles. Most taxi drivers and merchants in the Kathmandu valley have a working knowledge of English, as do most Sherpas. Elsewhere, you may find it difficult to make yourself understood, although the younger generation is fast acquiring a smattering of English-language words.

We strongly recommend that you learn a few basic words and expressions, such as those listed below. Like anywhere else, you will get big returns on this small investment, in terms of hospitality, friendship and respect.

Nepali is an atonal language. Whatever the length of the word, the accent is always placed on the first or second syllable. Words are pronounced exactly as they are spelled.

Consonants are pronounced as in English, with a few peculiarities:

ch is pronounced tch as in bench

chh	tch-h	pitch here
th	t-h	hot head
kh	k-h	dark hole
ph	p-h	top hat
j	dj	Jesus
dh	d-h	adhere

The t , d , thand dh with a dot beneath them are pronounced by rolling the tongue back and putting it in the center of the roof of the mouth, so that the sound produced is like "rt" in "cart" or "rd" in "card."

Vowels are pronounced either long or short:

e is always e (ay) as in cafe

u	oo	moon (never yu as in mute)
y	yi	yield (never ai as in my)
i	i	bin (never ai as in bind)
o	oh	toe

Nepalis do not use the greetings "Good morning," "Good afternoon" or "Good evening." Instead, when greeting someone, it is polite to clasp your hands together in front of you and say "Namaste" (pronounced "Na-ma-stay"). This simple phrase will evoke a smile and a warm greeting in return.

The letters of the Nepali alphabet are:

क	ख	ग	घ	ङ	च	छ
k	kh	g	gh	ng	ch	chh

ज	झ	अ	ट	ठ	ड	ढ
j	jh	n	t	th	d	dh

ण	त	थ	द	ध	न	प
n	t	th	d	dh	n	p

फ	ब	भ	म	य	र	ल
ph	b	bh	m	y	r	l

व	श	ष	स	ह
w	sh	sh	s	h

Nasalization is indicated by putting over the vowel, so that the sound is like the "n" in "conch"

Greetings from Civilities

hello, goodbye	धन्यवाद	namaste
thank you (very much)	धन्यवाद	danyabad
I'm sorry.	माफी माग्नोस	maaphi gavnus
please come in	भित्र आउनोस	bhitra aaunos
please sit down	बस्नोस	basnos
how are you?	तपाईलाई कस्तो छ	tapailai kasto chha
what is your name?	तपाईको नाम के हो	tapaaiko naam ke ho
my name is . . .	मेरो नाम........हो	mero naam . . ho.
where is your home?		
(where do you come from?)	तपाईको घर कहाँ हो	tapaaiko ghar kaha ho
my home is . . . (I come from . . .)	मेरो घर........हो	mero ghar . . . ma

Pronouns and Forms of Address

I	म	ma
You (singular)	तपाई	tapaai
	तिमी	timi (to children)
you (very respectful)	हजुर	hajur
he, she	उ	U (child)
	उहाँ	uhaa
	वहाँ	wahaa
we	हामी	haami
you (plural)	तपाईहरु	tapaaiharu
they	उहाँहरु	uhaaharu
	उनीहरु	uniharu (children)
to a woman meaning "sister"	ठिटि	didi (older than self)
	बहिनी	bahini (younger than self)
to a man meaning "brother"	दाजु	dajyu (older)
	भाई	bhai (younger)
Father	बाबु	babu
mother	आमा	ama
son	छोरो	chhoro
daughter	छोरी	chhori

(my) Friend	मेरो साथि	(mero) saat

Directions and Transport

pedicab	रिक्सा	rikshaw
car	मोटर	motor
bus	वस	bas
airplane	हवाइ जहाज	hawaaijahaaj
	प्लेन	plaain
boat	डुगा	dugaa
ship	पानी जहाज	paanijahaaj
bicycle	साइकल	saaikel
motorcycle	मोटर साइकल	motorsaaikel
where are you going?	कहाँ जाने	kahan jaane
where do you want to go?	तपाईंलाई कहाँ	tapaailaai kahaa
	जानु मन लाग्छ	jaanu man laagchha
I want to go to . . . मलाइ	जानु मन लाग्छ	malaai . . . jaanu man laagchha
stop here	यहिं रोक्नुस	yahaa roknos
turn right	दाहिने जानुस	dahine jaanos
which road leads to . . .	कुन वाटो . . . जाने	kun bato . . . janccha
how many kilometers	कति किलोमिटर हो	kati kilomatar ho
please go slowly	विस्तारि जानु	bistaare jaanos
straight	सिधा	sidhaa
left	वायां	bayaa
right	दायां	dahine
near	नजिक	najik
far	टाढा	tadhaa
from	वाट	baataa
to	मा	maa
inside	भित्र	bhitra
outside	वाहिर	baahira
between	विचमा	bich maa
under	मुनि	muni

326

English	Devanagari	Romanization
here	यहाँ	yahaa
there	त्यहाँ	tyehaa
in the front	अगाडी	agadi
in the back	पछाडी	pachaaadi
next to	को छेउमा मा	ko chheu maa
ascend	माथी जानु	maathi jaanu
descend	तल जानु	tala jaanu
to walk	हिरनु	hidnu
steep uphill (when trekking)	उकालो	ukaalo
steep downhill (when trekking)	ओरालो	oraalo
to drive	मोटर च्लाउनु	motor chhalaaunu
market, bazaar	वजार	bajaar
road (paved)	सडक	sadak

Important Places

hotel	होटेल	hotel
shop	पसल	pasal
airport	गीराउएड	giraund
cinema	सिनेमा	sinemaa
tourist office	टुरिष्ट अफिस	tourist ophis

Spending the Night

English	Devanagari	Romanization
room	कोठा	kotha
bed	ओछ्यान	ochhyaan
bedroom	सुत्ने कोठा	sutne kotha
toilet, latrine	लेट्रिन	latrin
bathroom, wash room	नुहाउने ठाउँ	nuhaaune thaau
towel	टालिया	tauliyaa
sheet	शट	sheet
pillow	सीरानी	siraani
water	पानी	paani
soap	साबुन	saaban
wash (self)	नुहाउनु	nuhaaunu

English	Nepali	Romanization
hot water, cold water	तातो पानी चिसो पानी	taato paani, chiso paani
wash clothes	धुनु	dhunu
iron	स्त्रि लाउनु	istri lagaaunu
clothes	लुगा	lugaa
trousers	पन्त	pyant
dress	फ्रक	frock (or just say "dress")
where is a hotel?	होटल कहाँ छ	hotel kahaa chha
How much for one night?	एक रातको कति	ek raat ko kati
Please wash these clothes	यो लुगा धुनु	yo lugaa dhuno
where is a place to stay the night (when trekking)	वास बस्ने ठाउं कहां छ	baas basne thaau kahaa chha

Eating

English	Nepali	Romanization
restaurant	रेष्टुरेन्ट	restaraant
food, meal	खाना	khaanaa
	भात	bhaat (traditional Nepali meal)
food and drink (colloq.)	खाना पिन	khaanaa pin
breakfast	बिहानको खाना	bihaanako khaanaa (or "breakfast")
dinner	बेलुकिको खाना	beluki ko khaanaa (or "dinner")
boiled water	उमालेको पानी	umaaleko paani
filtered water	फिल्टर भएको पानी	philtar bhaeko paani
tea	चिया	chiyaa
coffee	कफी	kaphi
beer	बीर	bir
	जाँड	jaad (local brew)
fresh orange juice	सुन्तलाको रस	suntalaako ras
milk	दुध	dudh
bread	रोती	rothi
	परोठा	paarothi
butter	मखन	mukkhan
yoghurt	दही	daahi
rice	भात	bhaat
noodles	नुडल	nudal
potatoes	नुडल	aalu

328

chicken	कुखुराको मासु	kukuraa ko maasu
pork	संगुरको मासु	sungurko maasu
mutton	मासु	maasu
goat meat	खसीको मासु	khasi ko maasu
liver	कलेजो	kalejo
fish	माछा	maachhaa
prawn	प्रान	praan
vegetables (curried vegetables)	तरकारी	tarkaari
fruit	फलफुल	phaalphul
egg	फुल	phul
sugar	चिनी	chini
salt	नुन	nun
pepper	मरीच	marich
vinegar	वीनेगर	chuk
sweet	गुलियो	guliyo
sour	अमिलो	amilo
bitter	तिटो	fito
hot (temperature)	तातो	fato
hot (spicy)	पीरो	piro
cold	चिसो	chiso
boiled	उमालेको	omaleko
fried	तारेको	taneko
sauce	झोल	jhol
drinking glass	गिलास	gilus
spoon	चम्चा	chamcha
knife	चक्कु	chakku
fork	कांटा	kanta
plate	थाल	thal
I am hungry.	मलाई भोक लाग्यो	maile bhog lagyo
I am thirsty.	मलाई तिर्खा लाग्यो	maile tirkha lagyo
Please cook . . .	पकाउनु होस	pakaaunos
The bill, please.	बिल दिनु होस	bil dinuhos

Shopping

shop	पसल	pasal
	दोकान	dokaan (in villages)
money	पैसा	paisaa
to change money	पैसा साटनु	paisaa saattnu
to buy	किन्नु	kinnu
price	मोल	mol
expensive	महगो	mahago
cheap	सस्तो	sasto
how much does this cost?	यस्को कति, यसलाई कती	yesko kati, yeslaai kati
very expensive	धेरै महगो	dherai mahago
is there a cheaper one	अर्को सस्तो छ	arko sasto chh
can you lower the price a little.	अली घटाउनोस न	alo ghataauno na
what is this?	यो के हो	yo ke ho
I'll take it	मैले लिन्छु	maile linchhu
I don't want it.	मलाई किन्नु मन लाग्दैन	malaai kinnu man laagdaina
I'll come back later	म पछी आउछु	ma pachhi aaunchhu

Time

day	दिन	din
night	राती	raati
today	आज	aaja
morning	विहान	bihaana
afternoon	दिउसो	diuso
late afternoon	सांझमा	saajhamaa
evening	वेलुकि	beluki
now	अहिले	ahile
soon, presently	एक छिन	ek chhin
after.	सधैं	sadhai
before	पहिले	pahile
when (interrogative)	कहिले	kahile
tomorrow	भोलि	bholi
yesterday	हिजो	hijo

330

minute	मिनेट	minut
hour	घण्टा	ghanta
hour (with exact time)	वजे	baje
day	दिन	din
week	हप्ता	haauptaa
month	महिना	mahinaa
year	वर्ष	barsa
a quarter past	सवा	. . . saba
half past	साढे	. . . sarhe
a quarter to	पाउने	. . . paune
Sunday	आइतवार	aitabaar
Monday	सोमवार	sombaar
Tuesday	मंगलवार	mangelbaar
Wednesday	बुधवार	budhibaar
Thursday	विहिवार	bihibaar
Friday	शुक्रवार	sukrabaar
Saturday	सनिवार	sansabaar
today	आज	aaja
what time is it?	कति वज्यो	kati bajyo

Handy Words and Phrases

yes	हो	ho
no	होईन	hoina
(that's) correct	ठिक छ	thik chha
(that's) wrong	ठिक छैन	thik chhaina
much, many	घेरै	dherai
very much, very many	घेरै घेरै	dheRai dherai
and	र	ra
but	तर	tara
with	संग	sanga
this	यो	yo
that	त्यो	tyo
like this	यस्तो	yesto

like that	तेस्तो	tyesto
nice	राम्रो	raamro
more	अरु	aru
less	तोरे	thorai
because	किन भने	kinabhane
perhaps	होला	holaa
good	राम्रो	raamro

Verbs

bring	ल्याउनु	lyaaunu
carry	वोक्नु	boknu
take	लिनु	linu
give	दिनु	dinu
buy	किन्नु	kinnu
sell	बेच्नु	bechnu
ask	सोध्नु	sodhnu
ask for or beg	माग्नु	maagnu
speak	बोल्नु	bholnu
hear	सुन्नु	sunnu
see	देख्नु	dekhnu
look at	हेनु	hernu
go	जानु	jaane
do	गनु	garnu
bathe	नुहाउनु	nuhaaunu
search	खोज्नु	khojnu
like	मन पर्छ	man parchha
need	चाहिन्छ	chahinchha
can (possible)	सकिन्छ	sakinchha
cannot (impossible)	सकिन्दैन	sakdaaina
say, tell	भन्नु	bhannu
I don't understand	मैले बुझेन	maile bujhdaina

English	Nepali	Romanization
I can't speak Nepali	मैले नेपाली बोल्न सक्दैन	maile nepaali bholnu sakdina
I only speak a little.	अलि मात्र बोल्छु	ali matre bholchhu
please speak slowly	बिस्तारै भन्नुस	bistaare bholnos
I am tired.	मलाई थकाई लाग्यो	maile thokai lagyo.
I am sick.	बिरामी छु	biraami chhu.

Interrogatives

English	Nepali	Romanization
who	को	ko
what	के	ke
where	कहाँ	kahaa
when	कहिले	kahile
why	किन	kina
how (in what manner)	कसरी	kasari
how much	कति	kati
which	कुन	kun

Useful Nouns

English	Nepali	Romanization
bridge	कुन	pul
hill	लेक, पहाड	lekh, pahaad
inn, lodging	भट्टी	bhatti
kerosene	मट्टीतेल	mattitel
lake	पोखरी, ताल	pokhari, tal
lamp, light	बत्ती	batti
load	भारी	bhaari
moon	चन्द्रमा	chandrama
pass (mountain)	भान्ज्याङ्ग	bhanjyang
porter	कुल्ली भरिया	kulli, bhariya
ridge	डाँडा	dandaa
river	खोला, नदि	khola, nadi
road (path)	बाटो	baato
snow	हिउँ	hiu
sun	सुर्य	surya

cigarette	चुरोट	churot
matches	सलाई	salaai
temple	मन्दीर	mandir
house	घर	ghar
newspaper	पत्र	patra
paper	कागत	kaagat
book	कीताव	kitaap
place	ठाउं	thaau
stamp (postage)	टीकट	tikat
electricity	वीजुली	bijuli
foreigner	परदेशी	paradesi
tourist	टुरीष्ट	turist
map	नक्सा	naksa
bank	बैंक	bank
immigration office	इमिग्रेसन अफिस	Immigration ophis

Useful Adjectives

big	ठूलो	thulo
small	सानो	saano
old (things)	पुरानो	paraano
new (things)	नयां	nayaa
nice, good	राम्रो	raamro
not good	नराम्रो	naraamro
hot	तातो	taato
cold	चिसो	chiso
hot (weather)	गरम	garam
warm (weather)	न्यानो	nyaano
cold (weather)	जाडो	jado
delicious	मिठो	mitho.
untasty	नमिठो	namitho
clean	सफा	saphaa
dirty	मैलो	mailo

334

red	गातो	raato
white	सेतो	seto
black	कालो	kaalo
green	हरियो	hariyo
yellow	पहेलो	pahelo
gold	सुन	sun
silver	चाँदि	chaadi
old woman/old man	बुढी बुढो	budhi, budho
male,/female	लोग्ने मान्छे स्वास्नी मान्छे	lognimaanchhe, swaasnimaanchhe

---

The Nepali numerical system reads like this:

१	२	३	४	५	६	७	८
1	2	3	4	5	6	7	8
ek	dui	tin	chaar	paach	chha	saat	aath

९	१०	११	१२	१३	१४	१५	१६
9	10	11	12	13	14	15	16
nau	das	eghaara	baara	tera	chaudha	pandhra	sora

१७	१८	१९	२०	२१	२२	२३	२४
17	18	19	20	21	22	23	24
satra	athaara	unnais	bis	ekkaais	baais	teis	chaubis

२५	२६	२७	२८	२९	३०	४०	५०
25	26	27	28	29	30	40	50
pacchis	chaabis	sattais	atthaais	unantis	tis	chaalis	pachas

६०	७०	८०	९०	१००	२००	१,०००	१०००,०००
60	70	80	90	100	200	1,000	100,000
saathi	sattari	ashi	nabbe	sae	dui sae	hajaar	laakh

ART/PHOTO CREDITS

140-141	Walter Andreae.
142	Hans Hoefer.
143	Hans Hoefer.
144-L	Walter Andreae.
144-R	Walter Andreae.
145-L	Walter Andreae.
145-R	Walter Andreae.
146	Hans Hoefer.
147	Hans Hoefer.
148	Hans Hoefer.
149	Hans Hoefer.
150-151	Hans Hoefer.
153	Hans Hoefer.
154	John Sanday.
155	Hans Hoefer.
156	Kalyan Singh.
157	Walter Andreae.
158	Bill Wassman.
161	Lithograph from Gustave LeBon's *Voyage au Nepal*, 1886.
162	Hans Hoefer.
163	Walter Andreae.
164-L	Walter Andreae.
164-R	Max Lawrence.
165	Walter Andreae.
166	Walter Andreae.
167	Walter Andreae.
168	Walter Andreae.
169	Walter Andreae.
170	Hans Hoefer.
171	Walter Andreae.
173	John Sanday.
174	Hans Hoefer.
175-L	Hans Hoefer.
175-R	Walter Andreae.
176-177	Hans Hoefer.
178	Bill Wassman.
180	Lithograph from Gustave LeBon's *Voyage au Nepal*, 1886.
181	John G. Anderson.
183-L	Walter Andreae.
183-R	Bill Wassman.
184	Jan Whiting.
185	Walter Andreae.
186	Bill Wassman.
188	Walter Andreae.
189-L	Walter Andreae.
189-R	Hans Hoefer.
190	Hans Hoefer.
191	Hans Hoefer.
192	Hans Hoefer.
193	Hans Hoefer.
194	Hans Hoefer.
195	Hans Hoefer.
196	Hans Hoefer.
197	Hans Hoefer.
198	Hans Hoefer.
199	Hans Hoefer.
200-201	Hans Hoefer.
202	Hans Hoefer.
204	Lithograph from Gustave LeBon's *Voyage au Nepal*, 1886.
206	From Henry Oldfield's *Views of Nepal 1851-1864*.
207	John Sanday.
208	Walter Andreae.
209	From Henry Oldfield's *Views of Nepal 1851-1864*.
210	Hans Hoefer.
211	Hans Hoefer.
213	Hans Hoefer.
214	Hans Hoefer.
215	Hans Hoefer.
216	Hans Hoefer.
217	Hans Hoefer.
218	Hans Hoefer.
219	Hans Hoefer.
220	Walter Andreae.
221	Walter Andreae.
222-223	Bill Wassman.
224	Max Lawrence.
227	Kalyan Singh.
228-229	Bill Wassman.
230	Max Lawrence.
231	Jan Whiting.
233	Thomas Schoellhammer.
234	Bill Wassman.
235	Max Lawrence.
236-L	Kalyan Singh.
236-R	Bill Wassman.
237	Bill Wassman.
238-239	Bill Wassman.
240	Thomas Schoellhammer.
242	Bill Wassman.
243	Jennifer Read, courtesy Himalayan River Exploration.
244-245	Desmond Doig.
246	Kalyan Singh.
249	Jan Whiting.
250-251	Jan Whiting.
252	John Cleare.
253	John Cleare.
254	John Cleare.
255	John Cleare.
256-257	Charles McDougal.
258	Wilhelm Klein.
259	John Sanday.
260	Ashish Chandola.
261	Philip Temple.
262-263	Hans Hoefer.
264	Hans Hoefer.
265	Bill Wassman.
266	Hans Hoefer.
267	Hans Hoefer.
268	Hans Hoefer.
269	Hans Hoefer.
270-271	Hans Hoefer.
272	Painting by W. Luker Jr., photo by|Kalyan Singh.
274	From the Harka Bahadur Gurung collection.
275	From Kirkpatrick's *Account of the Kingdom of Nepaul*, 1811.
276-277	Courtesy of the Rolex Watch Cox. Geneva.
278	John Cleare.
279	Courtesy of the Royal Geographical Society.
281	Lisa Van Gruisen.
282	John Cleare.
283	John Cleare.
284	Reinhold Messner.
287	Reinhold Messner.
289	Desmond Doig.
290	Sherpa painting from the Lisa Van Gruisen collection.
292	Kalyan Singh.
293	John Sanday.
294	John Sanday.
295	Kalyan Singh.
296	Hans Hoefer (telecommunications symbol).
End paper, back	Kalyan Singh (Gurkha symbol).

Charts of shrines and Durbar Squares copyright His Majesty's Government of Nepal.

(continued from page 13)

known of which are a biography of Calcutta's Mother Teresa and a volume co-authored with Sir Edmund Hillary, *High in the Thin Cold Air.* Doig accompanied Hillary on his yeti-hunting and schoolhouse expeditions in Sherpa country below Everest in the early 1960s. His photography is syndicated by Magnum; his painting has warranted several one-man shows in Nepal and abroad; and he is the designer of two of Kathmandu's leading hotels. Doig died in October 1983 while working on new books about Nepal.

Hillary himself has contributed a first-person article on his experiences with the Sherpa people, whom he has come to know so intimately since his historic first ascent of Mount Everest with Tenzing Norgay Sherpa in 1953. A native New Zealander, he has written numerous books and a multitude of articles for magazines throughout the world on his experiences in the Himalaya, first as a climber and later as founder of the Himalayan Trust, devoted to improving the living standards of the Sherpas in the Khumbu.

The executive officer of Hillary's Himalayan Trust is Elizabeth Hawley, a journalist and historian widely regarded as a one-woman Himalayan mountaineering institute. A resident of Kathmandu for more than 20 years, she writes for Reuters news service and *Time* magazine. Her files on every major mountaineering expedition ever undertaken in the Himalaya have made her office a meeting place for mountaineers. She has contributed this book's material on mountaineering history and a first-person interview with Reinhold Messner, as well as an update on contemporary Nepalese history.

If Hillary is the world's most famous mountaineer, Messner is its modern superstar. Raised in the Italian Alps, he is the only man to have climbed Everest solo. Twice he has reached the summit without the use of artificial oxygen. By October 1986, he had climbed all of the world's 8,000-meter giants — a giant achievement. Messner is the author of numerous books, and his writing and photography have appeared in a large number of magazines in several languages. In this book, he describes what drives him to climb. He has contributed several of his photographs, and has been very concerned and cooperative in this book's production from start to finish.

The other link in Apa's team of mountain experts is Al Read, former managing director of Mountain Travel in Kathmandu. Read's climbing career is distinguished by leading two Himalayan first ascents; Gauri Shankar in 1979 and Cholatse in 1982. A former American diplomat, Read also was a member of a 1969 Dhaulagiri expedition and a 1980 expedition to Minya Konka in China. During the Northern Hemisphere summer, he operates a climbing school in the Teton Mountains of Wyoming. He pioneered river rafting in Nepal with the establishment of Himalayan River Exploration. Much of the "Beyond the Valley" section of this book was prepared by Read, as well as all information on trekking, river rafting and climbing preparations.

Harka Gurung, who wrote about geography and Gurkhas and contributed his expertise to sections on Pokhara and the Terai, is one of Nepal's leading scholars and authors. Since completing his doctorate in geography at the University of Edinburgh (Scotland) in 1965, he has written more than 150 articles for magazines and journals as well as five books, including a travelogue called *Vignettes of Nepal.* He is currently preparing new books on Nepalese development, mountaineering history and the Pokhara Valley. Gurung was Nepal's first Minister of State for Tourism (1977-78); he has also held portfolios for Industry and Commerce, Education, Transport and Public Works.

Kunda Dixit, whose credits in this book include "Modern Nepal" and "Daily Life," is feature editor for *The Rising Nepal,* the nation's leading English-language newspaper. Trained as a microbiologist, Dixit was inspired to enter the field of journalism by his travels in Nepal and abroad. He finds himself increasingly concerned with Nepal's developmental and environmental dilemmas.

Dor Bahadur Bista, our expert on Nepal's "Ethnic Mosaic," is professor of anthropology at Tribhuvan University. Formerly, he was the Royal Nepalese Consul General in Tibet; director of the Research Center for Nepal and Asian Studies; and a Fulbright Scholar at Columbia University in New York. Among his many books and articles is *Peoples of Nepal,* the classic treatment of the country's many tribes, races and castes.

Biswa Nath Upreti, director general of the National Parks and Wildlife Conservation Department, Ministry of Forests, of His Majesty's Government of Nepal, also contributed significantly to this book. Upreti provided detailed information on flora and fauna throughout the country, as well as on the national park system.

Without the assistance of John Sanday, *Nepal* might never have gotten off the ground. One of the leading Western experts on traditional architecture in the Kathmandu Valley, Sanday acted as a consultant on all sections of the book. He also extensively rewrote the chapters on Kathmandu and Bhaktapur cities; prepared the listing of Valley walks; and contributed several photographs.

Sanday was trained at the Royal West of England School of Architecture. He came to the Valley as project leader of the UNESCO Hanuman Dhoka Restoration Project, and now acts as coordinator of the Programme for Conservation of the Cultural Heritage of the Kathmandu Valley. He also oversees restoration projects throughout the Indian subcontinent under the auspices of UNESCO, and is involved in the development of cultural tourism. He is the author of *Monuments of the Kathmandu Valley,* a guide to hundreds of ancient buildings.

Father John K. Locke, a Jesuit priest who has made a study of Hindu and Buddhist religious rites in the Valley, helped to prepare the section on religion.

While Hoefer, Wassman and Andreae were the chief photographic eyes involved in *Nepal,* they were not the only ones. More than a dozen photos were taken by Kalyan Singh, a young Indian who lives and works in Kathmandu. His work appears in several magazines in India and the Far East, as well as in Doig's 1976 biography of Mother Teresa. He recently completed shooting an entire photographic book on Nepal, and is now working on a visual biography of the leading Taiwanese actress, Lung Chun Erh.

John Cleare, a London-based alpine photographer rated among the world's elite, provided numerous mountain shots. The work of Max Lawrence, a native of New Zealand, and Jan Whiting, now living in Australia, has been represented by the Apa Photo Agency for several years; both have been featured in previous *Insight Guides.*

The brilliant photograph of the Bengal tiger was taken by Charles McDougal, director of wildlife for Tiger Tops. An anthropologist by training, McDougal's most noted publication is *The Face of the Tiger,* generally regarded as the classic study of the big cat.

The photo of Hillary and Messner preceding the mountaineering section comes courtesy of the Rolex Watch Co. of Geneva, Switzerland. The shot of Tenzing on the summit of Everest is from the Royal Geographical Society. Other photographs in this book were taken by Thomas Schoellhammer, Hugh R. Downs, Wilhelm Klein, Jennifer Read, Ashish Chandola, Philip Temple, Lisa Van Gruisen and John Anderson.

The book's thorough language section was prepared by American anthropologist Augusta Molnar. A former consultant to the U.S. Agency for International Development in Kathmandu, Molnar earned her doctorate from the University of Wisconsin in 1980 after field study on the economic and social roles of Magar women in Nepal.

Maps were drawn under the direction of Gunter Nelles of Munich, West Germany. The indexing was done by Linda Carlock.

Special thanks go to Boris Lissanevitch, the father of tourism in modern Nepal, for his unflagging encouragement. A native of the Ukraine, Lissanevitch came to Kathmandu in the early 1950s and opened the famous Royal Hotel. He and his wife Inger ran several Kathmandu restaurants, continuing a tradition of hospitality that has catered to queens and maharajahs for three decades. A legendary figure, known as a ballet dancer and tiger hunter as well as a restauranteur, Lissanevitch's life is described in Michael Peissel's book *Tiger for Breakfast.* Boris died on 20th October 1985.

His Majesty's Government of Nepal contributed Himalaya-sized assistance. Of special help were the Minister of State for Tourism, and his Ministry; the Department of Archaeology and Royal Nepal Airlines. Additional thanks must go to the Kaiser Library of Kathmandu, the National Museum, the Bhaktapur Museum, the Brigade of Gurkhas, and A.V. Jim Edwards and Tiger Tops Mountain Travel International.

Individuals who contributed in one or many ways were Dubby Bhagat, Prabal Shamsher Jung Bahadur Rana, Dr. J. Gabriel Campbell, British Ambassador John B. Denson, John Edwards, Bobby Chettri, Vira Mehta, Pertemba Sherpa, Tenzing Norgay Sherpa, Bob Gould, Basant Mishra, Bill March, K.K. Gurung, Col. Keith Robinson, Col. J.O.M. Roberts, Capt. Hardy Fuerer, Dave Peterson, Audrey Salkeld, Uschi Messner, Marge Dove, Theon Banos Cross, Corneille Jest, Stephen Bezruchka, Hemanta Mishra, Leonard Lueras, Leo Haks, Alice Ng, Raymond Boey, Sam Chan, Diana Tan, Magdelene Teo and Yvan Van Outrive.

A tip of the *topi* and a cheery *"Namaste"* to all.

Apa Productions

Glossary

agam—A family, patron or secret deity enshrined in a special building. No one can enter who is not an initiate.

akha—A traditional place where religious dancing is taught.

Ananda—The Buddha's chief disciple.

Ananta—A huge snake whose coils created Vishnu's bed.

Annapurna—The goddess of abundance; one aspect of Devi.

arak—A whisky fermented from potatoes or grain.

Asadh—The third month of the Nepalese year (June–July).

Ashta Matrikas—The eight mother goddesses said to attend on Shiva or Skanda.

Ashta Nag—Eight serpent deities who guard the cardinal directions and (if worshipped) keep evil spirits away.

Ashwin—The sixth month of the Nepalese year (September–October).

asla—A freshwater mountain trout.

Avalokiteshwara—A *bodhisattva* regarded as the god of mercy in Mahayana Buddhist tradition, and as the compassionate Machhendra in Nepal.

avatar—An incarnation of a deity on earth.

bahal—A two-story Buddhist monastery enclosing a courtyard.

bahil—A Buddhist monastery, smaller and simpler than a *bahal*.

Baisakh—The first month of the Nepalese year (April–May).

bajracharya—A Newar caste of Buddhist priests.

Bajra Jogini—A Tantric goddess.

Balarama—The brother of Krishna.

Balkumari—A consort of Bhairav.

betel—A stimulating mixture of araca nut and white lime, wrapped in a betel leaf and chewed. It is widely popular throughout South Asia.

Bhadra—The fifth month of the Nepalese year (August–September).

Bhadrakali—A Tantric goddess and consort of Bhairav.

Bhagavad-Gita—The most important Hindu religious scripture, in which the god Krishna spells out the importance of duty. It is contained in the *Mahabharata*.

Bhairav—The god Shiva in his most terrifying form.

bharad—A reverential title.

Bhimsen—A deity worshipped for his strength and courage

bhot—High, arid valleys in the Tibetan border region.

bodhi (also **bo**)—The pipal tree under which Gautama Buddha achieved enlightenment, and any tree so worshipped.

bodhisattva—In Mahayana tradition, a person who has attained the enlightened level of Buddhahood, but who has chosen to remain on earth to teach until others are enlightened.

Bon—The pre-Buddhist religion of Tibet, incorporating animism and sorcery.

Bonpo—A follower of the Bon faith.

Brahma—In Hindu mythology, the god of creation.

brahman—The highest of Hindu castes, originally that of priests.

Brahminism—Ancient Indian religion, the predecessor of modern Hinduism and Buddhism.

busadan—The anniversary of the founding of a temple.

Chaitra—The 12th and last month of the Nepalese year (March–April).

chaitya—A small stupa, sometimes containing a Buddhist relic, but usually holding *mantras* or holy scriptures.

chakra—A round weapon, one of the four objects held by Vishnu.

chapa—A small house annexed to a temple, in which feasts are held and rituals performed.

chapati—A type of bread made from wheat flour.

chhang—A potent mountain beer of fermented grain, usually barley but sometimes maize, rye or millet.

chhetri—The Hindu warrior caste, second in status only to brahmans.

chhura—Beaten rice.

chitrakar—A Newar caste of artists.

chiya—Nepalese tea, brewed together with milk, sugar and spices.

chorten—A small Buddhist shrine on high mountain regions.

chowk—A palace or public courtyard.

crore—A unit of counting equal to 10 million.

dabu—An urban roadside square, used for religious dancing during festivals and as a market place at other times.

Dalai Lama—The reincarnate high priest of Tibetan Buddhism and political leader of Tibetans around the world.

damais—A caste of tailors who form makeshift bands to play religious music for weddings and other occassions.

damaru—A small drum.

damiyen—A traditional stringed instrument, similar to a ukulele.

Dattatraya—A syncretistic deity variously worshipped as an incarnation of Vishnu, a teacher of Shiva, or a cousin of the Buddha.

Devi (or **Maha Devi**)—"The great goddess." Shiva's *Shakti* in her many forms.

dhal—A lentil "soup."

dhami—A soothsayer and sorcerer; also, the priest of a temple, especially a priest claiming occult powers.

Dharma—Buddhist doctrine. Literally, "the path."

dharmasala—A public rest house for travellers and pilgrims.

dharni—A weight measure equal to three *sers*, or about three kilograms.

dhoti—A loose loincloth.

dhyana—Meditation.

dighur—A Thakali system whereby a group of people pools its money to annually support one of its members in a chosen financial venture.

digi—A place of congregation and prayer.

doko—A basket, often carried on the head by means of a strap.

dorje—A ritual scepter or thunderbolt, symbol of the Absolute to Tantric Buddhists. (Also *vajra*)

dun—Valleys of the Inner Terai.

dungidara—A stone water spout.

Durga—Shiva's *shakti* in one of her most awesome forms.

dwarapala—a door guardian.

dwarmul—The main gate of a building

dyochhen—A house enshrining protective Tantric deities and used for common worship.

dzopkyo—A hybrid bull, the cross between a yak and a cow.

dzum—A hybrid cow, the cross between a yak and a cow.

dzu-tch—According to Sherpas, a type of yeti that is about eight feet tall and eats cattle.

ek—The number one, a symbol of unity.

Falgun—The 11th month of the Nepalese year (February–March).

gaine—A wandering, begging minstrel.

gajur—An often-ornate, bell-shaped finial crowning a *bahal*.

Ganesh—The elephant-headed son of Shiva and Parvati. He is worshipped as the god of good luck and the remover of obstacles.

Ganga—A Hindu goddess.

Garuda—A mythical eagle, half-human. The vehicle of Vishnu.

Gautama Buddha—The historical Buddha, born in Lumbini in the 6th Century B.C.

gelugpa-a Tibetan sect.

ghada—A type of club, one of the weapons of Vishnu and a Tantric symbol.

ghanta—A symbolic Tantric bell, the female counterpart of the *vajra*.

ghat—A riverside platform for bathing and cremation.

ghee—Clarified butter.

gompa—Tibetan Buddhist monastery.

gopala—A cowherd.

gopis—Cowherd girls; specifically, those who cavorted with Krishna in a famous Hindu legend.

Gorakhnath—Historically, an 11th Century yogi who founded a Shairite cult; now popularly regarded as an incarnation of Shiva.

granthakut—A tall, pointed brick and-plaster shrine supported by a one-story stone base.

gurr—A Sherpa food consisting of peeled raw potatoes, pounded with spices, grilled like pancakes and eaten with cheese.

guthi—A communal Newar brotherhood serving the purpose of mutual support for members and their extended families.

guthihar—The members of a guthi; also, a group of families with the same ancestry.

Hanuman—A deified monkey, Hero of the *Ramayana* epic, he is believed to bring success to armies.

hapa—A bamboo rice-measuring device made only in Pyangaon.

Harisiddhi—A fierce Tantric goddess.

harmika—The eyes on a stupa, placed to face the four cardinal directions.

hiti—A water conduit; a bath or tank with water spouts.
hookah—A water pipe through which tobacco or hashish is smoked.

impeyan—Nepal's national bird, a species of pheasant.
Indra—God of rain; the chief deity of Brahminism.

jadun—A large vessel for drinking water at public places.
Jagannath—Krishna, worshipped as "Lord of the World."
Jamuna—A Hindu goddess who rides a tortoise.
janti—The groom's party at a wedding.
jarun—A raised stone water tank with carved spouts.
jatra—Festival.
Jaya Varahi—Vishnu's *shakti* in his incarnation as a boar.
jelebi—A sweet Nepali snack.
Jesth—The second month of the Nepalese year (May–June).
jhaad—Traditional rice beer.
jhankri—A shaman or sorcerer.
Jhankrism—Traditional animism, incorporating occult practices.
jhya—Carved window.
jogini—A mystical goddess.
juga—leech.
jyapu—Newar farmer caste.

kalasha—A pot.
Kali—Shiva's *shakti* in her most terrifying form.
kapok—The silk cotton tree.
karma—The cause-and-effect chain of actions, good and bad, from one life to the next.
Kartik—The seventh month of the Nepalese year (October–November).
kata—A ceremonial scarf presented to high Tibetan Buddhist figures.
khat—An enclosed wooden shrine, similar in appearance to the portable shrines carried during processions.
khola—River or stream.
khukri—A traditional knife, long and curved, best known as the weapon of Gurkha soldiers.
Krishna—The eighth incarnation of Vishnu, heavily worshipped for his activities on earth.
kshepu—A snake-eating figure often depicted on temple *toranas*.
kumari—A young virgin regarded as a living goddess in Kathmandu Valley towns.
kunda—A recessed water tank fed by underground springs.

la—Mountain pass.
laddu—A sweet Nepali snack.

lakh—A unit of counting equal to 100,000.
lakhe—Masked dancing.
Lakshmi—The goddess of wealth and consort of Vishnu.
lama—A Tibetan Buddhist priest.
lingum (pl. *lingas*)—A symbolic male phallus, generally associated with Shiva.
Lokeshwar—"Lord of the World," a form of Avalokiteshwara to Buddhists and of Shiva to Hindus.
loo—A torrid desert wind which blows across India into the Terai.

Machhendra—The guardian god of

the Kathmandu Valley, guarantor of rain and plenty. The popular interpretation of Avalokiteshwara or Lokeshwar. Enshrined as the Rato (Red) Machhendra in Patan and the Seto (White) Machhendra in Kathmandu.
Magha—The 10th month of the Nepalese year (January–February).
Mahabharata—An important Hindu epic.
Mahabharat Lekh—A range of hills between the Himalayas and the Terai.
maharishi—Literally, "great teacher."
Mahayana—The form of Buddhism prevalent in East Asia, Tibet and Nepal.
Maitreya—The future Buddha.
makara—A mythical crocodile, often depicted on *toranas*.
mali—A Newar caste of gardeners.
mana—A measure for rice and cereals, milk and sugar, containing a little less than half a liter.
mandala—A sacred diagram envisioned by Tibetan Buddhists as an aid to meditation.
mandap—A roofless Tantric shrine of brick or wood.
mani—A Tibetan Buddhist prayer inscribed in rock in high-mountain areas.
Manjushri—The legendary Buddhist patriarch of the Kathmandu Valley, now often regarded as the god of learning.
mantra—Sacred syllables chanted during meditation by Buddhists.
Marga—The eighth month of the Nepalese year (November–December).
masheer—A large freshwater fish of Nepal.
math—A Hindu priest's house.
migyu—Tibetan name for the yeti.
mih-tch—According to Sherpas, a hostile, man-sized, ape-like yeti.
momos—Tibetan stuffed pastas, somewhat like ravioli.
mudra—A symbolic hand posture or gesture practiced in religious devotion.
munja—The sacred thread worn by brahman and chhetri males from the time of puberty.
muri—A dry measure equal to about 75 liters. It contains precisely 20 *paathis* or 160 *manas*.
muthi—A measure equal to "a handful."
naga—Snake, especially a legendary or a deified serpent.
nak—Female yak.
namaste—A word of greeting, often translated as: "I salute all divine qualities in you."
Nandi—A bull, Shiva's vehicle and a symbol of fecundity.
nanglo—A cane tray.
nani—A type of *bahal* containing a large courtyard surrounded by residences, also including a Buddhist shrine.

Narayan—Vishnu represented as the creator of life. A lotus from Narayan's naval issued Brahma.
Narsingh—Vishnu's incarnation as a lion.
nath—Literally, "Place."
nirvana—Extinction of self, the goal of Buddhist meditation.
Nriteshwar—The god of dance.

paathi—A dry measure equal to eight *manas*, about 3¾ liters.
padma—The lotus flower.
pahar—The heavily eroded central zone of hills and valleys between the Himalayas and the Mahabharat Lekh.
panchayat—A governmental system consisting of elected councils at local, regional and national levels.
Parvati—Shiva's consort, displaying both serene and fearful aspects.
pashmina—A shawl or blanket made of fine goat's wool.
Pashupati—Shiva in his aspect as "Lord of the Beasts." Symbolized by the *lingum*, he is believed to bring fecundity.
pasni—A rice-feeding ceremony conducted for seven-month-old babies, and repeated for old people of 77 years, seven months.
patasi—A sari-like dress, especially popular in Bhaktapur.
path—A small raised platform which shelters travelers on important routes and intersections.
pathi—A liquid measurement, slightly less than one gallon.
patuka—A waistcloth in which to carry small objects and even babies.
pau—A measure for vegetables and fruit, equal to 250 grams.
paubha—Traditional Newari painting, usually religious in motif.
pith—An open shrine dedicated to a Tantric goddess.
pokhari—A large tank.
Poush—The ninth month of the Nepalese year (December–January).
preta—A spirit of the dead.
puja—Ritual offerings to the gods.
pukhu—A pond.
punya—Merit earned through actions and religious devotion.
puri—Town.

rakshi—A homemade wheat or rice liquor.
Rama—The seventh incarnation of Vishnu. A prince, hero of the *Ramayana* epic.
Ramayana—The most widely known Hindu legend, in which Rama, with the aid of Hanuman and Garuda, rescues his wife, Sita, from the demon king Rawana.
Rawana—The anti-hero of the *Ramayana*.
rikhi doro—A golden thread which Shiva devotees tie around their wrists to ward off evil and disease.
rimpoche—The abbot of a Tibetan Buddhist monastery (*gompa*).
Rudrayani—A Kathmandu Valley nature goddess. Also known as Shekali Mai.

sadhu—A Hindu mendicant.
sajha—Cooperative, organized in the 1970s to deal with inequalities in land sharing.
sal—A strong timber tree of the lower slopes of Himalayan foothills.
sampradaya—A religious sect or community.
samsara—Literally, the universe.
sankha—The conch shell, one of the four symbols held by Vishnu. It is widely used in Hindu temples and shrines during prayer.

sanyasin—A religious ascetic who has renounced his ties to society.

saranghi—A small, four-stringed viola shaped from a single piece of wood and played with a horsehair bow.

Saraswati—Brahma's consort. worshipped in Nepal as the Hindu goddess of learning.

satal—A pilgrim's house.

ser—A unit of weight equal to four *paus*, or about one kilogram.

serow—A wild Himalayan antelope.

shaki (often cap.)—Shiva's consort, literally, power the dynamic element in the male-female relationship, and the female aspect of the Tantric Absolute.

Shaligram—A black ammonite fossil regarded as sacred by Vishnu devotees.

shandula—A mythical bird; a griffin.

shikhara—A brick or stone temple of geometrical shape, with a tall central spire.

Shitala Mai—A former ogress who became a protector of children, worshipped at Swayambhunath.

Shiva—The most awesome of Hindu gods. He destroys all things, good as well as evil, allowing new creations to take shape.

shrestha—A Newar caste.

sindur—A votive mixture made of red dust combined with mustard oil.

sirdar—A guide, usually a Sherpa, who leads trekking groups.

Sita—Rama's wife, heroine of the *Ramayana* epic. She is worshipped in Janakpur, her legendary birthplace.

Skanda—The Hindu god of war.

Srawan—The fourth month of the Nepalese year (July–August).

stupa—A bell-shaped relic chamber.

sudra—Lowest of the Hindu castes, commonly thought to have descended from Brahma's feet.

sundhara—A fountain with a golden spout.

Surjya—The sun god, often identified with Vishnu.

suttee—Former practice of immolating widows on their husbands' funeral pyres.

tabla—A traditional hand drum.

tahr—A wild Himalayan goat.

Taleju Bhawani—The Nepalese goddess, originally a South Indian deity; an aspect of Devi.

Tara—Historically a Nepalese princess, now deified by Buddhists and Hindus.

Terai—The Nepalese lowland region.

Thakuri—high Hindu caste.

thangka—A religious scroll painting.

thelma—According to Sherpas, a a small, reddish, ape-like yeti.

thukba—A thick Tibetan soup.

tika—A colorful vermilion powder applied by Hindus to the forehead, between the eyes, as a symbol of the presence of the divine.

tola—A metal measure equal to 11.5 grams.

tole—A street.

topi—The formal, traditional Nepali cap.

torana—A decorative carved crest suspended over the door of a sanctum, with the figure of the enshrined deity at its center.

trisul—The trident, chief symbol of the god Shiva.

tsampa—Raw grain, sometimes eaten dry, usually ground and mixed with milk, tea or water. A traditional mountain food.

tulku—In Tibetan Buddhism, a religious figure regarded as a reincarnation of a great *lama* of the past.

tulsi—A sacred basil plant.

tunal—The carved strut of a temple.

tympanum—A decorative crest beneath the triangular peak of a roof.

Uma—Shiva's consort in one of her many aspects.

Upanishads—Early Brahministic religious texts; speculations on Vedic thought.

vaisya—The "middle-class' caste of merchants and farmers.

vajra (also *dorje*)—In Tantric Buddhism, a ritual thunderbolt or curved scepter symbolizing the Absolute. It also represents power and male energy.

varahi—A god incarnated as a boar.

Vedas—The earliest Brahministic religious verses, dating from the second millennium B.C. They define a polytheistic faith.

vedica—A sacrificial altar.

vihara—A Buddhist monastery, encompassing a *bahal* and a *bahil*.

Vikrantha (also **Vamana**)—Vishnu in his fifth incarnation, as a dwarf.

Vishnu—One of the Hindu trinity, a god who preserves life and the world itself. In Nepal, he is most commonly represented as Narayan.

yab-yum—Tantric erotica, a symbol of unity and oneness.

yeh-tch—The Sherpa name for the yeti; literally, "man of the rocky places."

yeti—A mythical anthropoid of Nepal's highest elevations, often referred to in the West as "The Abominable Snowman."

yoni—A hole in a stone, said to symbolize the female sexual aspect. Usually seen together with a *lingum*.

zamindari—A system of absentee landlordism, officially abolished in 1955 but still perpetuated in some regions.

italy

france

crossing america

canada

bahamas

nepal

ireland

indonesia

florida

hong kong

burma

taiwan

northern california

new england

malaysia

republic of korea

thailand

alaska

singapore

mexico

california

australia